Apatura ilia [15]

Limenitis reducta [16]

Polygonia c-album [16]

Vanessa atalanta [17]

Inachis io [17]

Aglais urticae [17]

Vanessa cardui [17]

A FIELD GUIDE TO THE
BUTTERFLIES OF BRITAIN
AND EUROPE

The Peterson Identification System
The system of identification in this Field Guide is based on the
original system devised by Roger Tory Peterson, which emphasises
comparative patterns and diagnostic characters.

A FIELD GUIDE TO THE

Butterflies of Britain
and Europe

Lionel G. Higgins

and

Norman D. Riley

With 760 illustrations in colour by
Brian Hargreaves

COLLINS
St James's Place, London

First Edition 1970
Second Edition 1973
Third Edition 1975
Reprinted 1976
Reprinted 1977

D64,122

ISBN 0 00 219198 9

Printed in Great Britain
Collins Clear-Type Press
London and Glasgow

Preface

The need for a small but comprehensive book on European butterflies has been apparent for many years. The last English books of the kind, Kane's admirable *Handbook* of 1885 and Lang's *European Butterflies* of 1886, are both much out of date and long out of print. Wheeler's *Butterflies of Switzerland*, because of the richness of the Swiss fauna, has partially filled the gap, but is now also virtually unobtainable. A few large and expensive works exist, such as the volumes of Seitz's *Macrolepidoptera of the World* that cover the whole palearctic fauna, but in scope these go far beyond what is needed.

We have therefore set out to provide, both for the general public and for collectors, a compact handy book describing and illustrating all the butterflies of the western palearctic region—not a text-book, but essentially a guide with the emphasis on identification.

In the preparation of this guide we have enjoyed the willing help of many friends, acquaintances and correspondents at home and abroad.

At home we wish especially to thank R. F. Bretherton, Professor J. V. Dacie, K. M. Guichard, John Heath, E. C. Pelham-Clinton, Dr. J. F. Perkins and Baron Charles de Worms.

Abroad our thanks are particularly due to
D. Olegario Escola (Spain)
J. Bourgogne, Dr. G. Bernardi, P. C. Rougeot, Dr. H. de Lesse and Henri Stempffer (France)
B. J. Lempke (Holland)
Dr. W. Forster (Germany)
Professor O. Sotavalta (Finland)
Svend Kaaber and Niels Wolff (Denmark)
Professor Z. Lorković (Yugoslavia)
Charles Rungs (Morocco)

We are greatly indebted to the Secretariat of the International Commission on Zoological Nomenclature, and especially to their classical adviser Professor Jasper Griffin, for help with many problems of nomenclature, particularly those concerned with the derivation and genders of scientific names.

To the Trustees of the British Museum (Natural History), and in particular to the staff of the Entomological Department we owe an especial debt of gratitude for the free access to their unrivalled collections and library that we have enjoyed.

To the consummate skill and industry of Brian Hargreaves we owe all the beautiful colour plates. The specimens illustrated, with the exception of the male *Erebia serotina* lent to us by the National Museum of Natural History in Paris, and twenty one specimens in the British Museum, are all in the collection of Dr. Higgins.

Lionel Higgins
Norman Riley

Preface to Second Edition

Publication of this second edition has enabled us to take advantage of the considerable volume of new information that has reached us since the autumn of 1970. For this we have to thank again not only those friends and colleagues who contributed so much to the first edition but also many others, notably S. R. Bowden for advice on the difficult problems of the *Pieris napi* complex, and Dr. E. V. Niculescu, Dr. L. Gozmany, Dr. F. König and John Coutsis for their help with the detailed distribution of the butterflies of south-eastern Europe, from Hungary and Rumania through the Balkan peninsula to Greece. In some cases the new distributional data have been incorporated in the text, but more often they have been dealt with by alterations to the maps, 99 of which have been completely redrawn. Other important changes necessitated by recent advances in our knowledge of the European butterflies concern the genera *Apatura* and *Aricia*, while one species is added to the European fauna, namely the Pontic Blue, *Plebicula coelestina*, recently discovered in Greece. On p. 28 a few points are noted that we have been unable to incorporate in the text. A large number of very minor points—largely concerning details of distribution—must remain uncorrected in the present edition.

Lionel Higgins
Norman Riley

Contents

How to use this book

The *endpapers*, inside the front and back covers, illustrate butterflies characteristic of 8 of the 9 families occurring in Europe. For the 9th family see the unmistakeable species of Danaidae on Plate 14. Note the butterfly most like the specimen you want to identify and turn to the plates indicated by the numbers alongside the names. This should lead you to the correct group of illustrations.

On the *plates* are illustrated all the butterflies known to occur in Europe, including both sexes and all major subspecies. The left half of each illustration shows the upper sides of the wings, the right half the under sides. All are life size. When comparing specimens with the illustrations bear in mind that both pattern and colour are liable to variation and that colours are brightest in fresh specimens.

On the *caption pages*, facing the plates, will be found the names of the butterflies, their key characters, and page references to the full text descriptions. Sometimes it has not been possible to group together on a single plate all the varieties of a species that needed illustration. In all such cases cross references to other plates are given on the caption pages.

The *text descriptions* are restricted to characters important for identification. Pay particular attention to notes on 'Similar species' whenever these are given. Anatomical features are explained in the Introduction (p. 13) and Glossary (p. 29). *Flight periods* given are those normal to the species but are liable to considerable variation according to altitude and latitude. *Habitats* also vary and it has only been possible to give general indications of the kind of terrain in which the butterfly is normally found. Food plants of the caterpillars are also given here.

The text information on *Distributions*, necessarily condensed, is summarised on the *Maps* pp. 341-64. It should not be assumed that every species occurs everywhere throughout the area indicated on its map: it may be localised in widely separated colonies; it may regularly migrate beyond it, as indicated by the striped black and white areas. The map shows the whole range. The Atlantic islands are indicated by initials: A (Azores), C (Canary Islands) or M (Madeira).

Taken together, the descriptions and the information under flight, habitat and distribution, including the maps, should enable you to identify your specimens, to find a particular species you want, and also to know what to expect in any given area.

A *Checklist* of all the species described will be found on p. 23, and a selective *Bibliography* on p. 339. For *Abbreviations* see p. 33.

Introduction

Butterflies (*Rhopalocera*) and Moths (*Heterocera*) form together the very large Insect Order *Lepidoptera*, so-called because their wings are covered with scales. The coiled proboscis, through which nourishment is sucked up, is peculiar to Lepidoptera. In western Europe butterflies can be distinguished from moths by having clubbed antennae; by having the two wings on either side held together by the shape of the wings instead of the 'bristle and catch' frenulum of moths; by flying by day; and by sleeping with their wings closed together over the back. Brightly coloured day-flying moths and other similar insects that occur in Europe can be distinguished from butterflies by one or more of these characters.

European Butterflies. For the region covered in this book see the map on p. 34 and its explanatory note.

This region forms a subcontinent of great zoological interest. Of about 380 species of butterflies that are known to occur in it, at least 112 (just under 30%) are endemic, not found elsewhere.

Comparison of the distribution maps p. 341-64, will show a number of interesting recurrent patterns: groups of species confined to the central Alps, others dotted on isolated mountain ranges over a wide area, some almost confined within the Arctic Circle, many restricted to the Mediterranean sub-region or to one end of it, a few that hardly extend beyond the lowlands of central Europe, from France to Russia, and a wide-ranging group failing only to reach the Arctic and high alpine zones, and so on. These distribution patterns all mean something. They can be explained by, and help to explain, the great land movements and climatic changes to which Europe was subjected before and during the Great Ice Ages which began some 600,000 years ago.

Most European butterflies can be recognised fairly easily as belonging to one or other of the *species* described in this Guide. There are others, however, like the Brown Argus butterflies (p. 281) of which it is difficult to say whether they are a single species or a group of species so closely allied as to be virtually indistinguishable. Such a complex may be looked upon as a group still in the process of evolution, in which the various components are not yet separated and stabilised. On this view they are approaching the status of *subspecies*, i.e. geographical races which we define as differing populations of a single species that occur in different parts of the range of that species. By definition no two subspecies of any species ever fly together; but if and when their ranges meet they can, and usually do, interbreed and produce intermediate forms. This does not happen between species.

The large number of described and named subspecies has proved embarrassing, since only very few could find a place in this book. In the main only those that may be termed major subspecies have been described, i.e. those with clearly recognisable constant characters and well defined geographical distributions. Others, with less distinctive characters are referred to as 'forms', a term we use in a non-committal sense for any kind of recognisable variety of a species, whether expressly defined or not, such as a local race, a recurrent variety, an incipient subspecies, a seasonal, female or other special form.

In Europe there are many examples of a continuous type of variation that extends in a series of gradations throughout a butterfly's range. This kind of variation is known as a *cline*. No doubt clines are evolutionary stages that could give rise eventually to subspecies if the range of the species became interrupted by barriers to free movement. A good example is the Meadow Brown (*Maniola jurtina*, p. 201) which is large and brightly marked in southern Europe, small and dull in the north, the extremes linked by intermediates. There seems good reason to suppose that variation of this kind reflects the influence of climatic conditions.

Seasonal variation occurs only in butterflies that have two or more annual broods. Individual butterflies do not vary with the season. Most European butterflies are single-brooded, and this is particularly true of those that live at high altitudes and latitudes, where the season favourable to development is short. Double-brooded species are not numerous, and are mostly insects of the lower levels. Some species that are double-brooded in southern Europe are single-brooded in the north. Several of these differ greatly from one brood to the next. Good examples are the Green-veined White (p. 45) and the Map Butterfly (p. 89). A few species have more than two annual broods. Most of these will go on breeding so long as conditions are favourable. Good examples are the Bath White (p. 47) and the Long-tailed Blue (p. 250). In many species that have more than one annual brood a small proportion of each brood may hibernate as pupae or larvae till the following spring.

In most European butterflies the males and females are noticeably different, and in a few species the females themselves are dimorphic, as in the Clouded Yellows of the genus *Colias* (p. 57), many of which have both 'yellow' and 'white' forms.

Individual variations occur in all species, but are more common in some than others. In the Ringlets and Heaths (Satyridae) the characteristic eye-spots tend to increase or decrease in size and number; in the Fritillaries the black spots of the upperside tend to form streaks, or to overrun the whole wing, and the silver spots of the underside may do the same; in the

Blues the spots on the underside similarly may lengthen to form streaks between the veins, may be greatly reduced in number or even absent, and so on. Individuals with an excess of black pigment are melanics. Lack of pigment produces albinos. Curious specimens occur sometimes in which one side is male, the other female. These are gynandromorphs or intersexes, and are very rare. A male with scattered patches of female characters, or vice versa, is known as a mosaic. Pathological conditions, due to disease, which are common in some species, usually result in bleaching effects or the distortion of wings and veins.

All these freaks and 'aberrations' are worth keeping. Most of them have been given names, but they are far too numerous to be dealt with in this Guide.

Names (*nomenclature*). Less than a hundred of the European butterflies have English names. Our experience is that English names are especially welcome to beginners, so we have invented English names for all those that needed them. We have also included such Swedish, German, French and Spanish vernacular names as we have been able to find. For this we offer no apology. As knowledge grows these vernacular names will lead on inevitably to the use of the 'Latin' names that are the international currency of butterfly nomenclature.

One of the troubles with scientific names is their multiplicity. Which of the many names (synonyms, homonyms etc., see Glossary p. 30) given to any species is the *correct* name for that species is now fortunately determinable by the rules laid down in the International Code of Zoological Nomenclature (see Glossary p. 30). We have been at great pains to follow these Rules, as their purpose is to establish the stable nomenclature that we all need so badly. As a result we have had to make a few changes which we hope are final.

Of synonyms we have thought it most useful to include only those in current use.

THE BUTTERFLY

During its life a butterfly passes through four stages, from egg (ovum) to caterpillar (larva), chrysalis (pupa) and butterfly (imago), each stage undergoing a complete metamorphosis. This book is concerned only with the fourth stage—the adult butterfly.

To understand the characters used in the descriptions in this Guide you will need to know something about the structure of a butterfly. Take a common butterfly, like a Small Tortoiseshell, and run through the following paragraphs looking for the various structures as they are mentioned. Most of these can be seen with the naked eye, but a hand lens with a magnification of about ×10 will be a great help.

A butterfly has all its hard parts on the outside. This external covering (exoskeleton) is mainly composed of chitin, and to its inner surface the muscles are attached. The *head* is a small brittle capsule and its appendages are sensory. The proboscis, which takes the place of a mouth, is formed of two tubes joined together so as to form a third through which the insect drinks. There are no jaws. On either side of the proboscis is a sensory 3-jointed *palp*. Close behind the palpi are the two conspicuous *compound eyes*. The face between the eyes and below the antennae is called the *frons*. The *antennae* are wide apart in the Skippers, close together in all other butterflies; they are both sense organs and balancers.

The *thorax* bears the wings and legs and is made up of three segments. Each segment bears a pair of legs but only the second and third bear wings.

The three pairs of legs are all of the same pattern. They are made up of a basal hip-joint (coxa), which is immobile, and three mobile segments, the femur, tibia and tarsus, the last, corresponding to the foot, five-jointed and usually clawed. In the Nymphalidae and Satyridae the front legs are clawless and so small that butterflies of these two families seem to have only four legs.

Side view of a Pierid butterfly

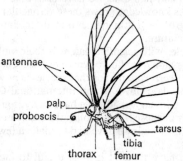

In the identification of butterflies the *wings* are of course of prime importance. The scales that cover them are minute flattened plates fixed to the wings by tiny stalks and overlapping like the tiles on a roof. These scales contain the pigments that give colour to the wings, and their arrangement forms the pattern of markings. The microscopic structure of some scales breaks up the light that falls on them, as does a thin film of oil, to produce the 'metallic' colours of the Blues and Coppers. These are interference colours and they disappear if the scales are wetted. Pigments are not affected in this way. Scattered amongst the ordinary scales are other scales peculiar to males and called androconia. At the base of such scales there are gland cells. These produce scents, believed to be attractive to females, which are diffused through the tufts of fine fibres at the tips of the scales. Very often these androconia are grouped together in patches to form sex-brands.

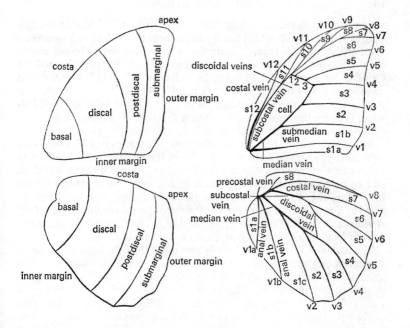

For descriptive purposes, the principal areas of the wing are the *costa* (front edge), *inner margin* (back edge), the outer margin, and the subdivisions of its surface, i.e., the basal, discal, postdiscal, submarginal, marginal, subapical and apical areas. The veins (fig. above) are of great importance. It is easiest to see them on the underside. If it is difficult, moisten the wing with a drop of benzene or alcohol. This will show them up momentarily and evaporate without doing any damage. Look first at the basal half of the wing towards the costa. You will see a largish clear area surrounded by veins. This is the *cell*, sometimes called the discal or discoidal cell. It is bounded in front by the *subcostal vein*, behind by the *median* vein, and outwardly by one to three short transverse veins called the discoidal or discocellular veins, one or even two of which may be absent. The veins of the fore-wing are numbered 1 to 12. Vein 1 arises from the base of the wing and runs roughly parallel to the inner margin. As it is largely hidden (when seen from beneath) behind the costa of the hind-wing it is best to start counting the veins from vein 2, which originates from the median vein about halfway along the lower edge of the cell. Count forwards from this vein and you will find that the last vein, which also arises from the base of the wing, is number 12. On the hind-wing start counting in the same way from vein 2; you will find that the last long vein is number 8, which usually has a short forward branch (precostal vein) arising near its base. This simple system contains one or two minor snags. Sometimes, particularly in the Lycaenidae, the fore-wing will be found to have only 10 or 11 veins. In such cases it is vein 7, 8 or 9 that is missing, or two of them. The veins we call 10, 11 and 12 are always present. Again, except in the Papilionidae there are two anal veins on the hind-wing, between the inner margin and vein 2; to avoid altering the numbers of the other veins these are called vein 1a and vein 1b.

The wing surfaces between the veins we call the *spaces*. Having learnt the veins, you should have no difficulty in identifying them. The system follows that of the veins. Space 2 (s2) lies above v2 and between it and v3, and so on to space 12 (s12). When only one anal vein is present on the hind-wing, the spaces starting from the inner margin, are numbered 1a and 1b; if two anal veins are present the third space so created is called slc. A statement such as 'ocelli in s2, 3 and (4)' implies that ocelli are always present in s2 and s3 but may or may not be present in s4.

The *abdomen* is much less heavily chitinised than the head and thorax. It is composed of 10 segments, only seven of which are externally recognisable, namely segments 2 to 8. Besides the organs of digestion and reproduction it contains the vascular heart (dorsally) and the nerve cord (ventrally) which both extend into the head. The chitinous parts of the genitalia, at the tip of the abdomen, are of very great importance in classification. They also provide a means of *sexing* specimens in difficult cases. Look at the tip of the body from beneath—it may be necessary to brush away the hairs and scales first. If it is a male the valves (claspers), one on each side, will be visible, and perhaps also the tip of the penis. The female abdomen is blunt-ended with at most the end of the ovipositor showing.

MAKING A COLLECTION

Apparatus. First essentials are a net, a killing bottle, forceps, pins, setting boards and store boxes, notebook and a labelling system.

Nets. A rigid circular frame about 15 inches in diameter, a short detachable handle, some two or three feet long, and a tapering bag of strong light-weight material are the basic requirements. A net of a different shape, known as a kite or balloon net is greatly preferred by many butterfly hunters. It has a rather larger opening and can be used without a separate handle, the brass Y-shaped frame holder serving this purpose. Black or dark green mosquito netting is best for the bag and it should be sewn to a much tougher material, such as calico, which passes over the frame. The length of the bag is important in two ways; it should be long enough to flick over the frame amply, so that the butterfly can't escape, and it should not be so long that one cannot easily reach the bottom with the killing bottle. Most types of net are made to fold up, or to take to pieces easily, and are to be had from dealers in natural history materials. When far afield it is wise to have spare bags and a spare frame—they are very liable to accident.

Killing Bottles. The standard killing bottle uses cyanide of potassium as the killing agent, embedded beneath a layer of Plaster of Paris. This is a deadly poison. Unless you are properly qualified to do so do not attempt to make a cyanide bottle yourself. Get a chemist to do it for you. A transparent unbreakable plastic bottle is far safer than a glass one. The bottle should have an opening about 2 inches wide, a depth of 4 to 5 inches and a cork bung. Such a bottle should last several years. Keep some crumpled tissue paper or cellulose wadding (*not* cotton wool) in the bottom, to give the insects a foothold and prevent them from rubbing around, but periodically remove and burn it. Carbon tetrachloride is an alternative, if cyanide is thought too dangerous. In a bottle, put a layer about one inch thick of bits of rubber, cover this with discs of thick blotting paper with a small central hole, drip the liquid through this, but don't over do it as it will spoil the specimens. The rubber will absorb the liquid, more of which will be needed fairly frequently, so always have some handy.

Some butterflies tend to die 'inside out', with their wings folded underneath, instead of over their backs. This is a great nuisance when it comes to setting them. As soon as they seem to be dead, grasp the legs with a fine-pointed forceps and gently blow between the wings. Usually they will spring over. If they don't, allow the points of the forceps to open and press gently downwards with the butterfly lying on its back. Wait a moment in case they spring back.

Keep the number of butterflies in the killing bottle at a time to the minimum. Having made quite sure that the butterfly you have bottled is a 'good' one, you will want to see that it stays good, so don't let it get thrown around in the bottle and rub its scales off. As soon as it is quiet (not necessarily dead) tip it out and with forceps—stamp collectors' forceps are good for this job—pick it up and slip it into a small transparent envelope—stamp collectors provide these too—and transfer it in the envelope unsealed to another larger killing bottle. A shallow glass jar about 4 inches in diameter with a tight-fitting screw cap is ideal for this purpose.

Pins. Most British collectors still refuse to accept the so-called continental pins, which are all of a standard length of 38 mm, vary in thickness, and are made of steel, preferably stainless. These pins are adopted by all important museums, leave plenty of room for labels, and allow specimens to be handled without forceps and exchanged with foreign collectors without recrimination. English entomological pins are made in a variety of lengths and gauges to suit individual tastes. A good all-round size is 30 mm long and known as a number 12. The only advantage of the English pin is that it saves space by allowing the use of shallower store-boxes. Ordinary household pins are too clumsy and should never be used.

With your fresh specimens still in their envelopes you must decide either to set them at once or to store them to set later (see below). The sooner a specimen is set the better it will be. Tip it out of the envelope, pick it up with forceps and place the thorax between finger and thumb of the other hand. Gently squeeze it. If it is in a fit state to set, i.e. properly relaxed, the wings will open slightly. Push a pin through the centre of the thorax at right angles to the long axis of the body, making sure that it does not lean to right or left. Leave about 10 mm of the pin clear above the body if you are using continental pins, less with the shorter English pins. It is now ready to set.

Setting boards. Your choice of setting boards will depend on your choice of pins: 'high' for continental pins, 'low' for English pins. They are made in various widths and the central groove varies accordingly. The top should be made of compressed cork about half an inch thick and papered. Cut some strips of tracing paper the length of the board but not quite as wide as the area to be covered, one for each side. Pin one strip firmly to the top of the board. The short domestic pins known as lill pins are ideal. Pin the specimen in the groove so that its wings will lie dead flat on the surface of the board and the pin is not sloping; then, with a setting needle, move the fore-wing forward under the paper till the inner margin is at right angles to the groove. Press the paper gently down to hold it there and put a pin alongside. Now move the hind-wing into position, and pin again. Put several more pins around the margins of the wings to stop them slipping while you repeat the process with the other wings. If the specimen tends to spin on its pin during these operations, push a long pin down into the groove close against the back of the thorax. Position the antennae neatly with further pins. Leave the specimens on the boards about 10 to 14 days. They will stay 'set' indefinitely if kept dry. Be especially careful when taking specimens off the boards not to touch the antennae, which will be very brittle and easily broken off. Travelling setting cases are available from dealers and are very convenient if you want to set your catch whilst away from home.

Storage. A butterfly, however perfect and well-set, loses much of its scientific value if not provided with proper data. Time (date), place, altitude (if relevant) and the name of the collector should be neatly written on stiff paper and pinned below on the same pin that carries the specimen. Use Indian ink, or if dealing with large numbers of specimens, have the labels printed. When labelled, specimens should be arranged in parallel columns, males on left, females on the right, and their names, written on thin card, pinned below. Wooden store-boxes are best, but they should be air-tight and have some provision for holding naphthalene to discourage insect pests. Entomological cabinets of ten or more drawers are even better than store-boxes, especially if they have glass bottoms as well as lids, but they are very much more expensive.

If you are unable to set your catch each day you can either put them between layers of cellulose wadding (not cotton wool) in a relaxing tin, or paper them. The type of relaxing tin known as a Newman tin is very good and will keep specimens relaxed and mould-free for several weeks. Be sure to put a locality label with each batch. To 'paper' a specimen take a rectangular piece of paper—ordinary newspaper is excellent as it is soft and slightly absorbent—and fold it to form a triangular envelope enclosing the specimen. Don't forget to write the data along the folded edge. Specimens stored in this way will keep indefinitely if put in a dry box with flaked naphthalene sprinkled among the papers. They can be relaxed and set when convenient. Any metal box with a fairly well-fitting lid will serve as a relaxing tin. Put about an inch of moist sterile sand in the bottom, cover it with a perforated false bottom and a sheet of blotting paper. Open the paper triangles and lay them on the blotting paper. Add a little naphthalene or thymol to prevent mould. The time needed for a specimen to become fully relaxed will depend on its size and the maintenance of constant high humidity at a temperature of 60° to 70° Fahrenheit inside the tin. Do not let moisture condense on the specimens: it will ruin them. Specimens that have been papered and relaxed before being set are never so good as those set 'fresh', especially the Blues, which are very apt to discolour. Relaxing is apt to be tricky, and in the case of the Skippers, sometimes very difficult. To set these, if they are trouble-some, make a short shallow cut on each side of the thorax immediately below the base of the wings. A good knife for this purpose is a broken piece of safety razor blade.

Other things to have or remember. A strong light-weight satchel that can be quickly and safely dropped is essential. If you take a lens with you when collecting, keep it on a sling round the neck. Tie a piece of red tape or wool to your forceps: they will be easier to find if dropped in the long grass. A wooden block about 2 inches square with a central hole of measured depth is useful for ensuring that data labels are all at the same height on the pins. You will think of other gadgets as experience grows, but there are very few that the dealers have not already thought of and can't supply.

Collecting. Chasing butterflies with a net is very good exercise, but it is not the most productive way to collect. It is better not to frighten the butterfly you want to catch. Stalk it and watch where it settles. Then, carefully avoiding sudden movements and taking care not to let your shadow fall on it, strike quickly. If you miss it the first time, have patience; it will very probably come back in time to the selfsame spot. Note carefully the kind of perch on which it has settled: it is disheartening to see it fly off unscathed whilst you are left to disentangle your net from a thorn bush. Don't strike too hard; a butterfly is very fragile and even the fabric of the net can damage it. Never strike at a butterfly head on; it will almost certainly dodge the net. Strike sideways or use a following shot, which is often best. When caught most butterflies will fly upwards towards the light, which is helpful when you are trying to bottle them. But there are some, notably the Graylings, which have a habit of diving down into the grass, or slipping out of the net sideways. The best way to catch these is often by slapping the net down on top of them for they are fond of settling on the ground.

When caught a butterfly should be got into the killing bottle without delay. Make sure that it is at the bottom of the net, if necessary sweeping the net backwards and forwards once or twice to get it there. Grasp the net above it and, holding it upwards, with the same hand take the bung out of the killing bottle which you have taken out of your pocket with the other hand. Slip the bottle up inside the net and manoeuvre the butterfly into it. Holding the net firmly, try to get a double fold of the net fabric over the mouth of the bottle, put the bung on top of this and gently withdraw the netting as you insert the bung. The stronger the killing bottle the better, for the less time a butterfly has to dash around inside the bottle the less damage it will do itself. For what to do next, see the paragraphs on pins, storage, etc.

All this may seem rather elaborate and complicated, but with a little practice you will soon get the hang of it. It takes longer to describe than to do.

Where to collect. For general collecting the best places are open glades in well established woodlands, heathlands and commons, flowery meadows and hillsides that have seldom been disturbed. Even roadside verges can be quite productive. Some butterflies are almost ubiquitous—because their food-plants are. Even within a radius of twenty-five miles of central London about half the indigenous British butterflies are to be found, though not so commonly as formerly. However, they don't all fly at the same time or in the same place.

If you are planning to go abroad, look through the distribution maps to see what species occur in the area you propose to visit, then check the dates when they are on the wing, their special food-plants and habitats. Many species are restricted to special habitats and food-plants, so you will need to be able to recognise these. When in the field look for blossoms that are particularly attractive to butterflies, such as bramble, thistles, thyme, clovers and trefoils, crane's bill and *Polygonum*, and remember that the females are most likely to be found hovering around the food-plants busy egg-laying. Only the Satyridae seem not to be greatly attracted by flowers, and these fly mostly in grassy places. In any new locality you visit make sure that you explore all the different kinds of habitat it affords, not forgetting swampy areas which are favourite places for some species and the slightly polluted mud puddles frequented by so many alpine butterflies.

In the bibliography (p. 339) you will find references to books and articles about the butterflies of the countries covered by this Guide. These will help you in planning a trip and point to species of special interest. But please do not be content just to follow in the footsteps of other collectors. Try other places that have not been visited. You may be disappointed, but you may also meet with some pleasant surprises, and certainly you will add to our knowledge of the detailed distribution of butterflies. Make sure that you have this Guide with you and do your best to identify at once everything you catch. Closely allied species, difficult to distinguish and easily confused, may be flying together, and if you only recognise this fact too late you will regret it. Don't neglect apparently 'common' species; they may be common where you find them but nowhere else. One tends to ignore the 'Small Whites' for example, yet in southern Europe there are several quite distinct species which are very difficult to identify on the wing. Blues, too, and the black and white Skippers of the genus *Pyrgus* present great difficulty even when set.

While collecting don't neglect any opportunities that occur to make notes about butterfly behaviour. Recorded information on flight habits, feeding preferences, courtship behaviour and mating, resting places and attitudes and so on are deplorably meagre. Observations of this kind are always welcomed by editors of entomological journals, of which there are many, and can be far more rewarding than just amassing specimens.

Why collect? With butterflies becoming scarcer every year this is a very pertinent question, the answer to which lies in the purpose of the intended collection. Making a small collection for personal satisfaction is forgivable provided that it is kept small enough not to jeopardise the species collected. Before starting a collection that is intended to form the basis of a scientific study of any kind it is well to seek advice as to whether the project in mind is worth while; and when the collection has served its purpose it should be offered to a suitable scientific institute or museum. Commercial collecting will be with us just so long as there are buyers: nothing can condone the use of butterfly wings in the manufacture of 'jewellery'. Neither can one find any excuse for the collector whose only objective would seem to be the possession of more specimens of every kind, and especially the rare kinds, than anybody else—these are the rogues who shame us all. One can collect butterflies with a camera. Why not try? If perfection is sought in the insects that form a collection, the best course is to rear them in captivity, and release any surplus to augment the wild stock.

Conservation. In some countries the collection of butterflies threatened with extinction is forbidden by law, and illustrations of these species are publicly displayed. In Britain the conservation movement is mainly voluntary, supported by the Nature Conservancy, and works, as far as butterflies are concerned, through a broadly based Joint Committee for the Conservation of British Insects (41 Queen's Gate, London, S.W.7), its only weapons precept, example and persuasion. Conservationists are however working towards the introduction of legislation that would protect all animals threatened with extinction in Britain.

This Guide has not been written to assist you to destroy wild life, but to enable you to identify the European butterflies that you find, so that you can talk about them, write about them, study them and add to knowledge. If you must make a collection, don't kill every butterfly you catch: butterflies can be stupefied in a killing bottle, and will quickly revive on release after examination. Spare them so that in years to come they are still with us and not just memories in a museum.

MAPPING SCHEME

An international scheme has recently been set up which will provide far more detailed information on the present distribution of European butterflies than is possible in this Guide. Maps are being produced on a 50 km basis, but it is hoped that the records from each European country will be collected on a 10 km basis. A special species-list card based on the check list used in this book is available with detailed instructions for those wishing to take part in the scheme. Further details are obtainable from The European Invertebrate Survey, c/o Biological Records Centre, Monks Wood Experimental Station. Abbots Ripton, Huntingdon, England.

Checklist of Species

NYMPHALIDAE [*contd.*]
Argynnis paphia
Argyronome laodice
Mesoacidalia aglaja
Fabriciana adippe
     niobe
     elisa
Issoria lathonia
Brenthis hecate
     daphne
     ino
Boloria pales
     napaea
     aquilonaris
     graeca
Proclossiana eunomia
Clossiana selene
     euphrosyne
     titania
     chariclea
     freija
     dia
     polaris
     thore
     frigga
     improba
Melitaea cinxia
     arduinna
     phoebe
     aetherie
     didyma
     deserticola
     trivia
     diamina
Mellicta athalia
     deione
     varia
     parthenoides
     aurelia
     britomartis
     asteria
Euphydryas maturna
     intermedia
     cynthia
     iduna
     aurinia
     desfontainii

SATYRIDAE
Melanargia galathea

russiae
larissa
occitanica
arge
ines
Hipparchia fagi
     alcyone
     ellena
     neomiris
     semele
     aristaeus
     azorina
     statilinus
     fatua
     hansii
Pseudotergumia fidia
     wyssii
Chazara briseis
     prieuri
Pseudochazara atlantis
     hippolyte
     mamurra
     anthelea
     geyeri
Oeneis norna
     bore
     glacialis
     jutta
Satyrus actaea
     ferula
Minois dryas
Berberia abdelkader
Brintesia circe
Arethusana arethusa
Erebia ligea
     euryale
     eriphyle
     manto
     claudina
     flavofasciata
     epiphron
     serotina
     christi
     pharte
     melampus
     sudetica
     aethiops
     triaria
     embla
     disa

medusa
polaris
alberganus
pluto
gorge
aethiopella
mnestra
gorgone
epistygne
tyndarus
cassioides
hispania
nivalis
calcaria
ottomana
pronoe
melas
lefebvrei
scipio
stirius
styx
montana
zapateri
neoridas
oeme
meolans
palarica
pandrose
sthennyo
phegea
Maniola jurtina
nurag
Hyponephele lycaon
maroccana
lupina
Aphantopus hyperantus
Pyronia tithonus
cecilia
bathseba
janiroides
Coenonympha tullia
pamphilus
corinna
dorus
austauti
vaucheri
arcania
gardetta
arcanioides
leander

glycerion
iphioides
hero
oedippus
Pararge aegeria
xiphioides
xiphia
Lasiommata megera
maera
petropolitana
Lopinga achine
Kirinia roxelana

NEMEOBIIDAE
Hamearis lucina

LYCAENIDAE
Cigaritis zohra
siphax
allardi
Thecla betulae
Quercusia quercus
Laeosopis roboris
Nordmannia acaciae
ilicis
esculi
Strymonidia spini
w-album
pruni
Callophrys rubi
avis
Tomares ballus
mauretanicus
Lycaena helle
phlaeas
dispar
Heodes virgaureae
ottomanus
tityrus
alciphron
Thersamonia thersamon
phoebus
thetis
Palaeochrysophanus hippothoe
Lampides boeticus
Syntarucus pirithous
Cyclyrius webbianus
Tarucus theophrastus
rosaceus
balkanicus

LYCAENIDAE [*contd.*]
Azanus jesous
Zizeeria knysna
Everes argiades
    decoloratus
    alcetas
Cupido minimus
    osiris
    lorquinii
    carswelli
Celastrina argiolus
Glaucopsyche alexis
    melanops
Turanana panagaea
Maculinea alcon
    arion
    teleius
    nausithous
Iolana iolas
Philotes baton
    abencerragus
    bavius
Scolitantides orion
Freyeria trochylus
Plebejus vogelii
    martini
    pylaon
    argus
Lycaeides idas
    argyrognomon
Vacciniina optilete
Kretania eurypilus
    psylorita
Eumedonia eumedon
Aricia agestis
    artaxerxes
    cramera
    morronensis
    nicias
    anteros
Albulina orbitulus
Agriades glandon
    aquilo
    pyrenaicus
Cyaniris semiargus
    helena
Agrodiaetus damon
    dolus
    ainsae
    admetus

    fabressei
    ripartii
Plebicula escheri
    dorylas
    golgus
    nivescens
    atlantica
    coelestina
    amanda
    thersites
Meleageria daphnis
Lysandra coridon
    hispana
    albicans
    caelestissima
    bellargus
    punctifera
Polyommatus icarus
    eroides
    eros
HESPERIIDAE
Pyrgus malvae
    alveus
    armoricanus
    foulquieri
    serratulae
    carlinae
    cirsii
    onopordi
    cinarae
    sidae
    fritillarius
    andromedae
    cacaliae
    centaureae
Spialia sertorius
    phlomidis
    doris
Muschampia tessellum
    cribrellum
    proto
    mohammed
    leuzeae
Carcharodus alceae
    lavatherae
    boeticus
    flocciferus
    orientalis
Erynnis tages
    marloyi

Heteropterus morpheus
Carterocephalus palaemon
    silvicolus
Thymelicus acteon
    hamza
    lineola

    sylvestris
Hesperia comma
Ochlodes venatus
Gegenes nostrodamus
    pumilio
Borbo borbonica

Further corrections to the Second Edition

The following are some further corrections which it has not been possible to incorporate in this edition.

The following additional MAJOR SUBSPECIES should be noted:

p. 158 *Erebia manto vosgesiaca* Christ 1882 TL: Vosges. ♂ upf usually lacks black subapical spots; ♀ unh markings often white (♂ form *bubastis* Meisner).

p. 220 *Coenonympha gardetta skypetarum* Rebel & Zerny 1931 TL: Albania. Large for a form of *C. gardetta* and perhaps more correctly associated with *C. leander katarae* Coutsis of the Pindus Mts.

p. 239 *Tomares nogelii dobrogensis* Caradja 1895 TL: Tultscha, Rumania Fw 15/16 mm. ♂ ups uniformly dark brown; unh grey with narrow orange bands bordered by black dots. Formerly in the Rumanian Dobrogea, now probably extinct.

p. 242 *Lycaena phlaeas phlaeoides* Staudinger 1901 TL: Madeira. Unh with narrow pale pd band.

p. 285 *Aricia nicias scandica* Wahlgren 1930 TL: Sweden. Slightly larger than alpine specimens; ♂ ups blue areas brighter and better defined on both wings, dark borders narrower. A striking race. Local and uncommon in S. Finland and eastern Sweden between 60°-65° N. latitude: July-August.

p. 281 *Agriades (glandon) dardanus* Freyer proves to be a subspecies of *Agriades pyrenaicus* and should be transferred to that species.

p. 296 *Agrodiaetus ripartii agenjoi* Forster 1965 TL: Catalonia, prov. Barcelona. Ups like *A.r.ripartii*; unh pale grey-brown, white stripe absent, rarely vestigial. July, in grassy places at valley levels. Catalonia. A similar form occurs in Greece.

p. 297 *Plebicula escheri ahmar* le Cerf 1928 TL: Tizi s'Tkrine, Middle Atlas, Morocco. Small. ♂ ups pale blue. June, at 5,400 ft.

The following SPECIES is an addition to the European list:

Pseudochazara sintenisi Staudinger 1895 TL: N.E. Turkey in Asia. As figured by Staudinger this species looks closely allied to *P. mamurra* (p. 149), but the ups is relatively darker. Specimens not available for description.

The following ALTERATIONS should be made:

p. 93 *Fabriciana (adippe) auresiana* Fruhstorfer proves to be a subspecies of *F. niobe* and should be transferred to that species.

p. 140 *Hipparchia aristaeus senthes* Fruhstorfer proves to be firmly established as a Grecian butterfly in many localities in the Peloponnesus and C. Greece.

p. 243 *Lycaena dispar batava* should be corrected to *Lycaena dispar dispar* as it is the extinct British Large Copper that is described.

p. 326 and elsewhere   The generic name *Muschampia* should read *Syrichtus*.

MAPS

Recent information extends the known range of *Leptidea sinapsis* to the Middle Atlas, Morocco; of *Erynnis marloyi* to Catalonia, prov. Barcelona; and of *Callophrys rubi* to the Canary Islands.

Glossary

Abdomen. The free part of the body behind the thorax.

Aberration. An individual variety of rare occurrence; a freak.

Allopatric. Occupying different, mutually exclusive geographical areas.

Anal Angle. The point of the hind-wing opposite the butterfly's anus; i.e. at the junction of inner and outer margins.

Anal fold. A fold in the hind-wing parallel to and close to the inner margin.

Androconia. Wing scales of special form, often tufted, occurring only in males and often grouped in patches to form "sex-brands".

Antennae. Paired sensory organs arising from the insect's head; feelers.

Apex, of wing. The point where costa and outer margin meet, usually angular on fore-wing, rounded on hind-wing.

Auct. (auctorum) used following a specific name indicates its use by authors otherwise than as intended by the original author.

Basad. Towards the base.

Base. Of a wing, the part nearest the body.

Caudal. Associated with the tail.

Cell. (i.e. in butterflies, the discoidal cell). The area in the basal half of each wing generally enclosed by veins. When the closure is incomplete the cell is said to be "open". See Fig. on p. 15.

Cephalic. Associated with the head.

Chevron. An arrow-headed mark.

Chitin. A horny material of which an insect's cuticle is composed.

Chrysalis. See *Pupa.*

Cline. A character gradient; a gradual and almost continuous change of size, colour or wing markings in a recognisable direction throughout a population or series of populations; often apparently related to climatic factors; especially common in such variable species as those of the genera *Erebia* and *Melitaea.*

Club. of antenna. The thickened terminal part of the antenna.

Code. See *International Commission.*

Conspecific. Belonging to the same species.

Costa. The front edge of a wing.

Costal fold. A fold of the fw costa enclosing androconia; confined to certain Skippers (Hesperiidae).

Cryptic. Camouflage intended to hide an animal from predators or prey.

Dimorphism. Occurrence within a species of two distinct forms., e.g. the 'white and 'yellow' females of *Colias.* See also *Polymorphism.*

Discal. Used of the disc or central area of the wing.

Discocellular. See *Discoidal.*

Discoidal. Used of the central area around the transverse discoidal veins at the end of the cell; discoidal spot, a conspicuous mark often present on these veins; discoidal cell, the central area enclosed by veins. See page 15.

Distad. Away from the the base (of the wing).

Distal. Distant from the centre of the body.

Endemic. Native to and always present in a particular area or country; in zoology, confined to that area and not found elsewhere.

Falcate. Hooked.

Family. In Zoology a group of genera all with certain similar characters and considered closely related on this account. Family names always end in -idae.

Fauna. Collective name for all the living creatures in a given region.

Fennoscandia. Geographical term embracing Norway, Sweden and Finland.

Filamentous. Like a fine thread.

Flora. Collective name for all the plants in a given region.

Form. Any recognisably distinct variant of a species, e.g. a female form, a seasonal or local form, a variety or aberration; an indefinite term unless qualified.

Frons. The front of the head between the eyes, often bearing a tuft of hair.

Fuscous. Dusky, grey-brown.

Fusiform. Spindle-shaped.

Genitalia. Sex organs. In butterflies the chitinous organs (partly external) at the end of the abdomen.

Genus. A unit including one species, or a group of species presumably of common origin, separated from related similar units by a different combination of characters.

Hibernation. Survival through winter in a dormant state.

Homonym. The same name used for different species are homonyms. The first published name only is valid.

Hyaline. Translucent; resembling glass.

I.C.Z.N. See *International Commission.*

Imago (pl. *imagines*). The fourth phase of a butterfly's life, the adult insect.

International Commission on Zoological Nomenclature. The body responsible for the International Code of rules that governs the application of the scientific names of animals.

Invalid name. A scientific name which does not conform with the international rules of nomenclature (the Code).

Irrorated. Minutely speckled: dotted with pale coloured scales.

Jullien Organ. A group of stiff rods (batons), formed from modified scales, on the dorsal surface of the last visible segment of the abdomen in certain Satyrid butterflies.

Larva. Caterpillar; an insect at the second (growth) stage of its life.

Linear. In the form of a line.

Lunule. A crescent-shaped mark.

Macular. Spotted.

Nacreous. Like mother-of-pearl.

Ocellus. Of markings, a round spot usually black with a central pale spot or pupil; if the pupil is absent the ocellus is termed "blind".

Palearctic Region. The zoogeographical region that includes Europe, Asia north of the Himalayas, northern Arabia and Africa north of the Sahara, i.e. most of the Old World north of the tropics.

Palpi. Paired sensory organs arising on each side of the proboscis.

Pilose. Covered with fine short hair.

Polymorphism. Occurrence of different individual forms in a single species; the forms may appear constantly or as rare exceptions ("aberrations").

Postdiscal. The area of the wing between the discal and submarginal areas. See Fig., p. 15.

Proboscis. The spirally coiled organ, composed of two minute tubes united side by side to form a third tube, through which a butterfly imbibes liquids; when not in use it lies coiled between the palpi.

Proximal. Near the centre of the body; opposite of "distal".

Pupa. An insect in the third (resting) stage of its life-cycle; the chrysalis.

Pyriform. Pear shaped.

Race. A local form, with distinctive characters, present in all or most individuals.

Reticulate. Marked with a network pattern.

Sagittate. Shaped like an arrow-head.

Sex-brand. See *Androconia*.

Space. An area of the wing lying between two veins and bounded outwardly by the wing margin; usually abbreviated to 's', e.g. s2, s3 etc. See diagram p. 15.

Species. The scientific term—which in practice cannot be precisely defined—for different kinds of butterflies. The specific name is written thus: *Pieris napi* or *P. napi*—*napi* being the name of the species, *Pieris* that of the genus.

Sphragis. A horny, pouch-like structure formed underneath the female abdomen during copulation.

Stria (pl. *striae*). A very slender streak.

Subspecies. Differing populations of a species that occupy separate, though often contiguous areas; geographical races. The subspecific name is written thus: *Pieris napi napi* (which can be abbreviated to *Pieris n. napi* or *P. n. napi*).

Symbiosis. Literally "living together", e.g. the association of the larvae of some Lycaenid butterflies with ants. The association may or may not be of mutual advantage.

Sympatric. Living in the same area; opposite of allopatric (q.v.).

Synonyms. Different names given to the same species. Only the first published name is valid.

Taxonomy. The classification of plants and animals.

Thorax. The part of the insect's body that bears the wings and legs; the chest.

Type locality. The locality in which the type specimen was collected.

Type specimen. The specimen actually described by the author of the name of a species (or subspecies or form).

Valid name. The name recognised as correct under the Code.

Vein. In insect wings, the minute rigid tubes that support the membrane of the wing. See Fig., p. 15.

Venation. The pattern of the veins in an insect's wing. See Fig., p. 15.

Abbreviations

♂ male
♀ female
dc   discoidal
esp. especially
f.   form
fw   fore-wing
fw22mm   length of fore-wing measured from apex to point
        of attachment to thorax, in millimetres.
gc   ground colour
hw   hind-wing
pd   postdiscal
s   space
subsp   subspecies
syn   synonym
TL   type locality
unf   underside of fore-wing
unh   underside of hind-wing
uns   underside
upf   upperside of fore-wing
uph   upperside of hind-wing
ups   upperside
v   vein
F: French
G: German
Sw: Swedish
Sp: Spanish

The area covered extends from the North Cape within the Arctic Circle to the southern slopes of the Atlas Mountains north of the Saharan Desert, and from the Azores, Canary Islands and Madeira to Tripoli, the Bosphorus and the western frontier of Russia but not to the Aegean islands or Cyprus. In Iceland there are no indigenous butterflies.

PAPILIONIDAE
Latreille 1809

A large family including species that vary greatly in appearance and in structural details. All are alike in two important characters: the butterflies (imagines) have six functional legs of nearly equal size and each tarsus has a single pair of claws. In the hind-wing there is a single submedian (or anal) vein and the inner margin is slightly concave.

PAPILIO MACHAON *Swallowtail*

F: Le Grand Porte-queue   G: Schwalbenschwanz   Sw: Makaonfjäril
Sp: Makaon
Range. From N. Africa across Europe and temperate Asia to the Himalaya Mts. and Japan. Represented in N. America by closely related species or subspecies.   Map 1

P. machaon Linnaeus 1758   TL: Sweden (Verity 1947)   Pl. 1
  syn: *sphyrus* Huebner 1823
Description. ♂fw 32/38mm.; *first brood* ups yellow with dense black markings; upf basal area black; uph inner margin and s1 black, blue spots in black pd band obscure; abdomen black. *Second brood* (f. *aestivus* Zeller 1847) ups markings dusted with pale scales; uph inner margin narrowly dark, s1 pale, black pd band less wide, blue markings better defined; abdomen yellow with black dorsal stripe. In S. Europe seasonal difference may be striking. ♀ similar.
Flight. April/May and July/August in two or three broods in S. Europe and N. Africa. In northern districts usually single-brooded.
Habitat. Meadows and flowery banks from lowlands to 6,000 ft. Larval food plants wild carrots, fennel and various umbelliferous plants.
Distribution. Throughout the region from N. Africa to North Cape; in England now confined to Norfolk, very local in fens, formerly more widely distributed. The species is a vagrant: continental specimens, usually of the second brood, occasionally reach England.
Variation. Apart from the seasonal changes the wing-markings are stable, showing little evidence of geographical variation in Europe. Rare abnormal forms include f. *nigra* Reutti, ups wings black except the uph blue spots in pd band; f. *nigrofasciata* Rothke, uph black pd band extends to blend with marginal border; f. *aurantiaca* Speyer ups wings deep yellow or orange-yellow.
Similar species. *P. hospiton* below, unf marginal band narrow, composed of dark-bordered grey-blue lunules; occurs only in Corsica and Sardinia.

PAPILIO HOSPITON *Corsican Swallowtail*
Range. Restricted to Corsica and Sardinia.   Map 2

P. hospiton   Géné 1839   TL: Tortoli, Sardinia   Pl. 1
Description. ♂fw 36/38mm., resembles *P. machaon* closely, but differs as follows: tail at v4 on hw shorter; uph blue spots in dark marginal border small and well defined; unf pd band composed of a series of grey lunules bordered black. On both surfaces the red anal spot is small, sometimes nearly absent. ♀ similar.
Flight. May/July in a single brood with prolonged emergence.
Habitat. Mountains at 2–4,000 ft. Larval food plants Umbelliferae, esp. fennel.
Distribution. Corsica and Sardinia only.
Similar species. *P. machaon* p. 35.

PAPILIO ALEXANOR   *Southern Swallowtail*
Range. From Provence, S. Italy and S. Balkans across W. Asia to Iran and Turkestan.   Map 3

P. alexanor   Esper 1799   TL: Nice, France   Pl. 1
Description. ♂fw 31/33mm., antennal club straight; ups bright yellow, outer margins narrowly bordered black; upf with four broad black transverse stripes, the black pd band with narrow blue central stripe; uph black pd band filled with blue and greatly enlarged in s2. ♀ often larger.
Flight. April to July in a single prolonged emergence.
Habitat. Mountainous districts to 4,000 ft. or more, attracted by thistles. Larval food plants Umbelliferae, esp. *Trinia vulgaris, Seseli montanum* and *Ptychotis heterophylla*.
Distribution. Alpine foothills in Provence to Ardèche, Drôme and Isère, esp. in Var and Basses Alpes, e.g. Draguignan, Beauvezer, St. Martin Vésubie, valley of the Tinée, etc. Italy, local and rare on eastern slopes of Maritime Alps, esp. San Martino Lantosca, also Aspromonte and E. Sicily. Yugoslavia in Istria and Dalmatia. Greece on Mt. Parnassus, Taygetos, Corfu, but generally very local and scarce in all eastern localities.

IPHICLIDES PODALIRIUS   *Scarce Swallowtail*
F: Le Flambé   G: Segelfalter   Sp: Chupa leche   Sw: Podaliriusfjäril
Range. From N. Africa across Europe and temperate Asia to China.
    Map 4

I. podalirius podalirius   Linnaeus 1758   TL: Livorno, Tuscany (Verity 1947)   Pl. 1
syn. *sinon* Poda 1761
Description. ♂fw 32/40mm., female larger; *first brood* ups very pale yellow, black markings heavy; upf six transverse stripes; uph wing-border along inner margin black but s1 narrowly pale, variable, sometimes obscured, anal ocellus with orange crescent above; unh double discal band filled orange; abdomen black. In *second brood* (f. *zancleus* Zeller)

ups cream-white; uph dark wing-border along inner margin clearly divided, s 1 pale and black stripes not heavy; unh double discal band not filled orange; apex of abdomen pale grey.

Flight. March/September in one or two broods, usually May/June and August/September.

Habitat. Lowlands to 6,000 ft. or more, often around fruit orchards. Larval food plants sloe and cultivated fruit trees.

Distribution. Pyrenees, excluding E. Pyrenees, thence eastwards through Europe to 54°N, including the Mediterranean islands. Occasional vagrants have occurred in Britain.

I. podalirius feisthamelii Duponchel 1832 TL: Barcelona and Algeria
Pl. 1

Description. ♂fw 35/42mm.; *first brood* ups grey-white, wings thickly scaled, black markings heavier; uph inner border broadly black; abdomen black. ♀larger, ups gc pale yellow. In *second brood* (f. *latteri* Austaut) wings less thickly scaled; ups black markings less dense; uph wing-border along inner margin clearly divided, s 1 pale and black stripes obsolescent; abdomen grey with black dorsal stripe. ♀ generally slightly flushed yellow, sometimes very large.

Flight and **Habitat** as for *P. p. podalirius*.

Distribution. Morocco, Algeria, Tunisia. Portugal and Spain northwards to southern slopes of Pyrenees. France, E. Pyrenees.

ZERYNTHIA POLYXENA *Southern Festoon*

F: La Diane G: Osterluzeifalter

Range. Local in S. Europe and W. Asia Minor. Map 5

Z. polyxena polyxena Schiffermueller 1775 TL: Vienna
syn: *hypsipyle* Schulze 1776; *hypermnestra* Scopoli 1763 (invalid homonym) Pl. 2

Description. ♂fw 23/26mm., ups gc yellow; upf black transverse markings with *small red costal spot in s*9, outer margin with border of deep lunules; uph a series of red pd spots and deep marginal lunules as on fw, the row of blue submarginal spots lying between sometimes vestigial or absent. ♀ similar.

Flight. End April/May in a single brood.

Habitat. Rough stony places, lowlands to 3,000 ft. Larval food plants *Aristolochia pistolochia*, *A. rotunda* and *A. clematitis*.

Distribution. Widely distributed but local in SE. Europe. Austria, Hungary, Rumania, Balkans to Greece. Sicily.

Z. polyxena cassandra Geyer 1828 TL: not stated Pl. 2
syn: *creusa* Meigen 1829

Description. Resembles *Z. p. polyxena* but ups *black markings slightly more* *extensive*; upf *red costal spot in s9 absent*; uph marginal lunules slightly wider and less deep; unh reddish suffusion more noticeable.

Flight and **Habitat** as for *Z. p. polyxena*.

Distribution. France in Var, Maritime Alps and Bouches du Rhône. Italy, common near Florence, Milan, Turin, etc., more rare in peninsular Italy and Sicily, upf sometimes with red costal spot.

Variation. Ups gc sometimes deep yellow, f. *ochracea* Staudinger.

Similar species. *Z. rumina* below, upf has red spots in cell; may be confusing in SE. France.

ZERYNTHIA RUMINA *Spanish Festoon*

Sp: Arlequin

Range. Confined to SW. Europe and N. Africa. Map 6

Z. rumina rumina Linnaeus 1758 TL: S. Europe Pl. 2

Description. ♂fw 22/23mm., ups gc pale yellow. Differs from *Z. polyxena* as follows: Upf *red spots are present at base of cell, in discal area in s1b* (usually), at cell-end and in pd area in s4, 5, 6, 9, with *vitreous cells beyond*, lunular marginal border less deep; uph with red spots on costa in s7 and pd red spots in s1–5. ♀ similar.

Flight. February/May depending upon altitude, etc., in a single brood.

Habitat. Rough places and rocky slopes on hills and mountains. Larval food plants various kinds of *Aristolochia*.

Distribution. SE. France, in Provence, Languedoc, Rousillon and E. Pyrenees. Spain and Portugal, widely distributed from sea-level to 5,000 ft., especially common on rocky coastal hills.

Variation. A red spot is sometimes present at the base of the cell on the hind-wing, almost constant in specimens from S. France, f. *medesicaste* Hoffmannsegg Pl. 2. Very rarely the red markings may be greatly enlarged, f. *honoratii* Boisduval Pl. 2; a recurrent variant with gc deep orange-yellow is more frequent, f. *canteneri* Staudinger, almost confined to females.

Z. rumina ornatior Blachier 1905 TL: Morocco Pl. 2
    syn: *africana* Stichel 1907

Description. ♂fw 25/26mm., larger, with brilliant markings, uph red pd spots larger and enclosed in the solid black marginal border; upf red spot in s1b absent. ♀ similar, f. *canteneri* common Pl. 2.

Flight. February or later.

Habitat as for *Z. r. rumina*.

Distribution. Morocco, Algeria, Tunisia, restricted to northern slopes of Atlas Mts., flying from sea-level to 5,000 ft.

Similar species. *Z. polyxena* p. 37.

ALLANCASTRIA CERISYI *Eastern Festoon*
Range. SE. Europe through Asia Minor (TL of *Thais cerisyi* Godart 1822), Lebanon, Iraq, Iran. Map 7

A. cerisyi ferdinandi Stichel 1907 TL: Bulgaria Pl. 2
Description. ♂fw 26/31mm., generally large; ups pale yellow; upf with scanty black costal and pd markings; uph with small red pd marks in s15- and on costa in s7. ♀ similar, ups black markings more extensive.
Flight. April/June in a single brood.
Habitat. Rough ground on hills or mountains to 4,000 ft. Larval food plants *Aristolochia* species.
Distribution. Crete and islands in the Aegean archipelago. N. Greece. Albania. SE. Yugoslavia. Rumania. Bulgaria.
Variation. Size varies in different localities; the Bulgarian race is the largest known. In Crete much smaller and paler, f. *cretica* Rebel.

ARCHON APOLLINUS *False Apollo*
Range. Bulgaria and the Near East. Map 8

A. apollinus Herbst 1798 TL: Ourlac (Bay of Izmir) Pl. 2
Description. ♂fw 27/30mm., largely hyaline, sometimes brownish; upf with fine transverse striae, large black spots in cell, at cell-end and on costa; uph yellowish, the dark marginal border enclosing six submarginal ocelli pupilled blue, bordered internally with red. ♀ darker, markings more complete.
Flight. March/April in a single brood, one of the first species to emerge in spring.
Habitat. Rough ground, usually in mountainous districts, to 5,000 ft. Food plant *Aristolochia hastata*.
Distribution. Recorded occasionally from Greece and European Turkey.

PARNASSIUS APOLLO *Apollo*
F: l'Apollon G: Apollo Sw: Apollofjäril Sp: Apolo
Range. On all major mountains from Spain through Europe, including Fennoscandia, to C. Asia. Map 9

P. apollo Linnaeus 1758 TL: Sweden Pl. 3
Description. ♂fw 35/42mm., ups white with markings of characteristic pattern; *upf round black pd spot in s1b*; uph spots red or more rarely yellow, usually large, ocellated. ♀ similar, ups usually with considerable grey suffusion, uph red spots often larger, sometimes with additional red spots in pd area of fw and at anal angle of hw. In both sexes *antennal shaft pale grey, ringed slightly darker grey*.
Flight. July/August.
Habitat. Among mountains at subalpine levels from 2,500–6,000 ft. in S.

and C. Europe, at lower levels in N. Europe. Larval food plants stonecrop
(*Sedum*, esp. *S. album*, *S. telephium*, *S. purpurascens* and *Sempervivum*).
Distribution. Widely distributed in mountains of W. Europe and S. Fennoscandia but extinct in some districts, e.g. C. Germany, Czechoslovakia
and Denmark. Absent from Britain.
Variation. A very large number of local races and subspecies have been
described and named. Description of these is beyond the scope of this
Guide. Those illustrated are *P. apollo hispanicus* Oberthur ♀, a large race,
usually only slightly suffused grey, a Spanish specimen with orange ocelli
on hw (Pl. 3); and *P. apollo rhodopensis* Markovic ♂, very large, uph ocelli
brilliant red with white pupils Pl. 3. Among other named subspecies the
following should be mentioned. *P. a. apollo* Linnaeus, TL: Sweden; large
♂ gc pure white. *P. a. geminus* Stichel, TL: Switzerland; ♂ gc faintly yellowish, red spots smaller. *P. a. bartholomaeus* Stichel, TL: Bavaria; small
♂ ups heavily marked (illustrated on front endpaper). *P. a. pumilus*
Stichel, TL Calabria, very small. *P. a. nevadensis* Oberthur, TL: S.
Spain; ♂ ups ocelli yellow. *P. a. siciliae* Oberthur, TL: Sicily; small.

PARNASSIUS PHOEBUS   *Small Apollo*

G: Alpen-Apollo
Range. Alps, Urals and through Siberia (TL of *P. phoebus* Fabricius 1793)
to Kamschatka. N. America to British Columbia and Rocky Mts.

Map 10

P. phoebus sacerdos   Stichel 1906   TL: Pontresina, Engadin   Pl. 3
   syn: *delius* Esper 1800 (invalid homonym)
Description. ♂fw 30/33mm., resembles *P. apollo*; *ups faintly yellowish-
white*; upf pd costal spot in s8 usually red-centred, spot in s1b usually
absent; uph pd area clear white, red spots often small. ♀ similar, more or
less suffused grey, more heavily marked and uph red spots larger, upf black
spot in s1b generally present, often red-centred. In both sexes *antennal
shaft white clearly ringed black*.
Flight. July/August.
Habitat. Grass slopes at 6,000 ft. or above. Larval food plants *Saxifraga
aizioides*, *Sempervivum montanum*.
Distribution. Maritime Alps and eastwards to Styria and Grossglockner,
rare in north, occasional in Allgäuer Alps, absent from Limestone Alps
of N. Tirol. Absent from Jura, Pyrenees, Julian Alps, Balkans and
Carpathians.
Variation. On uph red ocelli united by black bar, f. *cardinalis* Oberthur,
not rare in eastern Alps. The female illustrated is typical of the Styrian
race, f. *styriacus* Fruhstorfer.

P. phoebus gazeli   Praviel 1936   TL: Vallée du Boréon, Alpes Maritimes
Description. ♂ resembles *P. p. sacerdos*, but ups gc is chalk-white; upf grey

marginal border wide and extending nearly to the submarginal band, which is less dense than usual, pd costal spot in s 8 not red-centred; uph red spots small, without white pupils.
Flight and Habitat as for *P.p. sacerdos*.
Distribution. Known only from a few high valleys in the Maritime Alps, where it appears to replace the usual form.
Similar species. *Parnassius apollo* p. 39, shaft of antenna white indistinctly ringed pale grey; upf black pd spot in s 1b always present, usually large; flies at subalpine levels.

PARNASSIUS MNEMOSYNE   *Clouded Apollo*

F: Le semi-apollon   Sw: Mnemosynefjäril   G: Schwarzer Apollo
Sp: Blanca de Asso
Range. From Pyrenees and C. France across C. and N. Europe to 64°N and eastwards to Iran, Caucasus and C. Asia.   Map 11

P. mnemosyne mnemosyne   Linnaeus 1758   TL: Finland   Pl. 3
Description. ♂fw 26/31 mm., ups gc white without red spots; upf black markings reduced to two spots, upf wide marginal border grey; uph without marginal markings except on inner margin; uns glabrous. ♀ similar, often suffused dark grey, uph markings sometimes more extensive; dorsum of abdomen black and glabrous; sphragis large, extending from third abdominal segment to anal extremity.
Flight. May to July in a single brood.
Habitat. Hilly or mountainous districts to 5,000 ft. in C. Europe, a lowland species in the north, frequents damp meadows. Larval food plant *Corydalis*.
Distribution. Widely distributed in W. Europe to 64°N, including Pyrenees, Central Massif of France, Alps and Carpathians; Apennines, W. Sicily and Balkans. Very local and rare in Norway. Absent from Britain, Spain, Portugal, NW. Switzerland, Denmark (except Baltic islands).
Variation. Females with extensive fuscous suffusion are common in the Pyrenees and in other mountainous areas, f. *melaina* Honrath, Pl. 3.

P. mnemosyne athene   Stichel 1908   TL: Mt. Chelmos and Olenos, Greece   Pl. 3
Description. Resembles *P. m. mnemosyne*, but ups black markings less intense, usually smaller, the grey marginal border on upf divided by a chain of five or six faint white spots. ♀ sphragis noticeably longer.
Flight and Habitat as for *P.m. mnemosyne*.
Distribution. Southern Greece as a constant race; similar forms are not rare in the Apennines, Sicily, Alps of Provence and E. Pyrenees. This subspecies is clearly an outlier of the near-eastern races of the species.

Similar species. *Aporia crataegi* p. 42, easily distinguished by the absence of black markings.

PIERIDAE
Duponchel 1832

This is a very large family, but the species are generally easy to recognise, with white or yellow wings, the upper surface with scanty black markings. In nearly all species the sexes differ considerably, and many have two or more annual broods which may show marked seasonal variation. The butterflies have six functional legs of nearly equal size, each tarsus with a pair of double claws. In the hind-wing there are two anal veins, the inner margin slightly convex.

APORIA CRATAEGI   *Black-veined White*
F: Le Gazé   Sw: Hagtornsfjäril   G: Baumweissling
Sp: Blanca del Majuelo
Range. From N. Africa and W. Europe across temperate Asia to Korea and Japan.   Map 21

A. crataegi   Linnaeus 1758   TL: Sweden (Verity 1947)   Pl. 13
Description. ♂ fw 28/34 mm., ups gc white, veins pigmented dark brown or black, a narrow dark discoidal mark; uns similar, often with thin scattering of black scales, esp. on unh. ♀ larger, fw glabrous showing light brown membrane, veins brown, dark discoidal mark absent; hw thinly scaled.
Flight. May to July in a single brood.
Habitat. Open country, sea-level to 6,000 ft. Food plants hawthorn, *Spiraea, Prunus.* Sometimes an orchard pest.
Distribution. C. and S. Europe to 62°N, rarely farther north; extinct in Britain. Common locally in Morocco and Algeria. Absent from Corsica, Sardinia and Atlantic islands.
Variation. The dark scales along veins expand at outer margin of fw into dark triangles which may be exaggerated.
Similar species. *P. mnemosyne* p. 41.

PIERIS BRASSICAE   *Large White*
F: Piéride du Chou   Sw: Kålfjäril   G: Grosser Kohlweissling
Sp: Blanca de la Col
Range. From N. Africa across Europe and Asia to Himalaya Mts.
                                                                        Map 12

P. brassicae brassicae   Linnaeus 1758   TL: Sweden (Verity 1947)   Pl. 4
Description. ♂ fw 28/33 mm.; *first brood,* costa and apical border black powdered white, *the latter extending down outer margin to v3 or beyond;* uph with costal mark in s7; unf black spots present in s1b and s3; unh densely powdered with dark scales with greenish effect. ♀upf with black streak in s1a and round spots in s1b and s3; hw yellowish (f. *chariclea*

Stephens 1827). In *second brood* upf apical border intensely black; unh dark dusting slight if present. ♀hw usually white.

Flight. April/May and July/August in two or three broods.
Habitat. Gardens and flowery places, lowlands to 6,000 ft. Food plants various *Cruciferae*, esp. *Brassica*, and *Tropaeolum*
Distribution. Throughout N. Africa and W. Europe, including all Mediterranean islands, scarce or occasional north of 62°N. A well-known migrant, its abundance in Britain in late summer depends upon successful immigration in early months.

P. brassicae cheiranthi Huebner 1808   TL: Canary Islands   Pl. 4
Description. ♂fw 33 mm., uph costal mark enlarged; unf apex brilliant yellow, black spots in s 1b and s 3 enlarged and fused to form a large discal mark; unh bright yellow. ♀ all markings greatly enlarged; upf discal spots fused into a large black mark.
Flight. April and later, perhaps with several broods.
Habitat. Gardens and flowery places to 1,500 ft.
Distribution. Restricted to Canary Islands; Tenerife, La Palma, Gran Canary, etc. A less extreme form occurs on Madeira (*P. b. wollastoni* Butler 1886).

Similar species. *P. rapae*, below, upf apical dark border extends down outer margin to v6 only, but more widely along costa.

PIERIS RAPAE *Small White*

F: Petit Blanc du Chou   Sw: Liten Kålfjäril   G: Kleiner Kohlweissling
Sp: Blanquita de la Col
Range. From N. Africa across Europe and Asia to Japan; introduced into N. America and Australia.   Map 13

P. rapae Linnaeus 1758   TL: Sweden (Verity 1947)   Pl. 5
Description. ♂fw 23/27 mm.; *first brood* (f. *metra* Stephens 1827) upf markings grey, generally with spot in s 3, apical border extends along costa but only to v7 or v6 down outer margin; unf spots present in s 1b and s 3, apex yellow; unh yellow with grey dusting along lower margin of cell. ♀ups yellowish with grey suffusion at wing-bases; upf additional oblique mark in s 1b. In *later broods* ups markings dark grey or black; unh grey dusting greatly reduced.
Flight. March or later in two or more broods.
Habitat. Meadows, gardens, etc., from sea-level to 6,000 ft. Larval food plants *Brassica* and other Cruciferae and Resedaceae.
Distribution. From Canary Islands, Azores and N. Africa throughout Europe; generally common to 62°N, rarely to 70°N. Absent from Madeira.
Variation. In N. Africa generally small, unh in late broods plain white.

Similar species. *P. mannii*, below, only in S. Europe, upf apical border black and continued by a few dark scales down outer margin to v4 or v3. *P. napi* p. 45, esp. extreme summer form, upf apical border extends down outer margin as spots or triangles at vein ends, traces of pre-apical spot often present in s6. *P. ergane* below, unf unmarked. *P. brassicae* p. 42.

PIERIS MANNII *Southern Small White*

Sp: Blanca Catalana
Range. From Morocco across S. Europe to Asia Minor and Syria.

Map 14

P. mannii Mayer 1851 TL: Split (Spalato), Dalmatia   Pl. 5
Description. ♂fw 20/23mm.; *first brood* (f. *farpa* Fruhstorfer 1909) resembles *P. rapae*; upf apical *black border*, extending down outer margin to v4 or v3, outer margin of spot in s3 flat or concave, sometimes connected to dark outer margin by a few black scales along v4; uph costal mark in s6 moon-shaped, concave outwards; unh rather densely dusted with dark scales. ♀upf apical border wider, spot in s3 generally clearly connected with outer margin. *Later broods* generally larger, ♂fw 26mm., black markings enlarged esp. in ♀; unh dark dusting slight or absent.
Flight. March or later in three or four broods during summer.
Habitat. Rough rocky places from sea-level to 5,000 ft. Larval food plants *Iberis sempervivum*, *Sinapis*, etc. (Cruciferae).
Distribution. France, widely distributed S. of R. Loire. Spain, local and scarce in Catalonia. Switzerland, local in Tessin and Valais. Italy, widely distributed, including Sicily and Elba. Austria. Balkans, including Greece. Rumania in Retezat Mts. Morocco, very local in Atlas Mts. Absent from Corsica, Sardinia and small Mediterranean islands.

Similar species. *P. rapae* p. 43.

PIERIS ERGANE *Mountain Small White*

Sp: Blanca escasa
Range. SE. France and eastwards to Asia Minor, Syria, Iraq and Iran.

Map 15

P. ergane Geyer 1828 TL: Ragusa (Hemming 1937)   Pl. 5
Description. ♂fw 19/24mm., resembles *P. rapae*; upf markings grey, apical mark square, extending to v5, pd spot in s3 sometimes absent; uph a small grey mark on costa in s6, often absent; *unf apex yellow otherwise unmarked*, but pattern from ups may show through; unh yellow, lightly dusted with grey. ♀ups faintly yellowish esp. uph, usually with extensive grey suffusion; upf additional often ill-defined grey spot in s1b, spot in s3 larger; uph costal spot constant.
Flight. March or later in two or more broods.

Habitat. Rocky slopes with grass from lowlands to 6,000 ft. Food plant *Aethionema saxatile*.
Distribution. Balkans, including Bulgaria, Greece, Yugoslavia, esp. coastal areas. Italy, local in Apennines, occasional in hot valleys of S. Tirol, and near Cesena. France, E. Pyrenees and recorded from Briançon. Recorded from N. Spain. Rumania (Banat) and Crete.
Similar species. *P. rapae* p. 43.

PIERIS NAPI   Green-veined White

F: Piéride du Navet   Sw: Rapsfjäril   G: Rapsweissling
Sp: Blanca verdinervada
Range. N. Africa, Europe and east to N. America   Map 17

P. napi napi   Linnaeus 1758   TL: Sweden (Verity 1947)   Pl. 6
Description. Both sexes unh gc yellow, veins lined grey. First brood ♂ upf with or without pd spot in s3; ♀ ups veins lined grey, upf with additional spot in s5. Second brood often larger, unh grey stripes reduced or vestigial; ♀ ups veins not lined grey.
Flight and Habitat. March or later in 2 or 3 broods, often in light woodland. Food plants various crucifers.
Distribution. Europe, except southern and boreal regions.

P. napi meridionalis   Heyne 1895   TL: C. Italy   Pl. 6
syn: *dubiosa* Röber 1907 (part)
Description. First brood like *P. n. napi*, later broods often larger with extreme summer-brood characters. Distinction from *P. n. napi* is not entirely due to ecological conditions; larvae from Germany (*napi*) and from S. Italy (*meridionalis*) were bred alongside, but distinctive *meridionalis* characters remained very evident in Italian specimens (Bowden).
Distribution. Spain, S. France, Corsica etc.

P. napi adalwinda   Fruhstorfer 1909   TL: Finmark   Pl. 6
syn: *arctica* Verity 1911
Description. Like *P. n. bryoniae* but smaller. Cross-breeding with *P. n. napi* easy and successful, with *P. n. bryoniae* rarely satisfactory (Bowden).
Flight and Habitat as for *P. n. bryoniae*. Food plants *Draba*, *Arabis* etc.
Distribution. Fennoscandia north of 65°N latitude.

P. napi bryoniae   Hübner 1806   TL: Germany   Pl. 6♂; Pl. 13♀
Description. Like *P. n. napi*; ♂ ups veins firmly lined black. ♀ variable, ups more or less suffused grey along veins etc., upf a short marginal streak between v1 and v2 (bryo-streak) will confirm *bryoniae* in pale specimens.
Flight and Habitat. Occurs in a single brood at altitudes of 4,000 over. Foodplant *Biscutella*, rarely *Thlaspi*.
Distribution. In mountains, W. Alps, Jura, Tatra and Carpathians to Caucasus. Absent from Balkans.
Similar subspecies. *P. n. flavescens*, distinction very difficult. *P. n. neobryoniae*.

P. napi flavescens Wagner 1903 TL: Mödling, Vienna   Pl. 6
Description. ♂ like *P. n. napi*, ♀ extremely variable with all possible combinations of characters between *napi* and *bryoniae*.
Flight and **Habitat** as for *P. n. napi*, flying at low to moderate altitudes. Food plant *Biscutella*.
Distribution and **Variation.** Eastern Europe, extremely variable, f. *subtalba* Schima (Pl. 6g) common, unh gc white; genetically dominant. Different ♀-forms, varying from *napi* to *bryoniae*, may appear in offspring of a single ♀. Large races flying in the Karawanken Mts. often referred to *neobryoniae* Sheljuzhko, described from Maritime Alps.
Note. In its western range *P. n. bryoniae* is isolated ecologically; it can be crossed with *P. n. napi* but the broods have poor viability and f. *subtalba* is extremely rare; in its eastern range as *flavescens*, crossed with *napi*, the resulting broods have good viability, there is no evidence of ecological isolation, variation is extreme and the f. *subtalba* is common, often preponderating.
The following races of unknown genetic relationships are described here as subspecies of *P. napi*.

P. napi maura Verity 1911 TL: Glacières de Blida, Algeria
syn: *blidana* Holl 1912; *atlantica* Rothschild 1917   Pl. 13
Description. ♂ like *P. n. napi*, summer brood; unh veins weakly lined grey in first brood only. Flies at 3,500 ft., at Glacières de Blida, in 3 annual broods from April.

P. napi atlantis Oberthur 1923 TL: Azrou, Morocco   Pls. 6; 13
♂ fw 24–26 mm., ups black markings reduced but upf spot in s3 large. ♀ upf discal spot conspicuous as in ♂. In both sexes unh slightly or not at all lined grey.
Flight and **Habitat.** Occurs in May, only first brood known, flying at about 5000 ft. near Azrou.

P. napi segonzaci le Cerf 1923 TL: High Atlas   Pl. 6
Description. ♂ fw 25–26 mm., upf spots in s3, s5 and s6 constantly present, unh veins broadly striped. ♀ ups all veins lined grey.
Flight and **Habitat.** Flies from end June at 8,500 ft., Toubkal Massif only.

P. n. canidiaformis Drenowsky 1910 TL: Bosnia and Macedonia.
syn: *balcana* Lorkovíc.
Description. Like *P. napi napi* but unh suffused grey, veins not well defined. Cross breeding with *P. n. napi* proved sterile. (Lorkovíc).
Similar species. *P. rapae* p. 43; *P. callidice* p. 150.

PIERIS KRUEPERI *Krueper's Small White*
Range. S. Balkans and eastwards to Iran and Baluchistan.   Map 16
P. krueperi Staudinger 1860 TL: Arcana, Greece   Pl. 5
Description. ♂ fw 21/25 mm.; *first brood* upf *large round spot in s3*, pre-apical costal mark and border of marginal triangles on each vein from

apex to v3 all black; uph costal mark in s6 black; unh basal and discal areas grey-green, pd area white, with small grey marginal marks at vein endings. ♀similar. In *second brood* ups black markings often smaller; unh usually yellow, dark basal shade paler, yellow-green or absent, but dark costal mark in s5, 6, 7 always present.

Flight. March/April or later in two or more broods.

Habitat. Rocky or precipitous places from lowlands to 6,000 ft. or more. Larval food plant *Alyssum montanum.*

Distribution. SE. Europe, Bulgaria in Rumelia. Albania and SE. Yugoslavia. Greece, widespread.

PONTIA DAPLIDICE *Bath White*

Sw: Grönfläckig Kålfjäril G: Resedenfalter Sp: Blanquiverdosa

Range. From Africa and S. Europe to India and Japan. Map 18

P. daplidice Linnaeus 1758 TL: Africa and S. Europe Pl. 7

Description. ♂fw 21/24mm.; *first brood* (f. *bellidice* Ochsenheimer) upf with usual markings; uph dark pattern shows through from uns, sometimes with black mark in s7; *unf discoidal spot large, extending to costa, apical markings green*; unh basal, discal and marginal spots in series all dark green. ♀upf black markings larger; uph large post-discal and small marginal black spots in series; unh green markings generally confluent from base to discal series. *Second and later broods* uns green markings often less extensive; unh usually paler and suffused yellow but variable. Seasonal distinction often poorly defined.

Flight. February/March and later in two or more broods.

Habitat. Rough ground and flowery meadows from lowlands to 6,000 ft. Larval food plants *Arabis, Reseda, Sinapis*, etc., various Cruciferae.

Distribution. N. Africa and Europe to 66°N. The species is strongly migratory, and sometimes reaches Britain.

Similar species. *P. chloridice* below, only in S. Balkans, smaller, unf discoidal spot does not reach costa; unh marginal markings linear.

PONTIA CHLORIDICE *Small Bath White*

Range. From S. Balkans through Asia Minor, Iraq and Iran to Mongolia. N. America, in mountains of Oregon and California (*P. beckeri* W. H. Edwards). Map 19

P. chloridice Huebner 1808 TL: not stated Pl. 7

Description. ♂fw 20/22mm., *first brood* resembles *P. daplidice* but small, lightly marked; uph unmarked; unf discoidal spot narrow, not reaching costa; unh regular short green marginal stripes connected basally by green pd band. ♀upf apical markings better developed; uph with vestigial pd and marginal markings. In *second brood* slightly larger, ♀ups all markings

PLATE 1

1. **Iphiclides podalirius**   *Scarce Swallowtail*   **36**
   Ground-colour pale; upf six black stripes.

   1a. *I. p. podalirius* second brood ♂. Ground-colour faintly yellowish;
        uph dark border narrow; apex of abdomen white.
   1b. *I. p. feisthamelii* second brood ♂. Ground-colour grey-white;
        uph dark border wider; apex of abdomen white.

2. **Papilio alexanor**   *Southern Swallowtail*   **36**
   ♂. Upf wing-base yellow.

3. **Papilio machaon**   *Swallowtail*   **35**
   ♀. Upf wing-base broadly dark; unf submarginal band straight-
   edged.

4. **Papilio hospiton**   *Corsican Swallowtail*   **35**
   ♂. Like *P. machaon* but unf submarginal band wavy.
   For ups see front endpaper.

5. **Euchloe tagis**   *Portuguese Dappled White*   **52**
   E. tagis bellezina f. *castillana* ♀. Spain. See also Pl. 8.

6. **Euchloe belemia**   *Green-striped White*   **53**
   E. b. hesperidum ♀. Smaller than *E. b. belemia* (**Pl. 8**).

PLATE 2

1. Archon apollinus   *False Apollo*   39
  ♀. Uph with six large red, black and blue submarginal spots.

2. Allancastria cerisyi   *Eastern Festoon*   39
  Outer margin of hw deeply scalloped, short tail at vein 4.

  2a. ♂. Ups dark discal markings scanty on both wings.
  2b. ♀. Ups dark markings more extensive on both wings.

3. Zerynthia polyxena   *Southern Festoon*   37
  Upf lacking red spots in cell and at cell-end; no vitreous window.

  3a. *Z. p. polyxena* ♂. Ups dark markings not extensive; uph post-
    discal yellow band wide.
  3b. *Z. p. polyxena* ♀. Slightly larger, markings as in ♂.
  3c. *Z. p. cassandra* ♂. Ups dark markings extensive; uph post-
    discal yellow band narrow.

4. Zerynthia rumina   *Spanish Festoon*   38
  Upf red spots present in cell and at cell-end; vitreous window near
  apex. ♀ ground-colour pale yellow or (f. *canteneri*) brownish.

  4a. *Z. r. rumina* f. *honoratii* ♀. All red areas greatly extended.
  4b. *Z. r.* f. *medesicaste* ♂. Uph red basal spot present.
  4c. *Z. r. ornatior* f. *canteneri* ♀. Very large, ground-colour buff.
    For typical *Z. r. ornatior* (♀) see front endpaper.

larger, upf spot in s1b constant and pd and marginal spots well developed on both wings.

Flight. April/May and June in two broods.

Habitat. Rocky places from lowlands to 5,000 ft. Larval food plant not known.

Distribution. Bulgaria. Macedonia. Albania. European Turkey.

Similar species. *P. daplidice* p. 47.

PONTIA CALLIDICE   *Peak White*

G: Alpenweissling   Sp: Blanquiverdosa alpina

Range. From Pyrenees and Alps through Asia Minor and Lebanon to Himalaya Mts., Tibet and Mongolia. N. America, on high western mountains of Alaska, Colorado and California (*occidentalis* Reakirt), where it is associated with a lowland form (*protodice* Boisduval and Leconte).   Map 20

P. callidice Huebner 1805   TL: Swiss Alps   Pl. 7
Description. ♂fw 21/26mm., ups markings scanty; upf discoidal spot narrow; uph unmarked; unf markings as on ups; unh generally yellow with veins heavily lined greenish-grey, united in pd area by a series of V-shaped marks. ♀ups more heavily marked with well-developed pd and marginal markings; uns as in ♂.

Flight. End June/July/August.

Habitat. Grass slopes from 6,500 ft. upwards, restricted to higher alpine zone. Larval food plants *Erysimum pumilum*, *Reseda glauca*.

Distribution. Pyrenees, Hautes Alpes, Graian Alps and eastwards on higher summits to Dolomites, Austrian and Bavarian Alps. Absent from Tatra Mts., Balkans, Apennines and Cantabrian Mts.

Similar species. *P. napi* p. 45, which lacks a black discoidal spot.

COLOTIS EVAGORE   *Desert Orange Tip*

Range. Widely distributed in Africa and in S. Arabia (TL of *C. evagore* Klug) in a bewildering range of local and seasonal forms.   Map 22

C. evagore nouna Lucas 1849   TL: Djebel Aures, Algeria   Pl. 7
Description. ♂fw 15/18mm., ups white with variable black markings and vermilion apical patch; *first brood* upf with black streak along inner margin; uph with black shade at base and along costa. ♀ apex of fw rounded, red apical patch narrow with black proximal border. *Late broods* generally small, all black markings reduced, sometimes absent, thorax and abdomen pale.

Flight and Habitat. February/March or later in a succession of broods, flying in hot rocky gorges at 3–5,000 ft. Larval food plant caper bush.

Distribution. Morocco, Algeria and Tunisia, S. Spain.

EUCHLOE AUSONIA *Dappled White*
G: Mattfleckiger Falter; Glanzfleckiger Falter
Range. From N. Africa through Europe and Asia to Amurland; also in
N. America from Alaska to Colorado and Arizona (*ausonides* Lucas).
Map p. 23

E. ausonia ausonia Huebner 1804 TL: N. Italy Pl. 7
syn: *simplonia* Boisduval 1828; *marchandae* Geyer 1832
Description. ♂fw 20/24mm., ups white; upf *black discoidal spot narrow,
often externally concave and fusing with dark shade along costa*; *hw with
obtuse marginal angle at* v8; uph unmarked; unf discoidal spot angled and
white centred, apex green with white markings; unh with extensive irregular
green markings. ♀ similar, upf discoidal spot larger; uph yellowish.
Flight. June/July in a single brood.
Habitat. Subalpine meadows at 5–6,000 ft. Larval food plants *Iberis,
Sisymbrium, Barbarea,* etc. (Cruciferae).
Distribution. Cantabrian Mts., esp. Picos de Europa; Pyrenees and through
S. Alps to San Bernardino Pass and Splugen Pass. Absent from Jura, E.
Alps, Carpathians, Apennines and Balkans.

E. ausonia crameri Butler 1869 TL: S. Spain Pl. 7
syn: *belia* Stoll 1782 (invalid homonym); *esperi* Kirby 1871; *ausonia*
auct.; *orientalis* auct.
Description. Resembles *E. a. ausonia*; *first brood* (f. *kirbyi* Rothschild) upf
discoidal spot usually larger, extending to v12 but *not reaching costa*;
unf discoidal spot often round or square; unh green markings dense with
little yellow mixture, white spots sometimes shining (nacreous). ♀unf
discoidal spot generally very large. In *second brood* unh green markings
paler, green mixed with yellow, white spots not shining (matt). These
forms are not always well defined and may fly together.
Flight. March/April and May/June in two broods.
Habitat. Open meadows and hillsides from sea-level to 4,500 ft.
Distribution. Widely distributed in S. Europe to about 48°N. Switzerland,
only known from Rhône valley. Portugal. Spain, local but not rare south
of Cantabrian Mts. Morocco, Algeria, Tunisia, up to 8,000 ft. in Atlas
Mts. Malta, very rare.
Variation. In Balkans often very large, esp. second brood, upf with
enlarged discoidal spot.

E. ausonia insularis Staudinger 1861 TL: Corsica Pl. 7
Description. ♂fw 18/22mm., upf discoidal spot narrow with extension
along v12; white spots in s4 and s5 enclosed in black apical mark extend
to wing-margin; unf discoidal spot very small; unh white spots reduced
in size by extension of green markings. ♀ similar.

Flight and **Habitat.** March/April and May/June, local in mountains at about 3,000 ft.

Distribution. Confined to Corsica and Sardinia.

Similar species. *E. tagis* below, in which hw costa has a smooth even curve. *A. cardamines* p. 54, ♀ has superficial resemblance on ups; unf apex greenish-grey, unmarked; in *ausonia* unf apex clearly marked with green striae.

EUCHLOE TAGIS *Portuguese Dappled White*
Range. Confined to SW. Europe and N. Africa.   Map 24

E. tagis tagis   Huebner 1804   TL: River Tagus, Portugal   Pl. 8
  syn: *lusitanica* Oberthur 1909
Description. ♂fw 15/22mm., resembles *E. ausonia*; upf grey apical mark completely enclosing white spots in s4, 5; hw *costa in gentle curve without angle at* v8; unh gc grey-green, white spots small, nearly obsolete in some specimens. ♀ similar, fw apex less pointed.
Flight. February to April according to locality, probably a single prolonged generation.
Habitat. Flies from lowlands to 3,000 ft. or more in rough stony places. Food plants *Iberis, Biscutella.*
Distribution. Portugal, local on south bank of Tagus; Spain, widely distributed in south, but local. Algeria, Morocco.

E. tagis bellezina   Boisduval 1828   TL: Provence   Pls. 1, 8
Description. ♂fw 18/19mm., unf white markings in green apical area more extensive; unh gc green, white spots more numerous and larger. ♀similar.
Flight. April/early May.
Habitat. Rough open places in mountain foothills.
Distribution. France, in Provence, esp. Basses Alpes, Bouches du Rhône, etc.   Aix and Digne are well-known localities.
Variation. A small form, ♂fw 14/15mm., ♀larger, unh white markings slightly reduced, transitional to *E. t. tagis*, flies in a few localities in C. Spain, e.g. Aranjuez, f. *castillana* Verity Pl. 1.
Similar species. *E. ausonia* p. 51.

EUCHLOE PECHI *Pech's White*
Range. Confined to Algeria.   Map 25

E. pechi   Staudinger 1885   TL: Lambessa, Algeria   Pl. 8
Description. ♂fw 17mm., upf apex grey without white spots, grey discoidal mark extending along v12; unf apex smooth green, unmarked; unh *smooth green with small white discoidal mark.* ♀ not seen.
Flight. March/April.
Habitat. Recorded from Djebel Aures, flying at 6,000 ft.

Distribution. Algeria, recorded from Lambessa, El Kantara, Guelt-es-stel, El-Outaya, and Djebel Aures. A rare and very local species.

EUCHLOE FALLOUI *Scarce Green-striped White*
Range. N. Africa, including Tibesti, Fezzan, Tripoli and Egypt.

Map 26

E. alloui Allard 1867 TL: Biskra, Algeria Pl. 8
Description. ♂fw 18/19 mm., resembles *E. belemia*; upf black discoidal spot does not extend to costal margin; unf *discoidal spot small, dense black, without white central mark*; unh green markings forming well-defined stripes. ♀ similar, upf discoidal spot larger; unh green markings sometimes flushed yellow.
Flight. January/June, with a partial autumn brood in some localities.
Habitat. Atlantic coastal areas and southern slopes of Atlas Mts., recorded by Oberthur at 1,800 m. Food plant *Reseda muricata*.
Distribution. Morocco, Algeria, Tunis, esp. Biskra and Bou Saada. Range extends far into desert oases.
Similar species. *E. belemia* below.

EUCHLOE BELEMIA *Green-striped White*
Range. N. Africa, S.W. Europe, Tibesti to Iran and Baluchistan.

Map 27

E. belemia belemia Esper 1799 TL: Belem, Portugal Pl. 8
Description. ♂fw 19/22 mm.; *first brood*, apex of fw and anal angle of hw pointed; ups markings like *E. ausonia*; uns apex of fw and all hw green, marked with white transverse stripes, well defined, brilliant, often nacreous; unf discoidal spot large, enclosing narrow white curved crescent. ♀fw outer margin more rounded, apex less pointed. *Second brood* often larger, fw less pointed; unh green mixed with yellow, stripes less well defined. Both forms may fly together.
Flight. February/March and April/May in two broods.
Habitat. Rough places with flowers from sea-level to 3,000 ft. Larval food plants not known.
Distribution. N. Africa, on coastal plain and foothills of Atlas Mts., where it may fly in December. Portugal; local near Lagos, Lisbon, etc. Spain, from Mediterranean coast to Burgos but principally in south, Cadiz, Seville, Granada, Malaga, Cordoba, etc.

Similar species. *E. falloui* above, only in N. Africa; unf discoidal spot small, oval, dense black without central white crescent.

E. belemia hesperidum Rothschild 1913 TL: Canary Islands Pl. 1
Description. ♂fw 16/17 mm., wings less pointed; upf discoidal spot narrow; unh green stripes sometimes indefinite. ♀ similar.
Flight. End March/June in two broods.
Habitat. Mountains at 2,500–5,000 ft.

Distribution. Canary Islands, recorded from Gran Canary, Fuerteventura and Tenerife. There may be slight differences between the forms flying on different islands.

ELPHINSTONIA CHARLONIA   *Greenish Black-tip*
Range. Canary Islands, Morocco, Algeria, Tunisia, Tibesti, Macedonia, Egypt, Sudan, W. Asia to Iran, Baluchistan and Punjab.   Map 28

E. charlonia charlonia   Donzel 1842   TL: Emsilah, Algeria   Pl. 8
Description. ♂ fw 14/16mm., ups *gc sulphur-yellow*; upf with *large dark brown apical patch* with obscure paler markings and a large dark discoidal spot; unf red marginal lines along costa and outer margin, apex uniform grey-green, discoidal spot black; unh grey-green with a few obscure paler markings, most distinct along costa. ♀ similar.
Flight. February or later, often March/April with a series of two or more broods.
Habitat. Around cliffs or on rocky slopes, usually at considerable altitudes. Food plant not known.
Distribution. Morocco, Algeria, Tunisia, esp. in southern districts near desert, common in spring. Canary Islands, very local, flying at about 2,000 ft., recorded from Tenerife, Fuerteventura, Lanzarote.

E. charlonia penia   Freyer 1852   TL: not stated   Pl. 8
Description. ♂ fw 18mm., fw less pointed; upf pale markings in dark apex inconspicuous; unf red marginal lines absent.
Flight. April and June in two broods.
Habitat. Flies at low levels in rocky or precipitous places.
Distribution. SE. Yugoslavia, very local, Bitola, Skopje. Bulgaria. Greece.

ANTHOCHARIS CARDAMINES   *Orange Tip*
F: l'Aurore   Sw: Aurorafjäril   G: Aurorafalter
Range. From W. Europe eastwards through temperate Asia to China.
Map 29

A. cardamines   Linnaeus 1758   TL: Sweden (Verity 1947)   Pl. 8
Description. ♂ fw 19/24mm., *ups gc white*; upf small black discoidal spot just enclosed in wide orange apical area, apex and marginal border grey; uns with confused yellow-green markings at apex of fw and over hw. ♀ upf no orange apical patch; uph often flushed pale yellow; unf apex white or yellowish, *almost unmarked*.
Flight. April or later in a single brood.
Habitat. Flowery meadows from sea-level to 5,000 ft. Food plants Cruciferae, including cuckoo flower, hedge mustard, etc. (*Cardamine, Sisymbrium*, etc.).
Distribution. Throughout W. Europe to Arctic Circle. Absent from Crete, Elba, N. Africa and perhaps from S. Spain.

Similar species. *E. ausonia* p. 51, ♀ only.

ANTHOCHARIS BELIA *Morocco Orange Tip*
G: Gelber Aurorafalter
Range. N. Africa and SW. Europe.   Map. 30

A. belia belia Linnaeus 1767   TL: 'Barbaria' (Morocco)   Pl. 8
syn: *eupheno* Linnaeus 1767
Description. ♂fw 18/20mm., ups yellow; upf wide orange apical patch
with dusky proximal border enclosing a small black discoidal mark,
extreme apex dusky; uph yellow, unmarked; unh yellow with slightly
variable grey *markings indistinct except on costa*, sometimes slightly
suffused fuscous. ♀ups white, dark apical markings more extensive, with
orange scales between veins; uph flushed yellow; unh grey or reddish
markings as in male, sometimes better defined.
Flight. April/May in a single brood.
Habitat. Rough ground or light woodland, sea-level to 5,500 ft. Larval
food plant *Biscutella lyrata*.
Distribution. Morocco, Algeria, Tunisia, esp. from Atlas Mts. to Mediterranean coast.

A. belia euphenoides Staudinger 1869   TL: Gibraltar   Pl. 8
Description. ♂ups like *A. b. belia*; unh markings grey, more extensive and
well defined, transverse narrow sub-basal and discal bands joined by band
along anal vein, a series of white pd patches in s2–s7. ♀ ups resembles *A. b. belia*; unh markings as in ♂.
Flight. May/June/July.
Habitat. Usually in mountainous country from low levels to 5,000 ft.
Larval food plant *Biscutella laevigata*.
Distribution. Spain and Portugal, widely distributed, often common in
mountainous districts. France, from Pyrenees and Provence to Isère.
Italy, local in Maritime and Cottian Alps to Susa; Apennines, very local
on a few high mountains, Monte Majella, Gran Sasso, Monte Terminillo,
etc.; reported occasionally from warm valleys in S. Alps, Gondo, Lugano,
Locarno, etc. in Switzerland.

Similar species. *A. damone* below and *A. gruneri* p. 56, unh mottled green
in complicated pattern resembling *A. cardamines*.

ANTHOCHARIS DAMONE *Eastern Orange Tip*
Range. Sicily and S. Italy, Greece, Syria to Iran   Map 31

A. damone Boisduval 1836   TL: Sicily   Pl. 8
Description. ♂fw 19/20mm., ups resembles *A. belia*, gc *bright yellow*; unh
gc yellow with *confused greenish-grey markings* resembling those of *A.
cardamines*. ♀upf gc white, apex grey, orange apical patch absent; *uph gc*

yellowish; uns apex of fw and all hw gc yellow with markings as in ♂.
Flight. April/May.
Habitat. Rocky mountain slopes to 3,000 ft. or more. Food plant not
known.
Distribution. Sicily, local in neighbourhood of Mt. Etna absent from
W. Sicily; Italy, recorded from Aspromonte and Calabria. Greece,
common locally in rocky places to 1,500 ft. SE. Yugoslavia, Skopje
Similar species. *A. gruneri* below, ♂ smaller, unh gc white; ♀upf with
very large grey discoidal mark; *A. belia* p. 55.

ANTHOCHARIS GRUNERI   *Grüner's Orange Tip*
Range. Greece, Asia Minor and Syria to Iraq (Kurdistan). Iran.
                                                          Map 32

A. gruneri   Herrich-Schaeffer 1851   TL: 'Crete' (Greece?)   Pl. 8
Description. ♂fw 15/18mm., ups *gc light yellow*; upf orange-yellow apical
patch enclosing small black discoidal spot, apical border grey, base of
costa grey and fringe grey-chequered; unf apex yellow with grey mottling
along veins; *unh gc white*, marbled with green markings resembling those
of *A. cardamines*. ♀ white, upf a *large grey discoidal spot*, apical border wider
than in ♂; uph yellow flush along costa; uns as in ♂ but unf orange area
absent.
Flight. March/May.
Habitat. Lowlands to 3,000 ft., flying on open stony ground.
Distribution. Greece, esp. near Mt. Parnassus, Mt. Chelmos, etc. Albania.
SE. Yugoslavia, Vardar valley. Turkey in Europe.
Similar species. *A. damone* p. 55.

ZEGRIS EUPHEME   *Sooty Orange Tip*
Range. Morocco, Spain, S. Russia (TL of *Papilio eupheme* Esper 1782), Asia
Minor and eastwards to Iran.   Map 33

Z. eupheme meridionalis   Lederer 1852   TL: S. Spain   Pl. 9
Description. ♂fw 23/25mm., ups gc white; upf C-shaped discoidal mark
black, *apex broadly dark grey clouded white, enclosing an oval orange patch*;
unf apex yellow; unh gc yellow with irregular green-grey markings recalling
A. belia euphenoides. ♀ often slightly larger, orange apical patch reduced
or absent.
Flight. April/May in a single brood.
Habitat. Rough slopes with flowers, cornfields, etc., lowlands to 3,000 ft.
Food plant *Sinapis incana*.
Distribution. Morocco, Middle Atlas at Ifrane, Anosseur, Foum-Kharig,
5,500 ft.; High Atlas, at Oikemaden, 8,500 ft. S. Portugal. Spain, from
Mediterranean northwards to Lerida, Soria, Burgos, but absent in west.

CATOPSILIA FLORELLA   *African Migrant*

Range. All Africa south of the Sahara, Canary Islands and through Egypt to India and China.

C. florella   Fabricius 1775   TL: Sierra Leone   Pl. 13

Description. ♂fw 31mm., *ups pale greenish-white*, scaling appears mealy except over basal area of hw where surface is smooth; upf discoidal spot minute and margin of costa grey-brown; uph unmarked; uns apical and costal areas of fw and all hw pale yellow, *lightly irrorated pale grey-brown;* unf with hair-pencil arising from inner margin and associated with sex-brand on uph in s7 along upper margin of cell. ♀ dimorphic, closely resembling ♂ or with gc yellow-buff; upf discoidal spot brown, dark costal margin slightly more prominent and continued down outer margin as small dark marks on veins.

Flight and Habitat. In flowery places from sea-level to moderate altitudes, flying perhaps throughout the year. Larval food plant *Cassia*.

Distribution. Within the region recorded only from Gran Canary and Tenerife, for the first time in 1964.

COLIAS PHICOMONE   *Mountain Clouded Yellow*

G: Grünlicher Heufalter
Range. Restricted to Europe.   Map 34

C. phicomone   Esper 1780   TL: Styria   Pl. 9

Description. ♂fw 20/25mm., ups pale yellow-green *heavily suffused dark grey*; upf darker submarginal area enclosing yellow submarginal spots; uph grey-green from base to band of yellow submarginal spots, discoidal spot yellow. ♀greenish-white, markings as in ♂ but upf grey suffusion reduced.

Flight. End June/July/August in a single brood, occasionally in September.
Habitat. Grass slopes from 6,000 ft. upwards. Larval food plants vetches, esp. *Vicia* (*Leguminosae*).

Distribution. Cantabrian Mts., Picos de Europa. Pyrenees and main alpine chain eastwards to Hohe Tauern and N. Carpathians, including Bavarian and Salzburg Alps. Absent from Jura, Apennines, S. Carpathians and Balkans.

Similar species. *C. nastes* below, a purely arctic species.

COLIAS NASTES   *Pale Arctic Clouded Yellow*

Sw: Gröngul Höfjäril
Range. Arctic Europe, Greenland, Labrador (TL of *C. nastes* Boisduval 1832), probably circumpolar.   Map 35

C. nastes werdandi   Zetterstedt 1840   TL: Torne-Lapland   Pl. 9
Description. ♂fw 22/24mm., ups pale yellow-green *without general grey*

suffusion, veins lined fuscous; upf grey border enclosing pale submarginal spots; uph *yellow discoidal spot minute*. ♀ similar, ups gc less yellow, more variable, uph often suffused grey. In both sexes antennae, collar and fringes usually red but variable.

Flight. June.

Habitat. Rough ground, usually in hilly country at 1,000 ft. or more. Larval food plant *Astragalus alpinus*.

Distribution. NW. Scandinavia, from 66° to 70° N.

Similar species. *C. phicomone* p. 57, ups ♂ suffused dark grey; uph yellow, discoidal spot large; only flies in Pyrenees and Alps.

COLIAS PALAENO *Moorland Clouded Yellow*

Sw: Svavelgul Höfjäril   G: Zitronengelber Heufalter
Range. From C. and N. Europe through Siberia to Amur and Japan. Perhaps also in N. America.   Map 36

C. palaeno palaeno   Linnaeus 1761   TL: Sweden and Finland   Pl. 9
Description. ♂ fw 25/27 mm., ups gc pale sulphur yellow tending to white, fringes red; upf discoidal mark small, oval, black marginal band dense; uph black marginal border narrower; unf gc pale yellow; unh densely irrorated grey-green except the marginal band, discoidal spot small, white. ♀ ups white, dark marginal markings as in ♂ but less well defined.

Flight. Late June/July in a single brood.

Habitat. Bogs and moorland with *Vaccinium* bushes, usually at low levels. Food plant bog whortleberry (*Vaccinium uliginosum*).

Distribution. Fennoscandia, widely distributed, ups often very pale in far north.

C. palaeno europome   Esper 1779   TL: Saxony   Pl. 9
Description. ♂ fw 24/27 mm., resembles *C. p. palaeno* but ups gc sulphur yellow; upf dark marginal band usually wide, discoidal spot black or, more rarely, white; uns yellow, darker in tone at fw apex and over hw, which is finely irrorated with dark scales. ♀ gc generally white, occasionally yellow, f. *illgneri* Rühl.

Flight. Late June/July.

Habitat. Flies over bogs, etc., with *Vaccinium*, typically in lowland localities.

Distribution. Local in suitable localities NE. France in Vosges and Jura. Germany, esp. Bavarian moors. Rare in N. Czechoslovakia, Carpathians and Rumania. Absent from Central Massif of France, Pyrenees, Apennines and Balkans. Extinct in Belgium.

Variation. At high altitudes in main Alpine chain, smaller, unh more heavily irrorated with dark scales, f. *europomene* Ochsenheimer.

COLIAS CHRYSOTHEME *Lesser Clouded Yellow*

G: Hellorangegrüner Heufalter
Range. E. Europe and S. Russia to Altai Mts.   Map 37

C. chrysotheme Esper 1781 TL: Cremnitz, Hungary   Pl. 10
Description. ♂fw 20/24mm., apex of fw pointed; ups gc yellow with wide
black marginal borders regularly crossed by yellow veins; upf discoidal
spot small, often reddish; uph without sex-brand; *uns black pd spots in
regular series across both wings*; fringes red. ♀ resembles *C. crocea* and *C.
myrmidone* but fw more pointed; upf costal margin broadly and *con-
spicuously green-grey*.
Flight. May and July/August in two broods.
Habitat. Flies on grass slopes from lowlands to 3,000 ft. Food plant
Vicia hirsuta.
Distribution. Austria (Burgenland), Hungary, Czechoslovakia and
Rumania, in localised colonies. The species is a member of the Russian
steppe fauna, reaching its most westerly point near Vienna.
Variation. White or pale yellow female forms occur but are rare.

Similar species. *C. crocea* p. 60 and *C. myrmidone* below: ♂ups veins
crossing dark marginal bands only slightly or not at all lined yellow, uph
sex-brand present, ♀upf lacks broad grey-green band along costal margin.

COLIAS LIBANOTICA *Greek Clouded Yellow*

Range. From mountains of Greece to Asia Minor and Lebanon (TL
of *Colias libanotica* Lederer 1858).   Map 38

C. libanotica heldreichii Staudinger 1862 TL: Mt. Veluchi, Greece Pl. 10
Description. ♂fw 27/28mm., fw pointed, *ups gc dull orange with purple
reflections in oblique lights*; upf wide black marginal border crossed by
yellow-lined veins; uph prominent sex-brand above median vein, *veins
yellow-lined as they cross the black marginal border*; unh gc yellow-green,
pd spots if present reddish. ♀ resembles *C. myrmidone* but larger; ups wide
black marginal border broken by rather large greenish-yellow spots; uns
gc grey-green, almost unmarked, a small white discoidal spot and pale
submarginal spots.
Flight. June/early July.
Habitat. Rough open places at 5–8,000 ft. Larval food plant *Astragalus*.
Distribution. Greece, on Mt. Veluchi, Mt. Chelmos, Mt. Parnassus.
Variation. A white ♀ form occurs rarely.

COLIAS MYRMIDONE *Danube Clouded Yellow*

G: Orangeroter Heufalter
Range. From E. Europe through Russia to W. Asia (Steppe fauna).
                                                              Map 39

C. myrmidone   Esper 1781   TL: Turnau, Hungary   Pl. 10
Description. ♂fw 22/25mm., resembles *C. crocea*, ups *gc deeper, more
reddish orange-yellow*; upf discoidal spot smaller, dark border usually
dense, rarely v 5–8 lined yellow; uph narrow dark marginal border with
rather obscure pale orange submarginal lunules, conspicuous sex-brand at
base of s 7, discoidal spot red; uns resembles *C. crocea* but unf *black pd
spots in s 1b, 2, 3 small or absent.* ♀ups gc orange-yellow or greenish-white,
♀f. *alba* Staudinger, rarely with intermediate colour; uph yellow submarginal spots often prominent and tending to form a band. Specimens of
second brood perhaps slightly larger.
Flight. May and July/August in two broods.
Habitat. A lowland species flying over heaths and open spaces. Foodplant
Cytisus.
Distribution. Eastern Europe, mostly in Danube basin, Rumania, Hungary,
Austria and S. Germany to Munich. A very local species but often
abundant in an established colony.
Variation. In *first brood* slightly smaller, ♂fw 20/21mm., ups gc slightly
darker.

Similar species. *C. crocea*, below ♂upf black marginal border near apex
crossed by a few yellow veins, unf black pd spots in s 1b, 2, 3 conspicuous
in both sexes; ♀uph pale submarginal spots often irregular and series
incomplete. *C. chrysotheme* p. 59; *C. balcanica* p. 61.

COLIAS CROCEA   *Clouded Yellow*

F: Le Souci   Sw: Rödgul Höfjäril   G: Wandergelbling, Postillon
Range. N. Africa, including Fezzan and Cyrenaica, S. and C. Europe and
eastwards across W. Asia to Iran.   Map 40

C. crocea   Geoffroy 1785   TL: Paris   Pl. 10
    syn: *edusa* Fabricius 1787
Description. ♂fw 23/27mm., ups gc bright orange-yellow with wide black
marginal borders; upf veins near apex lined yellow across border; uph
body-groove pale yellow-green, black border rarely crossed by yellow
veins, conspicuous sex-brand near base in s 7. ♀upf with grey basal
suffusion, wing-border enclosing yellow spots in s 2 and near apex; uph gc
dusky yellow-grey with large orange discoidal spot, irregular yellow spots
in dark marginal band rarely in complete series. Unf pd spots black in
both sexes, well-marked in s 1b, 2, 3, fw outer margin and all hw yellow
tinted green; unh twin white red-ringed discoidal spots, pd spots small,
reddish.
Flight. April/May and later with succession of broods until autumn.
Habitat. Heaths and open places from lowlands to 6,000 ft. Food plants
various Leguminosae, esp. vetches.
Distribution. Throughout N. Africa and Europe to 60°N, including
Mediterranean islands, Canary Islands, Madeira and Azores.

Variation. A white ♀f. *helice* Huebner p. 81, is genetically controlled and behaves as a dominant to the common yellow form, in a balanced polymorphism with a ratio of about 10% in most populations. Rarely females with an intermediate yellowish-white gc occur, ♀f. *helicina* Oberthur.

Similar species. *C. myrmidone* p. 60.

COLIAS BALCANICA   Balkan Clouded Yellow
Range. Restricted to Balkan Mts.   Map 41

C. balcanica   Rebel 1903   TL: Bulgaria   Pl. 11
Description. ♂fw 25/27 mm., *slightly larger* than *C. myrmidone*; *ups gc deep reddish-orange with dense dark borders* lightly powdered yellow on fw; uph slightly dusky, oval sex-brand gleaming yellow above median v near wing-base, pale orange submarginal lunules generally present bordering black border; uns resembles *C. myrmidone*. ♀upf dark border fully encloses small yellow spots; uph gc slightly dusky, prominent pale yellow submarginal spots between veins; the 'white' form of the female is not common, f. *rebeli* Schawerda.
Flight. July in a single brood.
Habitat. Open spaces in light woodland at 4–5,500 ft. Food plant not known.
Distribution. Higher Balkan Mts. from Trebevic southwards to Durmitor in S. Yugoslavia; also Rilo, Rhodope Mts. and Pirin Mts. in Bulgaria. Not recorded from Greece.

Similar species. *C. myrmidone* p. 60, smaller, ♂ups gc paler orange-yellow, a lowland species occurring in the countries of Danube basin.

COLIAS HECLA   Northern Clouded Yellow
Sw: Högnordisk Höfjäril
Range. Arctic Europe and N. America, Greenland (TL of *C. h·cla* Lefèbvre 1836), probably circumpolar.   Map 42

C. hecla sulitelma   Aurivillius 1890   TL: Mt. Sulitelma, Sweden   Pl. 11
Description. ♂fw 20/23 mm., ups *gc orange-yellow with rosy reflection* in oblique light; upf discoidal spot small, black marginal border usually with yellow cross-veins and powdered with yellow scales; uph red discoidal spot indistinct, black marginal border only very rarely with crossing veins; unf discal area paler yellow, *apex and margin and all unh grey-green*; unh small white red-ringed discoidal spot; uns marginal pale grey-green borders paler in both sexes. ♀upf veins dark, marginal band enclosing yellow-green elongate spots between veins; uph suffused grey, yellow submarginal spots prominent and regular, orange discoidal spot indistinct.
Flight. Late June/July.
Habitat. Usually flies over rough grassy places from sea-level to 3,000 ft. Larval foodplant *Astragalus alpinus*.

Distribution. Fennoscandia, from 68°N to North Cape. On Mt. Nuolja flies at 3,000 ft., but on Porsanger Fjord at sea-level; often common in established colonies.

COLIAS HYALE   *Pale Clouded Yellow*

F: Le Soufre   Sw: Ljusgul Höfjäril   G: Gemeiner Heufalter or Goldene Acht
Range. From C. Europe, including Denmark and S. Sweden through S. Russia to Altai Mts. Range uncertain owing to confusion with *C. australis*.
Map 43

C. hyale   Linnaeus 1758   TL: S. England (Verity 1947)   Pl. 11
Description. ♂fw 21/25mm., ups gc pale yellow with dark grey or black marginal markings and red fringes. ♀ white with slightly yellow-green tint; uph discoidal spot pale orange; dark markings as in ♂. Females with yellow gc do occur but they are very rare.
Flight. May/June and August/September in two broods.
Habitat. Flowery meadows, clover fields, etc., lowlands to 6,000 ft. or over. The late brood is the more abundant. Larval food plants lucerne, *Coronilla*, *Vicia* and other Papilionaceous plants.
Distribution. Europe to 60°N, commoner in N. and E.; migrant to 65°, probably absent from Spain and S. Italy.

Similar species. *C. australis* below, identification may be very difficult but early stages are distinct. *C. erate* p. 63.
Note. The species is strongly migratory, dispersing northwards and occurring occasionally in southern England.

COLIAS AUSTRALIS   *Berger's Clouded Yellow*
Range. From S. and C. Europe through S. Russia to Asia Minor.   Map 44

C. australis   Verity 1911   TL: Andalusia, Spain   Pl. 11
Description. ♂fw 21/27mm., resembles *C. hyale*; ups *gc brighter yellow*; *upf dark apical markings less extensive*, dark basal shade *usually restricted to s1a* without spreading across base of cell; uph discoidal spot *bright orange*. ♀ white like that of *C. hyale*, very rarely yellowish.
Flight. May/June and August/September in two broods, often three broods in S. Europe.
Habitat. Rough ground, rocky slopes at moderate levels. Larval food plants *Hippocrepis comosa* (tufted horseshoe vetch), *Coronilla varia*.
Distribution. S. and C. Europe to 54°N, most commonly in SW., occasionally recorded from England and from Algeria; often flies with *C. hyale*.
Similar species. *C. hyale* above.
The wing-markings of *C. hyale* and of *C. australis* differ only slightly and identification may be difficult. The most useful distinctive characters are on the upper surface and are compared as follows:

Ground-colour: in *hyale* ♂ pale greenish-yellow; in *australis* ♂ brighter lemon-yellow. This character is not entirely constant.

Fore-wing shape: in *hyale* apex more pointed; in *australis* apex more rounded; distinction is not present in all specimens.

Fore-wing markings: in *hyale* dark apical markings more extensive, black basal shade fan-shaped extending into s1b; in *australis* apical markings less extensive, dark basal shade spreads below submedian vein in s1a along lower margin of wing.

Hind-wing markings: in *hyale* submarginal markings not infrequent and black marginal markings constant, orange discoidal spot pale, not prominent; in *australis* submarginal markings absent, black marginal markings small if present, orange discoidal spot more brilliant orange. Both species are variable and there is no reliable single external character for identification. The shape of the dark shading at base of fore-wing and the hind-wing markings are the most constant, most easily recognised and helpful characters. Identification of females may be very difficult. The two species may fly together.

COLIAS ERATE *Eastern Pale Clouded Yellow*

Range. E. Europe and across temperate Asia to Japan, Formosa and Kashmir. Recorded also from Abyssinia and Somalia. Map 45

C. erate Esper 1804 TL: Sarepta, S. Russia Pl. 11
Description. ♂fw 23/26mm., *ups bright lemon-yellow*; upf marginal black border dense, usually without yellow cross-veins; uph black marginal border narrower, orange discoidal spot often prominent. ♀upf dark margin broken by included yellow spots in s2 and near apex; uph marginal black border broken between veins and with clear yellow submarginal spots forming a somewhat indefinite band.
Flight. May/June and August/September in two broods.
Habitat. Open spaces and grass slopes at lowland levels. Larval food plants not recorded. All European specimens seen have been of the second generation.
Distribution. SE. Europe. Rumania, not rare in late summer. Bulgaria. Greece? Turkey in Europe. Occasional in Hungary.
Variation. In ♂form *hyaloides* Groum-Grshimailo, upf dark wing-borders broken by yellow spots as in ♀, a rare form in Europe.

Similar species. *C. australis* p. 62 and *C. hyale* p. 62, ups in both very like f. *hyaloides* but gc pale yellow.

GONEPTERYX RHAMNI *Brimstone*

F: Le Citron Sw: Citronfjäril G: Zitronenfalter
Sp: Limonera
Range. From N. Africa and W. Europe through Russia, Asia Minor and Syria to Siberia. Map 46

PLATE 3

1. Parnassius phoebus   *Small Apollo*   40
Antennae white, broadly ringed dark grey; ♂ uph lacks postdiscal markings, red ocelli prominent.

   1a. *P. p. sacerdos* f. *cardinalis* ♀. Ups dark markings extensive; uph red ocelli united by black bar.

   1b. *P. p. sacerdos* ♂. Ups less heavily marked; uph red ocelli smaller.

2. Parnassius mnemosyne   *Clouded Apollo*   41
Small, ups without red markings.

   2a. *P. m. athene* ♂. Ups black markings scanty; upf grey apical area enclosing small white spots.

   2b. *P. m. mnemosyne* ♀ f. *melaina*. Ups black markings more complete, extensively suffused dark grey.

3. Parnassius apollo   *Apollo*   39
Antennae white narrowly ringed pale grey; ♂ uph with grey postdiscal and marginal markings; red ocelli prominent.

   3a. *P. apollo* f. *rhodopensis* ♂. Upf lacking grey discal suffusion, uph ocelli large, red.

   3b. *P. apollo* f. *hispanicus* ♀. Upf with grey discal suffusion, all dark markings more extensive; uph ocelli orange-yellow. Red ocelli are much more common.

  See front endpaper for *P. a.* f. *bratholomaeus*

PLATE 4

1. Pieris brassicae *Large White* 42
Upf with extensive black apical border from costa down outer margin to vein 3.

    1a. *P. b. brassicae* first brood ♀. Upf with round black spots in spaces 1b and 3, apical black border powdered grey; unh grey.

    1b. *P. b. brassicae* second brood ♂. Upf lacks black discal spots, apical border black; unh yellow lightly powdered grey.

    1c. *P. b. cheiranthi* ♀. Large, fw black discal spots large and united on both surfaces.

    1d. *P. b. cheiranthi* ♂. Large, upf lacks black discal spots; uns as in ♀.

2. Lycaena helle *Violet Copper* 239
    ♀. Ups not suffused violet, markings well defined. For ♂ see Pl. 51.

3. Polyommatus icarus *Common Blue* 310
    ♀. Ups brown, wing-bases flushed blue; uns pale brown. For ♂ see Pl. 55.

4. Plebejus martini *Martin's Blue* 274
    4a. *P. m. martini* ♀. Ups brown, wing-bases flushed blue; uns brown, markings small. For ♂ see Pl. 55.

    4b. *P. m. allardi* ♀. Ups like *P. m. martini* ♀; uns markings larger.

G. rhamni Linnaeus 1758 TL: Sweden (Verity 1947) Pl. 12
Description. ♂fw 26/30mm., head and antennae red; ups *gc lemon-yellow* uniform on both wings, a small orange discoidal spot on each wing, veins marked at wing-margins by minute brown points, except at v1, 2, 3 on fw; uns markings similar; unh small brown pd points occasional between veins. ♀ greenish-white with similar wing-markings.
Flight. June or later in a single brood in Europe, hibernated specimens reappearing in early spring; a partial second brood in Africa flying in August/September.
Habitat. Light woodland and open places from sea-level to 6,000 ft. Food plant Buckthorn (*Rhamnus*).
Distribution. Widely distributed in N. Africa and in Europe to 67°N or beyond. Absent from Crete and Atlantic islands.
Variation. Large specimens with fw 33mm. occur in S. Europe and in N. Africa, f. *meridionalis* Roeber 1907.

Similar species. *G. cleopatra* below, ♀ only; *G. farinosa* p. 70.

GONEPTERYX CLEOPATRA *Cleopatra*

F: Citron de Provence Sp: Cleopatra
Range. From Madeira and Canary Islands through N. Africa and S. Europe to Syria.   Map 47

G. cleopatra cleopatra Linnaeus 1767 TL: Algeria Pl. 12

Description. ♂fw 25/30mm., resembles *G. rhamni*, but upf *vivid orange-red*, yellow marginal border 5–6mm. wide; uns costa of fw and all hw pale green or yellow (f. *massiliensis* Foulquier), both forms common in N. Africa. ♀ resembles *G. rhamni*, but unf with faint orange streak above median vein through cell.
Flight. May/June and later, depending upon locality.
Habitat. Frequent near light woodland and in open places, from sea-level to 6,000 ft.
Distribution. Morocco, Algeria, Tunisia, Sicily. Greece and all Mediterranean islands including Balearics and Crete.
Note. The angle at margin of hw at v3 is often feebly developed, sometimes scarcely noticeable.

G. cleopatra europaea Verity 1913 TL: Florence
Description. ♂upf orange discal field is slightly larger and deeper orange, yellow marginal border only 3–4mm. wide; angle at v3 on hw well defined, but distinctive characters slightly variable and not always well marked. Form *massiliensis* is recorded as a rarity from coastal districts of Mediterranean.
Flight. May/June, a partial emergence in August/September has been reported; hibernated specimens from March onwards.

Habitat. Usually in mountain foothills at 2-3,000 ft.
Distribution. Spain. Portugal. C. and S. France, northwards to Grenoble, Dordogne, etc. Italy, generally distributed; occasional in southern Alpine valleys.
Similar species. *C. rhamni* p. 63 and *C. farinosa* p. 70, ♀ only, unf lacks orange longitudinal flush from base through cell.

G. cleopatra maderensis   Felder 1862   TL: Madeira

Description. ♂ differs from the other subspecies in that the orange-red area on upf extends along the veins to reach the outer margin, spaces between veins being occupied by triangles of yellow. ♀ indistinguishable from *G. c. cleopatra*.
Flight and **Habitat.** No information.
Distribution. Confined to Madeira.

G. cleopatra palmae   Stamm 1963   TL: Canary Islands, La Palma

Pl. 12

Description. ♂fw 30/33 mm., outer margin nearly straight, apex slightly falcate; upf lemon-yellow with pale orange flush which fades to yellow near outer margin, red-brown marginal line and spots marking veins often conspicuous; hw margin bluntly angled at v3; uph lemon yellow; uns pale yellow-green, unf disc paler. ♀upf white, flushed yellowish at apex; uph palest orange; uns palest green, disc of fw white.
Flight. March/June, perhaps also later.
Habitat. Rough bushy ground at 2,000 ft.
Distribution. Canary Islands, confined to La Palma.

G. cleopatra cleobule   Huebner 1825   'Canary Island Brimstone'   Pl. 12
TL: Tenerife

Description. ♂fw 32/34 mm., resembles *G. c. palmae*, fw outer margin more sinuous and apex more falcate; upf orange area extending nearly to outer margin; hw angle at v3 faint or absent, veins marked by conspicuous red-brown spots; uph lemon-yellow slightly flushed orange. ♀ups lemon-yellow broadly flushed orange on fw and over pd area of hw.
Flight. February/March and later until mid-August.
Habitat. Rough ground at 2-6,000 ft. Larval food plants *Rhamnus crenulata* and *R. glandulosa*.
Distribution. Confined to Tenerife, Gomera. Females from Gomera are paler yellowish-white with minimal pale orange flush, probably a minor local race. In the Canary Islands the life-history of this species is not well understood. It is known to fly in January, February, March, May, June July, August and perhaps later. It seems possible that the butterfly flies throughout the year; the usual period of hibernation has not been reported.

PLATE 5

1. Pieris ergane   *Mountain Small White*   44
Unf without black markings but discal spot shows through from ups.

  1a. *P. ergane* ♂. Upf often with round black spot in space 3 (variable).

  1b. *P. ergane* ♀. Upf as in ♂ but with additional black spot in space 1b.

2. Pieris mannii   *Southern Small White*   44
Upf apical black mark extending down outer margin to vein 4.

  2a. *P. mannii* first brood ♂. Small, apical mark small; unh heavily powdered with dark scales.

  2b. *P. mannii* first brood ♀. Upf dark scales extend along veins to connect black spot in space 3 with outer margin; additional black mark present in space 1b.

  2c. *P. mannii* second brood ♂. Ups black markings larger; upf spot in space 3 tends to connect along veins to outer margin, appearing moon-shaped.

  2d. *P. mannii* second brood ♀. Ups all markings intense black and larger.

3. Pieris rapae   *Small White*   43
Upf apical mark grey, extending further along costa than down outer margin, spot in space 3 not connected with outer margin.

  3a. *P. rapae* first brood ♂. Upf apical grey mark small, not well defined; unh powdered with dark scales.

  3b. *P. rapae* second brood ♀. Upf apical mark and dark spots black, better defined; unh yellowish, dark shading slight.

4. Pieris krueperi   *Krueper's Small White*   46

  4a. *P. krueperi* second brood ♂. Upf with apical mark broken between veins, and dark costal bar before apex; unh dark costal mark at vein 7, basal area pale.

  4b. *P. krueperi* first brood ♀. Upf black markings larger; unh basal area dark, greenish.

1 a

1 b

2 a

2 b

2 c

2 d

3 a

3 b

4 a

4 b

PLATE 6

1. **Pieris napi**   *Green-veined White*

   Upf with or without black spot in space 3; apical mark broken, composed of grey expansions on veins along outer margin to vein 3; unh veins lined green or grey. See also Pl. 13.

   1a.-1d. *Pieris n. napi*. In ♀ ups white, lacking general fuscous suffusion but wing-bases powdered grey.

   1a. *P. n. napi* first brood ♂. Upf veins faintly lined grey near outer margin, unh ground-colour yellow, veins strongly lined green.

   1b. *P. n. napi* first brood ♀. Ups more heavily marked; upf with black spots in spaces 1b and 3; unh as in ♂.

   1c. *P. n. napi* second brood ♂ f. *napaeae*. Upf veins not lined grey, black spot in space 3 constant; unh ground-colour faintly yellow, veins partly lined grey (variable).

   1d. *P. n. napi* second brood ♀ f. *napaeae*. Ups veins slightly or not at all lined black, other black markings well-defined; uns as in ♂.

   1e. *P. n. adalwinda* ♂. Small, ups black markings greatly reduced; unh veins strongly marked on yellowish ground-colour.

   1f. *P. n. bryoniae* ♂ first brood. Ups veins lined grey, marginal dark markings distinct; unh ground-colour yellowish. For ♀ see Pl. 13.

   1g. *P. n. flavescens* f. *subtalba* ♂. Ups dark markings reduced; unh ground-colour white, veins lined grey.

   1h. *P. n. flavescens* ♀. Ups yellowish ground-colour prominent, fuscous suffusion extensive, veins lined grey.

   1i. *P. n. segonzaci* ♂. Large, upf black spot in s3 prominent; unh ground-colour yellowish, veins broadly lined greenish. See also Pl. 13.

   1j. *P. n. segonzaci* ♀. Large, upf black spots in spaces 1b, 3 and 5, veins lined grey in post-discal areas.

GONEPTERYX FARINOSA   *Powdered Brimstone*
Range. From SE. Europe through Asia Minor and Syria to Iran.

Map 48

G. farinosa Zeller 1847   TL: Macri (Fethiye), SW. Turkey   Pl. 12
Description. ♂fw 28/32mm., resembles *G. rhamni*; upf scales uneven (mealy), producing a slightly roughened appearance best seen with a hand lens; hw outer margin often rather deeply dentate between v1 and v3; upf gc lemon-yellow at base, becoming paler near outer margin, red discoidal spot minute or absent; *uph yellow gc distinctly paler than upf.* ♀ resembles *G. rhamni.*
Flight. May/June in a single brood.
Habitat. Usually in hilly or mountainous country from 1–5,000 ft. Larval food plant buckthorn.
Distribution. Only in extreme SE. Europe, Turkey, Greece, SE. Yugoslavia, Albania.

Similar species. *G. rhamni* p. 63, ♂ups yellow gc uniform in tone over both wings; in both sexes specimens from W. Europe usually have hw margin between v1b and v3 less deeply dentate; very rarely flies with *G. farinosa. G. cleopatra* p. 66.

LEPTIDEA SINAPIS   *Wood White*

F: Piéride de la Moutarde   Sw: Skogsvitvinge   G: Senfweissling
Sp: Blanca esbelta
Range. From W. Europe through Russia to Syria and Caucasus Mts.

Map 49

L. sinapis Linnaeus 1758   TL: Sweden (Verity 1947)   Pl. 13
Description. ♂fw 19/24mm., antennal club black, extreme tip chestnut-brown with white patch beneath; ups paper white. *First brood* upf apical mark large, grey; unf costa grey, apex yellowish; unh yellowish with obscure dusky markings across most of wing excepting cell and area beyond. ♀upf apical mark reduced to grey streaks along veins. *Second brood* (f. *diniensis* Boisduval) ♂upf apical mark black, smaller, round; unh markings reduced to obscure yellow-grey marblings but usually with grey band above anal region. ♀upf apical mark vestigial or absent.
Flight. April/May and later in two or more broods.
Habitat. Light woodland from lowlands to 5,000 ft. Larval food plants various Leguminosae, including tuberous pea, birds-foot trefoil, etc.
Distribution. Widely distributed through W. Europe to 66°N, rarely to 70°N, including the Mediterranean islands. Absent from Scotland, Malta and N. Africa.
Similar species. *L. duponcheli* p. 71; *L. morsei* p. 71 larger, fw in first brood slightly falcate but more rounded in second brood; unh paper-

white, unf veins lined grey near outer margin; unh grey pd markings better defined.

LEPTIDEA DUPONCHELI *Eastern Wood White*
Range. SE. France and Balkans to Asia Minor and Iran.   Map 50

L. duponcheli Staudinger 1871 **TL**: S. France   Pl. 13
syn: *lathyri* Duponchel (invalid homonym)
Description. ♂fw 17/21 mm., resembles *L. sinapis*, apex more pointed; antennal club without white spot beneath. *First brood* ups generally faintly flushed yellow; upf apical mark grey; uph extensive grey markings show through from uns; unh uniformly suffused grey-green except white mark at base of s5 and white area on outer margin. ♀ similar, upf apical mark pale grey. *Second brood*, f. *aestiva* Staudinger, ♂upf apical mark smaller, black; unh yellow flush generally well marked but dark markings absent. ♀upf apical mark often absent; unh as in ♂.
Flight. April or later in two broods.
Habitat. Open places generally at moderate altitudes, in mountainous districts. Larval food plants sainfoin and various Leguminosae.
Distribution. France in Var, Basses Alpes, Alpes Maritimes and Cantal. S. Yugoslavia. Greece. Albania. European Turkey.
Similar species. *L. sinapis* p. 70; *L. morsei* below. Both species have a white mark beneath antennal club.

LEPTIDEA MORSEI *Fenton's Wood White*
Range. From Europe across Siberia to Japan (TL of *L. morsei* Fenton 1881).   Map 51

L. morsei major Grund 1905 **TL**: Zagreb, Yugoslavia   Pl. 13
Description. *First brood*, f. *croatica* Grund, resembles *L. sinapis*; ♂fw 21/23 mm., slightly falcate at v6; upf apical mark grey, streaky, v3 and v4 darkened near margin; unf apex and all unh yellow-grey with darker markings as in *L. sinapis*; all veins grey except in basal half of fw. ♀fw falcate tip well marked. *Second brood*, f. *major*, ♂fw 23/25 mm., apex rounded with slight angle on outer margin at v6, not definite in all specimens; apical mark round, dark grey; unh paper-white with usual markings in palest grey. ♀upf apical mark of grey streaks along veins. Antennal club with small brown tip, uns white.
Flight. April and June/July in two broods.
Habitat. Light woodland at lowland levels. Food plant *Lathyrus niger*.
Distribution. Lower Austria. Czechoslovakia. Rumania, Mehadia. NW. Yugoslavia to Rijeka (Fiume) (farthest west).
Similar species. *L. sinapis* p. 70; *L. duponcheli* above.

DANAIDAE
Bates 1861

Large butterflies, characteristic especially of the tropics of Africa and the Far East, of which two species occur in the Canary Islands. They are distasteful to birds, have an unpleasant smell, tough leathery integuments and are extraordinarily tenacious of life. In both sexes the forelegs are small, useless for walking; antennal club slender and slightly flexed.

DANAUS PLEXIPPUS   Milkweed or Monarch
Range. America from Peru to Canada; Australia, New Zealand, Papua and larger East Indian islands; Canary Islands. Absent from Africa and continental Asia.   No map

D. plexippus   Linnaeus 1758   TL: Pennsylvania   Pl. 14
Description. ♂fw 47mm., variable; ups chestnut-brown, veins and wingborders lined black or dark brown, the latter including two marginal rows of small white spots; upf with scattered pale pd spots near apex; uph with small black sex-brand on v2; uns gc paler with similar markings. ♀gc paler, veins darker, esp. on hw, no sex-brand.
Flight. April or later in a succession of broods, perhaps throughout the year.
Habitat. Open places with flowers, etc., at low or moderate altitudes, very wide ranging. Usual foodplant *Asclepias curassavica*.
Distribution. Canary Islands, recorded from Tenerife, Gran Canary, La Palma, Hiero, sometimes common. Azores. Occurs as a rare vagrant in Portugal, Spain, France, Ireland and England.
This remarkable American migratory butterfly made spectacular extensions of its range during the nineteenth century. It reached New Zealand in 1840, Australia in 1870 and the Canary Islands in 1880, where it has been able to establish itself by accepting the indigenous African *Gossipium arboreum* and *Euphorbia mauretanica* as larval food plants.

DANAUS CHRYSIPPUS   Plain Tiger
Range. Africa, south of the Atlas Mts., Arabia and thence throughout tropical Asia to Australia. Canary Islands.   No map

D. chrysippus   Linnaeus 1758   TL: Egypt   Pl. 14
Description. ♂fw 35/42mm., variable; ups light tawny-brown; upf darker chestnut-brown near base, apex broadly black with white transverse band and small white marginal spots; uph with three small black discal spots, black sex-brand on v2, black marginal border enclosing small white spots; uns gc paler, markings similar. ♀ similar, without sex-brand.

Flight. Throughout warm months.

Habitat. Open places at low or moderate altitudes. Foodplant *Asclepias*.

Distribution. Appears to be resident in the Canary Islands on Tenerife, La Palma, Gomera. Occasionally reported from the Mediterranean area, esp. Greece and S. Italy; a rare migrant in Morocco. Not reported from Algeria or Tunisia.

LIBYTHEIDAE
Boisduval 1840

Rather small butterflies allied to the *Nymphalidae*, recognisable by the prominent tooth on the outer margin of the fore-wing, and by the great length of the palpi. They are migrants, and although the total number of species is small, they have become established on every continent and often occur on remote islands.

LIBYTHEA CELTIS *Nettle-tree Butterfly*
Range. From S. Europe and N. Africa through Asia Minor and Siberia to Chitral, Formosa and Japan. Map 52

L. celtis Laicharting 1782 TL: Bolzano, S. Tirol Pl. 22
Description. Palpi project nearly four times the length of the head. ♂fw 17/22mm., ups dark brown with orange-brown markings; upf a small white subapical mark on costa; unh neutral brown or grey with darker stripe along median vein, white mark often present at base of v4. ♀ similar. Markings are very constant.
Flight. June or later until hibernation, hibernated examples again in March/April.
Habitat. Low altitudes to 1,500 ft. near trees of *Celtis australis*, the larval food plant, but in late summer vagrants occur at much higher altitudes.
Distribution. Spain. France, in southern districts of Lozère, Basses Alpes and E. Pyrenees, etc., and in southern alpine valleys through Italy and Austria; widely distributed in peninsular Italy and Sicily. Rumania. Yugoslavia. Greece. Algeria.
Note. The butterflies disappear into a long hibernation in August/September until the following March/April, when they fly again and eggs are laid, which produce the single annual brood.

NYMPHALIDAE
Swainson 1827

This large family contains many of the best known European butterflies, such as the Tortoiseshells and Purple Emperor. They are conspicuously coloured and often common. In both sexes the fore-legs are small, densely hairy ('brush-footed'), useless for walking, the middle and hind legs normal.

CHARAXES JASIUS *Two-tailed Pasha*

F: Pasha à deux Queues   Sp: El Bajá
Range. From Mediterranean coastal districts across Abyssinia (*C. j. epijasius* Reiche) and into equatorial Africa as *C. jasius saturnus* Butler.
Map 53

C. jasius jasius Linnaeus 1766   TL: Barbaria (Algeria)   Pl. 15
Description. ♂ fw 38/41 mm., ups rich dark brown; upf with wide yellow-brown marginal border and vestigial pd spots; uph, marginal border continued, edged black, blue proximal spots in s 1c–s 4; uns basal area with elaborate pattern of spots and stripes outlined in white. ♀ similar, larger.
Flight. May/June and August/September in two broods.
Habitat. From sea-level to 1,500 ft. Larval food plant *Arbutus*.
Distribution. Mediterranean coastal districts from Greece westwards, including the larger islands. France, penetrates to Lozère, Cevennes, E. Pyrenees, not common. Italy, abundant locally on western coast, absent from Adriatic coast. Spain and Portugal, local and scarce in March and October in coastal areas. N. Africa, local and uncommon near coasts in Morocco and Algeria; more common in Tunisia.

APATURA IRIS *Purple Emperor*

F: Le Grand Mars   Sw: Stor Skimmerfjäril   G: Grosser Schillerfalter
Sp: Tornasolada
Range. W. Europe and across temperate Asia to China.   Map 54

A. iris Linnaeus 1758   TL: Germany, England   Pl. 15
Description. ♂ fw 31/37 mm., outer margin rounded at v 6; tip of antenna black; ups gc almost black, flushed brilliant iridescent blue; upf discal and pd spots white, *black spot in s 2 obscure*; uph oblique discal band white; uns brightly variegated with chestnut-brown, olive grey, etc.; unf pd fulvous mark enclosing a blue-pupilled ocellus in s 2; unh *white discal band with straight inner edge*, tapering towards anal angle. ♀ larger, ups without blue flush and white markings larger.
Flight. July/August in a single brood.
Habitat. Flies around tree-tops in old-established woodlands from sea-

PLATE 7

1. Euchloe ausonia   *Dappled White*   51
Upf grey apical border includes prominent white costal mark; unh ground-colour green, white markings irregular, marginal white spots irregular or rounded, costal margin bluntly angled at vein 8.

   1a. *E. a. crameri* ♂. Upf black discoidal spot rectangular, not extending beyond vein 12.
   1b. *E. a. ausonia* ♀. Upf black discoidal spot large, reaching costa; uph yellowish.
   1c. *E. a. ausonia* ♂. Upf discoidal spot narrow, angled, reaching costa; uph white.
   1d. *E. a. insularis* ♂. Upf discoidal mark narrow, angled; unh white markings small, numerous and well defined.

2. Pontia chloridice   *Small Bath White*   47
Unh with rather irregular continuous white postdiscal band; white marginal marks between veins regular and elongate.

   2a. *P. chloridice* second brood ♂. Ups black submarginal markings little developed.
   2b. *P. chloridice* first brood ♀. Ups black submarginal markings present on both wings.

3. Pontia daplidice   *Bath White*   47
Unf with black postdiscal spot in slb; unh with isolated round white white spot in cell.

   3a. *P. daplidice* second brood ♂. Upf lacks postdiscal black spot in slb; unh green ground-colour mixed with yellow.
   3b. *P. daplidice* first brood ♀. Ups black markings more extensive; unh ground-colour deep green.

4. Pontia callidice   *Peak White*   50
Unh elongate white mark in cell followed by row of white postdiscal chevrons.

   4a. *P. callidice* ♂. Upf black markings scanty; uph unmarked.
   4b. *P. callidice* ♀. Upf black submarginal markings well developed; uph dusky grey with black submarginal lunules.

5. Colotis evagore nouna ♂.   *Desert Orange Tip*   50
Upf apex red; unh ground-colour sandy-yellow or pinkish.

1a 5 1b

2a 6a 6b

2b 7a 7b

3 8a 8b

4a 7c 7d

4b 9a 9b

PLATE 8

1. **Euchloe tagis**   *Portuguese Dappled White*   52
   Like *E. ausonia* (**Pl. 7**) but hw costa evenly rounded at vein 8.
   1a. *E. t. tagis* ♂. Unh ground colour greenish with few small white spots. ♀ similar, often slightly larger.
   1b. *E. t. bellezina* ♀. Unh white markings larger and more numerous. Southern France. **See also Pl. 1.**

2. **Elphinstonia charlonia**   *Greenish Black-tip*   54
   2a. *E. c. charlonia* ♂. Small, yellow; upf apex broadly dark brown.
   2b. *E. c. penia* ♀. Larger, ground-colour slightly paler.

3. **Euchloe falloui**   *Scarce Green-striped White*   53
   ♂. Unf black discoidal spot small, lacks central white mark.
   ♀ slightly larger, otherwise similar.

4. **Euchloe belemia**   *Green-striped White*   53
   Like *Euchloe falloui*, but unf discoidal spot includes a slender white line.
   4a. *E. b. belemia* first brood ♂. Unh ground-colour dark green, white stripes clearly defined.
   4b. *E. b. belemia* second brood ♂. Unh ground-colour paler, yellowish, white stripes not clearly defined. **See also Pl. 1.**

5. **Euchloe pechi**   *Pech's White*   52
   ♂. Small; unh ground-colour green with small white discoidal spot.

6. **Anthocharis cardamines**   *Orange Tip*   54
   Ground-colour white; unh with mottled green markings.
   6a. *A. cardamines* ♂. Upf with broad orange-red apical patch.
   6b. *A. cardamines* ♀. No orange apical patch upf; apex rounded, grey apical border lacks distinct white spots (distinction from *Euchloe ausonia*, **Pl. 7**).

7. **Anthocharis belia**   *Morocco Orange-tip*   55
   Like *A. cardamines* but unh ground-colour yellow with markings reticulate.
   7a. *A. b. euphenoides* ♂. Ups yellow; upf with orange apical patch.
   7b. *A. b. euphenoides* ♀. Ups white, upf apex powdered orange; unh yellow, markings as in ♂.
   7c. *A. b. belia* ♂. Like *A. b. euphenoides* but unh reticulate markings grey or reddish-grey, usually obscure.
   7d. *A. b. belia* ♀. Ups as in *A. b. euphenoides* ♀; unh yellow, markings as in ♂.

8. **Anthocharis damone**   *Eastern Orange-tip*   55
   Like *A. cardamines* but unh yellow, with mottled green markings.
   8a. *A. d. damone* ♂. Ups yellow; upf with orange apical patch.
   8b. *A. d. damone* ♀. Ups white, lacking upf orange apical patch.

9. **Anthocharis gruneri**   *Gruner's Orange-tip*   56
   Like *A. cardamines* but small; unh green with irregular white spots.
   9a. *A. g. gruneri* ♂. Ups pale yellow; upf with orange apical patch.
   9b. *A. g. gruneri* ♀. Ups white; upf grey apical mark wide, extending to vein 2, discoidal grey spot large, extending to costa.

level to 3,000 ft. Larval food plants willow and sallow, esp. *Salix caprea*, also *S. aurita* and *S. cinerea*.
Distribution. N. Portugal. Spain in Guadarrama and Cantabrian Mts. From Basses Pyrénées across C. Europe, including S. England, Denmark and Baltic countries to 60°N. Migrant in Finland. Absent from Scandinavia and from much of southern Europe, including peninsular Italy and Balkans.
Variation. In a rare but recurrent form, ups white markings are nearly or quite absent, f. *iole* Schiffermueller.
Similar species. *A. ilia* below.

APATURA ILIA   Lesser Purple Emperor

F: Le Petit Mars   Sw: Liten Skimmerfjäril   G: Kleiner Schillerfalter
Sp: Tornasolada chica
Range. C. and S. Europe and across temperate Asia to Japan.   Map 55

A. ilia ilia   Schiffermueller 1775   **TL:** Vienna   Pl. 15
Description. ♂fw 32/35mm., resembles *A. iris* with similar blue flush on ups in males; outer margin of fw with blunt angle at v6; apex of antenna brown; upf discal markings white, a *well-defined pd orange-ringed spot in s2*; uph discal band white; unh inner margin of dull discal band not straight, a small dark spot present at base of cell. ♀ larger, pale markings larger. In nearly all localities and in both sexes dimorphic, upperside pale markings often yellow-brown (f. *clytie* Schiffermueller), but apical spots on fore-wing remain white. Extent of brown marking is variable, sometimes suffused over whole upperside. One or other colour may preponderate in a given colony. F. *clytie* rare in C. Italy, Spain and Portugal.
Flight. May/June and August/September in two broods in southern localities; a single brood in July in northern range. No seasonal variation has been reported.
Habitat. Light woodland at moderate altitudes. Larval food plants willows, poplar, etc., esp. *P. tremula* and *P. nigra*.
Distribution. Portugal; Geres. N. Spain, France; widely distributed from Pyrenees to Jura and Vosges. Belgium. Switzerland, rare in south. Germany to Rumania. Absent from England, Spain and Mediterranean islands.

A. ilia barcina   Verity 1927   TL: Antoni de Vilamajor, Catalonia
Description. ♂ like *A. i. ilia* but ups differs slightly in more complete white markings; upf white spot present in s1a and sometimes with obscure pale submarginal spots; uph white discal band wide at costa, outer edge straight, band tapering, directed to inner margin, pale submarginal spots often well defined; uns gc sandy-buff, markings white as on ups. ♀ larger, ups gc brown, white markings slightly larger, blue flush absent. Form *clytie* occurs rather rarely.
Flight and **Habitat** as for *A. i. ilia*.

Distribution. Catalonia, N.E. Spain, esp. in Province of Barcelona. In C. Italy somewhat similar.

Similar Species. *A. iris* p. 75, in which upf black spot in s2 is usually obscured by dark ground-colour.

APATURA METIS   *Freyer's Purple Emperor*
Range. From S.E. Europe across S. Russia and Siberia to China, Japan and Korea.

A. metis metis Freyer 1829   TL: Pecs (Fünfkirchen), Hungary   Pl. 15
Description. Like *A. i. ilia* but smaller; ♂ fw 30/32 mm., uph pale discal band sharply angled at v3, pale markings in slc and s2 displaced basad, pd dark band enclosing fulvous spots in spaces 2 and 3.
Flight and **Habitat** as for *A. ilia.*
Distribution. Austria, Hungary, Rumania, Bulgaria. Not recorded from Greece.
Note. Only seen in the f. *clytie,* ♀ entirely sandy yellow.

LIMENITIS POPULI   *Poplar Admiral*

F: Le Grand Sylvain   Sw: Aspfjäril   G: Grosser Eisvogel
Range. From C. Europe through C. Asia to Japan.   Map 56

L. populi Linnaeus   TL: Sweden (Verity 1950)   Pl. 15
Description. ♂ fw 35/40 mm., ups dark grey-brown with white spots, often indistinct, in cell and in pd areas, and with *orange-red and black submarginal spots*; uns gc *orange*, all markings better defined in white or blue-grey; unh with double row of dark pd spots. ♀ often larger, ups white markings much larger, uph with prominent white discal band.
Flight. June/July.
Habitat. Open woodland, from sea-level to 3,500 ft. Larval food plants aspen and other kinds of poplar.
Distribution. C. Europe to 66°N, often common. Absent from W. France, Pyrenees, Spain, Portugal, Britain, peninsular Italy and Greece.
Variation. Absence in ♂ of white markings on upf (except three apical spots), common in some localities, f. *tremulae* Esper.

LIMENITIS REDUCTA   *Southern White Admiral*

F: Le Sylvain Azure   G: Zaunlilienfalter   Sp: Ninfa de arroyos

Range. From S. and C. Europe across W. Asia to Syria, Caucasus and Iran.
   Map 57

L. reducta Staudinger 1901   TL: Armenia and Iran   Pl. 16
   syn: *rivularis* auct.
      anonyma Lewis 1872 (rejected by I.C.Z.N., Opinion 562)
      camilla auct.

PLATE 9

1. Colias phicomone   *Mountain Clouded Yellow*   57
Hw yellow discoidal spot well defined, generally prominent on both
surfaces.

  1a. *C. phicomone* ♂. Ups usually heavily suffused dark grey except
  the submarginal spots or band; unh bright yellow, basal and
  discal areas lightly suffused grey.

  1b. *C. phicomone* ♀. Ups greenish-white, lacking dark suffusion;
  unh as in ♂.

2. Colias nastes werdandi   *Pale Arctic Clouded Yellow*   57
Hw discoidal spot very small or vestigial on both surfaces.

  2a. *C. n. werdandi* ♂. Ups pale greenish-yellow; upf veins finely
  lined black; unh greenish-grey with light marginal markings.

  2b. *C. n. werdandi* ♀. Ups greenish-white, dark markings more extensive; unh as in ♂.

3. Colias palaeno   *Moorland Clouded Yellow*   58
Ups black marginal borders unspotted; unh discoidal spot small,
black or white, submarginal spots absent.

  3a. *C. p. palaeno* ♂. Ups ground-colour very pale yellow.
  3b. *C. p. palaeno* ♀. Ups ground-colour clear greenish-white.
  3c. *C. p. europome* ♂. Ups ground-colour bright yellow; upf discoidal spot often black.
  3d. *C. palaeno* ♀-form *illgneri*. Ups bright yellow; upf inner border
  of dark margin irregular, not well defined.

4. Zegris eupheme   *Sooty Orange-tip*   56
Upf with broad dark apical area enclosing small orange patch; unh
yellow, with reticulate pattern in dark grey-green.

  4a. *Z. e. meridionalis* ♂. Upf orange apical patch well developed.
  4b. *Z. e. meridionalis* ♀. Ups orange apical patch small or vestigial.

1a   1b

2a   2b

3a   3b

3c   3d

4a   4b

1a 1b

2a 2b

3a 3b

4a 3c

4b 4c

PLATE 10

In the species figured on this and the following plate males and females differ so greatly that it is not possible to give specific characters that cover both sexes.

MALES. Uph with oval sex-brand in space 8 except in *C. chrysotheme*; unf discal area yellow except 1a.

1a. **Colias libanotica heldreichii** *Greek Clouded Yellow*   59
Large; ups dusky orange with faintly rosy reflection, marginal dark borders crossed by yellow vein s; uns yellow-green, unf yellow discal area vestigial or absent.

2a. **Colias chrysotheme** *Lesser Clouded Yellow*   59
Small; ups orange-yellow, marginal dark borders crossed by yellow veins; uph sex-brand absent.

3a. **Colias myrmidone** *Danube Clouded Yellow*   59
Ups bright orange-yellow, marginal dark borders not crossed by veins; uph pale submarginal spots present internal to narrow black border.

4a. **Colias crocea** *Clouded Yellow*   60
Ups deep yellow; upf marginal dark border crossed by yellow veins at least near apex; uph lacks pale submarginal spots internal to dark marginal border.

FEMALES. Often polymorphic, orange or greenish-white.

1b. **Colias libanotica heldreichii.** Fw apex pointed; unhsmooth pale blue-green, white discoidal spot small.   59

2b. **Colias chrysotheme.** Small, fw apex pointed; upf costa broadly greenish-grey; white form not known.   59

3b. 3c. **Colias myrmidone.** Like *C. crocea* but uph large pale submarginal spots are present in regular series. 3c., ♀-form *alba*, greenish-white.   59

4b., 4c. **Colias crocea.** Uph pale submarginal spots irregular in size, series usually incomplete. 4c., ♀-form *helice*, greenish-white, uph suffused grey.   60

Description. ♂fw 23/27mm., ups gc blue-black, a submarginal series of small black spots edged blue on both wings; upf a prominent white spot in cell; uns gc reddish-brown; unh pale grey basal band and broad white central band followed by *single row of dark pd spots.* ♀ similar.

Flight. May or later in two or three broods in S. Europe, a single brood in July in N. Switzerland.

Habitat. Light woodland or bushy places, from lowlands to tree-line. Larval food plant honeysuckle (*Lonicera*).

Distribution. All S. Europe to 50°N.   Rare in N. and W. France.

Similar species. *L. camilla* below, unh with double row of dark pd spots.

LIMENITIS CAMILLA   *White Admiral*

F: Le Petit Sylvain   Sw: Tryfjäril   G: Kleiner Eisvogel
Sp: Ninfa de bosque
Range. C. Europe and across Russia and C. Asia to China and Japan.
Map 58

L. camilla   Linnaeus 1763   TL: Germany   Pl. 16
  syn: *sibilla* Linnaeus 1767
Description. ♂fw 26/30mm., white cell-spot faint or absent; uns markings varied blue-grey, white and tawny-brown; unh pd area tawny-brown with *double series of small black spots*; base and inner margin light grey. ♀ similar.

Flight. June/July.

Habitat. Flies in woodland from lowlands to 3,000 ft. Larval food plant honeysuckle (*Lonicera*).

Distribution. C. Europe to 56°N, including S. England and S. Sweden. Italy in Apennines south to 42°N. Absent from Htes and Basses Pyrénées, Portugal, S. Balkans, S. Italy and Mediterranean islands.

Similar species. *L. reducta* above.

NEPTIS SAPPHO   *Common Glider*

G: Schwarzbrauner Trauerfalter
Range. E. Europe, from Salzburg across Russia and C. Asia to Japan.
Map 59

N. sappho   Pallas 1771   TL: Volga, S. Russia   Pl. 16
  syn: *aceris* Esper 1783; *hylas* auct.
Description. ♂ and ♀fw 22/24mm., upf a narrow white stripe through cell with triangular mark beyond, both clearly marked; *uph discal and pd white bands present*; unh cinnamon red, broken pd band wider.

Flight. May/June and July/September.

Habitat. A lowland species flying in woodlands. Larval food plant *Lathyrus verna* (vetchling).

Distribution. E. Europe, esp. S. Hungary, N. Yugoslavia (Croatia) and Rumania, but extending westwards to Salzburg and Gradisca (Gorizia).

Similar species. *N. rivularis* below, uph with single white transverse band.

Note. *N. sappho* is commonly associated with Fenton's Wood White, *Leptidea morsei*, which has a similar distribution and food plant.

NEPTIS RIVULARIS *Hungarian Glider*

G: Schwarzer Trauerfalter

Range. From Piedmont in scattered colonies through Russia to C. Asia and Japan. Map 60

N. rivularis Scopoli 1763 TL: Graz, Austria Pl. 16
syn: *lucilla* Schiffermueller 1775

Description. ♂ and ♀fw 25/27mm., upf white stripe in cell vestigial; uph *a single oblique white discal band* crossed by black veins; uns cinnamon-brown, unh sometimes with traces of submarginal lunules.

Flight. June/early July.

Habitat. Light woodland, lowlands to 3,000 ft. Larval food plants *Spiraea*, perhaps meadowsweet.

Distribution. From Salzburg through Danube countries to Balkans and Bulgaria; S. Alps from Piedmont (Susa) in scattered colonies in southern alpine valleys, eastwards to NW. Yugoslavia (Gradisca).

Similar species. *N. sappho* p. 82.

NYMPHALIS ANTIOPA *Camberwell Beauty*

U.S.A.: Morning Cloak F: Le Morio Sw: Sorgmantel G: Trauermantel Sp: Antiopa

Range. From W. Europe across temperate Asia and N. America.

Map 61

N. antiopa Linnaeus 1758 TL: Sweden (Verity 1950) Pl. 17

Description. ♂fw 30/34mm., ups dark purple with wide cream-yellow marginal borders (white after hibernation), preceded by small blue spots. ♀ similar.

Flight. June/July or later and again in spring after hibernation.

Habitat. Open country but generally among hills or mountains. Larval food plants forest trees, willows, birch, etc.

Distribution. Europe, rarely common, most frequent in south but ranges north through Fennoscandia to North Cape. Occurs in Britain as a rare vagrant. Absent from S. Spain and Mediterranean islands.

Variation. In spite of the vast range of this species, geographical variation is practically non-existent.

NYMPHALIS POLYCHLOROS   *Large Tortoiseshell*

F: La Grande Tortue   Sw: Körsbärsfuks   G: Grosser Fuchs   Sp: Olmera
Range. From N. Africa across S. and C. Europe and Asia Minor to the
Himalayas.   Map 62

N. polychloros polychloros   Linnaeus 1758   TL: Sweden (Verity 1950)
                                                                    Pl. 17
Description. ♂fw 25/32mm., ups orange-brown with black markings and
dark marginal borders enclosing pale lunules; uph with blue lunules
internal to dark border; uns basal areas brown to blue-black, pd areas
paler. ♀ similar. In both sexes *hair covering palpi and legs very dark brown
or black.*
Flight. A single brood in June/July with long flight period, flying again in
spring after hibernation.
Habitat. Light woodland, lowlands to 5,000 ft. Larval food plants elms,
willows and other trees.
Distribution. W. Europe, including southern Fennoscandia, S. England
and Mediterranean islands. Absent from Ireland.

N. polychloros erythromelas   Austaut 1885   TL: Nemours, Algeria
Description. Size and markings as in *N. p. polychloros*; ups gc bright
fulvous-red; uns very dark, basal areas and marginal borders generally
black.
Flight and **Habitat** as in *polychloros*; recorded by Oberthur in August.
Distribution. Morocco, Algeria, Tunisia, mostly in Atlas Mts., flying at
5–6,000 ft.

Similar species. *N. xanthomelas* below, hair covering middle and hind-legs
dull buff; does not occur in W. Europe.

NYMPHALIS XANTHOMELAS   *Yellow-legged Tortoiseshell*

Sw: Videfuks
Range. E. Europe and through C. Asia to China and Japan.   Map 63

N. xanthomelas   Schiffermueller 1775   TL: Vienna   Pl. 17
Description. ♂fw 30/32mm., like *N. polychloros*; marginal angles slightly
more pronounced; ups orange-brown; uph black border before blue
marginal lunules slightly wider with inner margin less well defined. ♀
similar. In both sexes *middle and hind-legs and often palpi are dull brown
or buff.*
Flight. July/September in a single brood and again in spring after hibernation.
Habitat. A lowland species in E. Europe flying usually near willow trees
in which the silken larval nests are conspicuous. Larval food plants
willows, more rarely other forest trees.
Distribution. Rumania, Bulgaria, N. Yugoslavia, Hungary, Poland, E.

Germany, Czechoslovakia and Lower Austria, but rare in its western range. Occasional records, probably of migrant specimens, from Sweden, Finland, Denmark, Greece, etc.
Similar species. *N. polychloros* p. 84.

NYMPHALIS VAU-ALBUM *False Comma*

U.S.A.: Compton Tortoiseshell   G: Weisses L

Range. From E. Europe across temperate Asia to China and Japan; also in S. Canada and northern United States, where it is known as *N, j-album* Boisduval and Leconte.   Map 64

N. vau-album   Schiffermueller 1775   TL: Vienna   Pl. 17
  syn: *N. l-album* Esper 1781

Description. ♂ fw 30/33mm., ups resembles *N. polychloros* but *with prominent white costal marks near apex of fw and on hw*; uns usually yellow-brown with darker marbling; unh a small j-shaped white mark at cell-end. ♀ similar, uns pale markings predominantly grey.
Flight. July/September and again in spring after hibernation.
Habitat. A lowland species, most often in flowery meadows bordering woodland. Larval food plants forest trees, elm, beech, poplar, sallow, etc.
Distribution. Rare and local in E. Europe, most frequent in Rumania, esp. Retezat Mts. and Banat, also Bulgaria. Reported occasionally from other Danube countries westwards to 16°E and from S. Finland, Sweden and Baltic countries; probably vagrants.

Similar species. *N. polychloros* p. 84 and *N. xanthomelas* p. 84, both lacking the white costal mark on uph.

INACHIS IO *Peacock Butterfly*

F: Paon de Jour   Sw: Påfågelöga, or Jungfru   G: Tagpfauenauge
Sp: Pavo Real
Range. From W. Europe through temperate Asia to Japan.   Map 65

I. io   Linnaeus 1758   TL: Sweden (Verity 1950)   Pl. 17
Description. ♂ fw 27/29mm., size variable; ups chocolate-brown with *'peacock eye' ocellate marks on each wing*, impossible to confuse with any other butterfly. ♀ similar, slightly larger.
Flight. July or later and again in spring after hibernation.
Habitat. Flowery banks and gardens from lowlands to 6,000 ft. Larval food plant nettle, more rarely other low plants.
Distribution. W. Europe to 60°N, including all the larger islands of the Mediterranean. Absent from Crete and N. Africa.

VANESSA ATALANTA   *Red Admiral*

F: Le Vulcain   Sw: Amiral   G: Admiral   Sp: Numerada
Range. Azores, Canary Islands, N. Africa and through Europe and Asia
Minor to Iran. N. America to Guatemala. Haiti and New Zealand
(probably introduced).   Map 66

V. atalanta Linnaeus 1758   TL: Sweden (Verity 1950)   Pl. 17
Description. ♂fw 28/31 mm., ups black; upf with *unbroken red band across
cell to anal angle* and white apical markings; uph red marginal border in
s2–5; unh dark brown with confused markings. ♀ similar.
Flight. May to October; in S. Europe hibernated specimens appear in
spring.
Habitat. Flowery banks, gardens, etc., from lowlands to 6,000 ft. Larval
food plants nettle (*Urtica*); more rarely thistles.
Distribution. Throughout W. Europe to 62°N, more rarely to Arctic Circle
probably on migration. Morocco, Algeria, Tunisia. Canary Islands.
Azores.
Note. North of the Alps, and in England, survival of hibernating specimens
through winter is probably extremely rare. The abundant second brood in
England in late summer is due to the arrival in spring of immigrants from
S. Europe or N. Africa.
Similar species. *V. indica* below.

VANESSA INDICA   *Indian Red Admiral*

Range. Canary Islands and Madeira; India (TL of *Papilio indica* Herbst
1794), China, Japan and Korea.
  syn: *callirhoe* Millière 1867

V. indica vulcania Godart 1819   TL: Tenerife, Canary Islands   Pl. 17
Description. ♂fw 27/29 mm., like *V. atalanta*; upf *red band wider*, its lower
border *broken by black gc*; unh dark with confused cryptic markings.
♀ similar.
Flight. May/June or later in a succession of broods.
Habitat. Flowery banks, woodland borders, etc. Larval food plants not
recorded.
Distribution. Madeira. Canary Islands, widely distributed and often
common, probably absent from Fuerteventura and Lanzarote. Absent
from the Azores.
Similar species. *V. atalanta* above, upf red band narrower, unbroken.
Note. *V. indica* is not known from any locality between the Canary Islands
and India.

VANESSA CARDUI   *Painted Lady*

F: La Belle Dame   Sw: Tistelfjäril   G: Distelfalter
Sp: Bella Dama o Cardero
Range. Cosmopolitan, except S. America.   Map 67

V. cardui Linnaeus 1758 TL: Sweden (Verity 1950) Pl. 17
Description. ♂fw 27/29mm., ups rosy-buff; upf with small white spots at apex but not in s2; uph small black pd spots in s2–6 without pupils; unh pd area slightly darker than basal and discal areas and enclosing *five rather small ocelli.* ♀ similar.
Flight. In S. Europe from April onwards, may fly in any month in Africa. In N. Europe, including Britain, immigrants appear in June, followed by a single new generation in late summer.
Habitat. Flowery banks and mountain sides from lowlands to 6,000 ft. or more. Larval food plants thistles and nettles, rarely other plants.
Distribution. In Britain and in much of Europe only as an immigrant, rare in Ireland; has been recorded from Iceland.
Similar species. *V. virginiensis* below, unh pd ocelli in s2 and s5 very large.

VANESSA VIRGINIENSIS *American Painted Lady*
Range. Canary Islands and Madeira; throughout temperate N. America to Guatemala and Cuba. No map

V. virginiensis Drury 1773 TL: New York Pl. 17
syn: *huntera* Fabricius 1775
Description. ♂fw 20/25mm., size variable; ups resembles *V. cardui* but gc is orange-buff without rosy flush; upf white spot present in s2; uph pd spots in s2 and s5 enlarged to blue-pupilled ocelli; *unh pd ocelli in s2 and s5 very large* in well-defined darker pd band. ♀ similar.
Flight. June or later.
Habitat. Flowery places, generally in mountains. Larval food plants various Compositae, in America esp. *Gnaphalium* species.
Distribution. Canary Islands; Gran Canary, Gomera, La Palma, Tenerife. Recorded from Madeira. Rare vagrants occasional in SW. Europe and Britain.
Similar species. *V. cardui* above.

AGLAIS URTICAE *Small Tortoiseshell*
F: La Petite Tortue Sw: Nässelfjäril G: Kleiner Fuchs Sp: Ortiguera
Range. From W. Europe across Russia and Asia to Pacific coast.
Map 68

A. urticae urticae Linnaeus 1758 TL: Sweden (Verity 1950) Pl. 17
Description. ♂fw 22/25mm., ups gc red with black markings; upf with small black pd spots in s2 and 3; *uph basal area black*; unh basal area dark brown, pd area paler with dark marginal border. ♀ similar, slightly larger.
Flight. May or later in one or more broods; a single brood in N. Europe; hibernated specimens often appear in March/April.

Habitat. Flowery places from sea-level to 7,000 ft., frequent as a migrant on high mountains. Larval food plant nettles.
Distribution. All W. Europe to North Cape; absent from N. Africa and Atlantic islands.

A. urticae ichnusa Huebner 1824 TL: not stated   Pl. 17
Description. Resembles *A. u. urticae* but ups gc is brighter red and upf black spots in s2 and 3 are absent or obsolescent.
Flight and **Habitat** as for *A. u. urticae*.
Distribution. Corsica and Sardinia with characters constant. Peninsular Italy, occasional specimens only, more frequently transitional to *urticae*.
Similar species. *N. polychloros* p. 84, uph base fulvous, with black costal mark.

POLYGONIA C-ALBUM   *Comma Butterfly*

F: Robert le Diable   Sw: Vinbärsfuks   G: C-Falter   Sp: C-blanca
Range. From N. Africa across Europe to China and Japan.   Map 69

P. c-album Linnaeus 1758 TL: Sweden (Verity 1950)   Pl. 16
Description. ♂fw 22/24mm., ups orange-brown with darker markings; unh c-mark at cell-end. *First brood* (f. *hutchinsoni*) markings and uns marbling very bright in ♂ and ♀. *Second brood* markings duller; ♀unh very dark brown, markings obscure, with marked greenish tints.
Flight. June and end July/August in two broods; hibernated specimens fly in March/April.
Habitat. Flowery meadows, margins of woodland, gardens, etc., from lowlands to 6,000 ft. Larval food plants nettles, willow, hop and various trees.
Distribution. W. Europe to 66°N, including larger Mediterranean islands. N. Africa; Morocco, Algeria, Tunisia, not uncommon in Atlas Mts.
Similar species. *P. egea* below.

POLYGONIA EGEA   *Southern Comma*

G: Gelber C-Falter
Range. Provence and across S. Europe, Syria and Asia Minor to Iran.
                                                               Map 70

P. egea Cramer 1775 TL: Istanbul and Izmir   Pl. 16
Description. ♂fw 22/23mm.; *first brood* ups yellow-brown with small darker brown markings; uns confused brown markings on yellow ground, with bands of minute dark striae in pd areas; unh a small white y-mark on discoidal vein. ♀ similar. *Second brood* (f.*j-album* Esper) ups slightly darker, more fulvous brown with darker markings, uns darker, markings grey-brown.

Flight. May/June and August/September in two broods; again in spring after hibernation.
Habitat. Hot, dry stony valleys, around cliffs, etc., rarely above 4,000 ft. Larval food plant principally pellitory (*Parietaria*), more rarely nettles and various trees.
Distribution. Widely distributed in SE. France and in Italy. Common in SE. Europe to 46°N and extending to Hungary and Czechoslovakia.
Similar species. *P. c-album* p. 88, unh with white c-mark at cell-end.

ARASCHNIA LEVANA   *Map Butterfly*

F: La Carte Géographique   Sw: Kartfjäril   G: Netzfalter   Sp: Prótea
Range. From France across C. Europe, Russia and Asia to Japan.

Map 71

A. levana   Linnaeus 1758   TL: Germany   Pl. 16
Description. ♂fw 16/19mm.; *first brood* (f. *levana* Linnaeus) ups yellow-brown with irregular black markings; upf yellow pd mark on costa and small white pd spots in s2–4 and at apex; unh dark red-brown with confused markings, white veins and cross-lines. ♀ similar. *Second brood* (f. *prorsa* Linnaeus) ups black, discal bands pale yellow or white, broken on upf at v4; uns as in f. *levana*; ♀ similar.
Flight. May/early June and August/September; first brood flies in April in some districts and a third brood may occur, partly overlapping.
Habitat. Light woodland from lowlands to 3,000 ft. Food plant nettles. The larvae live gregariously.
Distribution. C. and E. Europe to Baltic coast. France, common in N. and C. districts southwards to Pyrenees. Rare in Switzerland and in N. Balkans. Italy, no recent records. Portugal, recorded from Coimbra. Absent from Britain, SE. France and S. Balkans.
Variation. Forms intermediate between *levana* and *prorsa* are not uncommon.

PANDORIANA PANDORA   *Cardinal*

F: Le Cardinal   G: Grünes Silberstrich   Sp: Pandora
Range. From Canary Islands, through N. Africa, S. Europe and S. Russia to Iran and Chitral.   Map 72

P. pandora   Schiffermueller 1775   TL: Vienna   Pl. 19
   syn; *maja* Cramer 1776
Description. ♂fw 32/40 mm., ups fulvous, more or less shaded with greenish-grey suffusion; upf sex-brands along v2 and 3 prominent; unf *discal area rose-red, apex green*; unh green with irregular sub-basal and narrow pd silver stripes and small white pd dots. ♀ larger with increased green-grey suffusion; unh silver stripes and dots better defined.
Flight. June/July in Europe; N. Africa in May/June and August/September in two broods.

Habitat. Flowery meadows from lowlands to 4,000 ft. in Europe, to 6,000 ft. in N. Africa; visits thistles, flowering lime trees, etc. Larval food plants violets, esp. *V. tricolor*, rarely rue.

Distribution. S. France, extending northwards in Atlantic coastal districts to Morbihan. Italy and Sicily, becoming rare along southern slopes of Alps. Corsica and Sardinia. Spain and Portugal, common in mountains. More widely distributed in E. Europe from Greece through Balkans to Austria, Hungary and Czechoslovakia. Common in Morocco, Algeria and Tunisia. Canary Islands, reported from Tenerife, La Palma, Gomera.

Similar species. *A. paphia* below.

ARGYNNIS PAPHIA   *Silver-washed Fritillary*

F: Tabac d'Espagne   Sw: Silverstreckad Pärlemorfjäril
G: Silberstrich or Kaisermantel   Sp: Nacarada
Range. From W. Europe and Algeria across temperate Asia to Japan.
Map 73

A. paphia paphia   Linnaeus 1758   TL: Sweden (Verity 1950)   Pl. 18
Description. ♂ fw 27/35mm., ups bright fulvous with black spots and striae; upf sex-brands conspicuous along v1–4; *unf pale fulvous-yellow*; unh greenish-grey with transverse silver discal and pd stripes, pd area mottled silver and lilac-grey with darker markings. ♀ occurs in two forms: ♀ f. *paphia* Linnaeus, like ♂, but ups fulvous duller, black markings large; unh silver markings as in ♂. ♀ f. *valesina* Esper pl. 18, ups pale grey with extensive greenish suffusion; uns dark markings and silver stripes as in f. *paphia*; behaves genetically as a dominant to ♀ f. *paphia*.
Flight. End June to August.
Habitat. Flies in woodland clearings from lowlands to 4,500 ft. Larval food plants mostly violets, rarely *Rubus idaeus* and other low plants.
Distribution. Europe to 63°N, Balkans and Greece. Absent from S. Spain, Morocco and Crete. The ♀ form *valesina* occurs sporadically, common in some localities, elsewhere absent as in Ireland or rare, e.g. in Britain.
Variation. In N. and C. Italy and in Spain, f. *anargyria* Staudinger, silver stripes on unh obsolescent, other markings unchanged.

A. paphia immaculata   Bellier 1862   TL: Corsica   Pl. 18
Description. Resembles *A. p. paphia*; unh markings greatly reduced but with general gleaming golden suffusion; pd area slightly darker with spots larger and better defined. ♀ similar, f. *valesina* not uncommon.
Flight and Habitat as for *A.p. paphia*.
Distribution. Corsica, Sardinia, Elba, Giglio, replacing *A.p. paphia*. In Sicily, and elsewhere near the Mediterranean coast, forms of *paphia* transitional to *immaculata* have been reported.

A. paphia dives Oberthur 1908 TL: Lambessa, Algeria
Description. ♂fw 34/36mm., large, ups boldly marked; unh markings well defined, most often without silver stripes, which are replaced by greenish-buff, but variable. ♀ larger, fw to 40mm., variable, tendency to *valesina-*colour uncommon.
Flight. June/July.
Habitat. Wooded valleys at 4–5,000 ft.
Distribution. Algeria, in mountains near Lambessa, Djebel Aures, Kabylia, Khenchela, Sgag. Absent from Morocco.
Similar species. *P. pandora* p. 89, unf discal area rosy red.

ARGYRONOME LAODICE *Pallas's Fritillary*

G: Grünlicher Perlmutterfalter
Range. From Baltic countries, Poland and Hungary across Asia to W. China and Japan. Map 74

A. laodice Pallas 1771 TL: S. Russia Pl. 19
Description. ♂fw 27/29 mm., ups bright fulvous with bold black markings; upf with sex-brand on v1 and 2; unh basal half light olive-green with brown markings, separated sharply by white striae from lilac-brown pd area, without silver spots. ♀ups paler fulvous-yellow, upf with white subapical costal spot.
Flight. July/August.
Habitat. Flies in woodland clearings at lowland levels. Larval food plants violets, esp. *V. palustris.*
Distribution. Lithuania, E. Poland, E. Prussia, Hungary, SE. Finland.

MESOACIDALIA AGLAJA *Dark Green Fritillary*

F: Le Grand Nacré Sw: Stor Pärlemorfjäril G: Grosser Perlmutterfalter
Sp: Lunares de Piata
Range. From W. Europe and Morocco across Asia to China and Japan. Map 75

M. aglaja aglaja Linnaeus 1758 TL: Sweden (Verity 1950) Pl. 19
 syn: *charlotta* Haworth 1802
Description. ♂fw 24/29 mm., ups markings of usual Argynnid pattern; uph pd spot in s4 small; unh gc yellow-buff with green overlay, all spots silver, *pd series absent.* ♀ups gc slightly paler.
Flight. June/July.
Habitat. Flowery meadows and heaths with violets, from lowlands to tree-line. Larval food plants violets; persicaria (*Polygonum*) also recorded.
Distribution. W. Europe from Mediterranean to North Cape, including British Isles. Absent from Crete and Mediterranean islands except Sicily.
Variation. Dark suffusion ups may be marked in some districts, e.g. Bavaria and Orkneys, esp. in ♀.

M. aglaja lyauteyi Oberthur 1920   TL: Azrou, Morocco   Pl. 19
Description. ♂fw 30/33 mm., large, ups gc paler yellow-buff with enlarged black markings; uns green suffusion more extensive and colour more intense, esp. over hw. up s gc pale buff with greenish reflections, fw 35 mm.
Flight. June/early July.
Habitat. Forest clearings at 5–6,000 ft.
Distribution. Morocco, in Middle Atlas; Azrou, Ain Leuh, Ifrane, etc. Not recorded from High Atlas, nor from Algeria.
Similar species. *F. niobe* p. 93; *F. adippe* below; in both unh submarginal spots, silver-pupilled, are distinctly separate from the large discal spots.

FABRICIANA ADIPPE   *High Brown Fritillary*

Sw: Allmän Pärlemorfjäril   G: Hundsveilchen-Perlmutterfalter   Sp: Puntos azules
Range. From N. Africa and W. Europe across temperate Asia to Japan.
                                                                    Map 76

F. adippe adippe Schiffermueller 1775   TL: Vienna   Pl. 18
  syn: *cydippe* Linnaeus 1761 (rejected name)
Description. ♂fw 25/31mm., ups bright fulvous; upf sex-brands on v2 and 3 thick; uph a fringe of long hair along v7; unh gc buff with darker shading and *reddish silver-pupilled pd spots*, small or absent in s4. ♀ similar, uph hair fringe along v7 absent. This subspecies occurs in two forms which may fly together: f. *adippe* Schiffermueller pl. 18, unh basal, discal and other spots brilliant silver; f. *cleodoxa* Ochsenheimer pl. 18, unh spots obscurely outlined against buff gc but without silver, except the pupils of pd series.
Flight. June/July in a single brood.
Habitat. Woodland clearings and meadows, from sea-level to tree-line, frequent in mountainous country. Larval food plant violets.
Distribution. All Europe except Arctic regions, Ireland, Spain (but see *F.a. chlorodippe* below), Portugal and the Mediterranean islands other than Sicily.

F. adippe chlorodippe Herrich-Schaeffer 1851   TL: Spain   Pl. 18
Description. ♂ups resembles *F. a. adippe*; uph hair fringe pronounced; unh gc olive-green, all spots fully silvered. ♀ similar, uph hair fringe absent.
Flight. June/early July.
Habitat. Flowery banks, woodland or heaths in mountains from 3,500 ft.
Distribution. Portugal. Spain south of Pyrenees and Cantabrian Mts., often common.
Variation. Unh green restricted to basal suffusion, spots without silver except pd series, outlined in brown, f. *cleodippe* Staudinger Pl. 18.

F. adippe auresiana Fruhstorfer 1908   TL: Djebel Aures, Algeria   Pl. 18
Description. ♂ resembles *F. a. chlorodippe*; ups sex-brand absent; uph hair fringe sparse; unh gc deeper green, silver spots often small, sometimes obsolescent. ♀ similar.
Flight. June/early July.
Habitat. Open woodlands and heaths at 5–6,000 ft., common locally.
Distribution. Morocco. Algeria.
Variation. In High Atlas, flying at 9,000 ft., small, ♂fw 25/26mm., f. *astrifera* Higgins. A *cleodippe*-like form has not been recorded from N. Africa.

The relative abundance of the forms *adippe* (with silver spots on unh) and *cleodoxa* and *cleodippe* (without silver spots) varies greatly from place to place. In northern and north-eastern Europe f. *adippe* is common, and f. *cleodoxa*, extremely rare in Britain, Belgium and Denmark, is rare in Fennoscandia. In northern and central France, Germany, Austria and N. Switzerland f. *cleodoxa* is less rare but still uncommon. On the southern slopes of the Alps the position is reversed, f. *cleodoxa* often preponderating in S. Switzerland, N. Italy and along the chain of the Appenines. In Sicily f. *adippe* appears to be absent. In the Pyrenees f. *cleodoxa* is common, but in Spain f. *cleodippe* (also without silver spots) is rare, especially in S. Spain, and the silver-spotted f. *chlorodippe* much more common. In Hungary, Romania and the Balkans f. *cleodoxa* becomes progressively more common until in Greece it apparently entirely replaces f. *adippe*.

Similar species. *F. niobe* below, often smaller and unh cell usually includes small yellow spot with black central point, unh veins black near outer margin; upf ♂ sex-brands often thin. *M. aglaja* p. 91.

FABRICIANA NIOBE   *Niobe Fritillary*

Sw: Bastardpärlemorfjäril   G: Stiefmütterchen-Perlmutterfalter
Sp: Niobe
Range. From W. Europe through Russia and Asia Minor to Iran.

Map 77

F. niobe Linnaeus 1758   TL: Sweden (Verity 1950)   Pl. 19
Description. ♂fw 23/30mm., ups as in *F. adippe*; upf slender sex-brands along v2 and 3 in N. and C. Europe, often absent in SW.; uph black pd spot small in s4, small or absent in s6; unh often flushed green near base with or without silver spots. *The small yellow spot below median vein near base of cell generally enclosing a minute black point* and black-lined veins are important specific characters. ♀ups black markings often heavy and more or less suffused dark grey.
Flight. June/July.
Habitat. Meadows and subalpine pastures to tree-line. Larval food plants violets, more rarely plantains.

Distribution. W. Europe, esp. in mountains, to 62°N. Local or occasional in NW. France, absent from Britain, Corsica, Sardinia and Crete.
Variation. In C. and S. Spain upf sex-brands may be absent. In many districts the species occurs in two forms, that may fly together, similar to those of *F. adippe*: f. *niobe* Linnaeus pl. 19, unh basal, discal and other spots brilliant silver; f. *eris* Meigen pl. 19, unh spots without silver, but outlined in black or brown against pale buff gc. Intermediate specimens with spots partly filled with silver are not uncommon. In most localities f. *niobe* is uncommon or rare, far outnumbered by f. *eris*. Form *niobe* is more common in females than in males, probably more common at low altitudes than in mountains. Form *niobe* is more common than f. *eris* in parts of C. France (Auvergne) and in C. Italy (Abruzzi), and in these and doubtless in other localities it may form about 70% of the population. No series exclusively of f. *niobe* has been seen from any locality. South of the Pyrenees the population appears to consist entirely of f. *eris*, and this is the situation also in the Asiatic range.

Similar species. *F. adippe* p. 92; *M. aglaja* p. 91.

FABRICIANA ELISA   *Corsican Fritillary*
Range. Confined to Corsica and Sardinia.   Map 78

F. elisa Godart 1823   TL: Corsica and Sardinia   Pl. 19
Description. ♂fw 23/26mm., ups gc bright fulvous, black markings mostly small, but upf pd spots well developed in s2, 3, 5 and 6, sex-brand absent; *unh spots all small and silver*, except pd row of white-pupilled brown spots. ♀ slightly larger, ups gc paler with somewhat reduced markings.
Flight. June/July.
Habitat. In light woodland and heathland areas from 3,000 ft. upwards. Larval food plant violets.

ISSORIA LATHONIA   *Queen of Spain Fritillary*
F: Le Petit Nacré   Sw: Storfläckig Pärlemorfjäril
G: Kleiner Perlmutterfalter   Sp: Sofia
Range. W. Europe, N. Africa and Canary Islands, and across C. Asia to Himalayas and W. China.   Map 79

I. lathonia Linnaeus 1758   TL: Sweden (Verity 1950)   Pl. 19
Description. ♂fw 19/23mm., fw without sex-brand, outer margin concave below v5; hw angled at v8 and anal angle often produced; uph with grey basal suffusions; *unh silver spots mostly very large*. ♀ similar.
Flight. February/March or later, in two or three broods throughout summer in the south, single brooded at higher latitudes.
Habitat. In rough places and meadows from sea-level to 7,000 ft. or more. Larval food plant violets.
Distribution. N. Africa and S. Europe, thence northwards as a migrant to

64°N or beyond, occasional in Britain but resident in S. Sweden. Canary Islands; Tenerife, La Palma, Gomera.

Note. The butterfly is a notable migrant. It is said to hibernate as an egg, larva or imago according to local conditions.

BRENTHIS HECATE *Twin-spot Fritillary*

G: Saumfleck-Perlmutterfalter Sp: Hechicera

Range. From SW. Europe to Russia, Asia Minor, Iran and C. Asia.

Map 80

B. hecate Schiffermueller 1775 TL: Vienna Pl. 20

Description. ♂fw 18/22mm., ups pd and submarginal black spots in regular and complete series on both wings; unh veins lined dark brown on buff gc, basal marks and spots of discal band all outlined brown or black; *pd and submarginal series of black spots both complete*, double marginal lines distinct. ♀ similar, ups often suffused fuscous.

Flight. End May/June.

Habitat. Rough ground and open slopes from 2–5,000 ft. Larval food plant *Dorycnium* (Leguminosae).

Distribution. SE. Europe, distributed in scattered colonies in Czechoslovakia, Hungary, Austria (rare) and southwards to Balkans. Reported from Greece (Sparta). S. France, very local to 45°N, esp. in Var, Alpes Maritimes, Basses Alpes, Bouches du Rhône; absent from Pyrenees. Spain, local as a mountain butterfly in Soria, Teruel, Cuenca and Andalusia. Italy, locally common in valleys of River Po and its tributaries; absent from peninsular Italy, Mediterranean islands and Portugal.

Similar species. *B. daphne* below; *B. ino* p. 98; both lack the double row of small dark pd spots on unh.

BRENTHIS DAPHNE *Marbled Fritillary*

Sp: Laurel G: Brombeer-Perlmutterfalter

Range. SW. Europe through Russia and C. Asia to China and Japan.

Map 81

B. daphne Schiffermueller 1775 TL: Vienna Pl. 20

Description. ♂fw 21/26mm., ups resembles *B. hecate*, upf spots of pd series uneven, small in s1 and s4, large in s2 and s3; unh veins and spots of discal band lined rather light brown against gc of yellow-buff, broad pd area marbled lilac-brown with markings rather obscure, *base of s4 mostly brown*. ♀ similar, ups gc paler.

Flight. June/early July.

Habitat. Warm valleys, rarely to 4,000 ft., often visits flowers of bramble. Larval food plants violets and bramble.

Distribution. S. Europe to 46°N in west, farther east extending to Austria,

PLATE 11

1a

5

2a

2b

3a

3b

1b

3c

4a

4b

PLATE 12

Czechoslovakia and Hungary, common in Balkans and Greece. Absent from S. Spain, Portugal and Mediterranean islands except Sicily.

Similar species. *B. ino* below; *B. hecate* p. 95.

BRENTHIS INO   *Lesser Marbled Fritillary*

F: La Grande Violette   Sw: Älggräsfjäril   Sp: Laurel menor   G: Violetter Silberfalter

Range. C. and N. Europe and through temperate Asia to N. China and Japan.   Map 82

B. ino   Rottemburg 1775   TL: Halle, Germany   Pl. 22
Description. ♂fw 17/20mm., smaller than *B. daphne*, ups black markings more linear, black marginal borders generally entire and continuous; unh *base of* s4 *usually yellow-buff*, pd spots and ocelli irregular. ♀ similar, slightly larger, ups often suffused fuscous with violet sheen in fresh specimens.
Flight. June/July.
Habitat. In marshy meadows and damp places, lowlands to 5,000 ft. Larval food plants principally meadowsweet, raspberry and great burnet.
Distribution. C. and N. Europe from Cantabrian Mts., Pyrenees and Alps to North Cape. Peninsular Italy, only in Calabria. Balkans, not rare, including Albania and Bulgaria. C. Spain, local in Teruel. Absent from S. Spain, Portugal, Britain, Mediterranean islands and Greece.

Similar species. *B. daphne* p. 95, larger, unf black pd spots large in s2 and s3; unh base of s4 mostly brown. *B. hecate* p. 95.

BOLORIA PALES   *Shepherd's Fritillary*

Sp: Perlada alpina
Range. Alpine levels from Cantabrian Mts. and Pyrenees, Alps, Carpathians and Caucasus to C. Asia and W. China.   Map 83

B. pales pales   Schiffermueller 1775   TL: Vienna   Pl. 21
Description. ♂fw 17/19mm., ups gc bright fulvous; upf *discal markings macular (not linear)*; uph black basal suffusion includes cell; unf *black markings scanty*, shadowy; unh brightly variegated, basal and pd areas generally dark red, yellowish discal band not conspicuous, spot in s4 and marginal spots silver, a yellow area from margin in s3. ♀upf gc sometimes paler.
Flight. July/August.
Habitat. From tree-line on mountains, flying over slopes of grass or *Vaccinium* to levels of 8,000 ft. or more. Larval food plant violets, esp. *V. calcarata*.
Distribution. E. Alps, Bavaria, N. Tirol and Dolomites, Austria, Tatras, Carpathians and Julian Alps.

B. pales palustris Fruhstorfer 1909 TL: Zermatt, Switzerland Pl. 21
Description. ♂fw 16/18mm., small, ups gc paler, yellowish; upf black discal markings thin; unh variable, sometimes nearly uniform red with obscure markings. ♀ generally similar, sometimes paler with slightly grey tint near wing-margins.
Flight and Habitat as for *B. p. pales*.
Distribution. S. Alps, from Alpes Maritimes to Ortler and Brenner. Apennines, local on a few high peaks, Gran Sasso, Monte Majella, etc. Balkans, on most high mountains, Rhodope, Prenj, Durmitor and in Albania. North of Rhône valley less typical, often transitional to *B.p pales*. Absent from Jura and Vosges.
Variation. At high levels in southern Alps often very small, upf markings linear, unh brightly coloured.
Similar species. *B. napaea* below, often larger, ups gc paler, upf markings more linear; ♀ups more or less suffused grey. *B. graeca* p. 103, only in SW. Alps and Balkans; ups gc orange-yellow with macular black markings, unf black spots present, unh colours pale. *B. aquilonaris* p. 102, unf black spots well developed.

B. pales pyrenesmiscens Verity 1932 TL: Gèdre, Htes Pyrénées Pl. 21
Description. ♂fw 18/20mm., ups gc orange-yellow with macular black markings; uph black basal suffusion less extensive, cell clear; unf *black markings variable*, generally small and scanty; unh markings not brilliant, yellowish, sometimes with distinctly greenish tints. ♀ups often paler, sometimes with slight general dusky suffusion.
Flight. End June/July.
Habitat. From 5,000 ft. upwards on grass slopes, etc.
Distribution. Pyrenees and Cantabrian Mts. on most higher slopes from Mt. Canigou to Picos de Europa, widely distributed on northern slopes of Pyrenees, more local on southern slopes.
Similar species. No similar species occurs in C. Pyrenees. In E. Pyrenees only *B. napaea* below occurs, very locally in the Cambre-d'Aze region.

BOLORIA NAPAEA *Mountain Fritillary*
Sw: Nordisk Gulfläckig Pärlemorfjäril
Range. E. Pyrenees, Alps and Fennoscandia to North Cape, eastwards to Altai Mts. and Amurland, probably extending throughout arctic Asia; Alaska and Wyoming. Map 84

B. napaea Hoffmannsegg 1804 TL: Alps of Tirol Pl. 21
Description. ♂fw 17/21mm., resembles *B. pales*; *ups gc fulvous yellow or pale buff*; upf *black markings linear*, discal series composed of confluent striae; uph black basal suffusion extensive; *unf black markings greatly*

PLATE 13

1. Leptidea duponcheli   *Eastern Wood White*   71
Fw apex pointed; ground-colour faintly yellowish; antennal club dark.
  1a. First brood ♂. Upf apex grey; unh mostly smooth, even grey.
  1b. Second brood ♀. Upf grey apical mark greatly reduced or vestigial; unh dark marking absent.
  1c. Second brood ♂. Upf apical mark dark grey (black).

2. Leptidea sinapis   *Wood White*   70
Fw apex less pointed; ups ground-colour dead-white; under surface of antennal club has large white area.
  2a. first brood ♂. Upf apex grey; unh grey with obscure markings
  2b. first brood ♀. Upf grey apical mark reduced.
  2c. second brood ♂. Upf apical mark black, rounded.

3. Leptidea morsei   *Fenton's Wood White*   71
Large; fw with blunt angle at vein 6; under surface of antennal club has large white area.
  3a. second brood ♀. Upf apical grey mark vestigial; unh yellowish with grey markings.
  3b. second brood ♂. (Small specimen). Dead white on both surfaces; upf apical mark dark grey; unh faint pale grey markings.

4. Pieris napi   *Green-veined White*   45
  4a. *P. n. atlantis* ♂. Large; upf prominent post-discal spot in space 3. **See also Pl. 6.**
  4b. *P. n. maura* second brood ♀. Ups dark markings complete.
  4c. *P. n. bryoniae* ♀. Ups extensively suffused grey along all veins and in basal areas. **See also Pl. 6.**

5. Tarucus rosaceus   *Mediterranean Tiger Blue*   252
Unf small black markings form almost continuous line.
  5a. ♂. Upf blue, with pinkish tint; narrow grey discoidal spot.
  5b. ♀. Ups with blue flush; uph with white markings clearly defined.

6. Kretania eurypilus   *Eastern Brown Argus*   280
♂. Upf brown, no discoidal spot; uns pale grey-brown, unf no cell-spot; unh green scales in marginal spots in spaces 1, 2 (3).

7. Lysandra albicans   *Spanish Chalk-hill Blue*   307
L. a. arragonensis ♂. Ups pearly-grey with faintly blue basal flush
See also Pl. 57.

8. Plebicula escheri   *Escher's Blue*   297
P. e. dalmatica ♂. Large, ups dark marginal borders 2 mm. wide on both wings. **See Pl. 57.**

9. Aporia crataegi   *Black-veined white*   42
♂. All veins lined black. ♀ fw mostly hyaline.

10. Catopsilia florella   *African Migrant*   57
♀. Ups greenish-white, costa and small discoidal spot dark.
♂ similar, costa pale.

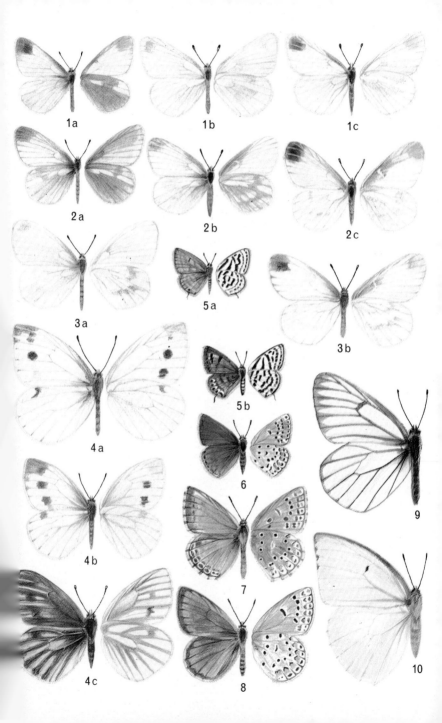

PLATE 14

1. **Danaus chrysippus**   *Plain Tiger*   72
   ♂. Ups veins not darkened; uph with small sex-brand on vein 2.
   ♀ similar but lacking sex-brand.

2. **Danaus plexippus**   *Milkweed* or *Monarch*   72
   ♂. Ups veins darkened; uph sex-brand on vein 2, very small.
   ♀ similar but lacks sex-brand.

3. **Kirinia roxelana**   *Lattice Brown*   230

   3a. ♂. Fw narrow, distorted by sex-brands; unh with 5 large, 2
       small postdiscal ocelli.
   3b. ♀. Fw shape normal; upf with pale apical markings; unh as in
       ♂.

4. **Melitaea didyma**   *Spotted Fritillary*   117
   M. d. occidentalis f. *dalmatina* ♂. Small, ups pale buff with small
   markings. See also Pl. 23

5. **Melitaea phoebe**   *Knapweed Fritillary*   114
   M. phoebe f. *pauper* ♂. Small, ups uniform pale fulvous with thin
   dark markings. See also Pl. 23

6. **Hamearis lucina**   *Duke of Burgundy Fritillary*   231
   H. lucina first brood ♀. Large, ups markings well defined, dark
   suffusion slight (f. *praestans*). For ♂ see Pl. 21

reduced or absent; unh pale or sandy red and yellow with little contrast, but sometimes brighter and darker in eastern Alps. ♀ generally larger, ups more or less suffused grey, often with violet reflections; unh pale, tinted green near base.

Flight. July/August.

Habitat. Near or above tree-line in mountains, often in damp places, rarely above 6,000 ft. Larval food plant alpine bistort (*Polygonum viviparum*).

Distribution. S. Alps from Alpes Maritimes to Hohe Tauern, often common. N. of Rhône valley from Bernese Alps to Bavaria, Innsbruck, etc., more local, often scarce. E. Pyrenees, extremely local on Cambre d'Aze, Val d'Eyne, Carlitte, etc. Fennoscandia, widely distributed from Hardanger Fjeld at 60°N to North Cape, usually small, f. *frigida* Warren Pl. 21. Absent from Styrian Alps, Tatra, Carpathians and Balkans.

Similar species. *B. pales palustris* p. 99, in W. Alps has rather linear black markings on ups, but unh is more brightly coloured than in any form of *napaea* and the females are not suffused with grey. *B. pales pyrenesmiscens* p. 99, in E. Pyrenees is larger, black markings ups larger and more macular, unf with some black spots. *B. aquilonaris* below; *B. graeca* p. 103.

BOLORIA AQUILONARIS   *Cranberry Fritillary*

Sw: Allmän Gulfläckig Parlemorfjäril

Range. Fennoscandia and C. Europe on Vaccinium moors, further range in Asia uncertain.   Map 85

B. aquilonaris   Stichel 1908   TL: Gellivare, Sweden   Pl. 21
   syn: *arsilache* Knoch 1781 (invalid homonym).

Description. ♂ fw 16/17mm., ups gc bright fulvous red; upf *black basal and discal spots prominent*, esp. in s1b, shaped like the letters V-V lying horizontally with apices joined; uph black basal suffusion covers cell; unf black spots well developed; unh gc sandy-red with darker areas, discal band not well defined, pd area red, usual yellow marginal mark in s3 small or absent; spot in s7, spots at apex of cell, in s1c near anal angle, and the six marginal spots all silver. ♀ often with slightly dusky suffusion.

Flight. June/early July.

Habitat. On bogs and in swampy places where larval food plant grows, from lowlands to 6,000 ft. depending upon latitude. Larval food plant cranberry (*Vaccinium oxycoccus*).

Distribution. Fennoscandia and Baltic countries to North Cape, usually common in suitable localities. More widely dispersed on *Vaccinium* bogs in Poland, Czechoslovakia, Austria, Germany (often common near Bavarian lakes), Jura, Vosges, Denmark, Belgium (in Ardennes) and France in the Massif Central. A few colonies are known at high altitudes in Switzerland, in Grisons and Engadin.

Variation. In Scandinavia small in arctic region; large with ♂fw 21 mm. or more in some localities in S. Sweden, Germany and France, f. *alethea* Hemming Pl. 21.

Similar species. *B. napaea* p. 99, ups black markings thin, linear, unf black markings absent. *B. pales* p. 98; *B. graeca* below.

BOLORIA GRAECA Balkan Fritillary
Range. Confined to Balkans and SW. Alps. Map 86

B. graeca graeca Staudinger 1870 TL: Mt. Veluchi, Greece Pl. 21
Description. ♂fw 19/20mm., hw anal angle slightly produced and margin more *sharply angled at v8* than in the other three species of *Boloria*; ups clear orange-fulvous; uph black suffusion does not include apex of cell; unf black spots small but *pattern over discal area complete*; unh yellowish with red and green marbling, discal band not well defined, silver spots present at cell-apex, in s7 and s1c, along outer margin and near costal angle, pd spots ocellate and prominent. ♀ups gc paler; unh greenish marbling more definite.
Flight. July.
Habitat. In subalpine meadows near tree-line at 5–6,000 ft. Larval food plant unknown.
Distribution. Greece on Mt. Veluchi, S. Yugoslavia on Mt. Perister, flying early in July.

B. graeca balcanica Rebel 1903 TL: Rilo Mts., Bulgaria
Description. ♂fw 16/17mm., small, ups gc less fiery orange and black markings smaller. ♀ups gc paler, yellowish with small black markings.
Flight and Habitat as for *B. g. graeca*.
Distribution. Balkan countries, widely distributed in Bulgaria, Bosnia, Serbia and Montenegro. Recorded from Rumania. SW. Alps (f. *tendensis* Higgins), widespread but local in Hautes Alpes, Basses Alpes, Savoie, etc., especially Pralognan, Valée du Boréon, Col di Tenda. Pl. 21

Similar species. *B. pales* p. 98; *B. napaea* p. 99, unf black markings greatly reduced; *B. aquilonaris* p. 102, gc bright reddish-fulvous with black markings heavy on both surfaces, not known from localities where *B. g. graeca* occurs. The smaller *B. pales palustris* flies on the same mountains as *B. graeca*, but at slightly higher levels.

PROCLOSSIANA EUNOMIA Bog Fritillary
G: Randring-Perlmutterfalter Sw: Svartringlad Pärlemorfjär
Range. A few scattered colonies in W. Europe, Fennoscandia, Russia and Siberia to Amurland; in N. America from Labrador to Alaska and along Rocky Mts. to Colorado. Map 87

P. eunomia eunomia   Esper 1799   TL: Kaliningrad (Königsberg)   Pl. 22
syn: *aphirape* Huebner 1799/1800
Description. ♂fw 20/23mm., ups gc clear fulvous yellow with neat markings; unh gc sandy-yellow, basal spots, discal band and marginal spots all gleaming yellow, sub-basal and narrow pd bands fulvous, pd spots in form of *small black circles filled white or pale yellow.* ♀ups often with some fuscous suffusion.
Flight. June/early July.
Habitat. Wet meadows and marshy places from lowlands to 5,000 ft. Larval food plant bistort (*Polygonum bistorta*), *Vaccinium*, etc.
Distribution. Very local in widely separated colonies. France, Vosges, E. Pyrenees. Belgium, Hertogenwald. Germany. Czechoslovakia. Austria. Bulgaria.

P. eunomia ossianus   Herbst 1800   TL: not stated   Pl. 22
Description. ♂fw 16/18mm., small, with dusky suffusion extending over ups; unh brightly marked, pale basal, discal and marginal spots white or gleaming silver.
Flight. End June/July.
Habitat. Rough moorlands and arctic bogs in lowlands.
Distribution. Fennoscandia, ups fuscous suffusion well marked from 65°N to North Cape, a common species on the tundra. Intermediate forms, brightly marked on uns but without heavy dusky suffusion on ups, are common in S. Scandinavia and in Baltic countries.

CLOSSIANA SELENE   *Small Pearl-bordered Fritillary*

F: Le Petit Collier Argenté   Sw: Brunfläckig Pärlemorfjäril
G: Braunfleckiger Perlmutterfalter   Sp: Perlada castaña
Range. From W. Europe across N. and C. Asia to Korea; widely distributed in N. America (*C. myrina* Cramer).   Map 88

C. selene   Schiffermueller 1775   TL: Vienna   Pl. 20
Description. ♂fw 18/21mm., closely resembles *C. euphrosyne*; ups gc orange-fulvous with few distinctive markings; uph round black spot usually present in cell; unh *yellow spot at cell base followed by round black spot*, gleaming metallic texture of discal band variable, sometimes absent, marginal spots yellow or silvered, pd spots dark, largest in s2 and s5. ♀ similar.
Flight. April/May and July/August in southern localities, the second brood often scanty; June/July in single brood in N. Europe and at high altitudes.
Habitat. Woodland margins or clearings from lowlands to 6,000 ft. Larval food plant violets.
Distribution. Widely distributed throughout W. Europe, including all Fennoscandia, Britain, E. Pyrenees to Andorra; N. and W. Spain to Sierra de Guadarrama; N. Portugal. Absent from Htes and Basses Pyrénées, Ireland, peninsular Italy, Greece and Mediterranean islands.

Variation. Upperside colour tones may be darker with more extensive black markings in extreme north, f. *hela* Staudinger p. 129.

Similar species. *C. euphrosyne* below; *C. thore* p. 107.

CLOSSIANA EUPHROSYNE   *Pearl-bordered Fritillary*

F: Grand Collier Argenté   Sw: Prydlig Pärlemorfjäril   G: Silberstrich
Sp: Perlada rojiza
Range. From W. Europe across Asia to Amurland and Kamschatka.

Map 89

C. euphrosyne Linnaeus 1758   TL: Sweden (Verity 1950)   Pl. 20
Description. ♂fw 19/23 mm., ups markings very like *C. selene*; unh sandy-red, including basal area of cell, discal band yellow, but *central spot in s4*, basal spot in s1c and marginal spots are all *bright silver* and prominent. ♀ similar.
Flight. April/May and July/August in southern areas, second brood often scanty; a single brood in N. Europe and at high altitudes in south.
Habitat. In light woodland from lowlands to 6,000 ft. Larval food plant principally *Viola*.
Distribution. Widely distributed throughout Europe to North Cape, including Britain, N. and C. Spain and Portugal. Very local in Ireland, absent from Mediterranean islands except Sicily.
Variation. The markings are constant over an enormous area. In high mountains and in northern range ups often slightly darker, ♀ with fuscous suffusion, f. *fingal* Herbst Pl. 20.

Similar species. *C. selene* p. 104, unh large round black spot in cell, all spots in discal band yellowish or silvery. *C. thore borealis* p. 110.

CLOSSIANA TITANIA   *Titania's Fritillary*

G: Natterwurz-Perlmutterfalter   Sw: Amathusias Pärlemorfjäril
Range. From W. Europe, including the Alps and S. Finland to Kentei and Altai Mts. in Siberia. Also in N. America, across Canada from Quebec to Alaska, thence along Rockies to New Mexico.   Map 90

C. titania titania Esper 1793   TL: 'Sardinia' (i.e. Piedmont)   Pl. 20
Description. ♂fw 21/23 mm., ups clear orange-fulvous with delicate black markings; unh marbled brown or yellowish, the six ocellate pd spots often joined to *marginal series of long V-shaped chevrons*. ♀ larger, ups gc paler; unh paler, yellowish, sometimes with greenish tints.
Flight. End June/July.
Habitat. In light woodland or forest clearings at 3,500–5,000 ft. Larval food plants *Viola, Polygonum*.
Distribution. Italy, in Cottian Alps, esp. Crissolo, Oulz. France; Isère, Auvergne, esp. on Mt. Mézenc, Col de Mayrand, etc.

C. titania cypris   Meigen 1828   TL: Bavaria and Switzerland   Pl. 20
syn: *amathusia* Esper 1784 (invalid homonym)
Description. ♂fw 21/24mm., ups gc fiery fulvous with heavy black markings; unh marbled purple-brown, yellow, etc., discal band pale and uneven. ♀ larger, gc ups paler.
Flight and Habitat as for *C. t. titania*.
Distribution. Through central and southern Alps to Bavaria and Austria. Yugoslavia, more local, Trebević, Durmitor, Maklen Pass; Transylvania.

CLOSSIANA CHARICLEA   *Arctic Fritillary*

Sw: Arktisk Pärlemorfjäril
Range. Arctic Europe, Greenland, boreal America, probably circumpolar.
Map 91

C. chariclea   Schneider 1794   TL: Lapland   Pl. 22
Description. ♂fw 16/18mm., ups gc fulvous with extensive black suffusion from wing-bases, esp. over hw; upf black discal markings fused into continuous band; unh gc red-brown with paler pd area, *discal band pale with spots prominent and mostly silvered*, small basal and marginal spots also silver. ♀ similar.
Flight. End June/July, depending upon weather.
Habitat. Dry tundra and hillsides at 1,000 ft. or more, well above valley levels. Larval food plant unknown.
Distribution. Fennoscandia, not south of 68°N, esp. Porsanger, Kilpisjärvi, Enontekiö, etc. The species has been taken at 81°42′N, probably farther north than any other butterfly.
Similar species. *B. freija* below, which may fly with *C. chariclea*, lacks prominent pale discal band on unh.

CLOSSIANA FREIJA   *Frejya's Fritillary*

Sw: Frejas Pärlemorfjäril
Range. From Scandinavia and Baltic countries across N. Siberia to Japan, boreal N. America and locally in western mountains to Colorado.
Map 92

C. freija   Thunberg 1791   TL: Sweden   Pl. 22
Description. ♂fw 18/22mm., upf black discal spots united to form an irregular discal band; uph black basal suffusion extensive; unh marbled light and dark brown with white markings, including white spot at base of s1c, white marks on costa in s7 and at base of s4 and seven white marginal spots, *prominent dark zig-zag marks in s1b, 1c, 2 and 3*. ♀ similar.
Flight. May to June, depending much upon weather.
Habitat. Moors, mountain heaths and tundra. Larval foodplants cloudberry (*Rubus chamaemorus*) and bog bilberry (*Vaccinium uliginosum*).

Distribution. Fennoscandia from 60°N to North Cape, widely distributed but more local in SE. Finland; reported also from Estonia.

Similar species. *C. chariclea* p. 106; *C. polaris* below, unh with numerous white marks.

CLOSSIANA DIA *Violet Fritillary*

F: La Petite Violette G: Hainveilchen-Scheckling Sp: Perlada Violeta
Range. From W. Europe across C. Asia to W. China. Map 93

C. dia Linnaeus 1767 TL: Austria Pl. 22
Description. ♂fw 16/17mm., margin of *hw sharply angled at v*8; ups black markings large; unh gc violet-brown, discal band with prominent spots in s1c, s4, s7 and six marginal spots, all silver, *pd spots dark, prominent.* ♀ similar.
Flight. April/May and throughout summer in two or three broods.
Habitat. Light woodland, heaths, etc., from lowlands to 3,000 ft., frequent in hilly districts. Larval food plants *Viola*, *Rubus* and other low plants.
Distribution. Europe from France, Belgium, Holland, eastwards through Switzerland to Rumania, Balkans and northern Greece; rare or occasional in N. Germany and Lithuania; uncommon in S. Europe, but occurs in SW. Alps, E. Pyrenees, Cantabrian Mts. and Catalonia (Montseny). Absent from Fennoscandia, Britain and Mediterranean islands.

CLOSSIANA POLARIS *Polar Fritillary*

Sw: Högnordisk Pärlemorfjäril
Range. Circumpolar, in boreal regions of Europe, Asia, Greenland and N. America. Map 94

C. polaris Boisduval 1828 TL: North Cape Pl. 22
Description. ♂fw 18/19mm., ups gc fulvous yellow; upf discal black spots fused into continuous irregular band; uph black suffusion covers basal and discal areas; unh mottled light and dark brown with *many small white marks in basal and discal areas*, white marks before each pd spot and seven white marginal marks. ♀ similar.
Flight. End June/July.
Habitat. On dry tundra and rough slopes above valley levels. Larval food plant possibly *Dryas octopetala*.
Distribution. Fennoscandia, not south of 68°N, esp. Petsamo, Maalselv, Pallastunturit, etc., very local and rare.

Similar species. *C. freija* p. 106.

CLOSSIANA THORE *Thor's Fritillary*

Sw: Gråkantad Pärlemorfjäril G: Alpen-Perlmutterfalter
Range. From N. Europe and Alps through Russia and N. Asia to Japan, mostly as *C. t. borealis* and nearly related forms. Map 95

PLATE 15

1. Apatura iris   *Purple Emperor*   75
♂. Ups with bright purple gloss; upf dark postdiscal spot in space 2 inconspicuous. ♀ ups grey-brown, no purple gloss, white markings larger.

2. Apatura ilia   *Lesser Purple Emperor*   98
Ups like *A. iris* but dark spot in space 2 conspicuous, ringed orange. ♀ like *A. iris* ♀, often tinted yellowish.

2a. *A. i. ilia* ♂.   Ups discal markings white.
2b. *A. i. ilia* f. *clytie* ♂. Ups discal markings yellow-brown.

2c. Apatura metis   *Freyer's Purple Emperor*
♂ Small, uph ocellar marginal dark spots reduced to narrow lunular band.

3. Limenitis populi   *Poplar Admiral*   99
♂. Ups dark with white and orange markings. ♀ similar but ups white markings larger.

4. Charaxes jasius   *Two-tailed Pasha*   75
♂. (Underside only.) Hw with two short tails; ups dark brown with wide fulvous borders. ♀ similar, larger.

1

2 b

2 a

2 c

3 b

3 a

3 c

4

6

5

7

PLATE 16

1. **Polygonia egea**   *Southern Comma*   88
   First brood ♂. Unh white discoidal mark very small, shaped like letter "**y**". Sexes similar.

2. **Polygonia c-album**   *Comma Butterfly*   88
   Unh white discoidal mark larger, shaped like letter "C".
   2a. *P. c-album* first brood ♂ (f. *hutchinsoni*). Ups ground-colour bright fulvous; uns markings in rather pale tones of brown, buff, etc. Sexes similar.
   2b. *P. c-album* second brood ♂. Ups darker; uns strongly marked in brown, buff, green, etc.
   2c. *P. c-album* second brood ♀. Uns very dark, markings obscure, mixed with green and very dark brown.

3. **Araschnia levana**   *Map Butterfly*   89
   Ups variable seasonally; uns with pale linear markings.
   3a. *A. levana* first brood ♂. Ups fulvous with black markings. Sexes similar.
   3b. *A. levana* second brood ♂ (f. *prorsa*). Ups black with prominent white discal markings.
   3c. *A. levana* second brood ♀ (f. *prorsa*). Ups like ♂ but with small fulvous postdiscal markings.

4. **Neptis sappho**   *Common Glider*   82
   ♂. Uph with white discal band and postdiscal spots; unh without black postdiscal spots. Sexes similar.

5. **Neptis rivularis**   *Hungarian Glider*   83
   ♂. Uph with single white discal band; unh without black postdiscal spots. Sexes similar.

6. **Limenitis camilla**   *White Admiral*   82
   L. camilla ♂. Unh with 2 rows of dark postdiscal spots. ♀ similar.

7. **Limenitis reducta**   *Southern White Admiral*   79
   L. reducta ♂. Unh with single row of dark postdiscal spots. ♀ similar.

C. thore thore Huebner 1803 TL: Alps of Tirol   Pl. 22
Description. ♂fw 20/23mm., ups fulvous almost obscured by black suffusion, markings indistinct; uph pd spots and marginal border generally fused into a wide black marginal band; unh gc brown, *discal band dull yellow*, pd and marginal markings gleaming lead-coloured. ♀ larger, ups black suffusion less dense.
Flight. End June/July.
Habitat. Flies at 3–5,000 ft., often near spruce woods. Larval food plant *Viola*.
Distribution. Restricted to Alps. Switzerland, local north of Rhône valley and in Graubünden. Germany, Bavarian and Allgäuer Alps. Austria, Arlberg, N. Tirol, Carinthia. Italy, Dolomites, esp. Canazei. E. Finland (f. *carelia* Valle).

C. thore borealis Staudinger 1861 TL: Lapland   Pl. 22
Description. ♂fw 19/20mm., small, ups gc yellow-fulvous, only slightly clouded darker; uph pd spots large; unh light brown markings indistinct without metallic marginal markings. ♀ similar, often larger.
Flight. End June/July.
Habitat. At low levels in birch zone in hilly country.
Distribution. Scandinavia, in mountainous districts, not south of 62°N, Abisko, Altenfjord, Inari, Saltdalen.

Similar species. *C. euphrosyne* p. 105, unh markings distinct, discal spot in s4 silvered. *C. selene* p. 104, unh basal and discal markings silvered.

CLOSSIANA FRIGGA *Frigga's Fritillary*

Sw: Friggas Pärlemorfjäril
Range. From Scandinavia across N. Asia, including Altai and Tarbagatai Mts. N. America, widely distributed in Canada and extending through Rocky Mts. to Colorado.   Map 96

C. frigga Thunberg 1791 TL: Lapland   Pl. 22
Description. ♂fw 20/23mm., ups gc orange-fulvous, black markings heavy and regular; uph with wide basal and discal black suffusions; unh gc red-brown, discal band pale with white spots in s1c, s4 and s7; pd area paler, lilac-tinted, pd markings not well defined. ♀ larger.
Flight. End June/July.
Habitat. At low levels on wet bogs and moors in mountain valleys. Larval food plant cloudberry (*Rubus chamaemorus*).
Distribution. Fennoscandia, not south of 60°N, most frequent in far north, esp. Dalecarlia, Maalselvdal, Abisko, etc., locally common. Recorded from Estonia and Latvia.

CLOSSIANA IMPROBA *Dusky-winged Fritillary*
Sw: Dvärgpärlemorfjäril
Range. N. Europe, N. America from Labrador to Alaska, Novaya Zemlya. No records available from boreal Asia. Map 97

C. improba Butler 1877 TL: Arctic America Pl. 22
Description. ♂ fw 15/17 mm., *ups yellow-grey, markings indistinct*, almost obliterated by fuscous suffusion; unh pale brown, discal band pale with white marks in s4 and s7 well defined, costa narrowly white. ♀ similar.
Flight. July.
Habitat. On dry mountain slopes and hill-tops from 1,200–3,500 ft. Larval food plant unknown.
Distribution. Fennoscandia, not south of 66°N, Abisko, on Mt. Nuolja at 3–3,500 ft., Altevand, N. of Kilpisjärvi at 1,200 ft.

MELITAEA CINXIA *Glanville Fritillary*
F: Le Damier Sw: Hökblomsternätfjäril G: Gemeiner Scheckenfalter
Sp: Doncella punteada
Range. From W. Europe and Morocco through Russia and W. Asia to Amurland. Map 98

M. cinxia cinxia Linnaeus 1758 TL: Sweden (Verity 1950) Pl. 24
Description. ♂ fw *first brood* 16/20 mm., *second brood* smaller; ups gc dull fulvous with complete black pattern; uph with a *black spot in each segment of sub-marginal band in* s1c–s5; unh yellow submarginal band with internal border of *proximally concave black lunules*, black marginal spots small. ♀ larger, ups black markings often heavier, sometimes with grey suffusion.
Flight. May/June and August/September in two broods in S. Europe; a single brood at high altitudes and in north.
Habitat. Flowery meadows from lowlands to 6,000 ft. or more. Larval food plants commonly plantain, more rarely hawkweed, knapweed (*Centaurea*), etc.
Distribution. S. and C. Europe, widely distributed to 60°N, flying at high altitudes in S. Alps. Local in N. and C. Spain, in S. Spain recorded from Murcia. Morocco and Algeria, local in Middle Atlas at 5–6,000 ft. Absent from Britain except in Isle of Wight, and absent from Mediterranean islands except Sicily.
Variation. At high levels in the Dauphiné Alps some specimens are small, ups with gc pale and heavily marked, transitional to *M. c. atlantis.*

M. cinxia atlantis le Cerf 1928 TL: High Atlas, Morocco Pl. 24
Description. ♂ fw 17/19 mm., ups gc pale yellow with heavy black markings. ♀ slightly larger.

PLATE 17

1. **Aglais urticae** *Small Tortoiseshell* 87
Ups red with black and yellow markings and blue submarginal lunules; uph with wide dark basal area. ♀ similar.

   1a. *A. u. urticae* ♂. Upf with black postdiscal spot in spaces 1b, 2, 3.

   1b. *A. u. ichnusa* ♂. No black postdiscal spots on upf.

2. **Vanessa virginiensis** *American Painted Lady* 87
♂. Unh with very large submarginal ocelli in spaces 2 and 5. ♀ similar.

3. **Vanessa cardui** *Painted Lady* 86
♂. Unh with 5 small submarginal ocelli. ♀ similar.

4. **Vanessa indica vulcania** *Indian Red Admiral* 86
♂. Upf red transverse band irregular, broken by black ground-colour. ♀ similar.

5. **Vanessa atalanta** *Red Admiral* 86
♀. Red transverse band intact, of even width throughout. ♂ similar.

6. **Nymphalis xanthomelas** *Yellow-legged Tortoiseshell* 84
♂. (Upperside only.) Ups inner edges of dark wing-borders indistinct; fore-legs buff; uns as in 7 but darker. ♀ similar.

7. **Nymphalis vau-album** *False Comma* 85
♂. Bright white marks present near apex of fw and on costa of hw. ♀ similar.

8. **Nymphalis polychloros** *Large Tortoiseshell* 84
♂. (Upperside only). Ups inner edges of dark wing-borders sharply defined; fore-legs black; uns as in 7 but darker. ♀ similar.

9. **Nymphalis antiopa** *Camberwell Beauty* 83
♂. Ups purple with wide cream-coloured border on both wings. ♀ similar.

10. **Inachis io** *Peacock*
♂. Ups with large "peacock eye" on each wing. ♀ similar.

1a

1c

1b

1d

2a

1e

2b

2c

PLATE 18

1. Fabriciana adippe   *High Brown Fritillary*   92
Unh with small silver-pupilled postdiscal spots.

   1a. *F. a. adippe* ♂, Unh ground-colour buff; basal, discal and marginal spots filled silver.

   1b. *F. a. auresiana* ♂. Unh green, spots filled silver but some basal spots missing. ♀ similar, larger.

   1c. *F. a. chlorodippe* ♀. Unh yellow-green, all spots present and filled silver. ♂ similar.

   1d. *F. a. cleodippe* ♂. Unh buff with green basal suffusion; spots paler buff, *not* filled silver.

   1e. *F. a. cleodoxa* ♂. Unh pale buff, spots (except postdiscal series) *not* filled silver. ♀ similar.

2. Argynnis paphia   *Silver-washed Fritillary*   90
Unh greenish with transverse bands and outer margin silvery.

   2a. *A. p. paphia* ♂. Upf with thick sex-brands along veins 1-4, other black markings rather small.

   2b. *A. p. paphia* ♀. Ups black markings larger and complete.

   2c. *A. p. immaculata* ♀ Unh suffused greenish-gold and markings obscure. Ups gc yellow-grey (♀-form *valesina*).

Flight and **Habitat.** End June/early July, at altitudes of 8,000 ft. or more. A second brood is not recorded.
Distribution. Morocco in the High Atlas.

Similar species. *M. arduinna* below.

MELITAEA ARDUINNA   *Freyer's Fritillary*
Range. Extreme SE. Europe through S. Russia (TL of *Papilio arduinna* Esper 1784) and Asia Minor to Iran and central Asia.   Map 99

M. arduinna rhodopensis Freyer 1836   TL: 'Turkey' (Macedonia) Pl. 24
Description. ♂fw 21/23mm., like *M. cinxia* but larger, ups bright fulvous; unh orange marginal band with large black spots in each segment, its inner border formed of *black lunules, flat or outwardly concave*, in s1c–4; thin semilunes between veins at margin. ♀ larger, ups black markings heavier.
Flight. May/June, only a single brood recorded in Europe.
Habitat. In Asia flies over flowery banks at moderate altitudes in foothills. Larval food plant uncertain, perhaps *Centaurea*.
Distribution. Very local in extreme SE. Europe. SE. Yugoslavia; Bitola, Katlanova, Selenokova. Bulgaria, Burgas. Rumania, Tultscha.

Similar species. *M. cinxia* p. 111, smaller, fw narrower, unh black proximal lunules of orange marginal band concave inwardly.

MELITAEA PHOEBE   *Knapweed Fritillary*
F: Le Grand Damier   G: Flockenblumenfalter   Sp: Doncella mayor
Range. From Europe and N. Africa across C. Asia to N. China.
                                                        Map 100

M. phoebe phoebe Schiffermueller 1775   TL: Vienna   Pls. 14, 23
Description. ♂fw *first brood* 20/24mm., *second brood* often smaller; ups gc generally bright fulvous with solid black margins; *upf marginal lunule in s3 much the largest*; uph orange submarginal band well defined, usually without enclosed black spots; unh each segment of yellow submarginal band enclosing a round red spot, a single row of orange marginal lunules, black marginal lunules joined to form a continuous wavy line. ♀ often larger.
Flight. End April or later and July or later in two or three broods at low levels, a single brood in July in mountains.
Habitat. Flowery meadows and slopes, lowlands to 5,500 ft. Larval food plants knapweed (*Centaurea*), more rarely plantain.
Distribution. C. and S. Europe to 50°N, except Spain and Portugal.
Variation. Mountain races in the S. Alps are generally large, f. *alternans* Seitz, heavily marked and brightly variegated with yellow and fulvous. Late broods in S. Europe may be very small with ♂fw 19mm. or less, ups black markings reduced, f. *pauper* Verity pl. 14, as in Italy, Sicily, etc.

M. phoebe occitanica Staudinger 1871 TL: 'Iberia' Pl. 23
Description. ♂fw 22/25mm., ups gc paler fulvous-yellow, the darker reddish-fulvous discal markings and submarginal bands producing a bright colour-contrast; black wing-markings may be heavy in mountainous localities.
Flight and Habitat as for *M. p. phoebe.*
Distribution. Spain, south of the Cantabrian Mts., and Portugal.
Variation. The full characters of *occitanica* are developed in the second brood, esp. in S. Spain, Granada, etc. First brood specimens (April) in which colour contrast is less marked are not greatly different from those of southern alpine localities. In all localities and in both broods there is considerable individual variation.

M. phoebe punica Oberthur 1876 TL: Lambessa, Algeria Pl. 23
Description. ♂fw 17/18mm., small, ups gc yellowish, black markings not heavy but discal spots upf well developed; unh gc gleaming white. ♀ similar.
Flight. May/June, probably first brood, a second brood has not been recorded.
Habitat. Flowery slopes from 3,500–7,000 ft.
Distribution. Algeria, Lambessa, Batna, Geryville. Morocco, Azrou, Ifrane and High Atlas at 8,500 ft., slightly larger, f. *gaisericus* Hemming.

Similar species. *M. aetherie* below, uph orange submarginal band not well defined.

MELITAEA AETHERIE *Aetherie Fritillary*

Sp: Doncella gaditana
Range. Confined to N. Africa, Iberian Peninsula and Sicily. Map 101

M. aetherie aetherie Huebner 1826 TL: not stated Pl. 23
Description. ♂fw 21/23mm., resembles *M. phoebe*; ups black markings reduced; upf discal spots small, pd spots often absent, submarginal and marginal markings complete, marginal lunule in s3 large; uph basal and discal markings small or absent, *orange submarginal band not defined*; unh submarginal band with a large round red spot in each segment. ♀ similar, ups grey suffusion on fw and over posterior area of hw common.
Flight. Late April/July. A second brood has not been recorded.
Habitat. In open woodland and flowery meadows at low levels. Larval food plant not known.
Distribution. Very local in S. Spain, Cadiz, Chiclana, Algiceras, etc. Portugal, Val de Rosal.

M. aetherie algirica Ruhl 1892 TL: Algeria Pl. 23
Description. Resembles *M. a. aetherie*, but unf black discal spots are

116   BUTTERFLIES OF BRITAIN AND EUROPE

generally prominent. ♀ups heavily suffused dark grey except the anterior half of hw.
Flight and Habitat. End May/June, flying at 5–8,500 ft.
Distribution. Local in Morocco, Algeria; in Tunisia it is said to fly at lower altitudes. Sicily, local in northern mountains.
Similar species. *M. phoebe* p. 114.

MELITAEA DIDYMA *Spotted Fritillary*
G: Roter Scheckenfalter   Sp: Doncella timida
Range. From S. and W. Europe and N. Africa to Russia, C. Asia, Turkestan and Amdo; also Tripolitania to Fezzan and Tibesti.

Map 102

This widely distributed butterfly occurs in Europe in a variety of biotopes from sea-level to over 6,000 ft. Its colonies show marked local variation, often confused by the presence of two or three annual broods, each with distinctive characters. The variation is best regarded as clinal, and the seasonal differences suggest that, in part at least, the basis is ecological. There is little evidence of the development of true geographical races, which is not surprising in a species with such a wide and continuous distribution. Nevertheless, it is possible to distinguish a northern 'European' form, a southern 'Mediterranean' form and an 'Alpine' form, but descriptions can apply only to average specimens, for intermediates occur nearly everywhere and defy analysis.

M. didyma didyma   Esper 1779   TL: Bavaria   Pl. 23
Description. ♂fw 18/21 mm., ups gc tawny red, black markings irregular and heavy, pd spots usually present; unh *basal orange band irregular but continuous, marginal black spots always round.* ♀ often larger, ups gc paler, esp. upf, with variable grey suffusion rarely quite absent.
Flight. May or later in one or two or even three broods.
Habitat. Flowery meadows from lowlands to 2,000 ft., common in hilly districts. Larval food plants principally plantains and toadflax.
Distribution. C. Europe to 55°N, esp. in NW. France. Belgium, Ardennes. N. Switzerland, Germany and Austria. Absent from Britain, Holland, Denmark and much of NW. Germany.

M. didyma meridionalis   Staudinger 1870   TL: Mt. Parnassus, Greece
Pl. 23
Description. ♂fw 20/22 mm., large, ups gc rich fulvous-red; pd spots rarely indicated. ♀ variable, ups usually heavily suffused dark grey, except anterior area of hw.
Flight. June/July, usually in a single brood.
Habitat. Most typical on subalpine meadows at 3–5,000 ft. At lower altitudes ♀ generally with less grey ups suffusion.

Distribution. The usual form in mountains of C. and S. Europe and foothills of Alps, Pyrenees, Apennines and Balkans.

M. didyma occidentalis Staudinger 1861 TL: Albarracin, Spain (Verity 1950) Pls. 14, 23
Description. ♂fw 20mm., or more, size variable; ups gc paler fulvous to yellow-buff; black markings often small, pd spots rarely present; unh orange basal band usually broken into several spots. ♀ similar, generally larger and without grey ups suffusion.
Flight. May and later in two or three annual broods.
Habitat. Open places and meadows from lowlands to 3,000 ft. in Europe, to 7,000 ft. in N. Africa.
Distribution. S. Europe, in low-lying warm southern districts, most typical in late summer broods in Spain, Portugal, Italy, Hungary and coastal areas of Balkans. N. Africa, local on northern slopes of Atlas Mts. at 3-7,000 ft.
Variation. Late broods may be small, ♂fw 15/17mm.; ups pale yellow-buff with black markings reduced, f. *dalmatina* Staudinger Pl. 14, in hot, low-lying localities in August/September, esp. in Italy and Balkans.

Similar species. *M. trivia* p. 118, unh black marginal spots triangular. *M. deserticola* below, easily confused in N. Africa, unh orange basal spots separated and bordered prominently in black.

MELITAEA DESERTICOLA *Desert Fritillary*

Range. N. Africa. In Atlas Mts., esp. southern slopes and in desert oases; Tripolitania, Fezzan; Egypt, Lebanon and Transjordan.
Map 103

M. deserticola Oberthur 1876 TL: Algeria Pl. 23
Description. ♂fw *first brood* 18/20mm., resembles *M. didyma*, but ups gc pale buff, with small but bold black markings; upf pd spots absent, unh gc white, *basal orange band completely broken up, each spot edged black*, pd orange band with double black proximal border in s2–s5. ♀ similar.
Flight. March/April and later. Second broods almost certainly, and perhaps third broods also occur in N. Africa, but have not been specifically recorded.
Habitat. Flies in hot valleys up to 6,000 ft. in Atlas Mts. Larval food plants unknown.
Distribution. Morocco, in High Atlas, Ourika, Amizmiz. Middle Atlas. Algeria, Mecheria, Biskra, Laghouat. Tunisian Sahara.

Similar species. *M. didyma* above.

MELITAEA TRIVIA   *Lesser Spotted Fritillary*
G: Braunlicher Scheckenfalter
Range. From S. Europe through S. Russia and W. Asia to Iran, Pakistan
and Baluchistan.   Map 104

M. trivia trivia Schiffermueller 1775   TL: Vienna   Pl. 23
Description. ♂ fw *first brood* 17/19 mm., *second brood* 14/16 mm., resembles
M. didyma; ups gc orange-yellow (*didyma* orange-red); orange marginal
lunules complete in regular series and fully enclosed by darker border;
uph pd black spots often prominent; *unh marginal black spots nearly
always triangular* (round in *didyma*); in hw lower dc vein present (absent
in *didyma*). ♀ larger, ups sometimes slightly flushed fuscous.
Flight. May/June and July/August in two broods.
Habitat. Flowery banks and rough ground to 5,000 ft. Larval food plant
mullein (*Verbascum thapsus*).
Distribution. E. Europe from Balkans to Czechoslovakia. Italy, Lake
Garda, and rarely in warm valleys in Alto Adige and E. Emilia; very
local in Apennines and Calabria.
Variation. First brood generally large, ♂ fw to 22 mm. in Balkan Mts., esp.
mountains of Bulgaria and Macedonia, f. *fascelis* Esper.

M. trivia ignasiti Sagarra 1926   TL: Portugal   Pl. 23
Description. ♂ fw 17/18 mm., ups gc paler orange-yellow, markings sharply
defined and without fuscous suffusion, yellow marginal lunules free, not
enclosed in dark border. ♀ similar, larger.
Flight and Habitat as for *M. t. trivia*; there is little difference between
broods.
Distribution. Italy, only recorded from Susa district, N. Piedmont. Spain,
common in northern and central districts, Catalonia, Cantabrian Mts.,
Cuenca, Sierra de Guadarrama. Portugal, Sierra de Estrela.
Similar species. *M. didyma* p. 116.

MELITAEA DIAMINA   *False Heath Fritillary*
Sw: Kovetenätfjäril   G: Silberscheckenfalter
Sp: Doncella oscura
Range. From N. Spain through C. Europe to 62°N and across central and
north-central Asia to Amur, principal colonies in mountains.   Map 105

M. diamina diamina Lang 1789   TL: Augsburg   Pl. 25
  syn: *dictynna* Esper 1779 (invalid homonym)
Description. ♂ fw 19/21 mm., ups wings dark, esp. uph, obscuring much of
fulvous gc, marginal spots when present often pale; unh gc pale, markings
orange-brown, submarginal band enclosing in each segment *a pale spot
with darker mark external to it*; *double marginal lines filled yellow*. ♀
similar, uph markings often pale yellow to white.

Flight. End May/July in a single brood.

Habitat. Grass banks and damp alpine meadows from lowlands to 6,000 ft. Larval food plants principally species of plantain, *Veronica* and cow-wheat (*Melampyrum*).

Distribution. France and C. Europe to 62°N, including N. Italy, Yugo-slavia and Bulgaria. In Hautes and Basses Pyrénées mostly transitional to following subspecies. Absent from peninsular Italy, Britain, Mediterranean islands and Greece.

Variation. In some warm alpine valleys in Ticino, Bergamasker Alps and Alto Adige, a second brood occurs in late summer, small, ♂fw 16/17mm., ups without black suffusion, unh markings chestnut-brown, f. *wheeleri* Chapman. The resemblance to small *M. athalia*, *M. aurelia* or *M. britom-artis* may be confusing.

M. diamina vernetensis   Rondou 1902   TL: Vernet-les-Bains, E. Pyrenees
Pl. 25

Description. ♂fw 17/19mm., ups black suffusion absent, resembles *M. athalia*; upf prominent club-shaped discal spot generally present in s1b; unh resembles *M. d. diamina* but markings in paler tones with small dark spot in each lunule of orange submarginal band in s1b–s4, these spots often far from obvious.

Flight and Habitat as for *diamina*.

Distribution. E. Pyrenees, esp. Mt. Canigou, Porta, etc.   Spain, Cantabrian Mts., Picos de Europa, Pajares.

M. diamina codinai   Sagarra 1932   TL: Tortosa, NE. Spain

Description. ♂fw 17/18mm., small, ups resembles *M. d. vernetensis* and *M. athalia*, ups without dusky suffusion, upf dumb-bell shaped discal black spot in s1b large; unh dark points in submarginal lunules vestigial or absent. ♀ similar or slightly larger.

Flight. May and July/August, probably with two annual broods.

Distribution. Spain, in Catalonia, very local, Planolas, Santa Fe, Tor-tosa.

Similar species. *M. athalia* p. 120, uph generally less suffused black, unh without vestigial dark spots in orange submarginal band. In *M. diamina vernetensis* ups colour and markings resemble *athalia* very closely. *M. britomartis* p. 124, size smaller than *diamina*, ups wing markings well defined (less black suffusion), unh spots in submarginal band less well formed; confusion with f. *wheeleri* is possible.

Note. *M. diamina* in most of its external characters agrees best with the species of the genus *Mellicta*, but in its genitalia is very similar to *M. cinxia* in the genus *Melitaea*.

MELLICTA ATHALIA   *Heath Fritillary*

Sw: Grobladsnätfjäril   G: Mittelwegerichfalter   Sp: Athalia
Range. From W. Europe through Russia and temperate Asia to Japan.
Map 106

This butterfly is the commonest and most widespread species of the
genus, as well as the most variable. In W. Europe it occurs mainly in two
subspecies, *athalia* Rottemberg and *celadussa* Fruhstorfer, superficially
similar but with clearly defined characters in the male genitalia. The
subspecific frontier between these varies in width from 30 to 100 miles
and is indicated on the map by a white line along which all grades of
intermediates occur.

M. athalia athalia   Rottemburg 1775   TL: Paris   Pl. 25
Description. ♂fw 18/20mm., ups black markings often heavy; unf yellow
marginal lunules irregular and with *heavy black internal border in s*2 (*and
s*3), pd markings often vestigial or absent, marginal band pale. ♀ often
larger, ups sometimes suffused fuscous.
Flight. May or later, sometimes a second brood in August/September.
Habitat. Flowery meadows from lowlands to 5,000 ft. Larval food plants
are species of plantain and cow-wheat, more rarely other low plants.
Distribution. Europe north of the Alps, including S. Scandinavia and S.
England, and all eastern Europe.

M. athalia boris   Fruhstorfer 1917   TL: Sliven, Rumelia   Pl. 25
Description. Markings upf are very regular, with wide, dark wing-borders.
In ♀ characters not always well defined; in ♂ often more marked with
extension of black suffusion invading all basal area of hind-wing. In some
areas dark ups suffusion may be very extensive in both sexes, f. *satyra*
Higgins Pl. 25.
Flight and Habitat as for *M.a. aihalia.*
Distribution. Bulgaria.

M. athalia norvegica   Aurivillius 1888   TL: Dovrefjeld, Norway
Pls. 21, 25
Description. ♂fw 17/18mm., small, ups markings very regular and com-
plete, upf discal spots often emphasised; unf marginal lunules vestigial.
♀ similar.
Flight. End June/July in a single brood.
Habitat. Moorlands from low levels to 3,000 ft.
Distribution. Norway, esp. on fjelds, Jotunheim, Hardanger, Dovrefjeld
and extending to North Cape.   Sweden. Finland in suitable localities.
Variation. In some districts in Fennoscandia upf postdiscal and sub-
marginal black bands widely separated, leaving a wide fulvous space, f.
lachares Fruhstorfer Pl. 25.

M. athalia celadussa Fruhstorfer 1910   TL: Maritime Alps   Pls. 21, 25
syn: *pseudathalia* Reverdin 1921

Description. Resembles *M. a. athalia* in size and general appearance, but genitalia are distinct. On ups gc generally bright fulvous, black markings thin. ♀ups fuscous suffusion uncommon.

Flight. June/July and August/September.

Distribution. SW. Europe and southern Alps eastwards to Venice, and south through Italy to Sicily; absent from Mediterranean islands.

Variation. In S. Europe specimens of late broods may be very small with thin black markings, f. *tenuicola* Verity (Pl. 21), easily confused with *M. parthenoides*. A local race, f. *nevadensis* Oberthur (Pl. 25), occurs in the Sierra Nevada, ups gc pale yellow-buff, upf with prominent dumb-bell shaped black spot in s1b, recalling *M. deione*.

M. athalia biedermanni Querci 1932   TL: Sierra de Estrela, Portugal
Pl. 25

Description. ♂fw 21/23mm., a very large form, ups black markings often thin, but upf discal band usually emphasised. ♀ larger.

Distribution. Portugal, Serra da Estrela. Spain, in Province Leon, large transitional forms occur in Sierra de Guadarrama, Sierra de Gredos, etc.

Similar species. Confusion may arise between *M. athalia* in its various forms and any other species of the genus except *M. asteria*. Identification of *M. athalia* depends largely upon noting the absence of the specific characters of these other species, and especially the presence in *M. athalia* of the well-developed dark internal border to the submarginal lunules in s2 (s3) on unf.

MELLICTA DEIONE *Provençal Fritillary*

Sp: Deion

Range. Confined to SW. Europe and N. Africa.   Map 107

M. deione deione Geyer 1832   TL: Aix-en-Provence   Pl. 24

Description. ♂ *first brood* 19/22mm., *second brood* 16/19mm. Resembles *M. athalia*; ups gc clear orange-yellow with thin black markings; upf last discal spot in *s1b often dumb-bell shaped* (not constant); unf yellow marginal lunules in s2 (3) *with minimal black proximal shade*, if any; unh discal and sub-marginal bands clear orange, the latter often with round, reddish spot in each space; terminal segment of palpi viewed from below fulvous (grey or slightly yellow in *athalia*). ♀ commonly with paler gc in cell and in pd area, producing a little colour contrast.

Flight. May/June and August/September in two broods.

Habitat. On flowery meadows from low levels to 5,000 ft., usually in mountainous districts. Larval food plants *Linaria*, *Antirrhinum semper-virens*.

Distribution. Spain and Portugal, widely distributed. S. France, widely distributed from Provence to Briançon, Auvergne, Cevennes, Pyrenees, esp. E. Pyrenees.

M. deione berisalii Ruhl 1891 **TL**: Simplon (error)   Pl. 24
Description. Size and general appearance as in *M. d. deione*; ups gc darker fulvous, black markings heavier, esp. dark marginal borders, which almost obliterate uph marginal lunules; unh vivid orange discal and sub-marginal bands contrast strongly with pale gc, black marginal lunules slightly enlarged, veins more distinctly black. ♀ similar; ups colour contrast little developed.
Flight and **Habitat** as for *M.d. deione*, often flies in vineyards. Larval food plants toadflax (*Linaria vulgaris* and *L. minor*).
Distribution. SW. Switzerland and in Rhône valley, Martigny, Saillon, etc. Also in Italy, Piedmont, local near Oulz. S. Tirol, in Eisaktal above Bolzano with characters somewhat intermediate to *M.d. deione*.

M. deione nitida Oberthur 1909 **TL**: Algeria   Pl. 24
Description. ♂ fw 18/20 mm., fw apex more rounded; ups gc paler fulvous yellow, lightly marked, black marginal lines clearly double. ♀ similar.
Flight. May, no record of a second brood.
Habitat. Probably flies in mountains at altitudes of 4–5,000 ft., but there is no precise information.
Distribution. Algeria, in Middle Atlas, Tlemcen, Sebdou. Morocco, not recorded from Atlas Mts., but probably flies in El Rif.

Similar species. *M. athalia* p. 120, in which unf black pd crescent in s2 is conspicuous (usually absent in *M. deione*).

MELLICTA VARIA *Grisons Fritillary*
Range. Confined to Alps and Apennines.   Map 108

M. varia Meyer-Dür 1851 **TL**: Graubünden Alps   Pl. 25
Description. ♂ fw 15/17 mm., ups gc bright fulvous; upf large black spot in s1b often dumb-bell shaped with *distal margin vertical* (oblique in *M. parthenoides*); unf a black streak to base of wing in s1b; uph pd area often clear fulvous, occasionally with included black spots; at high altitudes unh gc generally white. ♀ similar, ups often suffused grey.
Flight. End June/August in a single brood.
Habitat. Flies over short grass from 6,000 ft. upwards, rarely at 4,500 ft. in Apennines and Basses Alpes. Larval food plant gentians.
Distribution. From Maritime Alps to Savoie and Drôme and through S. Swiss and Italian Alps to Brenner, Landeck and Rieserferner Group. Apennines, local, esp. Gran Sasso, Monte Livata (Sulmona) at 4,500 ft., Sibillini Mts. Absent from Pyrenees, Carpathians, Balkans.
Variation. A larger form, f. *piana* Higgins, ♂ fw 17/19 mm., occurs as low as 4,500 ft. in the Maritime Alps and Abruzzi Mts.

Similar species. In SW. Alps only, *M. varia* overlaps the distribution of *M. parthenoides* below, which generally flies at lower levels and has ups markings thinner and more regular. *M. aurelia* below (subalpine), which also occurs in the same area is usually small, with broader wings and ups markings more complete. *M. athalia* p. 120, larger with ups markings less regular.

MELLICTA PARTHENOIDES   *Meadow Fritillary*

Sp: Minerva
Range. Confined to W. Europe.   Map 109

M. parthenoides Keferstein 1851   TL: Soucy, France   Pl. 24
  syn. *parthenie* Godart 1819 (invalid homonym)
Description. ♂fw 16/18mm., ups black markings regular with delicately drawn lines and striae; *upf black discal spots often emphasised, linear discal spot in s1b oblique* (distinction from *M. varia*); uph discal area clear orange-yellow. ♀ often larger, ups with grey suffusion and wider sub-marginal bands which are sometimes deeper orange; unf black markings resemble *M. varia* with heavy basal mark but pd area clear.
Flight. May/June and August/September in two broods at low levels, a single brood in June/July at high altitudes.
Habitat. Flies in foothills and mountains from 1,500–7,000 ft. Larval food plants plantain, scabious, *Melampyrum*, etc.
Distribution. SW. Europe. France, from Paris to Jura Mts. and Pyrenees; Bavaria, very local in SW. districts only. Switzerland, probably confined to SW. in Rhône valley, Tessin, Jura. Italy, only in Maritime Alps, Fenestrelle, Limone Piemonte. Widely distributed in Spain and Portugal.
Variation. Small specimens, ♂fw 15/16mm., are common in late broods. In the C. Pyrenees, f. *plena* Verity is slightly dusky, flying to 7,000 ft. and single brooded, with deceptive resemblance to *M. aurelia*.

Similar species. *M. varia* p. 122; *M. athalia* p. 120, ups black markings heavier and irregular.

MELLICTA AURELIA   *Nickerl's Fritillary*

G: Ehrenpreis-Scheckenfalter
Range. C. and E. Europe to Urals, Caucasus and C. Asia.   Map 110

M. aurelia Nickerl 1850   TL: Erlangen, Germany   Pl. 24
  syn: *parthenie* Borkhausen 1788 (invalid homonym)
Description. ♂fw 14/16mm., ups *black markings regular and complete* with tendency to dusky suffusion; unf pd spots variable, sometimes strongly marked; *unh double marginal lines sometimes filled yellow and slightly darker than adjacent lunules*; chequered cilia predominantly pale yellow or white. ♀ similar.

Flight. June/July depending upon altitude, perhaps partially double-brooded in some southern localities.

Habitat. Flowery meadows, moorlands, etc., from lowlands to 5,000 ft. Larval food plants plantain, *Veronica* and *Melampyrum*.

Distribution. Basses Alpes and through NE. France to Ardennes. Bavaria, esp. on peat-moors. Switzerland, including Valais, and east to Austria, Hungary and Balkans; becomes more rare in N. Germany. Italy, rare south of River Po. Absent from SW. and C. France, peninsular Italy, Spain, Portugal and Pyrenees.

Variation is slight apart from occasional individual abnormal wing-markings.

Similar species. *M. britomartis* below, usually slightly larger, darker, and has unh double marginal lines filled dark yellow; unf black markings rarely incomplete. The chequering of the fringes may also help. Dissection may be necessary for identification. *M. athalia* p. 120, black markings less regular, esp. unf.

MELLICTA BRITOMARTIS   *Assmann's Fritillary*

Sw: Veronikanätfjäril

Range. C. Europe and through C. Asia to Transbaickal and Korea.

Map 111

M. britomartis Assmann 1847   TL: Breslau, Germany   Pl. 24

Description. ♂fw *first brood* 17/18mm., *second brood* often very small. Resembles *M. aurelia*, generally slightly larger; ups strongly marked; unf gc darker fulvous; unh orange submarginal lunules often with *dark brown proximal border*, sometimes with traces of included darker spots within each lunule, which are rarely present in *M. aurelia*; double marginal lines *filled yellow or brown*; fringes chequered predominantly dark in most specimens. ♀ similar.

Flight. May and August in two broods in S. Europe, a single brood in northern range.

Habitat. Heaths and flowery places at low altitudes. Larval food plants plantain and *Veronica*.

Distribution. Italy, very local near Oulz, Turin, and here and there in valley of the River Ticino, esp. Galliate, Turbigo, etc. Commoner in E. Europe, often flying with *M. aurelia*, esp. in Danube countries, Bulgaria, Rumania, Hungary; Poland, esp. Wroclaw (Breslau); Germany, Berlin; recorded also from S. Sweden.

Similar species. *M. aurelia* p. 123; *M. diamina* p. 118, small second brood specimens of f. *wheeleri* may be confusing. Identification should be confirmed by examination of the male genitalia in specimens from any locality where *M. britomartis* is not already known to occur, since it may fly with *M. aurelia* and with *M. athalia*.

MELLICTA ASTERIA *Little Fritillary*
G: Kleiner Scheckenfalter
Range. Confined to Alps.   Map 112

M. asteria Freyer 1828 TL: Chur, Switzerland   Pl. 24
Description. ♂fw 14/15mm., ups wing-bases heavily suffused black, pd
and submarginal orange markings generally clear; unh gc pale yellow to
white, veins black, markings well defined, *a single black marginal line*.
♀ similar, ups less heavily suffused fuscous.
Flight. July.
Habitat. Flies over short grassy slopes at 7–8,000 ft. Larval food plant
unknown.
Distribution. Restricted to eastern Alps from Chur to Gross Glockner,
esp. Albula Pass, Guarda and Brenner. Reported also from the Niederer
Tauern near Turrach.

EUPHYDRYAS MATURNA *Scarce Fritillary*
Sw: Boknätfjäril G: Kleiner Maivogel
Range. From Europe north of Alps across Russia to Ala Tau and Altai
Mts.   Map 113

E. maturna Linnaeus 1758 TL: not stated   Pl. 26
Description. ♂fw 21/23mm., ups gc red; upf with cream-white spots on
costa, often also in cell; uph white spots in series beyond cell-end, and
prominent broad red pd bands; uns marginal borders red; *unf submarginal
lunules irregular in size, largest in s*3. ♀ usually larger.
Flight. May/June.
Habitat. A lowland species flying in open woodland, often at valley
bottoms, attracted by blossoms of privet. Larvae before hibernation live in
nests on ash, poplar or beech, after hibernation singly on plantain,
scabious, *Veronica*, etc.
Distribution. Paris (Ozoir), and eastwards through Germany, Austria, S.
Fennoscandia, Hungary, Rumania and Yugoslavia, esp. Bosnia and
Slavonia.

Similar species. *E. intermedia* below, ups more uniform red-brown, pd red
bands less prominent; unf submarginal lunules more regular. *E. cynthia*
♀ p. 126, which nearly always has small black spots in unh submarginal
band.

EUPHYDRYAS INTERMEDIA *Asian Fritillary*
Range. From Alps of Savoie to Julian Alps, Altai Mts., Amur (TL of *M.
intermedia* Ménétriès 1859), Sutschan and Korea.   Map 114

E. intermedia wolfensbergeri Frey 1880 TL: Maloja Pass, Engadine
                                                            Pl. 26

syn. *ichnea* auct. (misidentification)

Description. ♂fw 19/21 mm., ups gc uniformly yellow-brown with red cell-marks and pd bands, black lattice pattern uniform and rather heavy; uns gc paler, yellowish, marginal lines yellow-brown, unf lightly marked, submarginal black lunules regular; *unh pale discal band enclosing a thin black line.* ♀ similar, larger, ups markings often paler, esp. yellowish costal spots of fw and pd spots of hw.

Flight. End June/July.

Habitat. Mountains at 5,000–5,500 ft., often in light spruce woodland. Larval food plants unknown.

Distribution. Southern Alps, from Savoie to Julian Alps, esp. Pralognan, Saas-Fé, Preda, Bergün, Albula, Dolomites and Triglav.

Similar species. *E. maturna* p. 125, unf submarginal lunules irregular, flies at low altitudes north of main alpine chain, distribution does not overlap that of *intermedia*. *E. cynthia* below (♀ only), resemblance extremely close but unh pale yellow discal band without enclosed thin black line.

EUPHYDRYAS CYNTHIA *Cynthia's Fritillary*

G: Veilchen-Scheckenfalter

Range. Confined to Alps, and mountains of Bulgaria.   Map 115

E. cynthia cynthia Schiffermueller 1775 TL: Vienna   Pl. 26

Description. ♂fw 19/21 mm., ups pd bands red on *white* gc, but partly obscured by black suffusion; uph a black spot enclosed in each segment of red pd band; unh yellowish with orange-brown markings. ♀ resembles *E. intermedia*, ups gc *uniform orange-brown* with light black markings; uns resembles ♂, but unh pale pd band clear yellow-buff *without enclosed thin black line.*

Flight. End May/July depending upon altitude.

Habitat. On mountain heaths with juniper and *Vaccinium* from 1,200–7,000 ft. At highest levels generally small but brightly marked. Larval food plants plantain (*P. alpina*), lady's mantle (*Alchemilla*).

Distribution. Bavaria, Austria, widely distributed. Bulgaria in Rilo Dagh only, flying at 7,000 ft. or over.

E. cynthia alpicola Galvagni 1918 TL: Brenner, Tirol   Pl. 26

Description. ♂fw 16/20 mm., slightly smaller than *E. c. cynthia*, ups black suffusion more extensive, upf red pd bands often nearly obliterated and on uph reduced to small round spots. ♀ slightly larger, black suffusion ups less extensive.

Flight. Late June/early August.

Habitat. Above tree-line on high mountains, usually at 6–8,000 ft., attracted by low juniper bushes.

Distribution. From Maritime Alps and Savoie to Brenner and Oetztal, with intermediate forms in eastern range.

Variation. Extreme forms occur in the Maritime Alps with maximum extension of dark suffusion in ♂ups, ♀ups gc paler, sometimes with grey-white markings.

Similar species. *E. intermedia* p. 125, close resemblance in females.

EUPHYDRYAS IDUNA *Lapland Fritillary*

Sw: Lapsk nätfjäril

Range. Boreal Scandinavia, Caucasus, Altai Mts., Sajan Mts. in widely scattered local colonies. Map 116

E. iduna Dalman 1816 TL: Sweden Pl. 26

Description. ♂fw 18/19mm., ups gc pale yellowish with black markings and *broad orange-red cell-marks and pd bands*, double marginal lines filled orange; uns markings similar but better defined and without black suffusion. ♀ similar.

Flight. End June/July according to weather; butterflies emerge with onset of summer.

Habitat. Mountain sides and moorland at moderate altitudes, or near tree-line, often in light woodland with *Vaccinium*. Larval food plants not recorded.

Distribution. Fennoscandia, from 64°N to North Cape, esp. Abisko, Maalselv, Porsanger, etc. Always local, commonest in far north.

EUPHYDRYAS AURINIA *Marsh Fritillary*

Sw: Ärenprisnätfjäril G: Skabiosen-Scheckenfalter Sp: Ondas rojas

Range. W. Europe, Russia, Asia Minor and across temperate Asia to Korea. Map 117

This species and *E. desfontainii* differ in several ways from the preceding species. On uns the narrow coloured marginal band is replaced by the more usual black dots; black spots are always prominent in the red pd band of hw.

E. aurinia aurinia Rottemburg 1775 TL: Paris Pl. 26

Description. ♂fw 17/19mm., ups gc yellow-buff, cell-spots and pd bands orange-red, black markings variable; *uph with dark spots in each segment of pd orange band* in s1a to 6; uns paler, gc yellow-grey with light orange-brown bands, often pale with little colour contrast; *unf without prominent pd black spots.* ♀ generally larger, otherwise similar.

Flight. May/June.

Habitat. Very varied, bogs, flowery meadows, grassy banks, boggy margins of lakes, moors, etc., from lowlands to 5,000 ft. Larval food plants plantain, scabious, more rarely other low plants.

Distribution. All C. and E. Europe, including Britain, Balkans and Fenno-

PLATE 19

1. Mesoacidalia aglaja   *Dark-green Fritillary*   91
Unh with silver basal, discal and marginal spots, but no postdiscal spots.

   1a. *M. a. aglaja* ♂. Unh yellow-buff with green markings. ♀ ups often suffused grey.
   1b. *M. a. lyauteyi* ♂. Large, ups more heavily marked; unh green suffusion more extensive. ♀ larger, ups paler fulvous.

2. Fabriciana niobe   *Niobe Fritillary*   93
Like *F. adippe* (Pl. 18) but unh with a small silver or buff spot in centre of cell which often encloses a small black point (see 2b.); small postdiscal spots present. ♀ ups clouded with grey suffusion.

   2a. (uns only). *F. niobe* ♂. Unh all spots filled or pupilled with silver. ♀ similar.
   2b. (uns only). *F. niobe* f. *eris* ♂. Unh all spots buff except the small postdiscal spots. ♀ similar.

3. Fabriciana elisa   *Corsican Fritillary*   94
♂. Unh with numerous small silver spots. ♀ similar, larger.

4. Issoria lathonia   *Queen of Spain Fritillary*   94
♂. Unh with distinctive large silver spots. ♀ similar.

5. Argyronome laodice   *Pallas's Fritillary*   91
♀. Upf with small white costal mark near apex; unh base olive-yellow, distal area brown. ♂ similar.

6. Pandoriana pandora   *Cardinal*   89
Unf ground-colour rosy-red.

   6a. *P. pandora* ♂. Unh green with silver striae near costa.
   6b. *P. pandora* ♀. Unh green with wavy transverse silver stripes upf without sex-brands.

1b

1a

2a 2b

4

3

5

6b 6a

1a   1b

2a   2b

3a   3b

4a   4b

5a   5b

PLATE 20

1. Brenthis hecate   *Twin-spot Fritillary*   95

    1a. ♂. Unh with two rows of black postdiscal spots.
    1b. ♀. Similar, ups sometimes suffused grey.

2. Brenthis daphne   *Marbled Fritillary*   95

    2a. ♂. Unh with single row of black postdiscal spots, base of space 4
        usually brown (yellow in *B. ino* (Pl. 22).
    2b. ♀. Similar, usually larger.

3. Clossiana euphrosyne   *Pearl-bordered Fritillary*   105
Unh central spot in yellow discal band silver.

    3a. *C. euphrosyne* ♂. Ups clear fulvous, markings slender.
    3b. *C. euphrosyne* f. *fingal* ♀. Smaller, ups black markings heavier.

4. Clossiana selene   *Small Pearl-bordered Fritillary*   104
Unh spots of discal band uniformly yellow or silver.

    4a. *C. selene* ♂. Ups black markings slender.
    4b. *C. selene* f. *hela* ♀. Ups black markings heavier.

5. Clossiana titania   *Titania's Fritillary*   105

    5a. *C. t. titania* ♂. Ups orange-fulvous, black markings slender;
        unh colour contrast not striking. ♀ similar.
    5b. *C. t. cypris* ♂. Ups bright fiery fulvous, black markings larger;
        unh brightly marked in purple-brown, yellow, etc.

scandia, to 62°N. Absent from **Mediterranean islands and Greece**. Rare in peninsular Italy.

Variation. Individual differences and abnormal patterns are common, and even the characteristic features of a colony may vary from year to year. *E. a. aurinia* extends across Russia and far into Siberia with relatively slight geographical variation.

E. aurinia provincialis Boisduval 1828   TL: Provence, France

Description. ♂fw 19/22mm., often large, ups gc yellow-buff, pd bands little darker than gc with reduced colour contrast and thin black lattice pattern; unh pale, sometimes sandy-yellow overall with black markings obsolescent.

Flight. End April/May.

Habitat. Flowery banks and meadows at about 2,000 ft.

Distribution and Variation. France, only in Basses Alpes, Bouches du Rhône, Gironde and Var. N. Italy, a few colonies near Lake Como, small and paler, f. *comacina* Turati 1910, flying at about 3,500 ft. Yugoslavia, esp. Dalmatia, in a large form, f. *rotunda* Roeber 1926.

E. aurinia beckeri Herrich-Schaeffer 1851   TL: Cadiz   Pl. 26

Description. ♂fw 20/23mm., ups gc reddish-fulvous with or without yellow discal and pd markings, black lattice pattern often heavy; upf black marginal lines often single, marginal lunules large; ups pd red band wide and submarginal black spots large; unh gc pale yellow-grey, coloured bands bright orange, wide, black-edged, colour contrast brilliant. ♀ similar, sometimes very large.

Flight. End May/June.

Habitat. On rough ground, often among mountains, from lowlands (Gibraltar) to 5,000 ft. Larval food plants honeysuckle (perhaps also plantain, *Centaurea*, *Centranthus*).

Distribution. Portugal. Spain, widely distributed from Malaga and Granada to Catalonia; in Cantabrian Mts. transitional to *E. a. aurinia*. Morocco, common in Middle Atlas and El Rif, flying at 5–6,000 ft. Algeria.

Similar species. *E. desfontainii* p. 131, easily distinguished by series of black pd spots on unf.

E. aurinia debilis Oberthur 1909   TL: E. Pyrenees   Map 118   Pl. 26
  syn: *merope* de Prunner (invalid homonym)

Description. ♂fw 15/17mm., ups gc yellow, discal spots and submarginal bands orange-red; uns paler, gc yellow-grey with black markings reduced, often vestigial. ♀ often larger with fw to 19mm.

Flight. End June/July.

Habitat. Flies over grass slopes, usually at levels of 6,000 ft. and upwards, sometimes down to 4,500 ft. (Bavaria, Carnic Alps). Larval food plants gentian, *Primula viscosa*.

Distribution. E. Pyrenees, Basses Alpes to Hte Savoie and eastwards through the Alps to Bavarian Alps and Hohe Tauern (Gr. Glockner). Absent from Pyrenees west of Ariège, from Jura, Carpathians and Balkans. Variation. Brightly coloured in the E. Pyrenees, but at high altitudes in central Alps, ups with gc paler and black markings extended, often widely suffused fuscous but variable f. *glaciegenita* Verity Pl. 26.

Note. *E. a. debilis* appears to be a subspecies separated by altitude alone, as it is surrounded at lower levels by other subspecies of *E. aurinia*.

EUPHYDRYAS DESFONTAINII *Spanish Fritillary*

Sp: Dientes gualdos

Range. Confined to N. Africa, Spain and E. Pyrenees.   Map 119

E. desfontainii desfontainii Godart 1819 TL: Algeria   Pls. 22, 26
Description. ♂fw 20/24mm., fw apex rounded, ups gc red with paler discal and transverse bands; upf small yellow spots in red pd band, dark marginal border enclosing yellow lunules; *unf black pd spots prominent*, other markings as on ups, gc sandy-red. ♀ similar.
Flight. May/early June.
Habitat. Flies at 5–6,000 ft. on warm slopes among *Cistus*, etc., in Middle Atlas. Larval food plant in Algeria *Knautia*.
Distribution. Morocco. Algeria. Not recorded from Tunis. Specimens from Morocco are especially brilliant, f. *gibrati* Oberthur 1922 Pl. 22, local but not uncommon.

E. desfontainii baetica Rambur 1858 TL: Andalusia   Pl. 26
Description. Resembles *E. d. desfontainii*; ups gc paler red, cell-marks and pd bands yellow-buff and marginal lunules distinct; uns gc paler, often yellowish; unf black discal spots prominent, esp. near costa; unh markings mostly vestigial.
Flight and Habitat as for *desfontainii* but flies at 2–4,000 ft.
Distribution. In S. and E. Spain; Granada, Ronda, etc., and in widely separated colonies northwards to Catalonia and E. Pyrenees (Sournia). Variation. Different colonies show well-marked racial features. One illustrated is f. *zapateri* Higgins 1950 (Pl. 26) TL: Albarracin, Teruel, smaller, ups orange-fulvous; unh gc yellow with markings well defined by black striae.

SATYRIDAE
Boisduval 1833

This is a very large cosmopolitan family of grass-feeders, highly developed in the temperate regions of the Old World, the species occurring on open meadows, mountain slopes or light woodland, wherever their food plants can grow. In western Europe only seven or eight species of the genera *Oeneis* and *Erebia* are truly boreal, but there is a remarkable concentration of alpine species in the Pyrenees, Alps and Balkan mountains. The family is best represented in the warmer parts of Europe and it accounts for almost one-third of the butterfly fauna of the area. The species are generally of medium size, but some of the largest European butterflies are included in the Satyridae. There is a strong family likeness throughout the family, wings usually some shade of brown, varying from black to fulvous and yellow-buff, but white with black markings in the aberrant genus *Melanargia*. Characteristic markings are the postdiscal ocelli, of which that on the fore-wing in s5 is especially constant, often set in a paler mark or band.

MELANARGIA GALATHEA *Marbled White*
F: Le Demi-Deuil G: Schachbrett Sp: Medioluto norteña
Sw: Schackbräde
Range. N. Africa across Europe to Caucasus and N. Iran. Map 120

M. galathea galathea Linnaeus 1758 TL: Germany (Verity 1953) Pl. 27
Description. ♂fw 23/26mm., *upf cell without isolated black cross-bar*, white cell-patch occupying basal two-thirds only; unh markings black, ocelli enclosed in fuscous submarginal band broken at s4, dark discal band wide on costa at s7. ♀ larger, fw to 28mm., unh markings usually yellowish-brown with gc pale yellow.
Flight. June/July.
Habitat. Anywhere in grassy places, from sea-level to 5,000 ft. Larval food plants various grasses, e.g. *Phleum*, *Agropyron*, etc.
Distribution. Throughout W. Europe, except south-west, northwards to S. England and in Germany to Baltic coast, doubtfully recorded from Denmark. Absent from Fennoscandia and Estonia. In SE. France partially replaced by *M. g. lachesis* in Aude, Gard, Hérault, Ariège, Bouches-du-Rhône and E. Pyrenees, but recorded from all these. Present also in Cantabrian Mts. and locally on southern slopes of Pyrenees. Completely replaced by *M.g. lachesis* south of Pyrenees and Cantabrian Mts.
Variation. Recurrent abnormal wing markings include f. *galene* Ochsenheimer, in which unh ocelli are absent, and ♀ f. *leucomelas* Esper, in which the unh gc is plain white, unmarked, a common form in many

localities but rare in the north. In S. Italy and Balkans black markings more extensive, f. *procida* Herbst (Pl. 27), with corresponding reduction in white markings, sometimes associated with yellow ground-colour.

M. galathea lachesis Huebner 1790 TL: Languedoc (S. France) Pl. 27
Description. ♂fw 25/28mm., slightly larger than *M. g. galathea*; ups markings less heavy, esp. basal and discal markings, often vestigial; upf white cell-patch extending in a sharp point to cell-end, black mark at cell-end much reduced; unh markings grey, dark central band narrow on costa in s7. ♀ often larger.
Variation. Form *cataleuca* Staudinger, equivalent of the *leucomelas* form of *M.g. galathea*, with unh plain white, is common.
Flight and Habitat as for *M.g. galathea*.
Distribution. SE. France as recorded above, not east of the Rhône. Spain and Portugal, generally distributed south of Pyrenees and Cantabrian Mts. This subspecies is accorded specific rank by many authors. The distributional frontiers between *lachesis* and *galathea* are well defined and along them rather uncommon intermediate forms occur, esp. f. *duponti* Reverdin pl. 28, with black markings reduced on both surfaces.

M. galathea lucasi Rambur 1858 TL: Bougie, Algeria Pl. 28
Description. ♂fw 26/28mm., ups black markings heavy; white cell-patch extended, separated from cell-end by a small grey spot; unf cell closed distally by a black bar shortly before cell-end; unh black central band narrow on costa in s7. ♀ larger, unh slightly yellowish, with larger ocelli with blue pupils. No *leucomelas*-like form of the ♀ has been recorded from Africa.
Flight. June/early July.
Habitat. Local in grassy places in Atlas Mts., flying at 3–7,000 ft.
Distribution. Algeria, Morocco and Tunis. The usual form in Morocco is slightly larger than that of Algeria with heavier black markings.
Similar species. *M. russiae* below, cell of fw crossed by dark line.

MELANARGIA RUSSIAE *Esper's Marbled White*

Sp: Medioluto montañera
Range. Spain, Portugal and SE. France, and in widely scattered colonies across Italy and the Balkans to S. Russia, Transcaucasus and W. Siberia.
Map 121

M. russiae russiae Esper 1784 TL: Volga, SW. Russia Pl. 27
   syn: *suwarovius* Herbst 1796
Description. ♂fw 26mm., ups black markings delicate and complete (see *M. r. cleanthe* below). Occurred formerly in Pusta Peszer, Hungary, but is now extinct in that locality. It is unlikely that it occurs anywhere in W. Europe to-day.

M. russiae cleanthe Boisduval 1833   TL: Basses Alpes   Pl. 27
Description. ♂fw 26/30mm., ups with delicate complete black markings; upf black cell-end mark enclosing a white spot; *cell crossed by zig-zag black bar*; uph black central band continuous across s4; *unh pattern firmly outlined in black* with spaces filled pale grey; submarginal ocelli distinct, not enclosed in fuscous spaces. ♀ups black markings slightly more extensive, unh with yellow flush.
Flight. July.
Habitat. Dry stony places in hilly districts, to 5,000 ft., local.
Distribution. France, in Provence, Gironde, E. Pyrenees; in Aveyron and Lozère small. Spain, not uncommon in N. and C. mountains. Portugal, reported from Sierra de Estrela.

M. russiae japygia Cyrillo 1787   TL: S. Italy   Pl. 27
Description. ♂fw 25/27mm., black markings ups heavier, individually somewhat variable; uns distinction from *M. r. cleanthe* less definite. ♀ups black markings often tend to grey, unh yellowish.
Flight. July.
Habitat. Mountains, very local at 3–5,000 ft.
Distribution. Italy, from Bolognola southwards in Apennines, slightly larger in south, esp. in Sicily (rare), e.g. Fonte Larocca, Palermo, Monte Madonie.
Variation. At high levels in Abruzzi often darker. Also in Macedonia and Albania, a few colonies closely resembling the Italian forms reported near Lake Ochrid.
Similar species. *M. larissa herta* below; *M. galathea* p. 132.

MELANARGIA LARISSA *Balkan Marbled White*
Range. Perhaps confined to SE. Europe, but several closely allied species or subspecies widely distributed in W. Asia to Iran.   Map 122

M. larissa larissa Geyer 1828   TL: Cres (Cherso Is.), Istria   Pl. 28
Description. ♂fw 25/30mm., ups black markings heavy, *basal areas of both wings suffused dark fuscous* which may cover cell; *upf cell crossed by fine black line from between v2 and v3*; uph cell obscured by dark basal area; uns resembles *M. russiae*, unh basal area faintly grey, central band unbroken in s4. ♀ usually larger, uns fw apex and hw slightly yellow.
Flight. June/July.
Habitat. Rocky slopes, lowlands to moderate altitudes.
Distribution. Bulgaria, Greece, Albania, SE. Yugoslavia. Replaced in Dalmatia by following subspecies.

M. larissa herta Geyer 1828   TL: Dubrovnik (Ragusa)   Pl. 28
Description. Resembles *M. l. larissa* but all black markings greatly reduced,

esp. in pd areas; ups grey basal suffusion present on both wings; uph ocelli well defined. ♀ wing-markings grey, on unh often vestigial.
Flight and **Habitat** as for *M.l. larissa*.
Distribution. Occurs in the Karst regions of Dalmatia and Montenegro; unstable in some populations and forms intermediate between *M.l. herta* and *M.l. larissa* sometimes occur.

Similar species. *M. russiae japygia* p. 134, uph cell always white.

MELANARGIA OCCITANICA *Western Marbled White*

Sp: Medioluto herrumbrosa
Range. Restricted to SW. Europe and N. Africa.   Map 123

M. occitanica occitanica Esper 1793   TL: Toulouse   Pl. 28
   syn: *psyche* Huebner 1800; *syllius* Herbst 1796
Description. ♂fw 25/28mm., upf two small apical ocelli, black mark at cell-end encloses white centre, cell crossed by irregular black line; *uns veins lined brown*; unf discal markings black; unh cell closed by double oblique lines directed to v4, ocelli conspicuous, pupils blue, *marginal chevrons long and acute-angled*, longitudinal black line present in s1b. ♀ similar, uns often with heavy brown suffusion.
Flight. End May/June/July, depending upon altitude, etc.
Habitat. Mountainous rocky country, lowlands to 5,000 ft.
Distribution. France, E. Pyrenees, Var, Bouches du Rhône, Maritime Alps; Italian coastal areas at Capo Mele, Capo Berta, etc.; Spain, widely distributed southwards to Sierra Nevada, but local. Portugal, near Gerez, Coimbra. Reported from Corsica.

M. occitanica pelagia Oberthur 1911   TL: Sebdou, Algeria   Pl. 28
Description. ♂fw 23/25mm., size variable, often small; ups markings more delicate; base of s3 upf clear white, black bar across cell fully separate from cell-end markings.
Flight and **Habitat** as for *M. o. occitanica*.
Distribution. Algeria, in Oran, esp. Sebdou, Geryville, etc. Morocco, local in Middle Atlas, esp. Anosseur, Djebel Hebri, etc., sometimes larger and more heavily marked. Not recorded from Tunisia.

M. occitanica pherusa Boisduval 1833   TL: Sicily   Pl. 28
Description. ♂fw 25/27mm., ups black markings reduced; upf mark at cell-end usually enclosing a white spot, base of s3 always white; uph discal field whiter, ocelli small, sometimes absent (f. *plesaura* Bellier Pl. 28), unh veins delicately lined pale brown.
Flight. May/June.
Habitat. Mountains at 2–3,000 ft.
Distribution. Confined to Sicily, very local, recorded from Lupo, San

Martino, Palermo, etc. This subspecies is given specific rank by some authors.

Similar species. *M. ines* below, unh veins lined black.

MELANARGIA ARGE   *Italian Marbled White*
Range. Restricted to peninsular Italy.   Map 124

M. arge Sulzer 1776   TL: Kingdom of Sicily (which in 1776 included most of the Apennines)   Pl. 27
Description. ♂fw 25/26mm., resembles *M. occitanica* but more lightly marked; upf black bar across cell incomplete, mark at cell-end reduced, usually circular, enclosing white and blue scales; unh ocelli more prominent, more brightly coloured, their black circles distinct, veins lined dark brown (black), longitudinal dark line present in s1b; unf markings scanty, *marginal chevrons short, right-angled.* ♀ often larger, otherwise similar.
Flight. May/early June.
Habitat. Hills and mountains, flying in small localised colonies from quite low altitudes to over 4,000 ft.
Distribution. Peninsular Italy, from Gran Sasso southwards to Reggio; recorded also from Sicily near Messina.

Similar species. *M. ines* below, unh without dark longitudinal line in s1b; does not occur in Italy.

MELANARGIA INES   *Spanish Marbled White*
Sp: Medioluto Inés
Range. Spain and Portugal, Morocco, Algeria, Tunisia and Cyrenaica.
                                                              Map 125

M. ines Hoffmannsegg 1804   TL: 'Calabria' (error for Cantabria) Pl. 27
Description. ♂fw 23/25mm., resembles *M. occitanica* and *M. arge*; upf a broad black bar crossing middle of cell, blue-pupilled ocelli prominent; unf *marginal chevrons obtuse-angled,* nearly lunulate; unh without longitudinal dark line in s1b, fine black striae present along costa in s8. ♀ slightly larger, unh gc often yellowish.
Flight. End April/May/June, depending upon altitude.
Habitat. Rocky slopes with grass, usually in mountainous districts at altitudes of 3–4,000 ft.
Distribution. Spain, a common species in central and southern districts. Portugal. Tunisia. Morocco. Algeria.
Variation. Unusually large specimens with ♂fw to 27mm. occur at low altitudes in western Morocco. In Middle and High Atlas at altitudes of 7,000 ft. or more, the black markings of ups are extensive, f. *jehandezi* Oberthur Pl. 27.

Similar species. *M. arge* above.

HIPPARCHIA FAGI   *Woodland Grayling*

F: Le Sylvandre   G: Grosser Waldportier   Sp: Banda curva
Range. From France across C. Europe and Balkans to S. Russia.

Map 126

H. fagi   Scopoli 1763   TL: Carniola   Pl. 29
  syn: *hermione* Linnaeus 1764
Description. ♂fw 33/38mm., ups dark grey-brown; upf pale yellowish pd band suffused fuscous and enclosing small pd ocelli in (s2), s5; uph pd band better defined, usually white, often with small ocellus in s2, *outer edge of dark basal area nearly straight* or gently curved; unf pd band white or faintly yellowish near apex, dark basal area not sharply angled at v4; unh pd band white, becoming darker near outer margin, the whole irrorated with dark scales and striae. ♀ larger, ups pd bands paler and better defined, often slightly yellow near apex of fw.
Flight. July/August.
Habitat. Among trees or bushes, often rests upon tree-trunks, lowlands to 3,000 ft. Larval food plants grasses, esp. *Holcus*.
Distribution. C. and S. Europe to 52°N and including Bulgaria and Greece. Absent from NW. France, C. and S. Spain, Portugal, N. Germany, Fennoscandia and Atlantic islands.
Similar species. *H. alcyone* p. 138:

H. fagi and *H. alcyone*: comparative table of characters

These two species may fly together and often occur in the same districts. Identification may be difficult, especially in the Balkans. Distinctive external characters are contrasted in the following Key, but variation is great and no external character is entirely reliable.
Size. Length of fw under 33mm. = *alcyone*
      Length of fw over 33mm. = *fagi*
      This useful rule will apply to most specimens.
Altitude. *H. fagi* does not fly at altitudes over 4,000 ft. and usually occurs
      as a lowland species. *H. alcyone* up to 6,000 ft.
Markings.
  Pd band upf in ♂; well defined, yellowish: *alcyone*
                  clouded and suffused with fuscous: *fagi*
  Pd band upf in ♀; decidedly yellowish: *alcyone*
                  white or faintly yellowish near apex: *fagi*
  Outer border of dark basal area uph—
    Irregular with bulge at v3 and 4; pointing to inner
      margin above anal angle: *alcyone*
    Nearly straight or evenly curved; pointing near anal angle: *fagi*
Jullien Organs. *H. fagi*: three to five large rods on each side.
        H. alcyone: eight to eleven smaller rods on each side.

Distribution. *H. fagi* is absent from Fennoscandia, Germany, central and southern Spain and Portugal, but occurs in NE. Spain.
H. alcyone, much more widely distributed.

HIPPARCHIA ALCYONE   *Rock Grayling*

F: Le Petit Sylvandre   G: Kleiner Waldportier   Sp: Banda acodada
Range. C. and S. Europe, N. Africa, Asia Minor and Lebanon and Caucasus to Kurdistan.   Map 127

H. alcyone alcyone   Schiffermueller 1775   TL: Vienna   Pl. 29
   syn. *aelia* Hoffmannsegg 1804
Description. ♂fw 27/34mm., closely resembles *H. fagi*, generally slightly smaller; upf pd bands better defined, less clouded fuscous and often with distinct yellowish flush, esp. on fw; *uph outer edge of dark basal area irregular* with angle or bulge at v3, 4; unf pd band decidedly yellowish, dark basal area acutely angled at v4. ♀ slightly larger, upf pd bands wider, paler, often with small ocellus in s2.
Flight. June/July.
Habitat. Among rocks, precipices, etc., to 6,000 ft.; in southern range confined to mountains. Larval food plants various grasses, esp. *Brachypodium*.
Distribution. S. and C. Europe to 60°N, including extreme south of Norway. Replaced in Balkans by *H. a. syriaca*. Absent from NW. Europe, NE. Italy, Mediterranean islands and Crete.
Variation is not marked except in size. Northern specimens are small.

Similar species. *H. fagi* p. 137; see comparative table p. 137. Examination of Jullien organ may be necessary for certain identification.

H. alcyone syriaca   Staudinger 1871   TL: Syria   Pl. 29
Description. Resembles *H. fagi*; fw sometimes slightly more pointed; upf pd band paler, but much suffused dusky; uph outer edge of dark basal area slightly curved or nearly straight without the angle on v3, 4.
Flight and Habitat as for *H. a. alcyone*.
Distribution. Montenegro, Dalmatia, Albania, NE. Yugoslavia, European Turkey, Rumania (Orsova) and Greece. Generally less common than *H. fagi* in the Balkans.

H. alcyone   caroli Rothschild 1933 (June)   TL: Morocco
   syn. *natasha* Hemming 1933 (Dec.)
Description. Resembles *H. a. alcyone*; uph outer edge of dark basal area usually has a slight bulge in s4; upf obscure white pd spots present in most specimens in s3, 4. Jullien organ resembles that of *alcyone*, usually with 8–10 rods.
Flight and Habitat as for *H.a. alcyone*.
Distribution. Morocco, common in Middle Atlas, not recorded from High Atlas; absent from Algeria and Tunisia.

Similar species. *H. ellena* below; *H. fagi* p. 137, see comparative Table of Characters p. 137.

HIPPARCHIA ELLENA *Algerian Grayling*
Range. Confined to Algeria and Tunisia. Map 128

H. ellena Oberthur 1894 TL: Bône, Algeria Pl. 29
Description. ♂fw 30/34mm., ups gc very dark, *pd bands clear white, narrow*, inner border slightly irregular; upf ocelli well developed in s2 and s5; unh outer border of dark basal area straight below v5. ♀ups white bands wider, upf ocelli larger; unh dark basal area more mottled grey, white pd band wide.
Flight. End June/July/August.
Habitat. Among oak and cedar trees from 5,500 ft. upwards.
Distribution. Algeria. Tunisia at lower levels.

Similar species. *H. alcyone natasha* p. 138, upf pd bands suffused fuscous.

HIPPARCHIA NEOMIRIS *Corsican Grayling*
Range. Confined to Corsica, Sardinia and Elba. Map 129

H. neomiris Godart 1824 TL: Corsica Pl. 48

Description. ♂fw 23/25mm., ups gc brown with wide orange-yellow pd bands; upf apex suffused fuscous; unh white pd band narrow. ♀upf fuscous clouding less marked.
Flight. June/July.
Habitat. Mountains at 3–6,000 ft. on Corsica and Sardinia, at lower levels on Elba. Map 130

HIPPARCHIA SEMELE *Grayling*
F: l'Agreste Sw: Sandgräsfjäril G: Rostbinde Sp: Pardo-rubia
Range. W. and C. Europe and through S. Russia probably to Armenia. The distribution limits in Asia are little known.

H. semele and its close allies form a difficult complex, represented in W. Europe by *H. semele*, with large male genitalia, and by *H. aristaeus*, in which the genitalia are smaller. These two species resemble one another very closely. Both occur in Sicily, probably also in S. Italy, and certainly in Greece, but otherwise their distributions do not overlap.

H. semele semele Linnaeus TL: Europe (Sweden, Verity 1953) Pl. 30
Description. ♂fw 21/25mm., fringes pale, chequered brown; ups gc brown; upf with prominent sex-brand below median vein, yellow pd band often poorly defined, suffused and interrupted along veins by gc, enclosing ocelli in s2 and s5; uph *orange submarginal area broadly broken by veins* and enclosing small ocellus in s2; unh cryptic, marbled light and dark grey, darker

basal area generally defined and followed by pale grey or white pd band. ♀ larger, ups yellow markings more extensive with less dusky suffusion; unh markings more uniformly mottled and pale pd band poorly developed.
Flight. July/August.
Habitat. Open heaths and rough hillsides from sea-level to moderate altitudes; fond of settling in full sun on bare ground. Larval food plants various grasses, *Deschampsia, Agropyron*, etc.
Distribution. Southern Fennoscandia, Britain, N. Germany, Czechoslovakia and N. France.

H. semele cadmus Fruhstorfer 1908   TL: Valais, Switzerland   Pl. 30
Description. ♂ fw 27/30mm., larger, ups dusky suffusion more extensive; upf yellow pd band vestigial or confined to a few yellow scales around ocelli; uph orange submarginal markings usually bright; unh dark basal area and white pd band conspicuous. ♀ larger, ups brightly marked, with yellow areas around ocelli often forming a broken pd band.
Flight. End May or later.
Habitat. Lowlands to 5,000 ft. or more; the usual mountain form of the species.
Distribution. C. and S. Europe, esp. in Alps, Pyrenees and mountainous districts of Spain, Portugal and Balkans to Peloponnesus, but more stable on the whole than local races of *H. s. semele*. Absent from Sardinia, Corsica, Malta and Balearic Islands.
Variation. The unh markings are especially brilliant in some southern races, which have a conspicuous white pd band. Cretan males have noticeably different genitalia, *H. s. cretica* Rebel.
Similar species. *H. aristaeus* below. No reliable external characters have been found by which to distinguish between these two species; where they overlap examination of the genitalia will be necessary for certain identification.

HIPPARCHIA ARISTAEUS   *Southern Grayling*
Range. From Madeira, N. Africa and the larger Mediterranean islands, to Greece and Asia Minor.   Map 131

H. aristaeus aristaeus Bonelli 1826   TL: Sardinia   Pl. 30
Description. ♂ fw 25/27mm., resembles *H. semele*; ups gc brown with extensive generalised orange flush, pd markings orange-red; *uph pd area broadly orange, crossed by veins*; uns markings as in *H. semele*. ♀ ups brightly marked in orange-yellow which extends widely across disc of fw.
Flight. End June/July.
Habitat. In Corsica and Sardinia usually at about 3,000 ft. and upwards, flying over rough heathy land; at lower levels on Elba, Lipari Isles, etc. Larval food plants not known, but certainly grasses.
Distribution. Corsica, Sardinia, Elba, Lipari Islands, Sicily, S. Italy.

Variation. A large race, f. *siciliana* Oberthur, with ♂fw 27/28 mm. occurs in the Lipari Islands, Sicily and Giglio.

H. aristaeus algirica Oberthur 1876 TL: Algeria   Pl. 30
Description. ♂fw 26/27 mm., ups markings less bright, without orange flush, yellowish, resembling closely large forms of *H. semele* in both sexes; uns as in *H. semele*.
Flight. April/May/June, depending upon locality and altitude. Chneour records a partial second brood in Tunisia in autumn.
Habitat. Dry stony banks and heaths from 4,000 ft. to over 7,000 ft.
Distribution. Mountains of Morocco, Algeria and Tunisia. At very high levels slightly darker specimens appear to be more common.

H. aristaeus senthes Fruhstorfer 1908 TL: Taygetos Mts.
Description. Resembles *H. semele cadmus*. ♂ups yellow markings largely obscured by extensive dark suffusion; uph pd band grey, orange submarginal macules present in s3, 4, 5; unh as in *H.s. cadmus*. ♀ like *H.s. cadmus* on both surfaces.
Flight. June/July.
Habitat. From moderate altitudes to 3,500 ft., prefers hilly districts.
Distribution. Greece, widely distributed but rather uncommon. Peloponnesus and mainland, northwards to Struma valley and Naussa; also recorded from Isle of Khios.
Note. *H. a. senthes* is distinguished from *H. s. semele* by genitalia. Both species may fly in the same localities but *aristaeus* seems likely to appear first, with *semele* later in July.

H. aristaeus maderensis Bethune Baker 1891 TL: Madeira   Pl. 30
Description. ♂fw 24/25 mm., ups dark, both wings heavily suffused smoky-brown, ocelli and traces of usual pd markings present in most specimens; unh white pd band prominent. ♀ larger, fw 28/29 mm., very dark but ups pd markings present, approaching *H.a. algirica*.
Flight and **Habitat** as for *H.a. algirica*, flying at about 5,000 ft.
Distribution. Confined to Madeira.

Similar species *H. semele* p. 139

HIPPARCHIA AZORINA *Azores Grayling*
Range. Confined to the Azores.   No map

H. azorina Strecker 1899 TL: Azores   Pl. 30
Description. ♂fw 21/22 mm., ups very dark, fuscous suffusion nearly obscures very pale yellow gc and markings; upf small blind ocelli in s2, 5, sex-brand conspicuous, in isolated patches in s1b, 2, 3 and cell; unh basal area very dark brown, *pd band conspicuous, sinuous, white*, marginal area very dark and slightly mottled with fine striae. ♀ slightly larger, ups wing-pattern less obscure.

Flight. July/August.
Habitat. Grassy slopes of crater lip at 2,000 ft.
Distribution. Azores, on Fayal Island, Isle de Pico, Sao Miguel.
Note. *H. azorina* is regarded as a subspecies of *H. aristaeus* by some authors.

HIPPARCHIA STATILINUS   *Tree Grayling*

F: Le Faune   G: Eisenfarbiger Samtfalter   Sp: Satiro moreno
Sw: Vitbandad Gräsfjäril
Range. From N. Africa, Spain and Portugal through C. and S. Europe to
Asia Minor.   Map 132

H. statilinus statilinus   Hufnagel 1766   TL: Berlin   Pl. 31
Description. ♂fw 22/23mm., ups dark grey-brown obscurely marked; upf
with blind ocelli in s2, 5, and *small white spots in s*3, 4; unh suffused grey-
brown, discal area more or less defined by darker brown sinuous lines,
often incomplete, but colour contrast minimal; scalloped submarginal line
not sharp. ♀upf pd area with obscure yellowish markings, ocelli better
defined, usually with white pupils; unh brown, with very variable rather
indefinite markings.
Flight. July/August/September.
Habitat. Sandy heaths, bushy places or sparse woodland at low or
moderate levels. Larval food plants various grasses, esp. *Bromus sterilis*.
Distribution. C. and S. Europe to 50°N in west. In C. and N. Germany
local, becoming scarce and already absent from many earlier known
localities. Poland, very local. Absent from NW. Germany, Denmark,
Fennoscandia, Britain, Bavaria, NW. Switzerland, N. Tirol and Carpathians.
Variation. *H. statilinus* is a most variable species. In general, northern
races are small; in central Europe larger, f. *onosandrus* Fruhstorfer, unh
grey, discal area defined by dark lines but without much colour contrast.
In Portugal and S. Spain often very large, f. *allionia* Fabricius, unh
variegated with pale grey and dark brown. In f. *maritima* Rostagno
from C. Italy unh is almost uniform dark brown.

H. statilinus sylvicola   Austaut 1879   TL: Algeria   Pl. 31
Description. ♂fw 26/28mm., ups resembles *H. s. statilinus*, sex-brand very
broad; unh grey-brown, usually with an irregular dark pd line, but other
markings vestigial. ♀ similar, pd area vaguely paler, white spots in s3, 4
larger and apical ocellus with small white pupil.
Flight and Habitat as for *H.s. statilinus*, stony slopes at 5–6,000 ft. in early
July or later.
Distribution. Morocco, Algeria and Tunisia in Atlas Mts.

Similar species. *Hipparchia fatua* p. 143. Balkans only, unh scalloped submarginal line sharply defined.

HIPPARCHIA FATUA *Freyer's Grayling*
Range. Greece and SE. Yugoslavia, Lebanon, Syria.   Map 133

H. fatua Freyer 1844 TL: not stated   Pl. 31
  syn. *allionii* Huebner 1824 (invalid homonym)
Description. ♂fw 30/34mm., resembles *H. statilinus* but larger; uph dark
submarginal line of *externally concave lunules better defined*, usually
continuous; unh discal band clearly defined by irregular dark transverse
lines, the whole finely striated and irrorated with brown scales; outer
margin of hw deeply scalloped, submarginal line sharp. ♀upf pd markings
yellowish, prominent white pd spots in s3, 4; uph small ocellus in s2,
white spots in s3–6.
Flight. July/August.
Habitat. Among trees in hilly country but at moderate levels.
Distribution. This fine eastern species reaches Europe only in Turkey,
Greece and SE. Yugoslavia. A Lebanese specimen is figured, as a European
specimen in good condition was not available.
Similar species. *H. statilinus* p. 142.

HIPPARCHIA HANSII *Austaut's Grayling*
Range. From Morocco to Tunis, extending far into Tripolitania.
                                                                  Map 134

H. hansii hansii Austaut 1879 TL: Bône, Algeria   Pl. 32
Description. ♂fw 24/28mm., very variable; ups gc medium brown; upf
pd area usually paler with *yellowish suffusion around ocelli in s2, 5, and
white spots in s3, 4,* a smallish sex-brand below median vein; unh central
band defined by dark transverse lines. ♀ups yellow suffusion in pd area
more extensive, sometimes present also on uph, uph with small ocellus
in s2 and white spots in s3–6.
Flight. September/October.
Habitat. Rough ground and stony slopes at 5–7,000 ft. Larval food plant
grasses.
Distribution. Atlas Mts. in Morocco, Algeria and Tunisia, not recorded
from the Rif.
Variation. On unh ground colour varies from light to dark brown, often
with pale grey or nearly white pd area.

H. hansii powelli Oberthur 1910 TL: Géryville, Algeria   Pl. 31
Description. ♂fw 23/24mm., apex of fw slightly pointed; upf yellow
suffusion restricted to narrow ring around apical ocellus; unh all veins
lined grey, but dark transverse lines representing discal band are conspicuous in contrast with pale grey pd suffusion. ♀ups apical ocellus
enlarged, otherwise similar.
Flight and **Habitat** as for *H. h. hansii*.

PLATE 21

1. **Boloria napaea**   *Mountain Fritillary*   99
   Ups ground-colour fulvous with thin black markings; unf black markings scanty or vestigial.

   1a. *B. napaea* f. *frigida* ♂. Small, unh markings well defined; ♀ rarely heavily suffused grey.
   1b. *B. napaea* ♀. Ups usually heavily suffused dark grey; unh brightly variegated with yellow, greenish, red-brown, etc.; uph black basal shade rarely extends to cell-end.
   1c. *B. napaea* ♂. Ups ground-colour fulvous yellow.

2. **Boloria pales**   *Shepherd's Fritillary*   98
   Like *B. napaea*; ups black pattern more macular, discal spots firmly marked; unf black spots vestigial or absent.

   2a. *B. p. pales* ♀. Ups black markings heavy; uph black basal shade extends widely to cell-end, often includes body groove.
   2b. *B. p. pales* ♂. Ups clear bright fulvous; uph black basal shade as in ♀; unh markings lack greenish reflections.
   2c. *B. p. palustris* ♂. Small, ups markings less macular; unf black spots sometimes better developed.
   2d. *B. p. palustris* ♀. Ups often slightly paler, otherwise similar to ♂.
   2e. *B. p. pyrenesmiscens* ♂. Ups markings macular; uph black basal shade reduced; unf black markings present.

3. **Boloria graeca**   *Balkan Fritillary*   103
   Hw outer margin strongly angled at vein 8; unf black markings well developed.

   3a. *B. graeca* ♂. Unh with 6 round postdiscal spots well defined.
   3b. *B. graeca* f. *tendensis* ♀. Ups paler fulvous-yellow.

4. **Boloria aquilonaris**   *Cranberry Fritillary*   102
   Unf black markings complete; unh red postdiscal area invading usual yellow mark in space 3 and postdiscal ocelli well defined.

   4a. *B. aquilonaris* ♂. Upf marks strongly angled in space 1b.
   4b. *B aquilonaris* ♀. Ups often with faint violet gloss.
   4c. *B. aquilonaris* f. *alethea* ♀. Large.

5. **Mellicta athalia**   *Heath Fritillary*   120
   5a. *M. a. norvegica* ♂. Small, ups black eticulate pattern very regular. ♀ similar. See also Pl. 25.
   5b. *M. a. celadussa* f. *tenuicola* ♂. Small, ups pale, black markings thin and incomplete. See also Pl. 25.

6. **Hamearis lucina**   *Duke of Burgundy Fritillary*   231
   Second brood ♂. Ups fulvous spots partly obscured by extension of black ground-colour. See also Pl. 14.

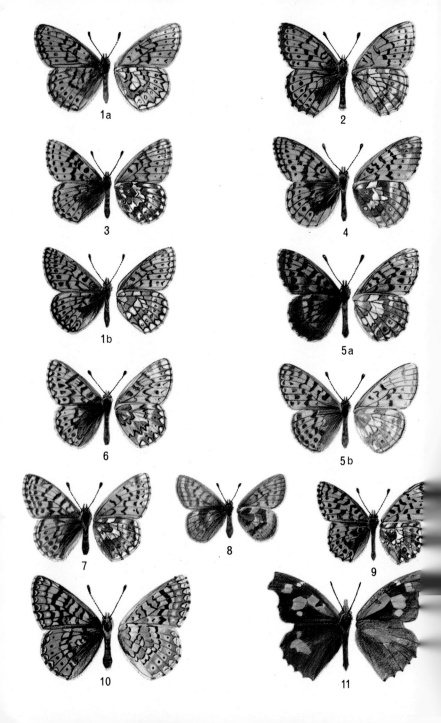

PLATE 22

1. Proclossiana eunomia *Bog Fritillary*   103
Unh with six white-centred postdiscal ocelli.

   1a. *P. e. eunomia* ♂ Ups ground-colour clear fulvous; unh pale
      discal spots and marginal lunules yellow. ♀ ups often slightly
      fuscous.
   1b. *P. e. ossianus* ♂. Ups slightly suffused fuscous; unh marginal
      lunules silvered. ♀ often darker and more heavily suffused
      fuscous.

2. Brenthis ino *Lesser Marbled Fritillary*   98
♂. Ups like *B. daphne* (Pl. 20) but smaller and black marginal lines
continuous; unh base of space 4 yellow. ♀ similar, ups sometimes
suffused fuscous.

3. Clossiana polaris *Polar Fritillary*   107
♂. Unh with many small white markings. ♀ similar.

4. Clossiana frigga *Frigga's Fritillary*   110
♂. Unh with conspicuous white costal and discal marks set in deep
brown. ♀ similar.

5. Clossiana thore *Thor's Fritillary*   107

   5a. *C. t. thore* ♂. Ups with very extensive black markings; unh
      yellow discal band conspicuous. ♀ similar.
   5b. *C. t. borealis* ♂. Ups ground-colour pale fulvous, less heavily
      marked; unh markings pale, not well defined. ♀ similar.

6. Clossiana freija *Freya's Fritillary*   106
♂. Unh with prominent zig-zag brown postdiscal line in spaces 1, 2,
3. ♀ similar.

7. Clossiana chariclea *Arctic Fritillary*   106
♀. Unh with prominent pale discal band. ♂ similar.

8. Clossiana improba *Dusky-winged Fritillary*   111
♂. Small, ups dusky, markings not well defined; unh like *C. frigga*.
♀ similar.

9. Clossiana dia *Violet Fritillary*   107
♂. Hw outer margin sharply angled at vein 8; unh marbled with
purple-brown. ♀ similar.

10. Euphydryas desfontainii *Spanish Fritillary*   131
♀. Uns suffused brick-red; unf with prominent discal band of black
spots; unh markings clearly defined by black striae (f. *gibrati*).
For ♂ see Pl. 26.

11. Libythea celtis *Nettle-tree Butterfly*   74
♂. Palpi very long; wings sharply angled. ♀ similar.

Distribution. Algeria, in southern and eastern districts; Tunisia.
Note. The taxonomic status of *powelli* is uncertain and the distribution is
not well known. While the ♂ genitalia do not differ from those of *H. hansii*,
external features are distinct and far more constant than those of other
forms of *H. hansii*.

PSEUDOTERGUMIA FIDIA   *Striped Grayling*

Sp: Festón blanco
Range. Confined to N. Africa and SW. Europe.   Map 135

P. fidia   Linnaeus 1767   TL: Algeria   Pl. 32
Description. ♂fw 28/31mm., outer margin of hw distinctly scalloped; friuge
of fw chequered; ups gc dark brown with markings as in *H. statilinus*; npf
with ocelli in s2, 5, white spots in s3, 4 and sometimes with vague yellow-
grey pd markings; *unh* variegated pale grey and brown with *striking pattern
of zig-zag dark lines*. ♀ larger, upf with white or yellowish pd markings
on costa and in s(1) 2, ocelli in s2 and 5, and rather large white spots in
s3, 4.
Flight. July/August according to locality.
Habitat. Stony slopes, often among trees, from lowlands to 6,000 ft. on
foothills or mountains. Larval food plants various grasses, esp. *Pip-
tatherium*.
Distribution. SE. France, local in Provence, Languedoc and E. Pyrenees,
northwards to Ardèche. Italy, only in Maritime Alps. Spain and Portugal,
widely distributed in suitable localities among mountains. N. Africa, local
but widely distributed in High and Middle Atlas in Morocco, Algeria and
Tunisia.
Variation. In N. Africa ups wing-markings are slightly more developed
and unh pale grey markings more prominent, sometimes with conspicuous
pale lining along veins, f. *albovenosa* Austaut.

PSEUDOTERGUMIA WYSSII   *Canary Grayling*
Range. Confined to Canary Isles.   No map

P. wyssii wyssii   Christ 1889   TL: Tenerife, Canary Isles   Pl. 31
Description. ♂fw 28/32mm., fw narrow, pointed, fringes chequered, sex-
brand conspicuous; hw outer margin slightly scalloped; ups gc dark
brown with slight golden lustre; upf cell very dark and markings obscure,
*blind ocelli in s2, 5 and white spots in s3 and 4 much better developed on
uns*; uph brown unmarked; unh paler brown finely irrorated with dark
scales, discal band defined by irregular dark transverse lines narrowly edged
white distally. ♀ups gc paler and markings more prominent, including upf
yellowish discal markings in s2, 5 and larger white spots in s3, 4.
Flight. July.

Habitat. Among trees at 6,000 ft., perhaps also at lower levels. Larval food plants not known.
Distribution. Tenerife, esp. Las Canadas, Parador de Tiede, etc.

P. wyssii bacchus Higgins 1967 TL: Hiero, Canary Isles Pl. 31
Description. ♂fw 30mm., ♀ 30/33mm., wings less pointed, outer margins of hw more deeply scalloped; uns gc darker more smoky brown, unh white pd markings more extensive and forming continuous irregular stripe. ♀ups dark brown with purple iridescence, slight golden lustre over basal area; upf conspicuous white costal spot and mark in s2 larger, yellowish; unh white markings enlarged, pd area richly marbled.
Flight. July/August.
Habitat. In vineyards and sparse woodland, at about 1,000 ft.
Distribution. Canaries on Hiero Island and Gomera Island.

CHAZARA BRISEIS *The Hermit*
F: L'Hermite G: Gemeinäugiger Falter Sp: Banda oblicua
Range. From N. Africa, Spain and S. France through Europe to W. Asia, Iran, Altai Mts. and Pamirs. Map 136

C. briseis Linnaeus 1764 TL: Germany Pl. 32
Description. ♂fw 21/30mm., size variable; ups gc dark brown, *pd bands cream-white, broken by gc along veins in fw,* but not in hw; upf costal margin almost white, more or less irrorated brown, a wide sex-brand below cell and often a pale area at cell-base; unh cream-white irrorated brown, large brown mark from costa to cell and another similar near inner margin, marginal border grey. ♀ larger, fw to 34mm., upf white pd band less regular; unh markings confused, irrorated and mottled grey-brown; dimorphic, white markings sometimes replaced by buff, f. *pirata* Esper, rare in S. Europe, not uncommon in Asia.
Flight. June or later.
Habitat. Dry stony places from lowlands to 6,000 ft. in N. Africa. Larval food plants grasses, esp. *Sesleria coerulea.*
Distribution. C. and S. Europe to about 50°N. Africa, common in Morocco, Algeria and Tunisia. Absent from N. and NW. France, Britain, Corsica, Sardinia, Elba.
Variation. In S. Europe and N. Africa often large, with ♂fw 29mm., f. *major* Oberthur.
Similar species. *C. prieuri* below, upf no white mark in s4.

CHAZARA PRIEURI *Southern Hermit*
Sp: Beréber
Range. Confined to Spain and N. Africa. Map 137

C. prieuri Pierret 1837 TL: Oran, Algeria Pl. 32

Description. ♂fw 27/33 mm., resembles *C. briseis*; upf costa and diffuse area in cell pale buff, white pd band more broken, with larger blind ocelli in s2, 5 but *no white mark in s4*; uph irregular white pd band broad in s5, not reaching costa; unh long pale v-shaped submarginal markings on v2-6, very long on v6. ♀ larger, upf blind ocellus in s2 often very large and buff mark in cell absent; unh dark irroration more general.

Flight. June or later.

Habitat. Rocky slopes in mountainous country from 3,000 ft. in Spain, to 7,000 ft. in N. Africa. Larval food plants not recorded.

Distribution. Morocco, Algeria, local in Middle Atlas. Spain, very local in central mountains, esp. Teruel (Albarracin, etc.) and Saragossa.

Variation. In Spain the ♀ is dimorphic, white markings sometimes replaced by buff, f. *uhagonis* Oberthur Pl. 32.

Similar species. *C. briseis* p. 147.

PSEUDOCHAZARA ATLANTIS   *Moroccan Grayling*
Range. Confined to Morocco.   Map 138

P. atlantis   Austaut 1905   TL: High summits of Moroccan Atlas
   syn: *maroccana* Meade-Waldo 1906   Pl. 48
Description. ♂fw 26/28 mm., ups gc light grey-brown with *wide, clear orange pd bands* and narrow grey marginal borders; upf black white-pupilled ocelli in s2, 5, sex-brand not conspicuous; unh gc pale yellow with grey and sandy brown irrorations. ♀ similar, unh striations better defined. Fringes not chequered.

Flight. June/early July.

Habitat. Mountains, flying on stony, barren slopes at 7-9,000 ft. Larval food plants not recorded.

Distribution. Morocco, local in Middle Atlas, High Atlas and South Atlas.

PSEUDOCHAZARA HIPPOLYTE   *Nevada Grayling*
Sp: Filabresa
Range. Isolated on the Sierra Nevada in Spain; S. Russia (TL of *P. hippolyte* Esper 1784), Asia Minor and east to Tian Shan.   Map 139

P. hippolyte williamsi   Romei 1927   TL: Sierra Nevada, Spain   Pl. 48
Description. ♂fw 25/26 mm., ups pale grey-brown with *broad pale straw-coloured pd bands*; upf ocelli in s2, 5; uph small ocellus in s2; unh gc yellow-grey with darker striations, basal area darker, dark lunular submarginal marks in series. ♀ slightly larger, upf darker basal area extended along v4.

Flight. End June/July.

Habitat. Stony slopes at altitudes of 7-9,000 ft.

Distribution. Spain, in Sierra Nevada and esp. on Mt. Mulhacen.

Note. The species was first known from Orenberg in southern Russia, distant about 3,000 miles as the crow flies from the Spanish colony. It is not known from any intermediate locality.

PSEUDOCHAZARA MAMURRA *Buff Asian Grayling*
Range. From Greece through mountains of Asia Minor (*Satyrus mamurra* Herrich-Schaeffer 1846, TL: Ararat) eastwards to Iran. Map 140

P. mamurra graeca Staudinger 1870 TL: Mt. Parnassus and Taygetos Mts. in Greece Pl. 48
Description. ♂fw 26/27mm., ups gc grey-brown; upf with yellow-brown pd band broken by gc along v4, crossed by dark veins, and enclosing blind black ocelli in s2, 5; *uph ocellus minute*, yellow-brown pd band in s2, 5, deeper orange near margin; uns pale yellow-grey; unh irrorated with fine darker scales and with greyish submarginal markings, without ocelli. The wide sex-brand on upf along median vein is not conspicuous. ♀ similar, larger.
Flight. July/August.
Habitat. Stony mountain slopes at 5,000 ft. or more.
Distribution. In Europe recorded only from Taygetos Mts., Mt. Chelmos, Mt. Parnassus and Veluchi Mts. in Greece.

PSEUDOCHAZARA ANTHELEA *White-banded Grayling*
Range. Southern Balkans and Crete through Asia Minor (TL of *P. anthelea* Huebner 1824) to Kurdistan. Map 141

H. anthelea amalthea Frivaldsky 1845 TL: Crete Pl. 35
Description. ♂fw 23/25mm., ups gc brown; upf conspicuous *black sex-brand* in cell, *narrow white pd band*, large ocelli in s2, 5 often blind; uph white pd band short, wide and suffused distally with fulvous; uns gc white; unh basal area and marginal border very dark, somewhat mottled darker. ♀ larger, unh less dark with confused irrorations and mottling, white pd area reduced or vestigial.
Flight. June/early July.
Habitat. Rough stony ground, usually among hills or mountains, lowlands to 5,000 ft. Larval food plants not recorded.
Distribution. Greece, SE. Yugoslavia, Albania, Crete (Psyloriti Mts.). The European white ♀ form does not occur in Asia, where all females have gc orange-yellow.

PSEUDOCHAZARA GEYERI *Grey Asian Grayling*
Range. From S. Balkans through Asia Minor (*Satyrus geyeri* Herrich-Schaeffer 1846, TL: Ararat) to Turkestan. Map 142

P. geyeri occidentalis Rebel and Zerny 1931 TL: Albania Pl. 48
Description. ♂fw 24mm., ups gc yellowish-grey, basal and submarginal markings slightly darker; upf ocelli white-pupilled; unf yellowish, boldly

marked; *unh submarginal area with sagittate brown chevrons.* ♀ups gc whiter, with bolder black markings; uns as in ♂.
Flight. July/August.
Habitat. Dry stony slopes at 4–6,000 ft. Larval food plants not known.
Distribution. In Europe known only from mountains in Albania and in SE. Yugoslavia north of Lake Ochrid

OENEIS NORNA   *Norse Grayling*
Sw: Gulbrun Gräsfjäril
Range. Lapland, Altai and Tarbagatai Mts., boreal W. Asia.   Map 143

O. norna   Thunberg 1791   TL: Lapland   Pl. 35
Description. ♂fw 26/28 mm., fringes slightly chequered; ups gc grey-brown with wide yellowish pd bands; upf ocelli, often blind, in s2, 5, additional ocelli frequent; uph commonly with small ocelli in s2, sometimes also in 3; unh dark brown *discal band edged white*, pd area mottled and irrorated with brown, white and yellow, best seen in fresh specimens. ♀ similar, gc often paler yellow-buff, pd ocelli variable, often with white pupils.
Flight. July.
Habitat. Rough moorland, from 3,000 ft. on Dovrefjeld to sea-level in far north. Larval food plants grasses, perhaps also sedge.
Distribution. Fennoscandia, from 62°N in Jotunheim to North Cape, locally common. Finland, less common, occurs principally in mountainous subarctic regions.

Similar species. *O. bore* below, slightly smaller, paler, markings unh similar but without ocelli. *O. glacialis* p. 151.

OENEIS BORE   *Arctic Grayling*
Sw: Grågul Gräsfjäril
Range. Northern Fennoscandia, northern Russia, Siberia, and N. America.   Map 144

O. bore   Schneider 1792   TL: Lapland   Pl. 35
Description. ♂fw 22/25 mm., fringes slightly chequered; ups gc pale fuscous, *ocelli absent* except rarely a very small, white-pupilled ocellus in s5 on upf; upf often with small yellow patches between veins in pd area, esp. in ♀; uph broad discal band usually present, lighter pd area often with small white or yellow spots between veins; unh dark discal band with white borders, pd area irrorated dark brown, yellow and white, with small pale spots between veins. ♀ similar, ups paler, sometimes with slight yellow flush on upf. *O. bore* is quickly worn, the wings losing scales and becoming nearly transparent.
Flight. June/July, depending upon weather.

Habitat. Stony slopes in hilly country, from sea-level to 2,000 ft. esp mountain summits. Larval food plant grasses, e.g. *Festuca ovina*.
Distribution. Norway and northern Finland, north of 67°N.
Similar species. *O. norna* p. 150.

OENEIS GLACIALIS   *Alpine Grayling*

G: Gletscherfalter
Range. Confined to Alps.   Map 145
O. glacialis Moll 1783   TL: Zillertal, Austria   Pl. 35
   syn: *aello* Huebner 1804
Description. ♂fw 25/28mm., fringes slightly chequered; ups gc light fuscous, yellowish in pd areas; upf ocelli in s2 and s5, often blind, inconspicuous, sex-brand along median vein conspicuous in fresh specimens; uph ocelli in s2 and s3; unh irrorated dark brown with *conspicuous white-lined veins*. ♀ larger, ups pale yellow-brown, wing-bases shaded grey, margins darker; unh pd area paler, ocelli usually white-pupilled on both wings.
Flight. End June/July.
Habitat. Rocky places, near tree-line, at 6,000 ft. or more, rarely at lower levels. Larval food plant *Festuca ovina*.
Distribution. Maritime Alps and eastwards to Carnic Alps, Bavarian Alps and North Tirol; commonest in Valais and Engadine. Absent from Jura and Vosges.
Similar species. *O. norna* p. 150, which does not show the distinctive white veins on unh.

OENEIS JUTTA   *Baltic Grayling*

Sw: Gråbrun Gräsfjäril
Range. From Scandinavia across N. Russia and Siberia to Alaska, Labrador and Nova Scotia, thence extending to Maine and New Hampshire.   Map 146

O. jutta Huebner 1806   TL: Lapland   Pl. 35
Description. ♂fw 27/28mm., fringes chequered; *ups gc dark smoky brown*, somewhat variable; upf sex-brand conspicuous, ocelli in s2(3) and 5 enclosed in yellow rings, usually blind; uph pd ocelli in s2, 3, sometimes absent, enclosed in yellow patches; *unh densely irrorated dark brown and mottled pale grey*, dark discal band often indicated by obscure grey shading. ♀ larger, pd ocelli ups larger and more constant, yellow pd patches often fused into a continuous band; unh resembles ♂.
Flight. End May to July.
Habitat. Among sparse pine trees growing around lowland bogs, etc.; the butterflies settle on the tree-trunks. Not a mountain species. Larval food plant not known.

Distribution. Fennoscandia, esp. around the lakes and bogs of Sweden and Finland, rare in Lithuania and East Prussia (Olsztyn).

SATYRUS ACTAEA   *Black Satyr*

F: l'Actaeon   Sp: Negra
Range. SW. Europe and again in Asia Minor, Syria and Iran.   Map 147

S. actaea Esper 1780   TL: S. France   Pl. 34
Description. ♂fw 24/28 mm., *sex-brand in s 1–3 erect*; ups gc black; upf a single white-pupilled ocellus in s 5 (rarely a small ocellus in s 2); unh wing-pattern often obscure, a dark basal area generally present followed by a grey band. ♀ slightly larger, ups gc pale brown; upf basal area dark, paler pd band grey and often a small ocellus in s 2; *unf gc light brown*, white spots in s 3, 4; unh dark basal area or discal band often followed by white band, but very variable.
Flight. July/August in a single brood.
Habitat. Dry stony slopes at 3–6,000 ft. Larval food plants various grasses (*Brachypodium*, *Bromus*, etc.).
Distribution. Spain and Portugal, widely distributed. France, from E. Pyrenees, Lot, Lozère and Aveyron to Maritimes and Basses Alpes. Italy, only in Maritime Alps and Cottian Alps northwards to Susa.
Variation. A variable species with many local races. Upf apical ocellus may be very large; in ♀ups yellow suffusion around ocelli is not uncommon and may extend to uph as a pd band, sometimes extensive.

Similar species. *S. ferula* below.

SATYRUS FERULA   *Great Sooty Satyr*

Range. Morocco and southern Europe (excluding Spain and Portugal) to Asia Minor, Iran and the Himalayas.   Map 148

S. ferula ferula Fabricius 1793   TL: Italy   Pl. 34
  syn: *bryce* Huebner 1800; *cordula* Fabricius 1793
Description. ♂fw 25/30 mm., *sex-brand absent*; upf gc black with *white-pupilled ocelli in s 2 and s 5*; uph a small ocellus often present in s 2; unh brown, usually strongly marked; unf white spots in s 3, 4 and ocelli as on ups; unh dark basal area usually distinct, followed by paler grey band and a dark pd band beyond, but variable, sometimes with very bright markings. ♀ larger, ups gc paler brown with more or less extensive yellowish suffusion around ocelli; *unf gc orange-yellow* with prominent black ocelli; unh grey or yellow-grey with light brown basal, discal and sub-marginal bands and dusting, the discal band sometimes clearly defined.
Flight. July/August.
Habitat. Rocky hillsides at 1,500–5,000 ft. Larval food plants various grasses.
Distribution. S. Europe, rarely north of 47°N. France, throughout southern

regions of Central Massif, Provence and northwards through the Alps to
Savoie and Isère, thence through the entire chain of southern Alps,
including Switzerland northwards to Rhône valley, Bolzano, Etschtal,
Trient, etc., but more local in Tirol. C. Italy in Apennines and south to
Aspromonte. Serbia. SE. Yugoslavia, Greece and Bulgaria. Absent from
Portugal, Spain, Pyrenees, except for a single colony in the Val d'Aran
in E. Pyrenees, and Mediterranean islands.

S. ferula atlanteus **Verity** 1927 (Sept.)   TL: Meknes, Morocco
   syn: *meknesensis* Strand 1927 (Oct.)
Description. ♂fw 24/28mm., upf a single apical ocellus in s5, closely
resembling *S. actaea, no sex-brand*; ♀upf a prominent white-pupilled
ocellus in s5, a smaller ocellus in s2, occasional faint traces of orange
suffusion around ocelli.
Flight. End June to August.
Habitat. Barren mountain slopes at 5–7,000 ft.
Distribution. Morocco, in High, Middle and South Atlas and El Rif.

Similar species. *S. actaea* p. 152, male upf with single apical ocellus and
sex-brand in s1–3; ♀ unf gc brown. *M. dryas* below.

MINOIS DRYAS   *Dryad*

Sp: Ojos azules   G: Blauäugiger Waldportier
Range. From N. Spain through central Europe and C. Asia to Japan.
Map 149

M. dryas Scopoli 1763   TL: Carniola   Pl. 34
   syn: *phaedra* Linnaeus 1764
Description. ♂fw 27/29mm., outer margin of hw scalloped; ups gc almost
black; *upf blue-pupilled ocelli in s2 and s5*; uph a small ocellus in s2 in
some specimens; unh dark brown, basal area sometimes followed by
vestigial pale band and vague darker submarginal markings. ♀ larger, fw
to 35mm., margin of hw deeply scalloped; ups gc paler brown, ocelli
larger; unh paler brown, traces of dark discal band usually present and
sometimes bordered with pale grey; unf white pd spots in s3, 4 very small;
unh markings variable in both sexes.
Flight. July/August.
Habitat. Grass slopes or light woodland from lowlands to 3,000 ft. Larval
food plants various grasses.
Distribution. Central Europe to 54°N, a local species absent from wide
areas. From N. Spain through France, including Pyrenees and Massif
Central to Fontainebleau and Vosges. Switzerland. N. Italy, Austria,
Yugoslavia, Bulgaria and Rumania. Germany, extending locally to Baltic
coast. Absent from S. Spain, Italy south of Florence, Greece and Mediter-
ranean islands.

Similar species. *S. ferula* p. 152, upf ocelli with white pupils; unh with pale bands.

BERBERIA ABDELKADER   *Giant Grayling*
Range. Confined to Africa north of the Atlas Mts.   Map 150

B. abdelkader abdelkader   Pierret 1837   TL: Constantine Province, Algeria   Pls. 33, 34
Description. ♂fw 35/39mm., ups very dark brown; upf blue-pupilled ocelli in s2 and s5, bluish-white spots in s3, 4; uph small blue-pupilled ocelli in s2, 5, bluish-white spots in s3, 4 sometimes absent; unh discal band defined by thick dark lines, the distal line strongly angled at v4, proximal line broken, sometimes absent. ♀ups gc paler; upf some yellowish suffusion common around ocelli; unh veins strongly lined pale yellow-grey. ♂upf with an extensive sex-brand in s2–4.
Flight. May/June and August/September in two annual broods.
Habitat. Rough ground and mountain slopes with esparto grass at 6–8,000 ft. in Morocco, at lower altitudes in Algeria. Sometimes congregates on lucerne fields. Larval food plants grasses, esp. *Stipa tenacissima* (l'Alfa).
Distribution. Morocco and Algeria in Middle and High Atlas Mts.
Variation. In some localities upf apex often cream-white, perhaps locally racial, f. *nelvai* Seitz (Pl. 33). Unh markings are slightly variable with dark lines and outer margin sometimes narrowly edged with yellow-buff.

B. abdelkader marteni   Chneour 1935   TL: Mines, Tunisia
Description. ♂fw 28mm., but size variable; wing-markings on both surfaces are said to be subdued.
Flight. In two broods like *B. a. abdelkader*.
Habitat. Recorded from relatively low altitudes.
Distribution. Known only from Tunisia.

BRINTESIA CIRCE   *Great Banded Grayling*
F: le Silène   G: Weisser Waldportier   Sp: Rey mozo
Range. From western Europe through Asia Minor to Iran and Himalayas.
                                                                     Map 151

B. circe   Fabricius 1775   TL: Europe (Germany, Verity 1953)
    syn: *proserpina* Schiffermueller 1775   Pl. 33
Description. ♂fw 33/36mm., ups black with single *milk-white broken pd band across both wings*; upf a single apical ocellus, generally blind; unh markings cryptic, white pd bands prominent. ♀ similar, larger, with fw to 40mm.
Flight. June/July.
Habitat. Light woodlands, lowlands to about 4,500 ft. Larval food plants various grasses, *Bromus*, *Lolium*, etc.
Distribution. South and central Europe to 50°N in west, but extending

farther to north in eastern Europe. Widely distributed and generally common from Spain, Portugal and France eastwards, with northern limits in central Germany. Czechoslovakia, Hungary and Rumania. Absent from Britain, Belgium, Holland and N. Africa.

ARETHUSANA ARETHUSA *False Grayling*

F: Le Petit Agreste G: Rotbinden-Samtfalter Sp: Pintas ocres
Range. N. Africa and western Europe to Asia Minor, S. Russia and central Asia.   Map 152

A. arethusa arethusa Schiffermueller 1775 TL: Vienna   Pl. 33
Description. ♂ fw 22/24 mm., upf sex-brand prominent; ups gc brown with broken *orange pd bands across both wings*, sometimes narrow or incomplete; upf a single blind dark ocellus in s 5; uph small ocellus often present in s 2; unh pale brown, irrorated with dark scales, basal area defined by a white band in many races. ♀ similar, ups orange bands better developed.
Flight. End July/August.
Habitat. On heaths and grassy places to 4,000 ft. Larval food plants various grasses, esp. *Festuca*.
Distribution. Local in S. Europe, esp. on calcareous soils. Widely distributed in Spain, Portugal and France. Switzerland, in Jura and perhaps in a few localities in south-west. Italy, Ligurian Apennines and in a few scattered colonies at Oulz and NE. Italy. Absent generally from central Alps. In eastern Europe more generally distributed, esp. in Danube countries and Balkans to Greece, but always local.

A. arethusa dentata Staudinger 1871 TL: Western France   Pl. 33
Description. ♂ ups orange bands wide (4 mm.) and bright, each segment pointed externally; uns markings more brilliant; unf with lunulate inner border to grey wing-margin. ♀ similar, wing-markings better defined, with firm distal edge to brown basal areas on both wings; unf with elbowed brown pd line.
Flight and Habitat as for *A. a. arethusa*.
Distribution. France, in the south-west, Gironde, Basses Pyrénées, Landes, etc. Transitional to *arethusa* in Basses Alpes, Alpes Maritimes, etc., also in N. and E. Spain and Portugal. Morocco, very local in High Atlas, like *A.a. dentata* but unh veins very pale.

A. arethusa boabdil Rambur 1842 TL: Andalusia   Pl. 33
Description. ♂ ups gc dark brown, orange pd markings vestigial; uns all markings more brilliant; unh veins lined white and white pd band sometimes conspicuous. ♀ ups orange markings slightly more developed.
Flight and Habitat as for *A. a. arethusa*.
Distribution. Spain, only recorded from Andalusia, esp. Sierra Nevada, Sierra de Alfacar, etc., flying at 4–5,000 ft. in mountains.

EREBIA LIGEA   *Arran Brown*

Sw: Skogsgräsfjäril   G: Milchfleck
Range. From Europe across Asia to Kamchatka and Japan.   Map 153

E. ligea ligea   Linnaeus 1758   TL: Sweden (Verity 1953)   Pl. 36
Description. ♂fw 24/27mm., ups gc black with wide red pd bands enclosing 3 or 4 ocelli on fw, generally white-pupilled, and 3 on hw; unh dark basal area limited by *white streak from costa to s5*, followed by white marks. ♀ups gc dark brown, pd bands orange-red; unh brightly marked, white streak longer and wider. In both sexes fringes chequered black and white. ♂ with *sex-brand* on *upf* from inner margin to s5.
Flight. End June to August.
Habitat. In hilly country from 1–5,000 ft., often in light woodland, esp. among spruce; a lowland species in northern range. Larval food plants grasses, *Digitaria* and *Milium effusum*.
Distribution. From Auvergne and SW. Alps through Jura and Vosges eastwards through the Alps, Carpathians and Balkans to Macedonia; also in lowland Fennoscandia and very locally in Ligurian and Roman Apennines (Monte Penna). Absent from Pyrenees, Spain, Portugal, Mediterranean islands, C. and N. Germany (except Harz Mts.), Poland and Greece. The reported occurence of *E. ligea* on the Scottish island of Arran has never been confirmed.
Variation. Only minor local variation occurs; races flying at high altitudes are often small with ups red markings somewhat reduced.

E. ligea dovrensis   Strand 1902   TL: Dovre, Norway   Pl. 36

Description. ♂fw 21/24mm., small, ups ocelli often small and blind; unh brown, markings reduced, white streak often obsolescent. ♀unh markings better defined, white streak from costa often reaching s2 but narrow and broken, 3 submarginal ocelli.
Flight. July.
Habitat. In mountainous country in S. Norway, from sea-level to 3,000 ft. in Dovrefjeld.
Distribution. Fennoscandia, chiefly Norway, from Hardanger and Dovrefjeld to North Cape. Sweden, Abisko. Finland, Ivalo.

Similar species. *E. euryale* below.

EREBIA EURYALE   *Large Ringlet*
Range. From Cantabrian Mts. through Pyrenees, Alps, Carpathians and Balkans to Urals and Altai Mts.   Map 154
E. euryale euryale   Esper 1805   TL: Riesengebirge   Pls. 28, 36
Description. ♂fw 21/23mm., resembles *E. ligea* but smaller and without

sex-brand; ups gc black with wide red pd bands enclosing small ocelli (usually blind); unh gc reddish-brown, paler submarginal band often irrorated white or yellow, enclosing three or four small red-ringed ocelli, often blind. ♀ups gc dark brown, pd bands paler, yellowish; unh dark discal band bordered externally by white or yellowish f. *ochracea* Wheeler; number and size of ocelli variable.

Flight. July/August.

Habitat. In mountains at 3–6,000 ft., often among spruce. Larval food plants various grasses.

Distribution. Cantabrian Mts., Pyrenees, Central Massif of France, Jura, N. Switzerland, Alps of Germany, Austria, Sudeten Mts., Carpathians and Balkans to SE. Yugoslavia.

Variation. The number of ocelli on upf varies locally, 4–6 spots in Riesengebirge, Erzgebirge and Böhmer Wald; farther south in much of Austria and Carpathians ocelli smaller, often absent in s3, f. *isarica* Rühl.

E. euryale adyte Huebner 1822 TL: Valais, S. Switzerland (Verity 1955)
Pls. 28, 36

Description. ♂fw 21/23mm., ups ocelli generally with conspicuous white pupils, red pd band constricted at v4; unh markings generally obscure. ♀ ups usually with white-pupilled ocelli on both wings, but distinction from *E. e. euryale* less marked.

Flight and **Habitat** as for *E.e. euryale*.

Distribution. Replaces *E.e. euryale* in SE. France and Italy, from Alpes Maritimes to Savoie, Cottian and Graian Alps. S. Switzerland to Ortler. Italy, local in Abruzzi, Gran Sasso, etc.

E. euryale ocellaris Staudinger 1861 TL: Styria and Carinthia Pl. 36
Description. ♂fw 20/22mm., differs from *E. e. euryale* on ups in reduction or absence of red pd bands, leaving only small blind red-ringed ocelli. ♀ups gc paler brownish, traces of normal markings more often present; unh as in *E.e. euryale*.

Flight and **Habitat** as for *E.e. euryale*.

Distribution. E. Alps, Dolomites and Alto Adige to Hohe Tauern.

Variation. Intermediate populations with ups red bands broken into separate spots often occur, with minor variation, between areas occupied by *E.e. euryale* and *E.e. adyte*, esp. at Bolzano, Glarus, Gemmi, Lenzerheide, Moléson, Gurnigel.

Similar species. *E. ligea* p. 156, which often flies with *euryale*, is larger with bolder markings, esp. unh, where conspicuous white mark on costa is distinctive. Males can be distinguished by the presence (*ligea*) or absence (*euryale*) of sex-brands on upf.

EREBIA ERIPHYLE   *Eriphyle Ringlet*

G: Ähnlicher Mohrenfalter
Range. Confined to European Alps.   Map 155

E. eriphyle eriphyle   Freyer 1839   TL: Grimsel Pass, Switzerland   Pl. 38
Description. ♂fw 16/18mm., upf pd red band obscure, sometimes with
small black dots in s4, 5; uph small red spot in s4 very constant; *unf red
flush extending towards base of wing*; unh red spot in s4 never with black
central spot. ♀ slightly larger, markings usually paler and often slightly
more extensive.
Flight. July.
Habitat. Among rocks in grassy places at 5–6,000 ft. or more. Larval food
plants unknown.
Distribution. Very local in SE. Switzerland, Grimsel Pass, Furka Pass,
Flüela Pass, Davos, Val Tschitta, etc.

E. eriphyle tristis   Herrich-Schaeffer 1848   TL: not stated   Pls. 28, 38
Description. Resembles *E. e. eriphyle* but markings better defined; upf red
pd band narrow but bright, often enclosing three or four black points;
uph red spot in s4 constant, smaller red spots often present in s2, 3, 5;
unf marked reddish suffusion extending from pd band towards wing-base;
unh generally three or four red pd spots, never with black central points.
Flight. July.
Habitat. On mountain slopes from 4–7,000 ft., seems to prefer damp places
often on northern slopes.
Distribution. Alps of Bavaria (Nebelhorn), Austria (Arlberg, Innsbruck),
Styria, Carinthia (Gr. Glockner, Gr. Sau Alp).
Variation. *E. e. tristis* is relatively constant in the eastern Alps and locally
not uncommon. In specimens from the Gr. Glockner all ups red markings
are greatly reduced but clearly defined.

Similar species. *E. melampus* p. 167, smaller with black dots in the red
spots on unh; *E. manto pyrrhula* p. 159, unh red spot in s4 elongate.
E. epiphron p. 162.

EREBIA MANTO   *Yellow-spotted Ringlet*

G: Gelbgefleckter Mohrenfalter
Range. Confined to Europe.   Map 156

E. manto manto   Schiffermueller 1775   **TL**: Vienna   Pl. 39
Description. ♂fw 20/21mm., upf pd band variable but usually present,
composed of *elongate red marks* long in s4, 5, shorter in s1a, 2, 3, each
enclosing a small black spot; uph small red marks generally present in
s4, 5, 6; unh gc distinctly reddish, markings more complete, often orange-
yellow, longest in s4, 5, 6, basal red markings variable, often absent. ♀ups
pd bands often paler and better defined; unh brown discal band bounded

proximally by yellow basal marks and distally by yellow pd markings. In Vosges (*E. m. vosgesiaca* Christ) ♂ upf usually lacks black subapical dots; ♀ unh pale markings often white, ♀-form *bubastis* Meisner, rare in other races.
Flight. July/August. **Habitat.** Subalpine meadows at 3-6,000 ft.
Distribution. Vosges, Alps and Tatra Mts., local in Balkans.

E. manto constans Eiffinger 1908 TL: Hautes Pyrénées Pl. 28
Description. Resembles *E. m. manto* but black, ups unmarked, uns very rarely with traces of usual markings. ♀ often slightly larger and more often with traces of uns red markings.
Flight. End June/July.
Habitat. Flies in subalpine meadows at 5-6,000 ft., usually in damp places.
Distribution. Hautes Pyrénées, Gavarnie, Luchon and eastwards to Aulus. Slightly smaller and local in Cantal and Auvergne, Le Lioran, Plomb de Cantal. etc.

E. manto pyrrhula Frey 1880 TL: Albula Pass, Engadine Pl. 38
Description. ♂fw 17/19mm., small and variable, markings always reduced or absent on both surfaces. ♀upf has twin subapical black spots in narrow red area.
Flight. July.
Habitat. High alpine meadows and slopes above tree-line at 6-7,000 ft.
Distribution. Engadine, Albula, Guarda, etc. Dolomites, rather local and not quite so small. Hte Savoie, Mt. Blanc, less extreme.
Similar species. *E. eriphyle* p. 158.

EREBIA CLAUDINA *White Speck Ringlet*
G: Weisspunktierter Mohrenfalter
Range. Confined to eastern Alps. Map 157

E. claudina Borkhausen 1789 TL: Austria Pl. 37
   syn: *arete* Fabricius 1787 (invalid homonym)
Description. ♂fw 17/18mm., upf pd red band narrow; uph two or three minute white submarginal points, sometimes traces of red submarginal band; *unh six white points forming a regular submarginal series.* ♀ups gc paler brown; upf pd band paler red, enclosing twin black spots in s5, 6; unh pale yellow-grey, white submarginal points larger.
Flight. July.
Habitat. Flies over short grass slopes at 6,000 ft. or more. Larval food plant grass, esp. *Deschampsia caespitosa.*
Distribution. Only in eastern Alps of Salzburg, Styria and Carinthia, including Zirbitzkogel, Gr. Sau Alp, Mallnitz.

PLATE 23

1. Melitaea phoebe   *Knapweed Fritillary*   114
Upf orange marginal lunule in space 3 very large; a most variable
species, ♀ ups sometimes suffused dark grey.

   1a. *M. p. phoebe* second brood ♂. Ups fulvous ground-colour
moderately constant in tone across both wings.

   1b. *M. p. phoebe* f. *alternans* ♂. Ups brightly marked with alternat-
ing bands of yellow and bright fulvous ground-colour, black
markings heavy.

   1c. *M. p. punica* ♂. Small; upf black discal spots prominent but
postdiscal area almost unmarked; unh ground-colour pale cream
to white.

   1d. *M. p. occitanica* second brood ♂. Ups brightly marked, ground-
colour pale buff, postdiscal bands orange-red, black markings
thin. **See also Pl. 14.**

2. Melitaea aetherie   *Aetherie Fritillary*   115
Ups like *M. phoebe*, postdiscal areas of both wings almost unmarked
in ♂. Sexes differ. Females very variable.

   2a. *M. a. algirica* ♂. Ups bright fulvous without colour contrast.

   2b. *M. a. algirica* ♀. Ups heavily suffused dark grey except the costal area of hw.

3. Melitaea didyma   *Spotted Fritillary*   116
Ups black markings macular, discrete; unh ground-colour pale yel-
low, marginal black spots round. ♀ very variable.

   3a. *M. d. occidentalis* second brood ♂. Ups ground-colour bright
fulvous, black markings scanty. ♀ generally similar with larger
black markings. **See also Pl. 14.**

   3b. *M. d. didyma* first brood ♂. Ups tawny red ground-colour
bright; black markings larger, including postdiscal spots.
♀ ups often powdered grey.

   3c. *M. d. meridionalis* first brood ♀. Ups ground-colour obliterated
by grey suffusion except the costal area of hw. ♂ ground-colour
reddish-fulvous, ups markings usually almost complete.

4. Melitaea trivia   *Lesser Spotted Fritillary*   118
Unh marginal spots triangular; in hw lower discocellular vein
always present. Sexes similar, ♀ often larger, slightly variable.

   4a. *M. t. trivia* second brood ♂. Ups ground-colour fulvous yellow,
black markings rather heavy.

   4b. *M. t. trivia* f. *fascelis* first brood ♂. Large, ground-colour darker
and black markings heavier.

   4c. *M. t. ignasiti* second brood ♂. Small, ground-colour paler, black
markings, smaller.

5. Melitaea deserticola   *Desert Fritillary*   117
♂. Ups like *M. didyma*; unh ground-colour white, basal orange
markings broken up, each spot bordered with black. ♀ similar.

1a

1b

1c

1d

2a

2b

3a

3b

3c

4a

4b

4c

5

PLATE 24

1. Melitaea cinxia *Glanville Fritillary* 111
Uph with 4 or 5 round black spots in submarginal band; unh marginal spots small, discrete; fringes chequered. Sexes similar, ♀ often larger.

1a. *M. c. cinxia* first brood ♀. Ups fulvous yellow.
1b. *M. c. atlantis* first brood ♂. Ups pale buff, markings intense black.

2. Melitaea arduinna *Freyer's Fritillary* 114
M. a. rhodopensis ♀. Ups like *M. cinxia*, larger, ups fulvous red; unh marginal black lunules joined. ♂ often smaller, ups sometimes paler.

3. Mellicta deione *Provençal Fritillary* 121
Upf discal spot in space 1b. dumb-bell shaped (inconstant): unf black inner border of orange marginal lunule in space 2, vestigial or absent.

3a. *M. d. deione* first brood ♂. Ups clear orange-yellow.
3b. *M. d. deione* first brood ♀. Large, ups colour contrast strong.
3c. *M. d. berisalii* first brood ♀. Ups darker, black markings heavy, black marginal borders wider.
3d. *M. d. nitida* first brood ♂. Ups orange-yellow; uph discal area almost unmarked.

4. Mellicta parthenoides *Meadow Fritillary* 123
Ups black pattern regular; upf black discal spot in space 1b oblique; uph postdiscal area often unmarked (inconstant); unf postdiscal area unmarked.

4a. *M. parthenoides* first brood ♂. Ups ground-colour clear fulvous.
4b. *M. parthenoides* ♀. Ups black markings heavier with slight colour contrast.
4c. *M. parthenoides* f. *plena* ♂. Ups darker, black markings heavier.

5. Mellicta britomartis *Assman's Fritillary* 124
M. britomartis ♂. Like *Mellicta aurelia*; unh orange submarginal lunules bordered internally by dark band. Identification may entail dissection. ♀ similar.

6. Mellicta aurelia *Nickerl's Fritillary* 123

6a. *M. aurelia* ♂. Like *M. britomartis*, usually slightly smaller; unf black postdiscal markings often complete; unh orange submarginal lunules bordered internally by grey.
6b. *M. aurelia* ♀. Like ♂; often slightly larger and ups fulvous paler.

7. Mellicta asteria *Little Fritillary* 125
M. asteria ♂. Small; unh marginal black line single.

Similar species. *E. epiphron* below; *E. melampus* p. 167.

EREBIA FLAVOFASCIATA   *Yellow-Banded Ringlet*
Range. Confined to Alps of S. Switzerland.   Map 158

E. flavofasciata   Heyne 1895   TL: Campolungo Pass, Tessin   Pl. 37
Description. ♂fw 17/18mm., ups gc black; upf small red-ringed black pd spots in s4, 5, often also in s2, 3, always in straight row; uph black red-ringed submarginal spots in s2–5; unf disc suffused reddish, pd spots better defined; *unh a wide yellow submarginal band* enclosing small black spots in s2–5. ♀ups gc paler, brownish; upf pd spots ringed yellow, series often complete.
Flight. July.
Habitat. On rocky slopes with grass at 7,000 ft. or more. Larval food plant grass, esp. *Festuca ovina*.
Distribution. Restricted to a few localities in S. Switzerland, Tessin (Campolungo Pass), Engadine (Pontresina), etc.
Variation. In the Engadine, f. *thiemei* Bartel, unh yellow band narrow, sometimes broken up.

EREBIA EPIPHRON   *Mountain Ringlet*
G: Mohrenfalter
Range. Mountains of Europe, excluding Fennoscandia.   Map 159

E. epiphron epiphron   Knoch 1783   TL: Harz Mts., W. Germany
                                                                   Pl. 38
Description. The species is probably extinct in the Harz Mts., and the following description is based upon the closely related Silesian form, *silesiana* Meyer-Dur 1852.
    ♂fw 17/19mm., fw pointed; *upf red pd bands brilliant, lustrous*, enclosing blind *round black spots in s2–5*; uph with similar pd band with three black spots; *unh brown*, generally with small dark submarginal spots narrowly red-ringed. ♀ similar, ups black spots usually larger and often with minute white pupils on upf.
Flight. July.
Habitat. Flies in clearings among fir trees at 2–3,500 ft. Larval food plants grasses, esp. *Deschampsia caespitosa*.
Distribution. S. Bavaria, Czechoslovakia, Tatra Mts. and Carpathians.
Variation. In Tatra Mts. and Carpathians slightly smaller with ups red pd bands slightly reduced, upf black spot in s3 often absent.

E. epiphron fauveaui   de Lesse 1947   TL: E. Pyrenees   Pl. 38
Description. ♂fw 19/21mm., resembles *E. e. epiphron* but fw less pointed upf red pd band reduced, rarely reaching s1b, enclosing four round black spots in most specimens. ♀ similar.

Flight. End June/July/August.
Habitat. Grass slopes at 6,000 ft. or more.
Distribution. E. Pyrenees, Mt. Canigou, Cambre d'Aze, etc., and westwards, with *aetheria*-forms becoming increasingly common, to Luchon.

E. epiphron mnemon   Haworth 1812   TL: Scotland   Pl. 38
  syn: *scotica* Cooke 1943
Description. ♂fw 17/19mm., size variable, general appearance dark; upf red pd band narrow and often incomplete, usually enclosing four small black spots. ♀ similar, ups markings sometimes better defined; unh gc grey-brown.
Flight. July.
Habitat. On rough moorland to 3,000 ft. or over. Larval food plants various grasses, esp. *Nardus stricta*.
Distribution. Scotland, on higher mountains in the Grampians, Ben Nevis, above Loch Rannoch, etc. England, Westmorland and Cumberland.
Variation. English specimens are small, ♂fw 14/17mm., upf markings so reduced that basic features may be obscured. Similar forms occur in the Vosges and in Auvergne.

E. epiphron aetheria   Esper 1805   TL: not stated   Pl. 38
Description. ♂fw 17/19mm., upf red pd band reduced, *constricted in s*3 with absence of black spot; sometimes only twin apical black spots present. ♀ups paler, markings better developed, upf often with four black spots, white pupils not rare in s4, 5; unh brown, pd area slightly paler.
Flight. July/August.
Habitat. Grass slopes on high mountains from 5,500 ft. upwards.
Distribution. S. Alps generally, including Tirol, S. Switzerland and Apennines. Central Pyrenees and Cantabrian Mts. West Balkans.
Variation. At very high altitudes smaller, ♂fw 16/17mm., markings very dark and obscure, f. *nelamus* Boisduval Pl. 38, a relatively constant form in many localities in Engadine, Oberland, Urschweiz, Dolomites, etc.

E. epiphron orientalis   Elwes 1900   TL: Rilo Mts., Bulgaria   Pl. 38
Description. ♂fw 18/20mm., fw narrow, pointed; upf red pd band narrow, broken, twin black white-pupilled ocelli in s4, 5; uph with round black red-ringed pd spots and generally white-pupilled ocelli in s2, 3, 4 (5); uns all ocelli small and white-pupilled. ♀ slightly larger, ups pd bands paler, unbroken, all ocelli larger, four ocelli on upf, four or five on uph.
Flight. July.
Habitat. Grass slopes at 5–7,000 ft.
Distribution. Bulgaria, in Rilo, Rhodope and Perim Mts. A little-known subspecies, habitats remote and difficult of access. In several respects it differs from other forms of *E. epiphron*, and perhaps would be better ranked as a distinct species. Also on Stara Planina.

PLATE 25

1. Mellicta athalia *Heath Fritillary*   120

Unf black inner border of yellow marginal lunules in spaces 1b, 2 (3) usually well developed. A most variable species.

  1a. *M. a. athalia* first brood ♂. Ups black markings regular and well defined.

  1b. *M. a. boris* f. *satyra* ♂. Ups black markings greatly extended.

  1c. *M. a. boris* ♂. Ups black markings regular, marginal black borders wider.

  1d. *M. a. norvegica* f. *lachares* ♀. Ups black markings thin, postdiscal fulvous band wide. See also Pl. 21.

  1e. *M. a. celadussa* ♂. Ups like *M. a. athalia*, but often brighter. The genitalia show subspecific characters.

  1f. *M. a. celadussa* ♀. Ups rather brightly marked with slight colour contrast. See also Pl. 21.

  1g. *M. a. biedermanni* ♂. Large, ups ground-colour bright fulvous, black discal spots prominent.

  1h. *M. a. celadussa* f. *nevadensis* ♂. Ups ground-colour pale orange-yellow, black markings thin.

2. Melitaea diamina *False Heath Fritillary*   118

Unh orange lunules of the submarginal band each enclose a small round spot; marginal line orange on both wings.

  2a. *M. d. diamina* ♂. Ups black markings heavy; uph base and discal areas black.

  2b. *M. d. diamina* ♀. Ups postdiscal and marginal spots usually pale.

  2c. *M. d. vernetensis* ♀. Like *M. athalia*, but ups without dark suffusion; unh marginal line pale, yellowish, but submarginal dark spots usually distinct.

3. Mellicta varia *Grisons Fritillary*   122

Upf discal black mark in space 1b. almost vertical (oblique in *M. parthenoides*); unf postdiscal area unmarked. ♀ ups often suffused grey.

  3a. *M. varia* f. *piana* ♂. Large, upf postdiscal markings present; unh discal band very pale.

  3b. *M. varia* ♂. Smaller, ups postdiscal areas unmarked; unh discal band yellowish (or white).

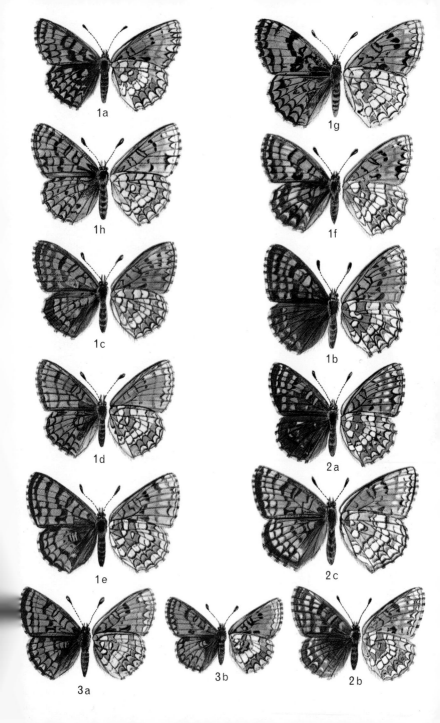

1a

1g

1h

1f

1c

1b

1d

2a

1e

2c

3a

3b

2b

PLATE 26

1. **Euphydryas aurinia** *Marsh Fritillary* 127
   Unf markings obscure, lacking black discal spots; unh submarginal
   band with a black spot in each space; unh margins pale; fringes not
   chequered. Sexes alike. ♀ larger. Very variable.

   1a. *E. a. debilis* f. *glaciegenita* ♂. Ups heavily suffused dark grey.
   1b. *E. a. debilis* ♂. Small; ups brightly marked in orange-red on
   yellowish ground-colour, black markings heavy.
   1c. *E. a. debilis* ♀. Like ♂ but larger.
   1d. *E. a. aurinia* ♂. Ups yellow with orange-brown bands and spots.
   black markings reduced and lacking dusky suffusion.
   1e. *E. a. aurinia* ♀. Ups pale yellow with reddish bands and spots;
   black markings increased.
   1f. *E. a. beckeri* ♂. Large, hw submarginal band wide with large
   black spots.

2. **Euphydryas iduna** *Lapland Fritillary* 127
   ♂. Ups ground-colour pale yellowish with orange-red spots and
   bands; hw sub-marginal band lacks black spots. Sexes similar.

3. **Euphydryas desfontainii** *Spanish Fritillary* 131
   E. d. baetica f. *zapateri* ♂. Like *E. aurinia* but unf black discal spots
   prominent.
   For ♀ see **Plate 22**.

4. **Euphydryas cynthia** *Cynthia's Fritillary* 126
   Unh marginal line orange; submarginal band includes small black
   spots.

   4a. *E. cynthia* ♂. Ups white with red spots and black markings.
   4b. *E. c. alpicola* ♀. Ups red-brown, spots and bands little or not at
   all darker; unh pale discal band includes fine black cross-lines
   in spaces 5, 6, 7; unf pale marginal lunules in regular series.

5. **Euphydryas maturna** *Scarce Fritillary* 125
   ♂. Ups black markings heavy; ground-colour red with prominent
   bands and small pale spots; unf pale marginal lunules irregular; unh
   marginal line orange. Sexes similar.

6. **Euphydryas intermedia** *Asian Fritillary* 125
   E. i. wolfensbergeri ♀. Ups like *E. cynthia* ♀; unh pale postdiscal
   band includes a fine black line running from costa to anal angle,
   marginal line orange. Sexes similar.

Similar species. *E. pharte* below, upf without pupils in red pd spots; *E. claudina* p. 159, unh with series of minute white pd spots; *E. christi* below, upf red pd band not constricted in s3, unh pd area distinctly paler; *E. eriphyle* p. 158, unh a round red spot always present in s4; *E. sudetica* p. 168 and *E. melampus* p. 167, both with orange submarginal spots on unh.

EREBIA SEROTINA   *Descimon's Ringlet*
Range. Only known from the Central Pyrenees at Cauterets.   Map 160

E. serotina Descimon and de Lesse 1953   TL: Cauterets   Pl. 44
Description. ♂fw 21/22 mm., resembles *E. epiphron fauveaui*, with three or four ocelli on upf of which the *apical pair have small white pupils*; uph with three or four small submarginal ocelli, red-ringed and sometimes with *white pupils*; unf red pd band clearly defined; unh basal area dark brown with a paler pd band which recalls *E. aethiopella*. The ♀ is not known.
Flight. September.
Habitat. All known specimens have been taken at about 3,000 ft.
Distribution. Near Cauterets in the Hautes Pyrénées. About twenty specimens, all males, are known. The rarity and unusual flight period of this insect are most difficult to explain. It may be a hybrid.

EREBIA CHRISTI   *Raetzer's Ringlet*
Range. Confined to S. Alps of Switzerland.   Map 161

E. christi Raetzer 1890   TL: Laquintal, Simplon   Pl. 38
Description. ♂fw 18/20 mm., resembles *E. epiphron*, upf *red pd band not constricted in s3*, crossed by dark veins, enclosing two to four black oval subapical dots in a straight row, the band of even width but slightly variable in extent; uph generally with three slightly oval red-ringed black dots; unh paler, with *vague grey-brown pd area without ocelli* or rarely with two or three small dark dots. ♀ all markings paler, upf pd band orange-yellow, wider; uph oval submarginal dots ringed fulvous; unh light brown, with paler pd area, sometimes a vague darker discal band.
Flight. End June/July.
Habitat. Grassy places among rocks at 4,500–6,000 ft. Larval food plant *Festuca ovina*.
Distribution. S. Switzerland, Simplon Pass, Laquintal, Alpien, Hossaz Alp, Zwischbergental, Eggen. Colonies very restricted.
Similar species. *E. epiphron aetheria* p. 163.

EREBIA PHARTE   *Blind Ringlet*
G: Unpunktierter Mohrenfalter
Range. Confined to European Alps and Tatra Mts.   Map 162

E. pharte pharte Huebner 1804 TL: Alps of Switzerland Pl. 38
Description. ♂fw 17/19mm., upf narrow red pd band of even rectangular spots continued on uph as a series of smaller rounded spots well separated; markings repeated on uns; *red spots are without black pupils or ocelli on either surface.* ♀ups gc paler, brownish-grey; uns suffused yellow.
Flight. July.
Habitat. Moist alpine meadows from 5,500 ft. upwards. Larval food plants unknown.
Distribution. Alps of Savoie, Valais, Vosges and N. Switzerland.
Note. The form illustrated in Huebner's original figure, of moderate size and with well-developed markings, occupies a central position on the cline of variation.

E. pharte eupompa Fruhstorfer 1918 TL: Schliersee and Tegernsee,
Bavaria Pls. 38, 44
  syn: *fasciata* Spuler 1901 (invalid homonym)
Description. ♂fw 19/20mm., large, brightly marked, upf pd band orange-red. ♀ups paler yellow-brown, pd bands and spots yellow.
Flight and **Habitat** as for *E. p. pharte.*
Distribution. Eastern Alps, Bavaria, Styria, Julian Alps, Tatra Mts.

E. pharte phartina Staudinger 1894 TL: Central Alps Pl. 44
Description. ♂fw 16/17mm., small, ups red markings greatly reduced, sometimes absent.
Flight and **Habitat** as for *E. p. pharte*, rarely seen below 6,000 ft.
Distribution. High mountains from the Dauphiné to the Gross Glockner, very typical at Pontresina, Guarda, Misurina and other localities in the Dolomites.
Variation. In all localities *E. pharte* is very variable in size and markings.
Similar species. *E. epiphron* p. 162.

EREBIA MELAMPUS *Lesser Mountain Ringlet*
G: Kleiner Mohrenfalter
Range. Confined to Alps of C. Europe. Map 163

E. melampus Fuessli 1775 TL: Switzerland Pl. 37
Description. ♂fw 15/18mm., upf red band narrow but extending from s1b–s6, crossed by dark veins and enclosing small black spots in s4, 5; uph two to four round red pd spots each enclosing a small black point, *spot in s3 displaced slightly outwards* and out of line with other spots in series, spot in s4 largest; uns pattern as on ups. ♀ similar, ups gc paler, uns often suffused yellow.
Flight. End June/July/August.
Habitat. Alpine valleys from 3,500 ft. upwards to over 6,000 ft., flying on grassy slopes and meadows. Larval food plants grasses, esp. *Poa annua.*

Distribution. Graian and Cottian Alps to Savoie and through Switzerland and N. Italian Alps to Dolomites, Styria and Carinthia. More local and scarce in Basses Alpes, S. Bavaria, N. Tirol and Lower Austria. Absent from Pyrenees, Apennines, Carpathians, Balkans, Jura and Vosges.

Variation. At higher altitudes often small, larger at lower altitudes. Additional black spots are sometimes present on upf.

Similar species. *E. eriphyle* p. 158; *E. sudetica* below. *E. claudina* p. 159, unh with series of minute white pd spots.

EREBIA SUDETICA   *Sudeten Ringlet*
Range. Confined to Europe.   Map 164

E. sudetica sudetica   Staudinger 1861   TL: Silesian Mts.   Pl. 37
Description. ♂fw 16/17mm., resembles *E. melampus* but uph with four to five red pd spots in regular series and *unh six spots conspicuously regular* and well graded, spot in s3 often largest, each spot usually enclosing a small black point. ♀ups gc slightly paler, otherwise similar.
Flight. July.
Habitat. Grassy places among woodland at 2–4,000 ft. Larval food plants not known.
Distribution. Altvater Mt., Carpathians, Retezat Mts.

E. sudetica liorana   de Lesse 1947   TL: Cantal, C. France   Pl. 37
Description. Resembles *E. s. sudetica* but markings less bright; uph series of red pd spots often reduced to four spots; unh four or five spots only, but the regular graded character of series fully maintained.
Flight and **Habitat** as for *E.s. sudetica*.
Distribution. France, in Massif Central, e.g. Lozère, Le Lioran, Puy-de-Dôme, etc. Another colony with markings even more reduced exists near Grindelwald in the Bernese Oberland of Switzerland.

Similar species. *E. melampus* p. 167, unh pd spots usually two to four in number, not regularly graded, spot in s3 displaced slightly distad, spot in s4 noticeably the largest. A black-centred small fulvous pd spot on upf in s6 is common in *E. sudetica*, rare in *E. melampus*.

EREBIA AETHIOPS   *Scotch Argus*

F: Le Grand Nègre   G: Mohrenfalter

Range. From W. Europe through Asia Minor, Urals and Caucasus to Sajan Mts.   Map 165

E. aethiops   Esper 1777   TL: S. Germany   Pls. 39, 44

Description. ♂fw 22/26mm., upf gc black, a conspicuous sex-brand from inner margin to s5 (6), pd band bright red, often constricted at s3 and enclosing white-pupilled ocelli in s2, 4, 5; uph with small white-pupilled pd ocelli in s2, 3, 4 (5), red-ringed or enclosed in red pd band; *unh* dark red-brown, pd band pale greyish with *minute white points in s2–4*. ♀ups gc paler brown, upf pd band orange or yellow; uph three or four larger red-ringed ocelli; unh yellow-brown, often with darker discal band defined by paler yellowish basal and pd areas; fringes slightly chequered light and dark brown.

Flight. August/September.

Habitat. In hilly districts, generally among coniferous trees from 1–6,000 ft. or more, exceptionally at sea-level on sand-dunes near Ostend. Larval food plants various grasses, including *Molinia caerulea*, *Agropyron*, etc.

Distribution. France, in woodlands, etc., in NE., also Auvergne, Cevennes (?), Jura and Vosges; Belgian Ardennes. From Hautes Alpes (Gap) northwards to Haute Savoie and throughout central Alps. N. England, Scotland, mountainous districts of Germany, Silesia, Baltic coast, Lithuania, Carpathians and Balkans. Italy, in Ligurian Apennines and Apuane Alps but absent from peninsular Italy. Absent from Pyrenees, Denmark, Fennoscandia, Greece.

Variation. Size is variable. A small race, f. *caledonia* Verity ♂fw 21/22mm. Pls. 39, 44, flies in S. Scotland and elsewhere at high altitudes. Large races are common on southern alpine slopes, ♂fw 23/26 mm. In ♀unh pale pd band varies in colour from yellow-buff to violet-grey, ♀ f. *violacea* Wheeler Pl. 39.

EREBIA TRIARIA *de Prunner's Ringlet*

G: Alpen-Mohrenfalter
Range. Confined to Europe.   Map 166

E. triaria triaria de Prunner 1798   TL: Exilles, Piedmont   Pl. 39
  syn: *evias* Godart 1823

Description. ♂fw 23/25mm., upf red pd band wide near costa, tapering towards anal angle, enclosing white-pupilled ocelli in s2–6, the small ocellus in s6 nearly constant; uph three or four ocelli enclosed in red pd band or widely ringed red; *unh* gc very dark, *obscurely irrorated grey*, with darker discal band. ♀upf pd band orange-red; unh gc and markings lighter, discal band better defined.

Flight. End May/June/July.

Habitat. Flies on open grassy slopes at 3–7,000 ft. often near tree-line. Larval food plants unknown.

Distribution. Very localised in scattered colonies. Portugal, Serra da Gerez. Spain, Cantabrian Mts., Guadarrama and Pyrenees. France, in Pyrenees, Vaucluse, Basses and Hautes Alpes. Switzerland, widely distributed in southern Alps, Simplon, Albula, Ofen Pass, etc. Austria. Italy, Alto Adige, Trentino. Yugoslavia, in Julian Alps, Hercegovina, Montenegro. Albania.

E. triaria hispanica Gumppenberg 1888 TL: Teruel
Description. ♂fw 22/24mm., small, ups pd bands yellowish and ocelli small. ♀ups gc paler; unh dark discal band usually well defined.
Flight. End May/June.
Habitat. On grassy slopes at 4–5,000 ft.
Distribution. Spain, in provinces of Logroño, Teruel and Cuenca, e.g. Sierra Alta near Albarracin, Canales.
Variation. The form from the Sierra de Guadarrama resembles *E. t. triaria* rather than *E.t. hispanica*, as does the large form that flies in the Picos de Europa and at Pajares.
Similar species. *E. meolans* p. 198, ♂unh black, nearly unmarked.

EREBIA EMBLA *Lapland Ringlet*
Sw: Gulringad Gräsfjäril

Range. Arctic Europe, Siberia to Altai Mts., Sajan Mts. and Kamschatka without notable variation.   Map 167

E. embla Thunberg 1791 TL: Västerbotten, Sweden   Pl. 38
Description. ♂fw 25/26mm., upf with large twin apical ocelli, often blind, small ocelli in s2, 3, rarely also in 1b, all ringed tawny-yellow; *uph* smaller *yellow-ringed ocelli in s*2–4 (5); unh brown with paler grey pd area, small white mark on costa and in s4, fringes slightly chequered. ♀ups gc and markings paler.
Flight. End May/June.
Habitat. On moorlands or among sparse pine trees, from 500–1,500 ft. Larval food plants unknown.
Distribution. Fennoscandia, from 60°N to North Cape, rather local, most common in S. Finland. Also recorded in Latvia.
Similar species. *E. disa* below, in which uph ocelli are absent.

EREBIA DISA *Arctic Ringlet*
Sw: Disas Gräsfjäril

Range. Arctic Europe, Sajan Mts., Irkutsk, Yakutsk, Yablonoi Mts. and arctic N. America in Alaska, Yukon, British Columbia and Alberta, circumpolar.   Map 168

E. disa Thunberg 1791 TL: Lapland   Pl. 38
Description. ♂fw 23/25mm., upf resembles *E. embla* but all four ocelli are approximately equal in size, ringed tawny and sometimes fused into a pd band; *uph brown, without ocelli*; unh grey, with wide dark brown discal band; fringes chequered grey and brown. ♀ resembles ♂, ups gc sometimes paler brown; unh markings well defined with increased contrast.
Flight. June/early July, according to season.

Habitat. Wet moorland and bogs, in Europe usually a lowland insect, sometimes at sea-level. Larval food plants not known.

Distribution. Fennoscandia, not south of 64°N, most common near coast and in far north, e.g. Saltdalen, Inari, Petsamo.

Similar species. *E. embla* p. 170.

EREBIA MEDUSA *Woodland Ringlet*

F: Le Franconien G: Blutgrasfalter

Range. Europe and Asia Minor.   Map 169

E. medusa medusa Schiffermueller 1775 TL: Vienna   Pl. 40

Description. ♂ fw 21/24 mm., upf white-pupilled ocelli in s4, 5 widely ringed tawny yellow and a smaller ocellus in s2, together making an incomplete band interrupted at v3, additional small ocelli in s1b and 6 in some specimens; uph three or four small ocelli ringed yellowish; *unh gc paler uniform brown* with four or five white-pupilled ocelli, otherwise unmarked. ♀ ups gc paler brown, markings orange-yellow, often larger, more or less confluent.

Flight. May/June.

Habitat. Moorlands, damp meadows and light woodland, in northern range often a lowland species, but flying to 4,000 ft. in hill country. Larval food plants grasses, esp. *Digitaria sanguinale* and *Milium effusum*.

Distribution. Belgian Ardennes. NE. France to Paris, Jura and Vosges, and southwards to Dijon, Savoy and Basses Alpes. Switzerland, in Geneva district. Italy, Susa in Piedmont, Etruscan Apennines. Poland, recorded from Baltic coast at Szczecin (Stettin) and Gdansk (Danzig) to 58°N. Germany, except in north-west. Austria. Czechoslovakia. Yugoslavia. Greece. Absent from W. France, Pyrenees, SW. Alps, peninsular Italy and Mediterranean islands.

Variation. Typical *E. medusa*, which flies at moderate altitudes near Vienna, occupies an intermediate position on the cline of variation in size and wing-markings. The two extreme forms are described below.

E. medusa psodea Huebner 1804 TL: Hungary   Pl. 44

Description. ♂ fw 23/25 mm., ups markings brighter, orange-yellow, often confluent; uns similar, gc smooth rather pale brown. Characters usually best marked in ♀, ocelli larger and orange-yellow areas more extensive, often six large ocelli and gc quite pale.

Flight and Habitat as for *E. m. medusa*, but flies to 5,000 ft. in Carpathians.

Distribution. Especially in E. Europe in favourable habitats. Hungary and Rumania in Carpathians, with tendency to smaller brightly marked races at high altitudes. Yugoslavia (very variable). Bulgaria. Often transitional to *E. m. medusa*, with which it blends insensibly farther west.

PLATE 27

1. Melanargia galathea   *Marbled White*   132
Upf discoidal cell lacks a black cross bar.

1a. *M. g. galathea* f. *procida* ♂. Ups ground-colour yellowish, black
    markings very heavy and extensive.

1b. *M. g. galathea* ♀. Ups ground-colour milk-white, black markings
    greatly reduced; unh grey discal band wide on costa, ground-
    colour yellowish.

1c. *M. g. lachesis* ♂. Ups black markings further reduced, uph discal
    markings vestigial; unh grey discal band narrow on costa. See
    also Pl. 28.

2. Melanargia arge   *Italian Marbled White*   136
♂. Upf with short incomplete cell-bar; unh veins lined black, a curved
black line in space 1b.

3. Melanargia russiae   *Esper's Marbled White*   133
Upf cell-bar irregular, complete; uph with conspicuous white basal
spot; ♀ unh markings yellowish or brown.

3a. *M. r. cleanthe* ♂. Large, ups black markings not heavy.

3b. *M. r. japygia* ♂. Smaller, ups black markings heavy and ex-
    tensive.

4. Melanargia ines   *Spanish Marbled White*   136
Ups cell-bar wide; unh veins black, no curved line in space 1b.
♀ unh yellowish.

4a. *M. i. ines* ♂. Ups black markings moderately heavy.

4b. *M. i. jehandezi* ♂. Ups black markings heavy and extensive.

1a   1b

1c   2

3a   4a

3b   4b

1b   1a

2b   2c

3b   2a

3a   2a

4

5   6

PLATE 28

E. medusa hippomedusa Ochsenheimer 1820   TL: Styria   PI. 40
Description. ♂fw 19/21 mm., ups gc dark brown to black, markings great-ly reduced, in extreme examples only two small subapical ocelli on upf, three on uph, all narrowly ringed orange-red; unh gc dark grey-brown. ♀ similar.
Flight. June/July.
Habitat. In mountains at high altitudes, usually near tree-line at 5–6,000 ft.
Distribution. In southern and eastern Alps and Balkans, Dolomites, Monte Baldo.
Variation. Still small but rather more brightly marked in Ticino (Fusio), Styria, Carinthia, Bosnia, S. Carpathians.

Similar species. *E. oeme* p. 195, usually smaller, ocelli ringed fulvous-red (yellowish in *medusa*), their pupils gleaming white; antennae in *oeme* tipped black (brown in *medusa*). *E. alberganus* below, small specimens of f. *caradjae* may resemble *hippomedusa*, but ocellar rings are oval. *E. polaris* below.

EREBIA POLARIS   *Arctic Woodland Ringlet*

Sw: Högnordisk Gräsfjäril
Range. Lapland, probably across boreal Asia to Lena River.   Map 170

E. polaris Staudinger 1871   TL: Lapland   PI. 40
Description. ♂fw 20/22 mm., ups gc dark brown; upf with small white-pupilled ocelli in s4, 5, often with additional small pd ocelli or fulvous spots in s2, 3; uph one to three fulvous-ringed submarginal ocelli; unf as above; *unh pd area faintly paler.* ♀ups gc slightly paler; uph ocelli often more numerous; unf brown to red-brown with brown outer margin, ocelli ringed paler; unh pale grey-brown, pd band better defined, usually enclosing ocelli.
Flight. End June/July.
Habitat. Lightly wooded valleys and hillsides from sea-level to 1,000 ft. Larval food plant unknown.
Distribution. Scandinavia, Porsanger, Utsjoki, Kautokeino, etc., not south of 68°N.

Similar species. *E. medusa hippomedusa* above, unh lacks the pale pd band There is no similar butterfly in the high north. The characters given above will distinguish *E. polaris* from specimens of *E. medusa* that lack data

EREBIA ALBERGANUS   *Almond-eyed Ringlet*

G: Gelbäugiger Mohrenfalter
Range. Confined to Europe.   Map 17

E. alberganus alberganus de Prunner 1798   TL: Piedmont   PI. 4
   syn: *ceto* Huebner 1804
Description. ♂fw 20/22 mm., ups dark brown, pd bands represented b

series of *orange-red lanceolate spots*, which enclose ocelli with minute white pupils, in s2, 4, 5 upf and s1–5 uph, additional ocelli often present on fw; uns the same pattern is repeated. ♀ups resembles ♂, uns gc yellowish-brown, pd spots often pale yellow, with markings as in ♂.

Flight. Late June/July.

Habitat. Alpine meadows at 3–6,000 ft. Larval food plants grasses, *Poa annua*, *Festuca*, etc.

Distribution. Alpes Maritimes to Savoie, Valais, Engadine, Dolomites, Oetztal, Hohe Tauern and locally in Apennines. In Switzerland rare and local north of the Rhône valley.

Variation. At 6–7,000 ft. in Engadine, Savoie, etc., very small, ♂fw 18/20mm., all orange markings greatly reduced, f. *caradjae* Caflisch, development of markings on ups very variable in many localities. On southern slopes of western Alps often large with very brilliant orange markings, f. *tyrsus* Fruhstorfer Pl. 42.

E. alberganus phorcys Freyer 1836 TL: Turkey (Bulgaria) Pl. 42
Description. ♂fw 23mm., ups orange markings extended; unh lanceolate spots long, pale yellow to white. ♀ similar.

Flight. Early July.

Habitat. Open woodland at 3,000 ft.

Distribution. Bulgaria, near Karlovo in Balkan Mts., not recorded elsewhere.

Similar species. *E. oeme* p. 195 and *E. medusa* p. 173.

EREBIA PLUTO *Sooty Ringlet*

G: Eismohrenfalter

Range. Confined to the Alps. Map 172

E. pluto pluto de Prunner 1798 TL: Val Varodisiana, Piedmont Pl. 41
syn: *belzebub* Costa 1839
Description. ♂fw 22/25mm., ups *velvet-black, unmarked*; unf margin of discal area sometimes indicated by a darker shade, pd area with faint deep-chestnut flush; ♀ similar, ups paler, unf with broad chestnut-brown pd band which may extend to base; unh basal area grey-brown, pd area paler.

Flight. End June/July/August.

Habitat. On stony screes and moraines from 6–9,000 ft. Larval food plants grasses, esp. *Poa annua*.

Distribution. Alpes Maritimes and through Cottian and Graian Alps northwards to Savoie, where it occurs mixed with *E. p. oreas*; also in Bernese Oberland (Dent de Morcles), Todi Group, W. Dolomites, Triglav massif and in the Abruzzi on Gran Sasso, Monte Rotondo and perhaps elsewhere.

PLATE 29

1. Hipparchia fagi   *Woodland Grayling*   137
Large, fw over 33 mm.;

   1a. *H. fagi* ♂. Upf densely suffused grey-brown; uph postdiscal pale
      band obscure.

   1b. *H. fagi* ♀. Upf pale postdiscal band better defined; uph white
      postdiscal band wide.

2. Hipparchia alcyone   *Rock Grayling*   138
Like *H. fagi* but smaller, fw 33 mm. or less, variable.

   2a. *H. a. alcyone* ♂. Ups like *H. fagi* but pale postdiscal bands
      yellowish and better defined.

   2b. *H. a. alcyone* ♀. Ups pale postdiscal bands well defined, yellowish
      on fw, white on hw.

   2c. *H. a. syriaca* ♂. Fw apex pointed, markings as in *H. fagi* ♂.
Note. It is not always possible to distinguish between *H. fagi* and
H. alcyone without dissection. See comparative table, p. 137.

3. Hipparchia ellena   *Algerian Grayling*   139
Like *H. alcyone*; ups postdiscal bands white and well-defined; uns
dark basal areas make strong contrast with white postdiscal bands.

   3a. *H. ellena* ♂. Fw apex pointed.

   3b. *H. ellena* ♀. Fw apex more rounded; postdiscal markings better
      developed; upf with ocellus in space 2.

1a

1b

2c

2a

3a

2b

3b

2d

3c

2e

PLATE 30

E. pluto alecto   Huebner 1804   TL: Lermoos, Bavaria   Pl. 41
Description. ♂fw 24/25mm., ups resembles *E. p. pluto* but *upf with white-pupilled ocelli in s*4, 5; unf reddish pd area usually present. ♀upf often with traces of red suffusion in pd area.
Flight and **Habitat** as for *E.p. pluto.*
Distribution. Widely distributed in the central and north-central Alps, but often with transitional characters towards other forms of the species complex. Most characteristic in the Allgäuer Alps, Bavarian Alps, Karwendel Alps and Dolomites. In Ortler Alps ups red pd bands usually broad, f. *velocissima* Fruhstorfer Pl. 41.

E. pluto nicholli   Oberthur 1896   TL: Campiglio, Brenta Alps
Description. ♂fw 20/23mm., ups sooty-black; upf dense black white-pupilled pd ocelli in s2–s5, usually small in s2, 3; uph similar ocelli in s2, 3, 4; uns black, markings as on ups. ♀ slightly larger; ups white-pupilled ocelli larger, often set in indistinct narrow brown pd bands; unf disc red-brown, outer margin and unh grey-brown to sooty-black, ocelli as on ups.
Flight and **Habitat** as for *E. p. pluto.*
Distribution. N. Italy (Trentino). Restricted to Alps of Brenta Group north of Lake Garda, also on Monte Baldo, with markings especially constant and well developed.
Variation. Farther north ocelli become less numerous with transitional forms blending with *E. p. alecto.*

E. pluto oreas   Warren 1933   TL: Chamonix, Savoie   Pl. 41
    syn: *glacialis* Esper 1804 (invalid homonym)
Description. ♂fw 21/24mm., ups gc very dark silky brown to black without ocelli; upf with *wide reddish pd band*; uph with or without broken red-brown pd band; unf pd band brighter with red flush to base; unh black, unmarked. ♀ups gc and markings paler and better defined; unf wholly reddish except margins; unh basal area brown with paler grey-brown pd band.
Flight and **Habitat** as for *E. p. pluto.*
Distribution. From Haute Savoie eastwards through Pennine Alps, Ticino and Grisons to the Albula Pass and Pontresina, also northwards in mountains of Upper Engadine. Farther east commonly transitional to *E.p. pluto* or *E.p. alecto.*

Similar species. *E. lefebvrei astur* and *pyrenaea* p. 188 and *E. melas* p. 187, none of which occurs in the Alps; unf not flushed chestnut-brown.

EREBIA GORGE *Silky Ringlet*
Range. Confined to Europe.   Map 17?

E. gorge gorge   Huebner 1804   TL: Switzerland and Tirol   Pl. 3?
Description. ♂fw 17/20mm., upf with inconspicuous sex-brand in s1–3, re?

pd band with gleaming texture, wide, enclosing two subapical ocelli; uph pd band narrower, sometimes with small submarginal ocelli; unf red with dark grey marginal border; *unh* variable, usually *marbled light and dark grey*, often with dark discal band. ♀ups gc and pd bands lighter in tone, unh gc paler, discal band more sharply defined.

Flight. End June/July.

Habitat. Moraines and rocky slopes from 5,000 ft. upwards. Larval food plants grasses.

Distribution. E. Pyrenees, Savoie, Pennine and Bernese Alps, Tirol, Styria, Carinthia. Reported from Albania and Bulgaria.

Variation. Large races with ♂fw 19/20mm., f. *gigantea* Oberthur, occur in the Cantabrian Mts., Allgauer Alps and Tatra Mts., apical ocelli usually small. Pl. 37.

E. gorge ramondi Oberthur 1909 TL: Gavarnie, Hautes Pyrénées Pls. 37, 44
Description. ♂fw 17/20mm., differs from *E. g. gorge* in having four to five well-formed white-pupilled ocelli on both surfaces of hw. Occasional specimens with triple apical ocelli on upf are not distinguishable from *E. g. triopes*.
Flight and **Habitat** as for *E.g. gorge*.
Distribution. Basses Pyrénées and eastwards to Andorra.

E. gorge triopes Speyer 1865 TL: Bernina Pass Pl. 37
Description. ♂fw 17/18mm., resembles *E. g. ramondi*, but upf ocelli in s4, 5, 6 conjoined, often nearly equal in size, forming a striking apical row, additional ocelli in s2, 3 may be present; uph three or four well-formed submarginal ocelli usually present near the outer border of the red pd band. ♀ similar.
Flight and **Habitat** as for *E. g. gorge*.
Distribution. Preponderates in Ortler group in Upper Engadine, Sulden, Pontresina, Monte Baldo. Occasional examples occur elsewhere in eastern Alps, Dolomites, etc. Rare in W. Alps.
Variation. Specimens with twin apical ocelli on upf, indistinguishable from *E.g. ramondi*, are not very uncommon.

E. gorge erynis Esper 1805 TL: Chamonix, Haute Savoie Pl. 44
Description. Differs from *E. g. gorge* in the absence of twin apical ocelli on upf, though occasional specimens occur with vestigial ocelli.
Flight and **Habitat** as for *E.g. gorge*.
Distribution. Alpes Maritimes, Basses Alpes. Abruzzi and Monte Sibillini.
Variation. Italian specimens are small, with unh very dark and obscurely marked, f. *carboncina* Verity Pl. 37.

In France the racial character of *E.g. erynis* is marked in the Maritimes and Basses Alpes with about 90% entirely without upf apical ocelli and the remaining 10% with one or two small ocelli, unlike *E.g. gorge*. North

of the Basses Alpes the incidence of *gorge*-forms increases to about 50%
in Savoy. In Switzerland *erynis*-forms are not rare in the Pennine and
Bernese Alps, and occasional eastwards to Pontresina.

Similar species. *E. aethiopella* below, resembles *E. gorge*, unh brown,
markings in regular bands, ocelli always small, frequents alpine meadows;
E. gorgone p. 181, larger, darker, unf deep chestnut, confined to Pyrenees;
E. mnestra p. 181, unh medium brown, almost unmarked.

EREBIA AETHIOPELLA *False Mnestra Ringlet*
Range. Confined to Europe.   Map 174

E. aethiopella aethiopella Hoffmannsegg 1806 TL: Piedmont   Pl. 37
  syn: *gorgophone* Bellier 1863
Description. ♂fw 18/20mm., with conspicuous sex-brand in s1a to 4, red
pd band wide, often extending to cell-end, with or (rarely) without small
white-pupilled ocelli in s4, 5; uph pd band wide on costa, tapering to s2,
ocelli absent; *unh rich brown with paler pd band,* the whole densely irrorated
with white scales in northern range, less so in Alpes Maritimes. ♀ups gc
paler brown, pd bands orange-red; upf ocelli constant, often larger; unh
brightly marked, gc grey or yellow-brown, paler at base, pale pd band conspicuous.
Flight. July/August.
Habitat. Grass slopes at 6,000 ft. or more. Larval food plants not known.
Distribution. Alpes Maritimes and northwards to Cottian Alps and Mont
Genèvre.

E. aethiopella rhodopensis   Nicholl 1900   TL: Rhodope Mts., Bulgaria
                                                            Pl. 37
Description. ♂fw 19/20mm., resembles *E. a. aethiopella*; upf apical ocelli
larger and small ocellus in s2; uph three submarginal ocelli; unh ocelli
very small or absent. ♀ups dark basal areas well defined; upf pd bands
orange-red; uph submarginal ocelli larger; unh markings much brighter,
brown and yellow-grey with paler irroration and marbling, submarginal
ocelli usually present but small.
Flight and **Habitat** as for *E.a. aethiopella*.
Distribution. Bulgaria. Stara Planina, Pirin Mts., Rilo and Rhodope Mts.
Variation. A slightly smaller brighter form, f. *sharsta* Higgins, with unh
grey and prominent white irroration, occurs in the Schar Planina, S.
Yugoslavia. The distribution of this species and its forms corresponds
closely with that of *Boloria graeca* Staudinger.

Similar species. *E. mnestra* p. 181, often slightly larger, upf ♂ sex-brand
inconspicuous, uph the red band shorter and more broken; unh markings
generally obscure in both sexes; range overlaps that of *E. aethiopella* in
the Hautes Alpes near Mont Genèvre; *E. gorge* p. 178.

EREBIA MNESTRA   *Mnestra's Ringlet*
G: Blindpunkt-Mohrenfalter
Range. Confined to central Alps of Europe.   Map 175

E. mnestra   Huebner 1804   TL: Swiss Alps   Pl. 37
Description. ♂fw 17/19mm., sex-brand very faint and inconspicuous; upf a broad red pd band extending in s4, 5 to cell-end, sometimes enclosing minute subapical twin ocelli; uph pd band narrow, broken, usually restricted to s3, 4, 5, without enclosed ocelli, sometimes vestigial; unf red with brown marginal border; *unh chestnut-brown, unmarked or (rarely) with vague paler pd band.* ♀upf twin white-pupilled subapical ocelli rarely absent, sometimes very small; uph with or without pd ocelli; unh paler brown, sparsely irrorated with white scales, mostly concentrated along veins and in pd band which is well defined in this way.
Flight. July.
Habitat. Grass slopes at 5,500–7,000 ft.
Distribution. France, in Isère, Savoie, Hte Savoie, Htes Alpes and eastwards through Switzerland (excepting NW.) to the Ortler, Oetztal and Adamello groups, and northwards to Allgäuer Alps, Salzburg Alps and Karwendel Mts. Recorded from High Tatra Mts. Colonies are mostly very localised and not too common.
Variation. There is individual variation in the presence or absence of ocelli, etc., but no local races have been described.
Similar species. *E. aethiopella* p. 180; *E. gorge* p. 178.

EREBIA GORGONE   *Gavarnie Ringlet*
Range. Confined to Pyrenees.   Map 176

E. gorgone   Boisduval 1833   TL: Pyrenees   Pl. 40
Description. ♂fw 20/21mm., sex-brand in s1a to 5 prominent; *ups very dark*; upf pd band dark mahogany-red enclosing twin apical ocelli and small ocellus in s2; uph red pd band in s2–4, divided by dark veins, each red mark enclosing a small ocellus; *unf dark red-brown* with brown marginal border; unh dark brown with obscure paler pd band, ocelli vestigial if present. ♀ups gc paler brown, pd band also paler; unf paler with orange-brown discal area and grey marginal border; unh gc speckled dark grey-brown, veins lined pale buff, pd area pale buff, ocelli if present very small, brown marginal markings irregular.
Flight. July/August.
Habitat. Grass slopes at 6–8,000 ft.
Distribution. Pyrenees, Puy de Carlitte (Lac Lanoux) and westwards through Ariège and Hautes Pyrénées to Luchon, Gavarnie and Basses Pyrénées.
Similar species. *E. gorge ramondi* p. 179

EREBIA EPISTYGNE *Spring Ringlet*
Range. Confined to SW. Europe.   Map 177

E. epistygne epistygne Huebner 1824   TL: not stated (Provence) Pl. 40
Description. ♂fw 22/25mm., *upf a small area in cell and all pd band
yellow-buff,* ocelli in s4–6 fused into a conspicuous row and small ocelli
often present in s2–3; uph four or five submarginal ocelli each broadly
ringed red; unf very dark brown, often reddish in cell and in pd area; unh
with dark discal band, basal and pd areas mottled paler grey-brown. ♀ups
markings slightly paler; unh basal and pd areas much marbled and
irrorated brown on grey or yellow-grey, and veins conspicuously lined
yellow-buff.
Flight. End March/April.
Habitat. Rough places and woodland clearings among low hills at 1,500–
3,000 ft. Larval food plant not recorded.
Distribution. France, in Alpes Maritimes, Basses Alpes, Var, Bouches du
Rhône, Hautes Alpes, Vaucluse, Gard, Hérault.

E. epistygne viriathus Sheldon 1913   TL: Losilla

Description. ♂fw 20/23mm., unf reddish suffusions more extensive, unh
gc paler brown, brightly marked.
Flight. May/June.
Habitat. At 4-5,000 ft.
Distribution. Spain, Teruel, Albarracin, Losilla, etc.

The Erebia tyndarus *group of species*

The six small species that form this group provide special features of
interest in their distribution and special difficulties in identification since
their wing-markings are very similar in all. The chromosome numbers
have been investigated by de Lesse and others and marked differences have
been found, confirming the existence in Europe of six distinct species.
Distribution patterns have been carefully checked, and it is found that, in
effect, only a single species occurs in any given locality. Flight places
rarely overlap, but the pattern is complicated especially in the Pyrenees
and western Alps. In some areas where an overlap appears on a map, it is
found that the species are separated by altitude. Individual variation can
be confusing, and it is not possible to define key characters for specific
identification by these alone, but with good data of place, date, altitude,
etc., confident identification is nearly always possible, especially if a series
of specimens is available. With the single exception of *E. ottomana*, the
species of this group are endemic Europeans. Closely allied species fly in
the Pontic Mts., in the Elburz, in C. Asia and in N. America.

EREBIA TYNDARUS *Swiss Brassy Ringlet*
G: Schillernder Mohrenfalter
Range. Confined to the Alps. Map 178

E. tyndarus Esper 1781 TL: Scheidegg, Switzerland Pl. 42
Description. ♂fw 17/18mm., apex blunt, gc dark brown with metallic greenish reflections, tawny pd band wide in s4, 5 and enclosing very small oblique twin subapical ocelli, but narrower below and extending to s2 or s1b, divided by brown cross veins, without additional ocelli; *uph without ocelli,* generally unmarked, small tawny spots occasional; uns apex of fw and all hw shining grey with bluish reflections in fresh specimens and brown striae, including a sinuous discal line across hw. ♀ similar, ups gc paler; upf subapical ocelli very small; uns apex of fw and all hw yellow-grey with brown markings.
Flight. July/August.
Habitat. High grassy slopes at 6,000 ft. or more.
Distribution. A restricted area in the central Alps from Val Ferret west of Mt. Blanc to the Oetztal, including Valais (Simplon), Oberland, Grisons, Engadine, Ortler, Brenner, Allgäuer Alps and Bergamasker Alps.
Variation. Specimens without upf ocelli are not rare in some districts, f. *caecodromus* Villiers and Guenée.
Similar species. *E. cassioides* below, a common species in the SW. Alps, can be distinguished by its more pointed fw with larger and less oblique subapical ocelli, pd tawny band usually short, rarely extending below s3 and white-pupilled ocelli present also on uph. The two species rarely fly together. *E. nivalis* p. 185.

EREBIA CASSIOIDES *Common Brassy Ringlet*
Range. Confined to Europe, from Cantabrian Mts. to Balkans. Map 179

E. cassioides cassioides Hohenwarth 1793 TL: Heilegenblut, Austria
Pl. 42
Description. ♂fw 16/19mm., resembles *E. tyndarus* but apex more pointed; *upf tawny band short,* rarely extending beyond v3 and not invading cell, enclosing larger white-pupilled twin subapical ocelli; *uph three pd ocelli,* well formed and white-pupilled, generally present, enclosed in tawny spots; unh grey, a darker discal band more or less clearly indicated by darker brown transverse lines. ♀ups gc and markings paler; upf pd band tawny-yellow; unh grey or yellow-grey irrorated with darker scales, sometimes with distinct darker discal band.
Flight. End June/July/August.
Habitat. Grass slopes at 5,500–6,000 ft. Larval food plants grasses.
Distribution. Widely distributed. France. Switzerland. Austria, Hohe and Niederer Tauern. Italy, Dolomites. Balkans, in S. Yugoslavia,

Albania and Pirin Mts. Rumania, Retezat Mts. Nearly every colony exhibits some minor racial peculiarity and many have been named.

E. cassioides arvernensis Oberthur 1908   TL: Mont Dore   Pl. 44
Description. Resembles *E. c. cassioides* very closely, slightly larger, upf subapical twin ocelli larger. ♀ unh usually distinctly yellowish.
Flight and Habitat as for *E.c. cassioides*.
Distribution. Auvergne, Mont Dore. Pyrenees, from Campcardos in the east to the Basses Pyrénées, but apparently absent between Salau and Gavarnie. Cantabrian Mts., Picos de Europa. Etruscan Apennines and Abruzzi.
Variation. External characters are not well marked, but the subspecies is of interest on account of its situation on mountains unconnected with the central Alps. The race of the central Pyrenees is referable to f. *pseudomurina* de Lesse Pl. 44.

Similar species. *E. tyndarus* p. 182; *E. nivalis* p. 185; *E. ottomana* p. 185.

EREBIA HISPANIA   *Spanish Brassy Ringlet*
Range. Confined to Spain and the Pyrenees.   Map 180

E. hispania hispania   Butler 1868   TL: Spain   Pl. 42
Description. ♂ fw 20/21mm., ups gc dark brown; *upf pd band orange-yellow*, wide in s 4–6, enclosing large twin ocelli, becoming rapidly narrower to s 1b or s 2; uph three smaller ocelli in fulvous spots; unh grey with rather indistinct discal line and other markings brownish. ♀ upf gc and markings in paler tones; uph markings vestigial or absent; unh grey to pale brown with transverse markings in darker brown more distinct.
Flight. End June/July.
Habitat. Stony slopes from 6,500 ft. upwards. Larval food plant not known.
Distribution. S. Spain on Sierra Nevada. Not recorded from central Sierras.

E. hispania rondoui   Oberthur 1908   TL: Cauterets, Hautes Pyrénées
                                                                  Pl. 42
Description. ♂ fw 17/19mm., smaller with fw shorter; upf pd orange band often wider; uph pd ocelli better developed; unh grey with darker discal and marginal bands often defined. ♀ uph orange submarginal markings and ocelli well developed.
Flight. July.
Habitat. Grassy slopes at 5–6,000 ft. or more.
Distribution. From Mt. Canigou in E. Pyrenees westwards to Basses Pyrénées.
Variation. In E. Pyrenees on French and Spanish slopes, often rather small and markings very brilliant, f. *goya* Fruhstorfer.

Note. *E. cassioides* and *E. h. rondoui* fly in contiguous areas but rarely occur together on the same ground.

EREBIA NIVALIS   *De Lesse's Brassy Ringlet*
Range. Confined to the Alps.   Map 181

E. nivalis   Lorkovic and de Lesse 1954   TL: Gross Glockner   Pl. 42
Description. ♂fw 15/17mm., resembles *E. tyndarus* with short square-cut fw; upf apical ocelli very small, scarcely oblique, with brilliant white pupils, pd band tawny, short, usually not beyond v3, but extending basad to cell-end in s4, 5; uph with or (generally) without small tawny blind pd spots; *unh with characteristic brilliant blue-grey* almost metallic lustre in fresh specimens. ♀unh also with bright silvery tone, veins paler.
Flight. July/August.
Habitat. Grass slopes at 7,000 ft. or over, flying about 1,000 ft. above *E. cassioides* often on the same mountain. Larval food plant not known.
Distribution. Austria, east of the Oetztal, including Hohe Tauern and Niederer Tauern. Switzerland, in a small area near Grindelwald (Faulhorn).

Similar species. *E. tyndarus* p. 182, which does not occur in the eastern Alps; upf basal extension of the tawny band in s4 5 less well marked, unh browner, without bluish-grey lustre; *E. cassioides* p. 183, fw more pointed with larger ocelli; ocelli present also on uph.

EREBIA CALCARIA   *Lorkovic's Brassy Ringlet*
Range. Confined to the eastern Alps.   Map 182

E. calcaria   Lorkovic 1953   TL: Julian Alps   Pl. 42
Description. ♂fw 18/20mm., resembles *E. tyndarus* but slightly larger with fw square-cut and apex rounded; *ups dark*, tawny markings subdued; *upf apical ocelli very small*; uph two or three small obscure ocelli sometimes present; unh smooth silver-grey with dark sinuous line across disc and dark marginal markings. ♀ups paler; unh gc silver-grey with some yellowish scaling.
Flight. July.
Habitat. Grass slopes from 4,000 ft. upwards. Larval food plants not known.
Distribution. Yugoslavia, on Karawanken and Julian Alps. NE. Italy, recorded from Monte Cavallo and Monte Santo near Piave di Cadore.

Similar species. No other species of this group is known from the Julian Alps.

EREBIA OTTOMANA   *Ottoman Brassy Ringlet*
Range. A few widely separated colonies in Europe, more generally distributed in Asia Minor (TL of *Erebia dromus* var. *ottomana* Herrich-Schaeffer 1851).   Map 183

E. ottomana bureschi Warren 1936 TL: Pirin Mts., Bulgaria   Pl. 42
Description. ♂fw 19/22mm., upf twin subapical ocelli enclosed in tawny
patch which rarely extends beyond v3; uph with small ocelli ringed tawny
in s2–4(5); unh gc silvery-grey with darker discal band outlined in brown,
brown marginal marks, and sometimes small dark vestigial pd ocelli.
♀ups gc and tawny markings paler; unh gc yellow-grey, a brown discal
band usually well defined and small brown pd ocellar spots and submarginal markings.
Flight. July.
Habitat. Grass slopes at 5–6,000 ft. Larval food plants not known.
Distribution. Greece on Mt. Veluchi. SE. Yugoslavia, Mt. Perister. Pirin
Mts. in Bulgaria. No doubt also on other mountains in this region.

E. ottomana balcanica Rebel 1913 TL: Rilo Mts., Bulgaria   Pl. 42
Description. ♂fw 19/20mm., slightly smaller and fw appears less pointed;
ups less brightly marked; upf ocelli small; unh with less colour-contrast,
often appearing brown, dusted with pale grey especially at base and in pd
area, and without vestigial ocelli.
Flight and **Habitat** as for *E. o. bureschi.*
Distribution. Widely distributed in Balkans. Bulgaria, Rilo and Rhodope
Mts. Yugoslavia, Serbia, Bosnia, Montenegro, Hercegovina and Mace-
donia on Schar Planina. Albania. NE. Italy.
Variation. Very small specimens with fw only 17mm. occur on the Schar
Planina at high altitudes on exposed mountain slopes. In Italy on Monte
Baldo, ups rather dark with tawny markings slightly reduced.

E. ottomana tardenota Praviel 1941 TL: Mt. Mézenc, Haute Loire
                                                              Pl. 42
Description. ♂fw 17/19mm., resembles *E. o. balcanica*, small in both
sexes; upf ocelli small; unh often well marked with distinct brownish
discal band. ♀unh yellow, usually with well-defined darker discal band
and marginal markings.
Flight. July.
Habitat. On grass slopes at 4,000 ft. or more.
Distribution. C. France, widely distributed in Massif Central esp. in
Ardèche and Haute Loire, e.g. Mont Mézenc, Gerbier de Jonc, Forêt de
Bauzon, etc.
Similar species. *E. cassioides* p. 183, which may be confusing in the
Balkans and in Italy, flies later, smaller, unf marginal band narrower.

EREBIA PRONOE *Water Ringlet*
Range. Confined to Europe.   Map 184

E. pronoe pronoe Esper 1780 TL: Styria   Pl. 4.
Description. ♂fw 21/25mm., sex-brand not conspicuous; upf red pd band

3–5mm. wide, generally clearly defined from s1b–s6, enclosing twin sub-apical ocelli and small ocellus in s2; uph two or three small red-ringed submarginal ocelli; *unh with scattered silver-grey irroration producing a violet-grey tone, dark brown discal band prominent.* ♀ups gc and markings paler; unh greyish to pale yellow-brown with discal band and marginal border darker.

Flight. End July/August/September. Larval food plant grasses, e.g. *Poa.*
Habitat. Woodland clearings and damp mountain slopes from 3–6,000 ft.
Distribution. Pyrenees. Bavarian, Karwendel, Innsbruck, Salzburg and Julian Alps. Styria and Carinthia. Tatra Mts. and Carpathians to S. Rumania. Recorded from Bulgaria.
Variation. In Pyrenees very local, ups red markings reduced, f. *glottis* Fruhstorfer.

E. pronoe vergy Ochsenheimer 1807 TL: S. Switzerland Pl. 43
  syn: *pitho* Huebner 1804 (invalid homonym)
Description. ♂fw 23/25mm., ups black, sometimes with inconspicuous sub-apical ocelli and traces of red pd band on fw; unf very dark, pd band vestigial, dull red-brown; unh as in *E. p. pronoe.* ♀ups gc brown, small subapical ocelli usually present; unh gc pale buff with brown discal band and marginal markings.
Flight and **Habitat** as for *E.p. pronoe.*
Distribution. Rather local. France, in Haute Savoie, Doubs (Jura), Grande Chartreuse. Switzerland, in Cantons Jura, St. Gall, Appenzell, Berne, Vaud, Valais, Grisons.
Variation. Races occur with intermediate characters of every grade.

Similar species. *E. styx* p. 190, unh pd area grey-brown or brown, discal band ill-defined; *E. aethiops* p. 168.

EREBIA MELAS *Black Ringlet*
Range. Confined to SE. Europe. Map 185

E. melas melas Herbst 1796 TL: Perzenieska, Rumanian Banat
Description. ♂fw 21/24mm., ups black; upf twin white-pupilled apical ocelli dead-black, a small ocellus often present in s2; uph two or three ocelli near outer margin; unh sometimes obscurely mottled, with traces of ocelli as on ups and obscure pale pd band. ♀ larger, usually strongly marked with large ocelli; upf fulvous pd band usually more or less present; unh brown, marbled with dark grey, paler pd band usually defined.
Flight. Late July/August.
Habitat. On moraines, rockfalls etc. from 600–5,000 ft. or more, uusally on calcareous mountains. Larval food plants not known.
Distribution. Rumania, at Herculiane in the Banat, Cernatal and surrounding mountains. S. Carpathians esp. Retezat Mts. Yugoslavia. Albania. Greece.

Variation. The species varies locally in development of ocelli and of the red pd band in ♀.

E. melas leonhardi Fruhstorfer 1918   TL: Velebit, Yugoslavia   Pl. 40
Description. ♂fw 21/22mm., smaller, ups ocelli variable, often well developed; ♀ with larger ocelli, upf red pd band vestigial or absent.
Flight and **Habitat** as for *E. m. melas*, usually at 4–5,000 ft.
Distribution. Yugoslavia in the Karst (Mt. Nanos), Velebit Mts.

Similar species. *E. lefebvrei astur* and *pyrenaea* below, perhaps only distinguishable by examination of the male genitalia. No species occurs in E. Europe that could be confused with *E. melas*. *E. pluto* p. 174.

EREBIA LEFEBVREI *Lefèbvre's Ringlet*
Range. Confined to Pyrenees and Cantabrian Mts.   Map 186

E. lefebvrei lefebvrei Boisduval 1828   TL: Pyrenees   Pl. 36
Description. ♂fw 22/24mm., ups gc deep black with *ocelli placed close to outer margins of wings*; upf red pd band (sometimes absent) poorly defined enclosing twin white-pupilled apical ocelli and small ocellus in s2; uph with three to four submarginal ocelli; uns very dark, black on hw, with markings as on ups. ♀ups gc dark brown, ocelli larger, often more numerous and red pd band better defined; unh brown with paler pd band.
Flight. End June/July.
Habitat. Moraines and rocky slopes at 6,000 ft. and upwards. Larval food plants unknown.
Distribution. Pyrenees, from Ariège westwards including most high mountains in Hautes and Basses Pyrénées.

Similar species. *E. meolans* p. 198, in the Pyrenees, upf brightly coloured with a wide red pd band.

E. lefebvrei astur Oberthur 1884   TL: Picos de Europa, Cantabrian Mts.   Pl. 36
Description. ♂fw 20/23mm., upf without or (rarely) with traces of red pd band, ocelli small; uph ocelli often absent or represented by white pupils only. ♀ups ocelli very variable, on uph reduced to white pupils or absent; unh heavily irrorated with pale grey with paler pd band.
Flight and **Habitat** as in *E. l. lefebvrei*.
Distribution. Known only from the Picos de Europa, Cantabrian Mts.

E. lefebvrei pyrenaea Oberthur 1884   TL: Mt. Canigou, E. Pyrenees

Description. ♂fw 20/21mm., upf as in *E. l. astur*; uph ocelli usually present but small; uns black, unmarked except for ocelli as on ups. ♀ups with normal ocelli; upf red pd band usually indicated, sometimes vestigial uph ocelli variable, often small or represented by white pupils; unh brown with paler pd area, ocelli variable, often absent.

Flight and **Habitat** as in *E.l. lefebvrei*.

Distribution. Eastern Pyrenees from Mt. Canigou to Fourmiguères, Pas de la Case and Pic Carlitte, on most high peaks and on French and Spanish slopes.

Similar species. *E. melas* p. 187, Balkans only; *E. pluto alecto* and *E.p. nicholli* p. 175, only in central Alps; *E. meolans* ♀p. 198.

EREBIA SCIPIO *Larche Ringlet*

G: Blassbindiger Mohrenfalter
Range. Confined to SW. Alps.   Map 187

E. scipio Boisduval 1832   TL: Basses Alpes   Pl. 39
Description. ♂fw 23/25 mm., fw pointed; upf red pd band pale, crossed by dark veins and enclosing twin subapical ocelli, sometimes with small ocelli also in s3, 4; uph pd band narrow, broken by dark veins, rarely with small ocelli; unf fulvous-red except the dark brown margins, apical ocelli conspicuous; *unh smooth dark brown*, usually with faint paler pd band, very rarely with minute ocelli. ♀ups red pd bands slightly paler and wider; unh pale grey, almost unmarked.
Flight. End June/August.
Habitat. Steep rocky places at 5–8,000 ft. Larval food plant not known.
Distribution. Maritime Alps, including the Italian slopes (rare), Basses Alpes and Vaucluse. Well-known localities include Digne, Beauvezer, Draix, Mont Ventoux, Mont de Lure, Col de Larche. It is said that the species has disappeared from some of its former localities.

EREBIA STIRIUS *Styrian Ringlet*

G: Weisskernaugen-Mohrenfalter
Range. Restricted to SE. Alps.   Map 188

E. stirius stirius Godart 1824   TL: Klagenfurt, Carinthia   Pl. 43
syn: *nerine* Freyer 1831
Description. ♂fw 24/26 mm., outer margin of hw often rather wavy, ups gc velvet-black; upf pd band dull red, not sharply defined, tapering below, rarely extending beyond v2, enclosing twin white-pupilled apical ocelli in s4, 5, rarely a small ocellus also in s2; uph broken red submarginal band with ocelli in s2, 3, 4; unf smooth chestnut brown with basal area limited by short darker mark from costa to about v4, marginal dark border narrowing in s1b; *unh smooth, very dark*, sometimes with pale scaling along margin of darker basal area which may be scarcely indicated, pd area generally slightly paler with three white-pupilled black ocelli. ♀ups gc dark brown, ocelli sometimes larger but additional ocelli rare, pd band orange-red, not well defined, often broken at v3 and with small red-ringed

ocellus in s2; *unh smooth pale grey* from base to wavy darker grey
discal line, three dark ocelli conspicuous in the pale pd area; fringes
slightly chequered.
Flight. Late July/August/September.
Habitat. Stony slopes from 2,500–5,000 ft. Larval food plants grasses
esp. *Poa alpina* and *Sesleria coerulea*.
Distribution. Eastern Alps. Widely distributed in Karawanken Alps,
Triglav and mountains near the Trenta Valley, Mt. Nanos in the Karst;
but not seen from anywhere west of Seiser Alp near Bolzano; also Mt.
Baldo. Report from Trafoi and Lower Engadine need confirmation.

E. stirius morula   Speyer 1865   TL: Seiser Alp, Dolomites   Pl. 43
Description. ♂fw 23/24mm., upf red markings reduced to an obscure area
round the twin ocelli; uph pd ocelli small; uns all markings rather small,
obscure, but unh paler grey pd area is distinct. ♀ markings better developed on both surfaces.
Flight and **Habitat.** No information, probably at high levels in late summer.
Distribution. Dolomites, on the Seiser Alp (Grodnertal) and Brenta;
recorded from the Gross Glockner, transitional to *E. s. stirius*. The
respective distribution ranges of *stirius* and *morula* are imperfectly known.
Note. The distinction between *E. stirius* and *E. styx* was defined first by
Lorkovic in 1952. Before that the species were so often confused that old
records are of little value. The distribution areas indicated here are based
as far as possible on specimens actually examined, and on Lorkovic's
records. In the Julian Alps (Trenta Valley) the specific distinction is very
obvious, but west of the Gr. Glockner the characters are less definite,
variation seems to be more common and identification may be difficult.
Similar species. *E. styx* below.

EREBIA STYX   *Stygian Ringlet*
Range. Confined to central and eastern Alps.   Map 189

E. styx styx   Freyer 1834   TL: not stated   Pl. 43
   syn: *reichlini* Herrich-Schaeffer 1860
Description. ♂fw 23/25mm., resembles *E. stirius* very closely but differs as
follows: upf red pd band well developed, extending generally to s1b
internally angled in s3 (inconstant in some races); unf darker basal area
usually defined by distinct distal border which often extends from costa
to inner margin, dark marginal border of even width to anal angle with
short projection basad in s1b (in *stirius* it tapers away and vanishes);
unh less smooth, markings better defined, dark basal area often bordered
with white. ♀unh often yellowish-grey, irrorated darker, basal area
usually defined, sometimes with white along distal border.
Flight. July/August.

Habitat. Among rocks, precipices, mountain paths etc. to 6,000 ft. Larval food plants grasses, probably *Poa annua* and *Sesleria*.
Distribution. Tirol and northern Alps. Among localities recorded are the following: Sulden, Cortina, Brenner Pass, Mendel Pass, Sorapiss, Allgäuer Alps, N. Switzerland, Karwendel Mts., Vosges (Ballon d'Alsace).

E. styx triglites Fruhstorfer 1918 TL: Monte Generoso
Description. ♂fw 23/24mm., upf red band wider, extending to inner margin and enclosing large apical ocelli; uph large ocelli in wide red submarginal band; unf and unh markings well developed. ♀fw apical ocelli larger, all red bands wide with brilliant ocelli; unf margin of basal area may be straight; unh with or without ocelli.
Flight and **Habitat** as for *E. s. styx*.
Distribution. Bergamasker Alps, Monte Generoso, Riva.

E. styx trentae Lorkovic 1952 TL: Trenta valley, Julian Alps Pls. 43, 44
Description. ♂fw 25/28mm., resembles *E. s. styx* but larger, ups ocelli prominent with brilliant white pupils, pd bands deep chestnut-red; unf gc dark mahogany-red with dark pd stripe from costa to inner margin; unh dark grey, discal band darker, the whole slightly marbled and irrorated with pale grey. ♀ups ocelli larger, conspicuous; upf usually with four or five ocelli; unh light grey, brightly marbled with darker, discal band prominent.
Flight. End July/August.
Habitat. Rocky slopes at 2,500–4,000 ft.
Distribution. Julian Alps, recorded only from Trenta valley and Mojstrovka Pass.
Note. This subspecies is full of character and differs greatly from the form that occurs in the central Alps of Austria etc.

Similar species. *E. pronoe* p. 186; *E. stirius* p. 189; *E. montana* below. Satisfactory definition of these three species is extremely difficult and the fact that the male genitalia are slightly variable does not help. The characters given above should permit identification of *stirius* and *styx*, at any rate in their eastern ranges. In both sexes of *E. montana* the brilliant marbling on unh is usually distinctive, but resemblance to *E. styx* can be very close in the central Alps. The shape of the brown marginal border on unf in s1b, when clearly defined, is a small but important character.

EREBIA MONTANA *Marbled Ringlet*
Range. Confined to Alps and Apennines. Map 190

E. montana montana de Prunner 1798 TL: Piedmont Pl. 40
syn: *homole* Fruhstorfer 1918
Description. ♂fw 22/24mm., upf pd band dull chestnut-red, narrow, taper-

PLATE 31

1. **Hipparchia statilinus**   *Tree Grayling*   142
   Upf ocelli usually blind; hw outer margin slightly scalloped, fringes paler. Unh very variable.

   1a. *H. s. statilinus* ♂. Ups very dark, markings obscure; unh smooth brown, discal band indicated by irregular dark lines.
   1b. *H. s. statilinus* ♀. Ups postdiscal areas paler, markings better defined; unh grey, markings vestigial.
   1c. *H. s. sylvicola* ♂. Unh grey-brown, markings obscure.

2. **Hipparchia fatua**   *Freyer's Grayling*   143
   Like *H. statilinus* but larger; unh densely striated and irrorated with dark scales, margin deeply scalloped.

   2a. *H. f. fatua* ♂. Ups very dark; uph dark submarginal lunules well defined.
   2b. *H. f. fatua* ♀. Ups ocelli ringed yellow, markings more complete.

3. **Hipparchia hansii**   *Austaut's Grayling*   143
   H. h. powelli ♂. Ups lacks yellow markings; unh veins conspicuously lined pale grey. See also Pl. 32.

4. **Pseudotergumia wyssii**   *Canary Grayling*   146
   Ups ocelli usually blind; unf with rather prominent pale mark in space 2; hw outer margin deeply scalloped, fringes white, chequered.

   4a. *P. w. wyssii* ♂. Fw pointed; ups medium brown, markings obscure; unh ground-colour yellowish-grey, white postdiscal band prominent.
   4b. *P. w. wyssii* ♀. Upf with pale postdiscal markings in space 2 and on costa, white spots in spaces 3, 4 larger; uns as in ♂.
   4c. *P. w. bacchus* ♀. Fw less pointed; ups dark brown, postdiscal markings better developed; unh as in *P. w. wyssii* but darker.

1a   1c   1b   2a   2b   3   4a   4b   4c

PLATE 32

1. Chazara briseis   *The Hermit*   147

   1a. *C. briseis* ♂. Upf costa pale yellow-grey; unh grey basal area bounded by dark mark on costa.

   1b. *C. briseis* ♀. Unh pale brown, markings obscure, heavily dusted with fine dark striae.

2. Chazara prieuri   *Southern Hermit*   147

   2a. *C. prieuri* ♂. Upf with buff flash in cell; unh white postdiscal band followed by saggitate dark markings.

   2b. *C. prieuri* ♀. Upf lacks buff flash in cell; unh marbled dark grey, brown, etc.

   2c. *C. prieuri* ♀-form *uhagonis*. Ups white markings replaced by orange-brown.

3. Hipparchia hansii   *Austaut's Grayling*   143

   3a. *H. hansii* ♂. Ups medium brown; upf with white-pupilled ocelli in spaces 2, 5, and white spots in spaces 3, 4, in obscurely yellow postdiscal band; unh postdiscal band pale grey. See also Pl. 31.

   3b. *H. hansii* ♀. Like ♂ but ups markings better defined.

4. Pseudotergumia fidia   *Striped Grayling*   146

   4a. *P. fidia* ♂. Ups grey-brown, ocelli inconspicuous; unh with striking dark zig-zag lines.

   4b. *P. fidia* ♀. Ups markings better defined.

ing to v2 or s1b, enclosing small twin white-pupilled apical ocelli; uph pd band variable with ocelli in s2, 3, 4; unf slightly darker basal area clearly defined by dark discal line, brown marginal border tapering slightly to v1; unh gc dark brown, with darker discal band, the whole *mottled and irrorated white*, esp. in paler pd area. ♀ *fringes chequered*; outer margin of hw slightly wavy; ups pd bands orange-red and ocelli larger; unh gc paler yellow-brown, *brightly mottled with pale grey and white*, veins lined white.

Flight. July/August.

Habitat. Rocky mountain slopes, generally at 5–7,000 ft., sometimes at lower levels. Larval food plant grasses (not identified).

Distribution. SW. Alps from Alpes Maritimes northwards to Savoie and Graian Alps. Italy, in Ligurian Apennines and Abruzzi, but more local, Gran Sasso, Mt. Portella and Corno Grande.

E. montana goante Esper 1805 TL: Switzerland Pl. 40
Description. ♂fw 23/25mm., upf pd band brighter red and wider with larger ocelli, often with small ocellus in s2; unh very dark, white irroration less extensive but border of basal area usually defined. ♀ups resembles *E. m. montana* but unh white lining of veins much less prominent. The features of *E. goante* are most definite in the Alps of E. Switzerland and Austria.

Flight and **Habitat** as for *E.m. montana*.

Distribution. From southern Switzerland eastwards through the Alps to the Engadine, Brenta Group, Brenner Pass and Oetztal Alps. Less common in N. Switzerland and occasional only in Allgäuer Alps.

Similar species. *E. styx* p. 190.

EREBIA ZAPATERI *Zapater's Ringlet*
Range. Confined to mountains of Central Spain, Teruel and Cuenca.
Map 191

E. zapateri Oberthur 1875 TL: Sierra de Albarracin Pl. 41
Description. ♂fw 19/20mm., *upf pd band orange-yellow, wide* on costa and tapering to anal angle, enclosing twin apical ocelli; uph dark brown with occasional traces of red submarginal markings; unh brown with paler pd band. ♀ups gc paler brown, pd band yellow; unh light brown with grey pd band.

Flight. End July/August.

Habitat. Open woodland and rough ground at 3,500–5,000 ft. Larval food plant not known.

Distribution. Central Spain. Recorded from Bronchales, Griegos, Albarracin, Tragacete, Noguera etc.

EREBIA NEORIDAS   *Autumn Ringlet*
Range. Confined to southern Europe.   Map 192

E. neoridas neoridas Boisduval 1828 TL: Grenoble   Pl. 41
Description. ♂fw 20/23 mm., upf fulvous-red *pd band wide near costa and tapering to anal angle*, enclosing twin apical and other ocelli; uph with ocelli in s2–4 enclosed in red rings or a narrow interrupted fulvous-red band; unh dark brown with paler pd area. ♀ similar with markings on both surfaces in paler tones.
Flight. August/September.
Habitat. Hill country and mountain foothills at 2–5,000 ft.
Distribution. E. Pyrenees, Maritime Alps and northwards to Isère and Hautes Alpes, Gard, Vaucluse and Var, Lozère and Cantal (Puy de Dôme). Italy in Cottian Alps and north to Susa valley. Spain, recorded from Val d'Aran, Pyrenees.
Variation. Specimens from the Central Massif of France (Lozère) are small with ♂fw 18/19 mm., unh paler brown with little contrast.

E. neoridas sibyllina Verity 1913 TL: Monte Sibillini, C. Italy.
Description. ♂fw 19/20 mm., ups ocelli small; unh more brightly marked with dark discal band bordered grey.
Flight and Habitat as for *E. n. neoridas*.
Distribution. C. Italy, recorded from Monte Sibillini, Monte Rotondo, Gran Sasso, and Apuane Alps.

Similar species. *E. aethiops* p. 168.

EREBIA OEME *Bright-eyed Ringlet*
G: Doppelaugen Mohrenfalter
Range. Confined to Europe.   Map 193

E. oeme oeme Huebner 1804 TL: Tirol   Pl. 40
Description. ♂fw 20/22 mm., ups gc black or very dark brown; upf with small white-pupilled twin subapical ocelli enclosed in a small red patch, and a small ocellus in s2; uph three red-ringed submarginal ocelli, the *white pupils conspicuously brilliant*; uns markings of ups repeated, often with larger ocelli; unf gc paler grey-brown, often with reddish flush; unh with five ocelli in a very even row. ♀ups paler with larger ocelli; unf flushed cinnamon-brown; unh yellow-grey, generally with six ocelli set in yellow band or yellow spots. *Antennae black-tipped.*
Flight. June/July.
Habitat. Wet meadows or damp woodland at 3–6,000 ft. Larval food plant wood-rush (*Luzula*).
Distribution. France, widely distributed throughout the Pyrenees, Mont Dore, Monts du Forez, Aveyron, Isère, Savoie, S. Jura. Bavaria. Upper Austria. Reported occurrence in Czechoslovakia needs confirmation.

PLATE 33

1. **Arethusana arethusa**   *False Grayling*   155
   Ups medium brown with orange-yellow postdiscal markings; ♂ up
   with single blind apical ocellus.

   1a. *A. a. arethusa* ♂. Ups orange postdiscal markings vestigial; unh
       brown with obscure paler postdiscal band.
   1b. *A. a. arethusa* ♀. Larger; ups postdiscal orange markings slightly
       better developed.
   1c. *A. a. boabdil* ♂. Ups obscurely marked; unh strongly marked
       with white postdiscal band and white veins.
   1d. *A. a. dentata* ♀. Ups with well developed orange postdiscal bands;
       unh veins lined with pale grey.

2. **Brintesia circe**   *Great Banded Grayling*   154
   ♂. Large, ups almost black; upf with single blind ocellus and white
   interrupted postdiscal band. ♀ similar, larger.

3. **Lopinga achine**   *Woodland Brown*   229
   ♂. Ups with large yellow-ringed blind ocelli on both wings. ♀ similar,
   ocelli slightly larger.

4. **Aphantopus hyperantus**   *Ringlet*   207
   ♂. Ups almost black, ocelli obscure; unh paler, ocelli prominent,
   yellow-ringed, white pupilled, absent in space 4. ♀ ups paler, ocelli
   usually larger; uns yellow-brown.

5. **Berberia abdelkader**   *Giant Grayling*   154
   ♀. Upf outer margin pale yellow-grey (form *nelvai*); unh veins pale
   yellowish, transverse lines obscure. **For ♂ see Pl. 34.**

PLATE 34

1. Satyrus actaea   *Black Satyr*   152

    1a. *S. actaea* ♂. Ups dark brown (black), upf with single apical ocellus and sex-brand below cell; unh basal area bordered pale grey.

    1b. *S. actaea* ♀. Ups paler brown; upf apical ocellus often ringed orange-yellow, a small ocellus in space 2 often present.

2. Satyrus ferula   *Great Sooty Satyr*   152

    2a. *S. ferula* ♂. Ups very dark brown (black), upf with 2 ocelli, sex-brand absent; unh basal area bordered pale grey.

    2b. *S. ferula* ♀. Ups paler brown; upf ocelli strongly ringed orange or set in orange postdiscal band; unh pale brown, markings obscure.

3. Minois dryas   *The Dryad*   153

    3a. *M. dryas* ♂. Ups very dark brown; upf with 2 small blue-pupilled ocelli; hw outer margin scalloped.

    3b. *M. dryas* ♀. Ups paler brown; upf ocelli large; hw outer-margin deeply scalloped

4. Berberia abdelkader   *Giant Grayling*   154

    ♂. Ups ocelli blue-pupilled, with small blue spots between; unh brown with dark pale-edged postdiscal line and pale marginal markings. For ♀ see Pl. 33.

E. oeme lugens Staudinger 1901 TL: Gadmen, Switzerland   Pl. 37
Description. ♂ fw 19/21 mm., ups ocelli very small or partly obsolete; all red markings reduced on both surfaces. ♀ ups ocelli small, better developed on uns and ringed yellow.
Flight and Habitat as for *E. o. oeme.*
Distribution. Switzerland, widely distributed esp. north of R. Rhône. Bavaria esp. in Allgäuer Alps, with some colonies transitional to *E.o. oeme.*

E oeme spodia Staudinger 1871 TL: Austria   Pl. 40
Description. ♂ fw 19/23 mm., ups ocelli and red pd band usually better developed; unf gc reddish-brown; unh with six ocelli widely red-ringed. ♀ ups pd bands generally complete and enclosing ocelli with large white pupils; upf often with additional ocellus in s 6; unh markings exceptionally brilliant, submarginal ocelli large and enclosed in a yellow band.
Flight and Habitat as for *E. o. oeme.*
Distribution. Eastern Alps, esp. Styria, and locally in Balkans (Velebit). Bulgaria.
Similar species. *E. medusa* p. 171; *E. meolans valesiaca* p. 199, ♂ unf red pd band usually well defined; *E. alberganus* p. 174, ocellar rings almond-shaped.
Note. *E. oeme* shows very marked variation on a cline, of which the main forms are described above, from rather small dark forms sometimes almost without markings to larger specimens with large bright ocelli.

EREBIA MEOLANS *Piedmont Ringlet*

G: Gelbbindiger Mohrenfalter
Range. Confined to Europe.   Map 194

E. meolans meolans de Prunner 1798 TL: Piedmont
syn: *calaritas* Fruhstorfer 1918   Pls. 39, 44
Description. ♂ fw 19/21 mm., upf red band entire, enclosing white-pupilled subapical ocelli in s 4, 5, a smaller ocellus in s 2 and sometimes others; uph red band narrower, broken by dark veins and with three or four ocelli; unf gc very dark, the *pd band wider and well defined* in s 1b–6, enclosing ocelli as on ups; unh black when fresh, pd area usually slightly paler, ocelli without red rings. ♀ ups gc brown, pd bands orange-red with larger more prominent ocelli, usually five on fw, four on hw; unh paler brown, the basal area separated by a white band (sometimes absent) from the paler pd area, three inconspicuous ocelli.
Flight. End June/July.
Habitat. Stony slopes with grass, precipices etc., at 5–6,000 ft. Larval food plants various grasses.
Distribution. Alpes Maritimes and Basses Alpes and northwards through Savoie to Jura with minor local variation. Massif Central of France, present on most mountains and often small and variable, esp. Mont Dore,

Le Lioran, etc. More brightly marked and often with more numerous ocelli in Black Forest. Ligurian Apennines, central Apennines (rare).

E. meolans bejarensis Chapman 1902 TL: Sierra de Gredos, Spain
Pl. 39
Description. ♂ fw 22/27mm., upf tawny bands wide and bright, extending often below v1, with four or five ocelli; unh slightly marbled dark grey in some specimens, pd area distinctly paler. ♀ often very large, all colour tones paler with conspicuous ups ocelli; unh white border to darker basal area reduced or vestigial.
Flight and **Habitat** as for *E. m. meolans*.
Distribution. C. Spain, Sierra de Gredos, Sierra de Guadarrama, Sierra de la Demanda.
This subspecies represents the maximum development in size, brilliance of markings and in number of ocelli. These characters diminish further north in the Cantabrian Mts. to blend insensibly into the smaller races flying in the Hautes Pyrénées.

E. meolans stygne Ochsenheimer 1808 TL: Alps of Tirol and Switzerland
Description. ♂ fw 21/23 mm., upf red pd band narrow, often incomplete and interrupted by dark veins; upf usually with three ocelli; uph ocelli small and inconstant; unf pd band reduced in size but remaining well defined and entire; unh pd area sometimes faintly paler with vestigial ocelli. ♀ gc brown, unh basal area slightly darker, rarely bordered white.
Flight and **Habitat** as for *E. m. meolans*, sometimes at lower levels.
Distribution. Local and uncommon in the E. Alps, Thuringia, Allgäuer Alps, Hochschwab, Brenner district, etc. Switzerland, widely distributed north of Rhône valley. Carpathians?

E. meolans valesiaca Elwes 1898 TL: Valais, Switzerland   Pl. 39
Description. Smaller ♂ fw 20/21 mm., markings reduced to very small red-ringed apical twin ocelli on fw, on hw ocelli vestigial or absent; unf red pd band narrow, short. ♀ ups markings only slightly increased.
Flight and **Habitat** as for *E. m. meolans*.
Distribution. Switzerland, in Graubünden (Grisons) and westwards to Rhône Valley.

Similar species. *E. oeme* p. 195; *E. triaria* p. 169; *E. palarica* below; *E. lefebvrei* ♀ p. 188, unh paler pd area not clearly defined.

EREBIA PALARICA *Chapman's Ringlet*
Range. Confined to NW. Spain.   Map 195

E. palarica Chapman 1905 TL: Pajares, Cantabrian Mts.   Pl. 41
Description. ♂ fw 28/30mm., closely resembles *E. meolans* but larger; unh

dark brown, *slightly mottled with 'roughened' appearance*, discal dark band often present, sometimes defined by scanty pale grey markings before the faintly paler pd area which contains small inconspicuous ocelli. ♀ sometimes smaller, with gc and markings in paler tones; unh much paler grey-brown, discal band edged darker and bordered pale grey, ocelli small and variable.

Flight. End June/July.

Habitat. Rough places among rocks and long grass, especially associated with tall broom (*Cytisus*). Larval food plant not known.

Distribution. Cantabrian Mts., in Provinces of Oviedo and Leon.

Similar species. *E. meolans* (p. 198) smaller, unh surface smooth, unf pd band with proximal border straight (slightly concave in *E. palarica*).

EREBIA PANDROSE   *Dewy Ringlet*

Sw: Fjällgräsfjäril F: Le Grand Nègre Bernois G: Graubrauner Mohrenfalter

Range. Arctic and Alpine zones on high mountains from E. Pyrenees to central Asia and in Fennoscandia.   Map 196

E. pandrose Borkhausen 1788 **TL:** Styria   Pls. 39, 44
  syn: *lappona* Thunberg 1791

Description. ♂fw 20/25 mm., ups gc dusky-brown; upf with dark striae in cell, dark transverse pd line, and *broad tawny pd area enclosing blind black spots* in s 2–5; uph sometimes with similar spots ringed reddish-brown; unh gc silver-grey, discal band more or less distinctly outlined by irregular dark transverse lines. ♀ similar with paler gc; upf pd spots sometimes absent; unh more variable, gc yellowish-grey with discal band sometimes filled darker.

Flight. End June/July.

Habitat. Stony slopes and pastures at 6,000 ft. or more in Pyrenees and Alps, at lower levels in Fennoscandia. Larval food plants grasses, esp. *Festuca* and *Poa*.

Distribution. From eastern Pyrenees through the whole Alpine chain to Julian Alps and higher Carpathians. More local in Balkans, but recorded from Prenj and Durmitor in S. Yugoslavia and Belmeken in Bulgaria. Fennoscandia, in the south as a mountain insect at 3,000 ft.; in the High North from sea-level. Italy, Monti della Laga. Absent from Jura, Vosges and Spanish Sierras.

Variation. This is slight through most of the range. In the Carpathians the ♀unh has a stronger pattern with discal band filled dark brown and edged pale grey ♀-f. *roberti* Peschke Pl. 44.

Similar species. *E. sthennyo* below.

EREBIA STHENNYO   *False Dewy Ringlet*
Range. Confined to Hautes and Basses Pyrénées.   Map 19⁻

E. sthennyo Graslin 1850 TL: Bagnères de Bigorre, Pyrenees Pl. 39
Description. ♂fw 20/22mm., resembles *E. pandrose* but differs as follows; smaller; upf dark pd spots nearer to outer margin, dark striae in cell and dark pd line absent or vestigial; unh pale grey nearly unmarked. ♀ resembles ♂; ups slightly paler brown; unh pale grey.
Flight. End June/July.
Habitat. Grass slopes at 6,000 ft. or more. Larval food plants not known.
Distribution. Basses and Hautes Pyrénées eastwards to Andorra at Pic de Coullac near Salau.
The distributions of *E.* [*sthennyo* and *E. pandrose* (p. 200) do not overlap although in Andorra and in Aulus the species fly in close proximity. The small differences in markings and in male genitalia appear to be constant.

EREBIA PHEGEA *Dalmatian Ringlet*
Range. Dalmatia and S. Russia (*Papilio phegea* Borkhausen 1788 TL: Volga) to C. Asia.   Map 198

E. phegea dalmata Godart 1824 TL: Sibenik, Dalmatia Pl. 44
  syn: *afer* Esper 1783 (invalid homonym)
Description. ♂fw 22/24mm., ups gc brown; upf apex and most of outer margin yellowish-grey; fused twin white-pupilled ocelli in s4 and 5, additional ocelli placed more distally in s1b (twin) 2, 3, and 6; uph ocelli in s1b–6 in regular series, small; uns brown; unf apex paler with veins lined pale yellow-grey and disc slightly reddish; unh veins conspicuously yellow-grey, 8 small pale-ringed ocelli. ♀ similar with markings in paler tones.
Flight. May.
Habitat. Rocks and boulder-strewn slopes at comparatively low levels.
Distribution. Dalmatia, Zara, Sibenik, appears to be very local and rare.
Note. This species has several unusual features including a precostal vein in the hind-wing. It is not well placed in the genus *Erebia*.

MANIOLA JURTINA *Meadow Brown*
F:Le Myrtil Sw:Allmän Slåttergräsfjäril G:Ochsenauge Sp:La Loba
Range. Canary Islands and N. Africa through Europe to Urals, Asia Minor and Iran.   Map 199

M. jurtina jurtina Linnaeus 1758 TL: Europe and Africa Pl. 45
(Sweden, Verity 1953)
Description. ♂fw 22/25mm., a large black sex-brand from near wing-base extending along and below median vein; *ups* gc dark brown nearly or quite *without orange markings; upf a single white-pupilled apical ocellus* unh grey to yellow-brown, basal area darker, small black dots in s2 and s5 in paler pd band. ♀fw 24/26mm., upf with yellow or orange discal and

pd areas; unh often yellowish and brightly marked, without small black spots in paler pd band.

Flight. June to August with long flight period, females appearing late.

Habitat. Meadows and grassy places from sea-level to 6,000 ft. Larval food plants various grasses, esp. *Poa*.

Distribution. Europe, S. of 62°N; northern specimens slightly smaller than those from southern areas; replaced in SW. by *M. j. hispulla*.

M. jurtina hispulla Esper (*ante* 1805) TL: Lisbon   Pl. 45
Description. ♂fw 24/27 mm., large, sex-brand appears very large; resembles *M. j. jurtina*; unh additional small dark spots are common in paler pd band. ♀fw 26/29 mm., ups orange markings much extended and upf apical ocellus large; uph orange pd band wide; unh darker brown basal area often bordered with yellowish suffusion.

Variation. In Africa and Canary Islands mostly very large, females brightly coloured, f. *fortunata* Alpheraky. Local races of large size with brightly coloured females, transitional to *M. j. jurtina*, occur in many districts in S. Europe.

Flight and **Habitat** as for *M.j. jurtina*.

Distribution. Canary Islands, Morocco, Algeria, Tunisia, Portugal, Spain, E. Pyrenees and Provence, Mediterranean islands to Malta.

M. jurtina splendida White 1872 TL: Lunga Island, W. Scotland
Description. ♂fw 21/22 mm., upf brightly marked, with fulvous pd area in s2-4 usually well developed, often enclosing the ocellus in s5; uph very dark, basal area vaguely indicated; unf apical ocellus a little larger; unh sometimes with very small black pd ocelli in s2, 5. ♀ larger, upf fulvous pd area extends into cell; uph often with slightly fulvous pd flush.

Flight and **Habitat** as for *M. j. jurtina*.

Distribution. N. Scotland in Western Isles—Canna, Lunga, S. Uist, etc., on mainland to W. Sutherland—Lochinver, etc. Orkneys. Ireland. Isle of Man. Scilly Isles. South of the Firth of Forth, *M. j. splendida* does not occur, and is replaced by *M. j. jurtina*, sometimes with traces of fulvous pd flush.

Similar species. *M. nurag* p. 203. *H. lycaon* and *H. lupina* p. 206, in which upf apical ocellus is blind. *P. janiroides* p. 211, upf apical ocellus twin-pupilled.

Note. Typical *jurtina* and typical *hispulla* are so different in appearance that they have often been regarded as distinct species. However, between the north-eastern *jurtina* and the south-western *hispulla* a wide belt occurs which is populated by races with intermediate characters that link them together.

MANIOLA NURAG *Sardinian Meadow Brown*
Range. Confined to Sardinia. Map 200

M. nurag Ghiliani 1852 TL: Mt. Gennargentu, Sardinia Pl. 46
Description. ♂fw 20mm., *resembles M. jurtina hispulla but smaller*; upf sex-brand conspicuous; ups brown with broad yellow pd suffusions on both wings; unh gc paler, grey-brown, almost unmarked, a trace of yellow in pd area where very small dark spots may be present. ♀ larger, upf broadly orange with brown marginal border and darker transverse striae from costa; uph with broad yellow pd band; unh without dark spots in pd area.
Flight. End June/July, flight of females prolonged.
Habitat. Open bushy places at moderate altitudes. Larval food plant grasses.
Distribution. Local in Sardinia, probably most frequent in northern areas.
Similar species. *M. jurtina* p. 201, ♂ distinguished by larger size and absence of yellow suffusion on uph. The rather similar species of *Pyronia* can be distinguished by having twin white pupils in the fw apical ocellus.

HYPONEPHELE MAROCCANA *Moroccan Meadow Brown*
Range. Confined to Morocco. Map 202

H. maroccana maroccana Blachier 1908 TL: High Atlas Pl. 45
Description. ♂fw 21/22mm., ups gc medium brown; upf narrow sex-brand bordering median vein, *orange-yellow pd suffusion sometimes extending towards base of wing*, small ocellus often present in s2, larger ocellus constant in s5; uph unmarked; unf single white pupil in apical ocellus; unh pale grey-brown, discal band generally indicated by slightly darker broken transverse lines. ♀hw outer margin wavy; upf orange-yellow pd area brighter, extending to wing-base, dusky basal area clearly defined by brown elbowed discal line, ocelli larger, sometimes very large, apical ocellus occasionally with white pupil; uph vague darker discal and submarginal lines sometimes present; unh pale grey-brown, discal band indicated by brown striae.
Flight. June/July.
Habitat. Rough ground at 6–7,000 ft. Larval food plants not recorded, probably grasses.
Distribution. Local in the High Atlas.

H. maroccana nivellei Oberthur 1920 TL: Taghzeft and Pl. 45
Djebel Hebbri, Middle Atlas.
Description. ♂fw 18/20mm., resembles *H. m. maroccana* but smaller; upf apical ocellus small, often double; unh paler grey with brown discal striae less regular. ♀unh gc pale grey.

PLATE 35

1a

1b

2a

3a

2b

3b

4a

4b

5a

5b

PLATE 36

1. Erebia euryale   *Large Ringlet*   156
Fringes chequered; ♂ upf lacks sex-brand; markings very variable.

   1a. *E. e. euryale* ♂. Ups with small blind ocelli in fulvous postdiscal bands; uns ocelli white-pupilled; unh dark, ocelli very small, fulvous-ringed.

   1b. *E. e. euryale* ♀. Ups markings paler, ocelli white-pupilled; unh dark basal area followed by pale band enclosing ocelli.

   1c. *E. e. ocellaris* ♂. Ups fulvous markings reduced to narrow rings round small blind ocelli. ♀ similar.

   1d. *E. e. adyte* ♂. Ups with white-pupilled ocelli in fulvous postdiscal bands.

   1e. *E. e. adyte* ♀. Ups like male, but more brightly marked; unh postdiscal band wide, yellow or white. **See also Pl. 28.**

2. Erebia ligea   *Arran Brown*   156
Fringes chequered; upf with sex-brand below median vein.

   2a. *E. l. dovrensis* ♂. Ups like *E. euryale*; unh with white costal mark before obscure postdiscal band.

   2b. *E. l. ligea* ♂. Large; ups ocelli white pupilled; unh very dark, white postdiscal band strongly developed.

   2c. *E. l. ligea* ♀. Ups more brightly marked; unh brown with paler postdiscal band and white costal stripe.

3. Erebia lefebvrei   *Lefèbvre's Ringlet*   188

   3a. *E. l. astur* ♂. Ups black; upf with very small white-pupilled apical ocelli, and minute white points in space 2 and uph near margin; uns markings similar. ♀ unh grey.

   3b. *E. l. lefebvrei* ♂. Ups black with white-pupilled ocelli close to margins; upf ocelli weakly fulvous-ringed. ♀ similar but more brightly marked.

Flight and **Habitat** as for *H.m. maroccana.*

Distribution. Middle Atlas on Taghzeft Pass, etc. Appears to be confined to Middle Atlas in Morocco; not recorded from Algeria. In series distinction from *H.m. maroccana* is quite marked.

Similar species. *H. lupina mauretanica* p. 207, common in Morocco, is a larger species, and lacks orange-yellow suffusion on upf.

HYPONEPHELE LYCAON   *Dusky Meadow Brown*

G: Kleines Ochsenauge   Sp: Lobito   Sw: Gråbrun Slåttergräsfjäril

Range. From W. Europe through S. Russia, Asia Minor, Lebanon and Caucasus, to Central Asia.   Map 201

H. lycaon Kuehn 1774   TL: Berlin   Pl. 45

Description. ♂fw 20/24 mm., ups gc grey-brown; upf a *narrow brown sex-brand* below median vein *cut by paler* gc on v2 *and* v3, and often with slightly fulvous flush in pd area; uph unmarked; unf apical ocellus with single white pupil; unh grey-brown, irrorated darker to pale grey, darker discal band often vaguely indicated by vestigial brown elbowed pd transverse line. ♀hw slightly scalloped; *upf disc orange-yellow* with dusky basal area defined by dark distal edge; uph gc grey-brown, basal area defined by darker transverse line followed by paler, often yellowish, pd band.

Flight. July/August; female emerges late.

Habitat. Dry, rocky places, often at low altitudes, exceptionally to 6,000 ft. Larval food plants grasses, esp. *Poa.*

Distribution. C. and S. Europe from Mediterranean to Finland. Absent from Britain, France, Belgium, Holland, Denmark, Scandinavia, Mediterranean islands (except Sicily), and N. Africa.

Variation. Variation is slight. Males with an ocellus on upf in s2 are not rare in some colonies; ♀ups varies in extent of yellow-suffusion.

Similar species. *H. lupina* below; *M. jurtina* p. 201.

HYPONEPHELE LUPINA   *Oriental Meadow Brown*

Sp: Lobito anillado

Range. From N. Africa and south-western Europe, S. Russia and Asia Minor to Iran, perhaps to the Himalayas and Mongolia.   Map 203

H. lupina lupina Costa 1836   TL: Otranto, Naples   Pl. 45

Description. ♂fw 21/24 mm., resembles *H. lycaon*; ups gc yellow-brown with brassy reflection; upf a conspicuous *dark sex-brand, not cut by veins,* small blind apical ocellus, otherwise unmarked; hw outer margin scalloped, uph unmarked; unf light orange-brown with grey marginal border, black apical ocellus conspicuous, white pupilled; unh light grey-brown with fine darker irrorations, position of discal band often indicated by darker striae. ♀hw outer margin scalloped; *ups gc grey-brown* with blind ocelli in s2 and s5 on upf each surrounded by pale yellow, but always separated by *brown gc along* v4; uph generally with darker basal area followed by paler band.

Flight. July/August.

Habitat. Hot rocky places from lowlands to 3,000 ft. The butterflies shelter in bushes and fly out when disturbed, but vanish immediately into a different shelter. Larval food plants not recorded.

Distribution. Italy, very local in Apennines, etc. France, in Vaucluse, Gard, Alpes Maritimes, very local. Hungary, Flamenda, Deliblat. Dalmatia, Krk.

H. lupina rhamnusia Freyer 1845 TL: Etna, Sicily
Description. ♂fw 26/28mm., resembles *H. l. lupina* but larger; ups gc yellow-brown with brassy-golden pile at wing-bases; upf dark sex-brand conspicuous; hw outer margin deeply scalloped. ♀ups as in *H.l. lupina.*
Flight and **Habitat** as in *H.l. lupina.*
Distribution. Sicily. SE. Yugoslavia, Mt. Perister, slightly smaller. Greece, Mt. Parnassus, Mt. Olympus.

H. lupina mauretanica Oberthur 1881 TL: Algeria Pl. 45
Description. ♂fw 21/24mm., ups gc nearly uniform dark grey-brown with little brassy reflection; upf dark sex-brand less conspicuous on darker gc. ♀upf yellow markings slightly paler in tone and often reduced in extent, but distinction from *H. l. lupina* less marked in this sex.
Flight and **Habitat** as for *H.l. lupina,* but flies in Spain at 3–4,000 ft. and up to 6,000 ft. in Morocco.
Distribution. Morocco. Algeria. Spain, common in mountainous districts. Portugal, in the Sierra de Estrela.

Similar species. *H. lycaon* p. 206, ♂ sex-brand upf inconspicuous, narrow, and cut by veins 2 and 3; ♀upf orange-yellow markings more extensive, generally without dark shade along v4 in pd area; *M. jurtina* p. 201.

APHANTOPUS HYPERANTUS *Ringlet*

F: Le Tristan Sw: Luktgräsfjäril G: Brauner Waldvogel
Sp: Sortijitas

Range. Europe, except Mediterranean and arctic regions, and across N. Asia to Ussuri. Map 204

A. hyperantus Linnaeus 1758 TL: Europe (Sweden Verity 1953) Pl. 33
Description. ♂fw 20/24mm., ups gc almost black; upf with inconspicuous sex-brand along median vein, and with or without obscure ocelli in s3 and s5; uph obscure ocelli in s2, 3; fringes very pale; uns gc pale brown with golden reflection, *conspicuous yellow-ringed ocelli* with white pupils in s3, 5 on fw, and s(1), 2, 3, 5, 6 in uneven series on hw. ♀ups gc paler brown with ocelli, constantly present, usually white pupilled on hw.
Flight. June/July.

PLATE 37

1. **Erebia flavofasciata**   *Yellow-banded Ringlet*   162
   ♂. Unh with yellow postdiscal band enclosing small ocellar spots.
   ♀ paler, markings better defined.

2. **Erebia mnestra**   *Mnestra's Ringlet*   181
   ♂. Upf ocelli absent (or very small), no sex-brand; unh cinnamon-
   brown, unmarked. ♀ upf with twin apical ocelli; unh often with pale
   grey postdiscal band.

3. **Erebia aethiopella**   *False Mnestra Ringlet*   180
   Uph with fulvous postdiscal band; ♂ with sex-brands below median
   vein.
   3a. *E. a. aethiopella* ♂. Upf with very small white-pupilled apical
       ocelli; unh brown, dusted with scattered white scales.
   3b. *E. a. aethiopella* ♀. Like ♂ but more brightly marked and ocelli
       larger.
   3c. *E. a. rhodopensis* f. *sharsta* ♂. Upf ocelli larger (sometimes
       present on hw); unh brown or grey. ♀ more brightly marked.
   3d. *E. a. rhodopensis* ♂. Ups more brightly marked with larger ocelli;
       hw postdiscal ocelli present on both surfaces.

4. **Erebia sudetica**   *Sudeten Ringlet*   168
   4a. *E. s. liorana* ♂. Unh with 5 to 6 orange postdiscal spots in
       regular graded series. ♀ unh ground-colour yellow-brown.
   4b. *E. s. sudetica* ♀. Unh postdiscal spots larger, separated only by
       brown veins.

5. **Erebia melampus**   *Lesser Mountain Ringlet*   167
   ♂. Like *E. sudetica* but unh orange postdiscal spot in space 4 dis-
   placed slightly basally, series irregular. ♀ similar, unh paler.

6. **Erebia claudina**   *White Speck Ringlet*   159
   6a. *E. claudina* ♂. Unh brown with 6 or 7 minute white submarginal
       points between veins.
   6b. *E. claudina* ♀. Ups paler brown; uph with 4 larger submarginal
       white points; unh pale yellow-grey.

7. **Erebia gorge**   *Silky Ringlet*   178
   Upf with gleaming silky texture; male sex-brands present.
   7a. *E. g. gorge* ♂. Upf fulvous-red postdiscal bands well developed;
       twin apical ocelli prominent; uph with or without postdiscal
       ocelli; unh dark grey marbled paler, dark discal band some-
       times present. ♀ fringes chequered, unh much paler.
   7b. *E. g. ramondi* ♂. Like *E. g. gorge* but on hw white-pupilled post-
       discal ocelli prominent on both surfaces. For ♀ see Pl. 44.
   7c. *E. g. erynis* f. *carboncina* ♂. Small, upf ocelli greatly reduced (or
       absent); unh very dark. See also *E. g. erynis* Pl. 44.
   7d. *E. g. triopes* ♂. Like *E. g. ramondi* but upf with 3 united ocelli.
   7e. *E. g. gorge* f. *gigantea* ♂. Like *E. g. gorge* but larger, unh usually
       dark.

8. **Erebia oeme**   *Bright-eyed Ringlet*   19
   E. o. lugens ♂. Ups black, ocelli reduced to vanishing point; uns with
   small blind ocelli present on both wings. ♀ similar. **See also Pl. 40.**

1a 1b 2

3a 4a 4b

3b 5d 5c

5a 5b 5e

5f 5g 5h

6 7

PLATE 38

1. Erebia eriphyle   *Eriphyle Ringlet*   158
   1a. *E. e. eriphyle* ♂. Unf discal area orange-brown; uph postdiscal
     orange spot in space 4 prominent.
   1b. *E. e. tristis* ♂. Like *E. e. eriphyle*; ups fulvous markings brighter
     and more extensive. For ♀ see Pl. 28.

2. Erebia manto   *Manto Ringlet*   158
  E. m. pyrrhula ♂. Small, with obscure fulvous elongate marks on
  both wings. ♀ similar. See also Pls. 28, 39, 44.

3. Erebia pharte   *Spotless Ringlet*   166
   3a. *E. p. pharte* ♂. Ups broken fulvous postdiscal bands lack in-
     cluded black spots. ♀ paler, unh broadly yellowish. See also Pl.
     44.
   3b. *E. p. eupompa* ♂. Larger, upf fulvous postdiscal bands wide. For
     ♀ see Pl. 44.

4. Erebia christi   *Raetzer's Ringlet*   166
   4a. *E. christi* ♂. Like *E. epiphron* but unh postdiscal band slightly
     paler, ocelli represented by small black spots.
   4b. *E. christi* ♀. Upf orange postdiscal band wider; unh pale grey-
     brown, 4 small dark spots in pale postdiscal area.

5. Erebia epiphron   *Mountain Ringlet*   162
  Unh ground-colour uniform brown, with or without 3 small postdiscal ocelli.
   5a. *E. e. epiphron* f. *silesiana* ♂. Upf fulvous postdiscal band wide,
     enclosing 4 blind ocelli; uph 3 blind ocelli ringed fulvous.
   5b. *E. e. epiphron* f. *silesiana* ♀. Like ♂ but more brightly marked;
     upf post-discal ocelli usually with white pupils.
   5c. *E. e. aetheria* ♂. Upf fulvous band dull, narrow, and generally
     lacking ocellus in space 3; hw usually with small postdiscal
     ocelli.
   5d. *E. e. aetheria* ♀. Ups paler brown; upf ocelli larger, sometimes
     with white pupils.
   5e. *E. e. aetheria* f. *nelamus* ♂. Markings almost obsolete on both
     surfaces.
   5f. *E. e. fauveaui* ♂. Like *E. e. silesiana* but all markings less bright;
     upf generally with 4 blind postdiscal ocelli.
   5g. *E. e. orientalis* ♂. Upf fulvous postdiscal band narrow, enclosing
     twin apical ocelli; uph with 3 ocelli, all with minute white pupils.
     ♀ similar with larger ocelli.
   5h. *E. e. mnemon* ♂. Upf markings dull, reduced, but usually with 4
     black spots in the fulvous band.

6. Erebia disa   *Arctic Ringlet*   170
  E. disa ♂. Uph unmarked. ♀ similar, ups slightly paler.

7. Erebia embla   *Lapland Ringlet*   170
  E. embla ♂. Uph with 3 or rarely 4 blind postdiscal ocelli. ♀ nearly
  similar.

Habitat. Damp grassy places, often in light woodland, from lowlands to 5,000 ft. Larval food plants grasses, e.g. *Milium, Poa*, also *Carex* and more rarely sedges.
Distribution. Western Europe to 64°N. Cantabrian Mts. France including Pyrenees and generally through C. Europe, Britain, Ireland and S. Scotland. Absent from Portugal, C. and S. Spain, peninsular Italy, Mediterranean islands; local and scarce in central Balkans.
Variation. Individual variation occurs in the development of the ocelli on uns.

Similar species. *Coenonympha oedippus* p. 223, smaller with an ocellus on unh in s4.

PYRONIA TITHONUS *Gatekeeper*

F: l'Amaryllis   G: Gelbes Ochsenauge   Sp: Lobito agreste   Sw: Rödgul Slåttergräsfjaril
Range. From Spain and western Europe to Asia Minor and Caucasus.
Map 205

P. tithonus Linnaeus 1771   TL: Germany   Pl. 46
Description. ♂fw 17/19mm., upf sex-brand in and below cell in s1–4, base of wing not suffused fuscous; uph base dusky, orange pd area variable, sometimes small, occasional ocellus in s2; unh gc reddish to pale yellow-brown, margin of dark basal area bounded by paler yellowish area with very *small white-pupilled ocelli in s2 and s5* both enclosed in yellow-brown shades. ♀ larger, ups gc brighter orange-yellow, unh gc yellow.
Flight. July/August in a single brood, females appear late.
Habitat. Around bramble-bushes, etc., in lowlands, rarely to 3,000 ft. Larval food plants various grasses, e.g. *Poa, Milium*.
Distribution. Local but widely distributed in western, central and southern Europe, including southern Ireland and Britain, to about 52°N; Sardinia, Corsica and Elba; eastwards to the Balkans. Broadly absent from the Alps except along their southern slopes; absent from S. Italy, Sicily and other Mediterranean islands. Spanish Morocco, El Rif.
Variation. On upf in ♂ additional ocelli are not uncommon.

Similar species. *P. cecilia* below, unh without ocelli.

PYRONIA CECILIA *Southern Gatekeeper*
Range. From Morocco and Spain through S. Europe to Asia Minor (Bursa).   Map 206

P. cecilia Vallantin 1894   TL: Morocco   Pl. 46
    syn: *ida* Esper 1785 (invalid homonym)
Description. ♂fw 15/16mm., ups resembles *P. tithonus*; upf with striking *quadrilateral sex-brand*, usually divided by fulvous veins, extending into outer angle of cell; uph without ocelli; *unh no ocelli*, gc pale grey marbled

olive-brown, irregular darker basal area bounded by pale gc in pd area but sometimes indistinct in ♂. ♀ larger with fw 20mm., uns as in ♂.

Flight. May/August perhaps in a succession of broods.

Habitat. Rough, bushy places in hot localities, usually in lowlands but rising in Spain to 4,000 ft., and to 6,000 ft. in Morocco. Larval food plants grasses, esp. *Deschampsia caespitosa*.

Distribution. Morocco, Algeria, Tunisia, Portugal. Spain, absent in N. but present in Balearic Islands. France in south-east, Alpes Maritimes, Var, Bouches du Rhône, Hte. Garonne, Hérault, Lozère, E. Pyrenees. Corsica, Sardinia, Elba, Giglio. Italy, local and scattered in north, more common in peninsular Italy and Sicily. Recorded from Dalmatia, Albania, Greece and Turkey in Europe. Records from Rumania need confirmation.

Similar species. *P. tithonus* p. 210.

PYRONIA BATHSEBA   *Spanish Gatekeeper*

Sp: Lobito listado

Range. Confined to W. Europe and N. Africa.   Map 207

P. bathseba bathseba   Fabricius 1793   TL: Morocco ('Barbaria')   Pl. 46
  syn: *pasiphae* Esper 1781 (invalid homonym)

Description. ♂ fw 18/19mm., upf orange gc partly obscured by dark basal suffusion which encloses sex-brand; uph small submarginal ocelli in s2, 3, 5; unf basal area not usually defined; *unh* gc brown, a very *narrow pale yellow discal stripe* with sharply defined inner border followed by obscure, yellow-ringed white-pupilled ocelli, sometimes very small, in s1c, 2, 3, 5, 6. ♀ larger, fw to 23mm., upf dark basal suffusion less extensive; unh gc paler, pale discal stripe wider, ocelli more conspicuous.

Flight. May/June or later.

Habitat. Rough places, hedges, etc., to 5,500 ft. in Middle Atlas. Larval food plants grasses, esp. *Brachypodium*.

Distribution. Morocco, Algeria, widely distributed. Not recorded from Tunisia.

P. bathseba pardilloi   Sagarra 1924   TL: Barcelona   Pl. 46

Description. Slighter larger, unf distal margin of basal area more clearly defined; unh yellow discal line wider, generally extending along v4 into pd area; ocelli on both surfaces more conspicuous esp. in the larger female.

Flight and Habitat as for *P. b. bathseba* but at lower altitudes.

Distribution. Portugal, Algarve, Torres Vedras, etc. Spain, widely distributed except in NW. France, in Lozère, Bouches du Rhône, Var, E. Pyrenees. In S. Spain often transitional to *P.b. bathseba*.

PYRONIA JANIROIDES   *False Meadow Brown*

Range. Confined to eastern Algeria and Tunisia.   Map 208

P. janiroides Herrich-Schaeffer 1851   TL: 'Spain' (error)   Pl. 46
Description. ♂fw 23mm., upf brown, with narrow orange pd band re-
stricted by wide dark basal area covering sex-brand; uph orange pd band
much wider; unh gc grey-brown, discal band slightly darker with paler pd
area enclosing *three or four very small blind yellow ocelli*. ♀ slightly larger,
upf dark basal suffusion greatly reduced.
Flight. May/June or later.
Habitat. Rough ground, esp. near coast and at low altitudes. Larval food
plants not known.
Distribution. Algeria, Blida, Bone, Collo, etc.   Tunisia, common in July/
September.
Similar species.   *Maniola jurtina* p. 201.

COENONYMPHA TULLIA   *Large Heath*

F: Le Daphnis   Sw: Starrgräsfjäril   G: Grosser Heufalter
Range. From NW. Europe across temperate Asia to Pacific; N. America,
local in eastern States, but extending through western mountains to
California.   Map 209
This variable species occurs within the region in two subspecific groups.
In north, west and central Europe the *tullia* group of subspecies fly over
peat mosses and damp mountain meadows from lowlands to moderate
altitudes. In this group there is marked local variation on a cline. Five
forms are described below as subspecies, but all are connected by transitional forms. In central Italy, Rumania and Balkan countries the species is
widely distributed as a mountain butterfly, *C. t. rhodopensis* Elwes, flying
at 4,500–7,000 ft. over high subalpine meadows. In a few localities *C.t.
tullia* is known to fly on marshes at low levels within the area of *C.t. rhodopensis*, but the habitats of the two subspecies never overlap.

C. tullia tullia   Mueller 1764   TL: Fridrichsdal (Seeland),   Pl. 47
Denmark
   syn: *philoxenus* Esper 1780.
Description. ♂fw 19/20mm., ups gc dingy grey-brown, variable; upf with
small yellow-ringed apical ocellus and paler orange-brown suffusion over
base and disc, *but without dark margin*; uph yellow-ringed submarginal
ocelli (variable) in s1, 2, 3; unf gc pale golden-brown with yellow or white
pd stripe and white-pupilled ocelli in s(2), 5; unh grey, sometimes flushed
fulvous, an irregular white pd band generally broken in s2/3 and black
white-pupilled yellow-ringed submarginal ocelli in s1–6, often very small
in s4, 5. ♀upf gc paler orange-brown, yellow pd stripe of uns indicated
on costa; uph often darker with pale pd mark in s3, 4, 5; two or three submarginal ocelli present in some specimens.
Flight. June/early July.
Habitat. Bogs, peat mosses and rough meadows, esp. among cotton grass,

from lowlands to lower mountain slopes. Larval food plants cotton grass (*Eriophorum*) and beaked rush (*Rhynchospora alba*).

Distribution. Denmark, becoming extinct. Germany, esp. in NW, Hanover, Hamburg, etc. England in NE counties from Northumberland to Yorkshire and in Cumberland. Scotland in southern counties to about 56°N. Wales, in northern districts, now rare. Ireland, widely distributed and very variable. Scandinavia, lowland districts in S. and W.

Variation. It is difficult to give precise characters as nearly every colony shows minor local features and individual variation is also marked. Some specimens from north-eastern England and southern Scotland closely resemble *C.t. tiphon*.

C. tullia rothliebii Herrich-Schaeffer 1851 TL: not stated Pl. 47
syn: *philoxenus* auct.

Description. Compared with *C. t. tullia* ♂ups darker grey-brown, upf orange-brown suffusion reduced; uph variable, usually with 3 to 5 ocelli; unf gc darker orange-brown, 2–4 submarginal ocelli; unh grey-brown, six large pd ocelli. ♀ similar, ups gc slightly paler, pale pd markings well-defined, uph generally with 4–5 ocelli.

Flight and **Habitat** as for *C.t. tullia*.

Distribution. England, in a restricted area in N. Shropshire, Lancashire and Westmorland. Extinct in Cheshire and Staffordshire. Extent of remaining habitat rapidly shrinking.

C. tullia tiphon Rottemburg 1775 TL: Halle, W. Germany Pl. 47
Description. ♂fw 17/20 mm., ups gc light orange-brown, pd area of fw and much of hw slightly grey; upf apical ocellus usually present; uph with or without submarginal ocelli; unf ocelli present in (2), 5; unh grey but often with brown flush over disc, pd ocelli usually well developed. ♀ups gc paler ochre-yellow; uph slightly grey with pale discal mark and ocelli more clearly marked.

Flight. End June/July.

Habitat. Wet meadows, moorland, etc., in lowlands.

Distribution. Belgium, Ardennes. Jura. Switzerland, north of Rhône valley. Bavaria. Austria. Yugoslavia, Bosnisch-Brod, Jaice. Rare or absent in south Tirol.

C. tullia scotica Staudinger 1901 TL: Scotland Pl. 47
Description. ♂fw 18/19 mm., ups gc pale yellow-brown or yellow-grey; upf single apical ocellus sometimes present; uph pale discal mark nearly constant; unf pale pd band enlarged, ocelli small or absent, grey apical area more extensive; *unh grey, ocelli small or absent*. ♀ups gc golden-buff, pale whitish areas often enlarged on both surfaces.

Flight. End June/July.

Habitat. Bogs and rough grassy places from lowlands to about 2,500 ft.

Distribution. Scotland north of 56°N but including Argyll, also Hebrides and Orkney Islands; characters are best marked in northern areas.
Variation. Less typical south of 56°N and transitional to *C. t. tullia.*

C. tullia demophile Freyer 1844 TL: Lapland   Pl. 47
  syn: *suecica* Hemming 1936
Description. ♂fw 15/18mm., upf gc light yellow-brown, outer border and uph tending more to grey, rarely a small apical ocellus; unf paler, a single apical ocellus, pale pd stripe well-marked, outer border and all hw grey; unh ocelli reduced or absent. ♀ups yellow with rather grey hw; pale markings show through from uns.
Flight. End June/July.
Habitat. Rough grassy places, moorland, etc.
Distribution. Fennoscandia at lowland levels on fjelds and in arctic regions to 70°N, with transitions to *C. t. tiphon* in Baltic countries.

C. tullia rhodopensis Elwes 1900 TL: Bulgaria   Map 210 Pl. 47
Description. ♂fw 16/19mm., ups gc *clear orange-buff*, slightly variable, often with small black basal suffusion; upf apical ocellus usually shows through faintly from uns, fuscous shading along outer margin slight or absent; uph sometimes slightly darker, rarely with ocelli in s2, 3 (Balkan Mts.); unf broadly orange-yellow, pale pd stripe absent or (rarely) vestigial; unh grey with fulvous discal flush, *small white mark in s4–5 constant*, pd ocelli well developed. ♀ups paler, upf clear orange-yellow without black basal suffusion; uph pale discal mark plainly visible.
Flight. July.
Habitat. Mountain meadows at 4,500–7,000 ft.
Distribution. Confined to SE. Europe and C. Italy. Probably flies on all higher mountains from Sarajevo (Trebević) southwards to Mt. Perister; not recorded from Greece. Markings vary slightly in different colonies. Italy, local on a few high mountains in Abruzzi, Monte Sibillini and Monte Baldo, closely resembling Balkan specimens, f. *italica* Verity Pl. 47. Rumania, only at high altitudes in Retezat Mts.

Similar species. *C. pamphilus* below, nearly always smaller and ups gc clear yellow-buff with narrow grey wing borders, unh small submarginal ocelli indistinct if present; ocelli always well formed in s2 and s6 in all European forms of *C. tullia.* *C. glycerion* p. 221.

COENONYMPHA PAMPHILUS *Small Heath*

F: Le Procris   Sw: Kamgräsfjäril   G: Kleiner Heugrassfalter
Sp: Nispola
Range. All Europe and N. Africa, Asia Minor, Lebanon, Iraq, Iran and Turkestan, perhaps further east into Siberia.   Map 21

C. pamphilus pamphilus Linnaeus 1758 TL: not stated Pl. 48
(Sweden, Verity 1953)

Description. ♂fw 14/16mm., ups gc bright yellow-buff with *grey marginal borders* 1–2mm. wide; upf, apical ocellus small, grey; uph a pale discal mark may show through from uns; unf apical ocellus black, white-pupilled and yellow-ringed, indications of pale pd line sometimes present; unh grey nearly unmarked in many northern specimens, basal area often darker and followed by pale pd mark and obscure submarginal ocelli in s1–6. ♀ similar, larger.

Flight. Throughout summer with succession of broods from April in N. Africa and Spain and from end May in N. Europe. Some larvae from each brood hibernate until following spring.

Habitat. Open grassy places from sea leval to 6,000 ft. Larval food plants various grasses, e.g., *Poa annua*, *Nardus stricta*, etc.

Distribution. Throughout W. and N. Europe and N. Africa.

Variation. In some districts of S. Europe summer broods have conspicuous dark grey ups marginal borders. In such specimens unh gc is often brown instead of grey, f. *latecana* Verity.

C.p. pamphilus f. *lyllus* Esper 1805 TL: Portugal Pl. 48

Description. ♂Differs on ups in wider grey marginal borders; unf with black shade along outer margin near anal angle and pd transverse line reddish; unh gc pale buff with dark basal area, markings brown, often indistinct. ♀ similar, unh basal area slightly darker, pd area usually unmarked.

Flight. May or later.

Distribution. The common summer form in the W. Mediterranean region, including the islands, but not fully developed in all localities. It occurs constantly in N. Africa, Spain and Portugal, and often with commoner intermediate forms in S. France and peninsular Italy, uph sometimes with small ocellar pd points.

C. pamphilus thyrsis Freyer 1845 TL: Crete Pl. 46

Description. ♂fw 13/14mm., resembles f. *latecana* Verity; ups dark marginal borders conspicuous; uph frequently with small pd ocellar points; unf dark pd line well defined; unh gc pale buff, dark brown basal area sharply defined, 5 or 6 small black white-pupilled pd ocelli, fuscous shade in s2, 3, 4 followed by metallic antemarginal line. ♀ similar, slightly larger, uph black pd dots constantly present.

Flight. End May and later.

Habitat. Waste ground and rough places among grass, from sea-level.

Distribution. Isle of Crete.

Note. *C. p. thyrsis* is regarded as a distinct species by some authors.

Similar species. *C. tullia* p. 212.

COENONYMPHA CORINNA   *Corsican Heath*

Range. Corsica, Sardinia, Elba.   Map 212

C. corinna corinna   Huebner 1804   TL: Sardinia   Pl. 48
Description. ♂fw 14/15mm., ups bright fulvous with dark fuscous apical
and marginal borders, including costal margin of hw; upf with small blind
yellow-ringed apical ocellus and narrow yellow antemarginal line; uph
unmarked fulvous, apart from black costal border; unh gc fulvous with
margin of darker grey, basal area defined by *very irregular yellowish pd
line often incomplete*, small yellow-ringed ocellus in s6, other pd ocelli
absent or if present very small in a *straight row in s*2, 3, 4. ♀ similar, ups
dark wing-borders often reduced; unh markings better defined and basal
area usually more grey.
Flight. May/June and later with succession of broods through summer.
Habitat. Open grassy places, commonest at about 3,000 ft. Larval food
plants not recorded.
Distribution. Corsica and Sardinia.
Variation. In Corsican specimens unh gc is more fulvous, and there is a
small pale mark in cell opposite origin of v2.

C. corinna elbana   Staudinger 1901   TL: Isle of Elba   Pl. 48
Description. Uph with blind pd ocelli in s2, 3 and 4; unh ocelli larger and
also present in s1b and s5; basal area grey-buff, followed by narrow pale
yellow irregular band.
Flight and Habitat. As for *C. c. corinna*.
Distribution. Elba and locally on Italian mainland near Monte Argentario.

COENONYMPHA DORUS   *Dusky Heath*

Sp: Velado de negro
Range. N. Africa and SW. Europe to C. Italy.   Map 213

C. dorus dorus   Esper 1782   TL: Toulouse, France   Pl. 48
Description. ♂fw 16/17mm., upf grey-brown with yellow undertones,
yellow-ringed apical ocellus blind, pd spaces sometimes partly filled yellow;
uph gc orange-yellow with wide fuscous costal border, blind *ocelli in s*1–4
in internally convex curve, a very small ocellus in s6; uns metallic antemarginal and orange marginal lines; unf a single black white-pupilled
apical ocellus; unh basal area yellow-grey, bordered by slightly irregular
pale yellow or white pd band with distal bulge in s4, 5, pd area paler with
black white-pupilled yellow-ringed ocelli as on ups. ♂ with a wide sex-brand
on upf partly obscured by fuscous gc. ♀upf orange-fulvous, marginal
borders grey with double lines in some races, uph often with fuscous
shading along costa.
Flight. End June/July, in a single brood.
Habitat. Dry stony places from lowlands to 5,000 ft. or more. Larval food
plants not recorded.

Distribution. France, Provence to Aveyron, Lozère and E. Pyrenees. Spain, widely distributed south of Pyrenees, replaced in NW. by *C. d. bieli* (see below). Portugal, common except in north. Local in C. Italy.
Variation. A very variable species with many named local races.

C. dorus bieli Staudinger 1901 **TL: N. Spain** Pl. 48
Description. ♂ fw 15/16mm., ups dark smokey brown, ocelli small or absent; unf apical ocellus small; unh markings grey or yellow-grey, pale pd band variable and often extending into pd area, ocelli small, grey and inconspicuous. ♀ upf orange-brown with dark brown marginal border, with or without apical ocellus; uph fuscous flushed orange-brown, one or two yellow-ringed ocelli present in s2, 3; unh as in ♂ with small ocelli.
Flight and Habitat as for *C. d. dorus*.
Distribution. NW. Spain in Galicia and Leon. N. Portugal, widespread in Minho and Tras os Montes.
Variation. In ♂ ups orange-brown discal flush not rare, esp. uph; small yellow-ringed ocellus uph in s2 common, more rarely also apical ocellus upf.

C. dorus aquilonia Higgins 1968 TL: l'Aquila, C. Italy
Description. ♂ fw 14/16mm., upf grey with fulvous-yellow pd band 2–3mm. wide; uph yellow area includes most of cell, ocelli small, sometimes incomplete; unf apical ocellus small, usual dark markings reduced; unh gc yellow-grey with darker basal area, ocelli small but in complete series. ♀ ups light orange-fulvous, lightly marked with small ocelli; uns resembles ♂ but gc paler.
Flight and Habitat. July, on rough ground at 3,000 ft.
Distribution. C. Italy, local in Marche and Abruzzi, Bolognola, l'Aquila.

C. dorus fettigii Oberthur 1874 TL: Tuelagh, Algeria Pl. 48
Description. ♂ fw 15/16mm., ups resembles *C. d. aquilonia*; upf fulvous-yellow pd patch sometimes extending basad; uph pd ocelli small; unf apex pale grey, dark antemarginal line obsolete; unh gc pale grey, dark basal area defined only near costa, ocelli small or minute but rarely absent. ♀ upf fulvous patch extended to cover base and discal area.
Flight and Habitat. End June/July, on rough ground at 5–6,000 ft.
Distribution. Algeria, in Oran. Morocco, more widely distributed in Middle and High Atlas. Not recorded from Tunisia.
Variation. In High Atlas unh almost uniform pale grey with very pale pd area and minute ocelli.
Note. *C. d. fettigii* is regarded as a distinct species by some authors.

Similar species. *C. austauti* p. 218, unh white discal band narrow, almost straight.

COENONYMPHA AUSTAUTI   *Austaut's Algerian Heath*
Range. Confined to Algeria.   Map 214

C. austauti   Oberthur 1881   TL: Nemours, Algeria   Pl. 46
Description. ♂fw 14/15mm., resembles *C. dorus*, upf with sex-brand, but apex of fw more rounded, apical ocellus large, clearly yellow-ringed; unh gc yellow-grey, *distal border of darker basal area not uneven*, followed by a narrow nearly straight white or pale yellow stripe, ocelli enclosed in yellow-grey band, a yellow antemarginal patch in s1c, 2, 3. Metallic antemarginal lines very bright on uns of both wings. ♀ups fuscous suffusion greatly reduced, resembling *C. dorus*.
Flight. June/July, and perhaps later with continuous emergence.
Habitat. Probably at low or moderate altitudes but little information.
Distribution. Only recorded from Province of Oran in Algeria, in neighbourhood of Nemours, e.g., Masser Mines, Lalla Marnia, Zough-el-Beghal, etc.
Remarks. The relationship between *C. fettigii* and *C. austauti* is confusing. Both forms have been recorded from Lalla Marnia, but whether flying together or not is not known. Existing records suggest that *austauti* is more generally distributed near the coast, perhaps at low altitudes, and *fettigii* is known to fly more commonly in mountains at levels of 4,000 ft. or more.

Similar species. *C. dorus* p. 216.

COENONYMPHA VAUCHERI   *Vaucher's Heath*
Range. Confined to Morocco.   Map 215

C. vaucheri vaucheri   Blachier 1905   TL: High Atlas, Morocco   Pl. 46
Description. ♂fw 17/18mm., ups gc sandy-orange with slight fuscous shading; upf a large blind apical ocellus across s4, 5; uph small blind ocelli in s1c–s4 (5); unf gc much paler beyond darker basal area, apical ocellus with twin silver pupils; unh *striking dark basal area with pale mark in cell*, bordered by pale discal band and regular series of six ocelli enclosed in fuscous pd area. ♀ similar.
Flight. June/July in a single brood.
Habitat. Rough stony ground at altitudes of 8–9,000 ft. Larval food plant unknown.
Distribution. Only in High Atlas esp. on Toubkal Massif, e.g., Amizmiz, etc.

C. vaucheri annoceuri   Wyatt 1952   TL: Annoceur, Middle Atlas
Description. ♂fw 15mm., small, ups without fuscous suffusion; upf blind apical ocellus smaller; uph two or three very small submarginal ocelli; unf gc paler with little contrast between basal and pd areas; unh pd area mostly pale sandy yellow, ocelli small. ♀ similar.

Flight. June.
Habitat. Barren mountain-sides at 5–7,000 ft.
Distribution. Middle Atlas, local, esp. Taghzeft Pass, Annoceur.

COENONYMPHA ARCANIA *Pearly Heath*

Sp: Mancha Leonada Sw: Pärlgräsfjäril G: Perlgrasfalter
Range. From W. Europe through Asia Minor and S. Russia to southern
Urals. Map 216

C. arcania arcania Linnaeus 1761 TL: Sweden Pl. 47
  syn: *amyntas* Poda 1761
Description. ♂fw 17/20mm., ups gc yellow-orange; upf fuscous marginal
borders wide; uph dark fuscous, usually with traces of orange marginal
line at anal angle and sometimes a small pd ocellus; unf dark border reduced, sometimes replaced by orange marginal and metallic antemarginal
lines; unh gc orange-brown to grey, *conspicuous white irregular pd band
wide in s4, 5*, black white-pupilled yellow-ringed ocelli in s2–3 in pd area,
often with additional small ocelli in s1c, 4, 5, *prominent ocellus proximal
to pd band in s6*, orange marginal and metallic antemarginal lines as on fw.
♀ similar.
Flight. June/July usually in a single brood, partial second broods may occur
in southern localities.
Habitat. Grassy banks and light woodland from lowlands to 4,000 ft. in
Alps to Jura, to over 6,000 ft. in Pyrenees, commonest in hilly country.
Larval food plants grasses, esp. *Melica*.
Distribution. W. Europe, widely distributed to 60°N. Spain, local in
northern and central districts, San Ildefonso, Cuenca, etc. Portugal.
Absent from S. Spain, Britain, Sicily, Corsica, Sardinia, Elba and Crete.
Variation. In C. Spain uph often with a slight fulvous flush.

C. arcania darwiniana Staudinger 1871 TL: Valais, Switzerland p. 268
Description. ♂fw 16/17mm., resembles *C. a. arcania* but usually smaller;
unh gc greyish-fulvous, pd band white or yellowish, *narrow, often slightly
irregular*, ocelli mostly well developed, encircled with wide yellow rings,
small in s5, *ocellus in s6 in ♂ usually proximal to pale band*, but in ♀ more
often enclosed within it. ♀ otherwise resembles ♂.
Flight. July/August in a single brood.
Habitat. Subalpine meadows at 5,000 ft. or more, rarely at lower altitudes.
Distribution. Maritimes and Basses Alpes. Switzerland on southern alpine
slopes in Valais, Tessin, Graubünden and eastwards locally to Mendel,
Schlern and Dolomites. Also recorded from Massif Central of France and
Monts de Forez.

Similar species. *C. gardetta* p. 220, unh ocelli without external yellow rings.

COENONYMPHA GARDETTA *Alpine Heath*
Range. Confined to Alps and N. Balkans.   Map 217

C. gardetta de Prunner 1798 TL: Val Varaita, Alpes Maritimes
                                                                Pl. 47
  syn: *satyrion* Esper 1804; *philea* Huebner 1800 (invalid homonym);
  neoclides Huebner 1805
Description. ♂fw 15/16mm., upf grey-brown with slight fulvous discal
flush in some specimens; uph grey, orange marginal line at anal angle
vestigial; unf gc tawny, apex and outer border grey, often with small
apical ocellus; unh grey with *regular white submarginal band* enclosing
ocelli in s1–6, and metallic antemarginal and orange marginal lines. ♀upf
orange-brown with fuscous border from apex down outer margin; uph
grey-brown, orange marginal line usually present.
Flight. July/August.
Habitat. High alpine meadows at 5–7,000 ft., often very abundant; exceptionally at lower levels, e.g., Gimel, Switzerland at 2,700 ft. Larval food
plants not known.
Distribution. Hautes Alpes, Savoie and Haute Savoie and eastwards
through the higher Alps including Bavarian Alps, Dolomites and Hohe
Tauern to Karawanken Mts.
Variation. At high altitudes in northern Alps ♂ ups may be plain grey without fulvous and ♀ paler with upf fulvous area reduced. At lower altitudes
upf fulvous area is often increased, sometimes with enlarged submarginal
ocelli on unh, f. *macrophthalmica* Stauder, esp. in eastern Alps from
Berchtesgaden, Dolomites, etc.
Similar species. *C. arcania darwiniana* p. 219.

COENONYMPHA ARCANIOIDES *Moroccan Pearly Heath*
Range. Confined to Morocco, Algeria and Tunisia, north of Atlas Mts.
                                                                Map 218

C. arcanioides Pierret 1837 TL: Oran, Algeria   Pl. 47
Description. ♂fw 14/15mm., upf gc fulvous, dark fuscous border along
outer margin wide, extending over apex and enclosing blind apical
ocellus; uph fuscous with orange marginal line at anal angle; unf a large
white-pupilled apical ocellus preceded by transverse yellow pd line; unh
gc dark brown with *narrow irregular white pd stripe* followed by small
ocelli; metallic antemarginal lines along outer margins of both wings.
♀ similar.
Flight. April to September in continuous broods without obvious seasonal
variation.
Habitat. Uncultivated grassy places; especially common near coast and
up to 5,000 ft. Larval food plants not recorded.
Distribution. Morocco, Algeria and Tunisia, in coastal regions and on
northern slopes of Middle Atlas.

COENONYMPHA LEANDER *Russian Heath*

Range. From Hungary and Bulgaria through S. Russia, Asia Minor and Armenia to Iran. Map 219

C. leander Esper 1784 TL: Russia, Volga Pl. 47

Description. ♂fw 16/17mm., ups gc dark brown; upf fulvous flush often present from base to cell-end; uph sometimes with two or three submarginal blind ocelli and an orange mark at anal angle which may spread into s2, 3; unf gc light fulvous with small white-pupilled apical ocellus; unh light fulvous with pale grey basal shade, six white-pupilled yellow-ringed black submarginal ocelli in regular series, and *prominent orange band between ocelli and metallic antemarginal line.* ♀upf yellow-buff, more or less shaded fuscous towards outer margin, often with small apical ocellus; uph *yellow anal submarginal marks* often expanded into a band sometimes enclosing small ocelli; uns markings as in ♂.

Flight. May/June, in a single brood.

Habitat. Rough grassy places from lowlands to moderate altitudes. Larval food plants unknown.

Distribution. Carpathians, Rumania, Bulgaria and SE. Yugoslavia.

Similar species. *C. iphioides* p. 222.

COENONYMPHA GLYCERION *Chestnut Heath*

G: Rostbraunes Wiesenvögelchen Sw: Darrgräsfjäril

Range. From W. Europe across Russia to Siberia. Map 220

C. glycerion Borkhausen 1788 TL: not stated (Bavaria)
syn: *iphis* Schiffermueller 1775 (invalid homonym) Pl. 47

Description. ♂fw 16/18mm., ups gc chestnut brown; upf without apical ocellus; uph usually unmarked, occasionally with one or two blind submarginal ocelli; unf tawny brown with wide grey border at apex and down outer margin; unh grey, *with white discal marks in s(1c) and s4,* six pale-ringed pd ocelli of uneven size *with brilliant white pupils* (rarely very small or absent in s4, 5), and usually an orange antemarginal line near anal angle. ♀ both wings ups and uns with faint orange antemarginal lines, usually preceded on unh by a narrow metallic line; *upf orange-buff; uph dark grey,* sometimes with two or three small ocelli; unf gc as upf; unh pale grey, ocelli larger, with brilliant pupils.

Flight. June/July in a single brood.

Habitat. Grassy places from foothills to 5,000 ft., not uncommon, but local. Larval food plants various grasses, e.g., *Melica, Brachypodium, Cynsurus,* etc.

Distribution. N. Spain (Huesca). E. Pyrenees and central France, through Switzerland and central Europe to S. Finland, Baltic countries, Rumania, Bulgaria and N. Yugoslavia. Italy in northern Alps and Apennines, but very local. Absent from Britain, W. and N. France, Basses and Hautes

Pyrénées, Spain (except Huesca), Portugal, Belgium, Holland, NW. Germany, Scandinavia, S. Italy and Greece.

Similar species. *C. pamphilus* p. 214 and *C. tullia* p. 212, both of which have an apical ocellus on upf. *C. iphioides* below.

COENONYMPHA IPHIOIDES   *Spanish Heath*

Sp: Castaneo morena
Range. Confined to northern and central Spain.   Map 221

C. iphioides   Staudinger 1870   TL: Castile, Spain   Pl. 47
Description. ♂ fw 17/20mm., resembling *C. iphis* but larger; ups gc dark brown; upf a tawny flush from base across disc; uph with or without two or three blind submarginal ocelli, a narrow orange marginal line near anal angle; unf fulvous, apex grey with small ocellus; unh gc grey with white pd mark in s4, often small sometimes absent, *six white-pupilled yellow-ringed ocelli of nearly uniform size in s1c–s6*, and metallic antemarginal and *orange marginal line* from anal angle to s5. ♀upf gc orange-buff with grey outer margin and *yellow marginal line*, often with small apical ocellus; uph dark grey with yellow marginal line, with or without ocelli; unh ocelli conspicuous.
Flight. June/July.
Habitat. Rough moist grassy uplands to 5,500 ft. Larval food plants not known.
Distribution. Spain, northern and central districts south of Pyrenees, including southern slopes of Cantabrian Mts. to Leon (Brañuelas) and south to Teruel and Sierra de Guadarrama. Not recorded from Portugal.
Variation. There is slight minor variation principally in development o' ocelli on hw.
Similar species. *C. glycerion* p. 221, smaller, ♂ups markings similar; unl white mark in s4 often larger, ocelli relatively smaller and less uniform i size, orange marginal line often poorly defined. ♀uns ocelli much les prominent than in *iphioides* and orange marginal line much less brillian *C. leander* p. 221, with very different distribution, unf without grey apex unh without orange marginal line but with orange submarginal band be yond the very regular ocelli.

COENONYMPHA HERO   *Scarce Heath*

G: Wald-Wiesenvögelchen   Sw: Brun Gräsfjäril
Range. From N. France and Scandinavia across C. Europe and Asia t Amur, Korea and Japan.   Map 22

C. hero   Linnaeus 1761   TL: S. Sweden   Pl. ·
Description. ♂ fw 15/17mm., *ups uniformly dark grey-brown*; upf u marked; uph usually with *yellow-ringed generally blind submargin ocelli* in s1c, 2, 3, (4) (variable) and orange marginal line at anal angl

unf grey-brown with pale pd transverse shade and small apical ocellus; unh an irregular white pd line before a series of six black white-pupilled yellow-ringed ocelli, metallic antemarginal and orange marginal lines. ♀ slightly larger and paler; upf a small apical ocellus; uph ocelli more prominent.
Flight. End May/June in a single brood.
Habitat. Damp meadows, moorlands, etc., at moderate altitudes. Larval food plants various grasses, esp. *Elymus arenarius*.
Distribution. Southern Scandinavia. France, only in NE. Belgium. Holland. Germany (rare). Baltic countries, Lithuania, etc. An extremely local species with colonies widely scattered.
Similar species. *C. oedippus* below.

COENONYMPHA OEDIPPUS *False Ringlet*

G: Moor-Wiesenvögelchen   Sp: Lindos ojos
Range. From W. Europe through Russia and C. Asia to China and Japan
Map 223

C. oedippus oedippus Fabricius 1787 TL: S. Russia   Pl. 47
Description. ♂ fw 17/21 mm., resembles *A. hyperantus* but smaller; ups gc dark brown (black), fw unmarked; uph small ocelli often dimly visible in s2, 3; uns gc yellow-brown; unf small pd ocelli usually present in s2, 3 and (4); unh silver-pupilled pd ocelli present in s1–4 and s6 (*large, displaced basad*), ocellus in s5 small or absent, *metallic antemarginal line* constant on hw, vestigial on fw. ♀ similar, larger, with ocelli better developed on both surfaces, often bordered proximally by pale band.
Flight. June/July in a single brood.
Habitat. Wet meadows and boggy places in lowlands, but sometimes also in dry woodland or scrub with open grassy places. Larval food plants include *Lolium, Carex, Iris pseudacorus*.
Distribution. France, very local in widely distributed colonies in Isère, Hte Garonne, Basses Pyrénées, E. Pyrenees, Landes, Deux Sèvres, Charente, etc. Belgium (rare). Italy, near Turin, etc., Venezia Giulia. Germany, no recent records.

C. oedippus hungarica Rebel 1900 TL: not stated
Description. ♂ fw 17/19 mm., ups ocelli absent; uns ocelli rudimentary on fw, small on hw, but ocellus in s6 remains conspicuous, with pale proximal bar present in both sexes.
Flight and **Habitat** as above.
Distribution. Austria ('Vienna'), Hungary.
Variation. Minor local variation in size and development of markings occurs in most colonies.
Similar species. *C. hero* p. 222, smaller, ocelli usually well developed on

PLATE 39

1. **Erebia pandrose**   *Dewy Ringlet*   200
   E. pandrose ♂. Upf with dark transverse discal line; unh ground-
   colour grey, discal band defined by two irregular dark lines. **For ♀ see
   Pl. 44.**

2. **Erebia sthennyo**   *False Dewy Ringlet*   200
   E. sthennyo ♂. Upf discal markings indistinct; unh pale grey, almost
   unmarked.

3. **Erebia manto**   *Manto Ringlet*   158
   3a. *E. manto* ♂. Ups fulvous bands well developed, enclosing small
       black points between veins; unh with wide yellowish marks in
       spaces 4, 5 and 6.
   3b. *E. manto* ♀. Ups ground-colour paler brown; unh basal and
       discal markings yellow, elongate. See also Pls. **28, 38, 44.**

4. **Erebia meolans**   *Piedmont Ringlet*   198
   4a. *E. m. meolans* ♂. Ups brightly marked; unh very dark, post-
       discal area faintly paler; ocelli small or absent. **For ♀ see Pl. 44.**
   4b. *E. m. bejarensis* ♂. Large, ups fulvous bands wide, bright, ocelli
       conspicuous.
   4c. *E. m. valesiaca* ♂. Small, ups fulvous markings reduced; unf
       fulvous band short.

5. **Erebia triaria**   *de Prunner's Ringlet*   169
   E. triaria ♂. Upf with 3 apical ocelli in series; unh very dark, rough,
   with obscure black transverse markings (distinction from *E. meolans*).
   ♀ unh paler brown, darker discal band defined.

6. **Erebia aethiops**   *Scotch Argus*   168
   6a. *E. a.* f. *caledonia* ♂. Small, ups fulvous markings reduced; unh
       with 3 small white spots in paler postdiscal band. **For ♀ see Pl. 44.**
   6b. *E. a. aethiops* ♀. Fringes slightly chequered; ups brightly
       marked; unh pale grey, brown discal band wide.

7. **Erebia scipio**   *The Larche Ringlet*   189
   7a. *E. scipio* ♂. Upf with twin apical ocelli in fulvous band; unf
       discal area chestnut-red; unh dark chestnut brown, unmarked.
   7b. *E. scipio* ♀. Ups paler, more brightly marked; unh pale grey.

PLATE 40

1. Erebia polaris *Arctic Woodland Ringlet* 174
E. polaris ♂. Unh red-brown (contrasting with smooth uniform grey-brown of *E. medusa*); postdiscal area faintly paler. ♀ unh markings better defined.

2. Erebia epistygne *Yellow Spring Ringlet* 182
E. epistygne ♂. Upf postdiscal band pale yellow; unf ground-colour red-brown. ♀ similar.

3. Erebia oeme *The Bright-eyed Ringlet* 195
    3a. *E. o. oeme* ♂. Ups fulvous markings small, pupils of ocelli gleaming white; tip of antenna black (distinction from *E. medusa*). See also Pl. 37.
    3b. *E. o. spodia* ♀. Ups ocelli very large with brilliant white pupils; unh ground-colour yellowish-brown.

4. Erebia montana *The Marbled Ringlet* 191
    4a. *E. m. goante* ♂. Upf fulvous band rather narrow; unh ground-colour very dark, marbled white and sprinkled with white scales.
    4b. *E. m. montana* ♀. Ups paler, brightly marked; unh brightly marbled dark on pale grey; fringes slightly chequered; veins white.

5. Erebia medusa *The Woodland Ringlet* 171
    5a. *E. m. medusa* ♂. Ups markings orange-yellow; unh uniform smooth brown; tip of antenna brown (distinction from *E. oeme*). ♀ similar, brighter. See also Pl. 44.
    5b. *E. m. hippomedusa* ♂. Small, ups dark brown, ocelli very small, ringed fulvous. ♀ similar.

6. Erebia gorgone *The Gavarnie Ringlet* 181
    6a. *E. gorgone* ♂. Ups dark, upf postdiscal band red-brown, male sex-brand conspicuous; unh with distinctly paler postdiscal band.
    6b. *E. gorgone* ♀. Ups paler, ocelli larger; unh marbled yellow-grey, veins lined paler.

7. Erebia melas *The Black Ringlet* 187
Uph ocelli, when present, are near outer margin.
    7a. *E. m. leonhardi* ♂. Ups black ocelli lack fulvous circles; uph ocelli indicated by small white spots between veins.
    7b. *E. m. leonhardi* ♀. Ups dark brown, upf apical ocelli large, widely ringed fulvous; unh base dark with paler postdiscal area.

uph, and on unh preceded by conspicuous white band. *A. hyperantus* p. 207, larger, unh large ocellus in s 4 absent.

PARARGE AEGERIA   *Speckled Wood*

F: Le Tircis Sw: Kvickgräsfjäril G: Laubfalter Sp: Maculada
Range. From W. Europe through Asia Minor, Syria and Russia to C. Asia.   Map 224

P. aegeria aegeria Linnaeus 1758 TL: S. Europe and N. Africa Pl. 49
Description. ♂ fw 19/22 mm., fw outer margin concave below v 5; hw outer margin rather deeply scalloped; ups gc orange-yellow with dark criss-cross markings; upf a small apical ocellus and a broad sex-brand from inner margin below median vein to v 4 and extending along v 2 and v 3; uph ocelli in s 2, 3, 4 (5); *unh* yellow-brown with *greenish tint*, markings confused, darker area along outer margin enclosing small white spots between veins. ♀ similar.
Flight. March or later with successive broods until October.
Habitat. Shady places and woodland from sea-level to 4,000 ft. in Europe, to 5,500 ft. in Africa. Larval food plants various grasses, esp. couch grass (*Agropyron*), also *Triticum repens*, etc.
Distribution. S. and C. France; S. Switzerland. Italy, esp. peninsular Italy. Spain and Portugal. Mediterranean islands. Morocco. Algeria. Tunisia.

P. aegeria tircis Butler 1867 TL: France   Pl. 49
    syn: *egerides* Staudinger 1871
Description. Resembles *P. a. aegeria* but gc on ups pale yellow to white, on uns cream-white, paler in late broods. ♀ similar.
Flight and Habitat as for *P.a. aegeria* but appears first about April.
Distribution. Northern, central and eastern Europe to 63°N, including British Isles and Balkan countries.
Variation. The distribution areas of the two colour forms are not clearly defined; late broods of the northern *P.a. tircis* incline in the southern range to *P.a. aegeria*. The *aegeria*-form is constant in the western Mediterranean as far east as Sicily, reappearing in Lebanon.

PARARGE XIPHIOIDES   *Canary Speckled Wood*
Range. Confined to Canary Islands.

P. xiphioides Staudinger 1871 TL: Canary Islands   Pl. 4
Description. ♂ fw 21/24 mm., size variable, smaller in late broods; resemble *P. aegeria* in colour but outer margin of fw not concave at v 5; upf apical ocellus small; unh light brown with darker chestnut markings, prominen white costal mark generally extending to cell; pd ocelli often strongl marked. ♀ similar, larger, ups gc paler; unh gc yellow-grey with brow markings as in ♂.

Flight. May to September or later.
Habitat. Widespread and common.
Distribution. Canary Islands, but not known from Hierro, Fuerteventura or Lanzarote.

PARARGE XIPHIA *Madeiran Speckled Wood*
Range. Restricted to Madeira.

P. xiphia Fabricius 1775 TL: Madeira   Pl. 46
Description. ♂fw 26/27mm., fw bluntly pointed with outer margin gently convex; hw outer margin rather deeply scalloped; ups resembles *P. aegeria* but dark criss-cross markings more extensive, orange gc darker and reduced to small spots; upf apical ocellus vestigial, narrow sex-brand below cell extends from v1 to v4, covered with long hair that fills cell; unf gc orange-fulvous; unh bright chestnut-brown with small white mark on costa and grey marginal border. ♀unh gc paler grey-brown, basal area darker with larger white costal mark.
Flight. May and later to August.
Habitat. From sea-level to 2,500 ft. or more, often common in Funchal.

LASIOMMATA MEGERA *Wall Brown*
F: Le Satyre Sw: Svingelgräsfjäril G: Mauerfuchs
Sp: Saltacercas
Range. From W. Europe and N. Africa through Russia and Asia Minor to Syria, Lebanon and Iran.   Map 225

L. megera megera Linnaeus 1767 TL: Austria and Denmark Pl. 49
Description. ♂fw 19/25mm.; *ups gc orange-yellow* with black lattice wing-pattern; upf apical ocellus and sex-brand conspicuous; uph smaller pd ocelli in s1c, 2, 3, 4; unh grey with confused basal and discal markings including brown-ringed pd ocelli in s1c–s6. ♀ similar, ups often slightly paler.
Flight. March or later, two broods in C. Europe, three in S. Europe.
Habitat. Rough ground, gardens, woodland glades, etc., from sea-level to 5,000 ft. Larval food plant grasses esp. *Poa* and *Dactylis*.
Distribution. Widely distributed in N. Africa and Europe to 60°N, including Ireland and Mediterranean islands. Absent from Madeira and Canary Islands; replaced in Corsica and Sardinia by following subspecies.

L. megera paramegaera Huebner 1824 TL: Sardinia (Verity 1953)
                                    Pl. 49
  syn: *tigelius* Bonelli 1826
Description. ♂fw 18/19mm., resembles *L. m. megera*, but upf black pd line in s1b and s2 thin, sometimes incomplete; uph fuscous pd line internal to ocelli lacking.

Flight. April to September, probably three broods.
Habitat. Rough places esp. open moorland at about 3,000 ft.
Distribution. Sardinia and Corsica.
Variation. Corsican specimens are more lightly marked, and on upf the pd line in s1c and s2 is usually absent; the thin, partly obsolete appearance of the black markings on ups is especially noticeable in females. Similar forms have been reported from Sicily and Majorca.
Similar species. *L. maera* below, ♀ larger, upf with single dark bar in cell.

LASIOMMATA MAERA *Large Wall Brown*

F: Le Nemusian (♂) et l'Ariane (♀) Sw: Vitgräsfjäril
G: Braunauge Sp: Pedregosa
Range. From N. Africa and W. Europe across Russia, Asia Minor and Syria to Iran, central Asia and Himalayas. Map 226

L. maera maera Linnaeus 1758 TL: Sweden (Verity 1953) Pl. 49
  syn: *monotonia* Schilde, 1885; *hiera* Fabricius 1777
Description. ♂ fw *first brood* 25/28 mm., *second brood* 22/23 mm., ups brown; upf a large white-pupilled apical ocellus in s4 and 5, sometimes with two pupils, and sometimes a small ocellus in s6, fulvous pd area broken by dark veins, sex-brand somewhat obscured by brown discal area; *uph* yellow-ringed white-pupilled ocelli in s2, 3, 4, *discal area unmarked*; unh grey with confused markings and small brown-ringed pd ocelli in s2–s6. ♀upf fulvous pd band brighter and wider, enclosing apical ocellus.
Flight. June/July in a single brood in northern range; May/June and August/September in two broods in southern range.
Habitat. Rough places and rocky paths in hills and mountains from lowlands to 6,000 ft. Larval food plants various grasses, e.g., *Poa annua, Glyceria fluitans*.
Distribution. Common and widely distributed in W. Europe from Mediterranean coasts to 68°N. Absent from Britain, Corsica, Sardinia, Crete and Atlantic islands.
Variation. In S. France, Spain and Portugal fulvous markings are more extensive in both sexes, in ♀upf orange-yellow, lightly marked, f. *adrasta* p. 272 Illiger. In all localities late broods emerging August/September are generally small with ups fulvous markings more extensive. In northern Scandinavia males are small, often dark but in ♀upf pale yellowish apical patch is well defined, f. *borealis* Fuchs.

L. maera meadewaldoi Rothschild 1917 TL: Algeria
  syn: *alluaudi* Oberthur 1922
Description. ♂ fw 28 mm., large with exaggerated *adrasta*-features; ups fiery orange-fulvous and uns more brown than grey, suggesting a well-defined subspecies. Smaller specimens, probably of late broods, have been

taken occasionally in the Middle Atlas and in the Rif. Very similar forms occur in S. Spain.

Distribution. Algeria and Morocco on High Atlas June and July.

Similar species. *L. petropolitana* below; *L. megera* p. 227.

LASIOMMATA PETROPOLITANA *Northern Wall Brown*

Sw: Berggräsfjäril G: Braunscheckauge
Range. From Pyrenees through Alps and Fennoscandia, Russia and N. Siberia to the Amur. Map 227

L. petropolitana Fabricius 1787 TL: Petrograd Pl. 49
  syn: *hiera* auct.
Description. ♂fw 19/21 mm., like *L. maera* but smaller; upf with two, often obscure, dark cross-bars in cell; unf dark line between apical ocellus and cell-end close to ocellus; *uph with dark curving wavy transverse discal line.* ♀ similar.
Flight. May/July, according to locality, in a single brood.
Habitat. Frequent in open spaces in woodland of pine or spruce, from sea-level in the high north to 6,000 ft. in southern Alps. Larval food plants grasses, esp. *Festuca.*
Distribution. Fennoscandia to 68°N; as a mountain butterfly in Pyrenees, Alps and probably on all higher mountains to Bulgaria, SE. Yugoslavia and Greece (Pindus Mts.), though not certainly known in southern Carpathians. Not recorded from Spain, Jura, Vosges, Apennine or Tatra Mts.

Similar species. *L. maera* p. 228, uph without wavy transverse discal line.

LOPINGA ACHINE *Woodland Brown*

F: La Bacchante Sw: Dårgräsfjäril G: Bacchantin
Range. From N. France and S. Scandinavia through C. Europe, Russia and north-central Asia to Amur, Ussuri and Japan. Map 228

L. achine Scopoli 1763 TL: Carniola Pl. 33
  syn: *deianira* Linnaeus 1764
Description. ♂fw 25/27mm., outer margins of wings slightly wavy; ups gc uniform light grey-brown, each wing with an evenly curved *row of large yellow-ringed blind ocelli* in pd area; uns paler, ocelli as on ups with or without white pupils and prominently yellow-ringed, preceded on fw by pale buff and on hw by a white stripe; both wings with double pale buff antemarginal lines. ♀ similar, slightly larger and paler. Males are without a sex-brand but androconia are abundant on uph.
Flight. Early June/July in a single brood; females emerge later than males.
Habitat. Shady woodland from lowlands to 3,000 ft. Larval food plants various grasses, *Lolium, Triticum.*
Distribution. Very local in widely scattered colonies. S. Fennoscandia, Germany, Baltic countries. France, widely distributed esp. in N. and E.;

Belgium; Switzerland; Italy, north of the Po and eastwards. Recorded from N. Yugoslavia. Not recorded from Poland or Czechoslovakia.

KIRINIA ROXELANA *Lattice Brown*
Range. From SE. Europe through Asia Minor to Cyprus, Syria and Iraq.

Map 229

K. roxelana Cramer 1777 TL: Istanbul   Pl. 14
Description. ♂ fw 29/31 mm., fw narrow, pointed; hw cell long; ups gc brown; upf with fulvous flush and small apical ocellus in s5, a complicated pattern of sex-brands occupies basal and much of discal areas causing distortion of v1 and shape of wing; uph ocelli show through faintly from uns; unh series of white-pupilled yellow-ringed pd ocelli smallest in s4 and s5. ♀ fw of normal shape; upf with white costal and apical spots; unh wing-markings much better defined.
Flight. End May/June/July from lowlands to 3,500 ft.
Habitat. Rough ground, hill paths, etc., prefers to sit in low bushes and rarely flies unless disturbed. Larval food plant not known.
Distribution. Eastern Hungary, Rumania, southern Balkans including Yugoslavia, Bulgaria, Greece, Albania and Turkey.

NEMEOBIIDAE
Bates 1868

Closely related to the Lycaenidae, but differing in important respects; male fore-leg greatly reduced, useless for walking. An extensive family which reaches its maximum development in the American tropics. In the Old World it is represented by a few genera in tropical Asia and Africa, and in Europe by a single species.

HAMEARIS LUCINA   *Duke of Burgundy Fritillary*

Sw: Gullvivefjäril   **G**: Perlbinde   **Sp**: Perico

Range. From C. Spain widely distributed through S. and C. Europe to C. Russia.   Map 230

H. lucina Linnaeus 1758   TL: England (Verity 1943)   Pls. 14, 21

Description. ♂fw 14/17mm., ups gc dark brown to black with small fulvous spots arranged in transverse series, well-marked on fw, on hw sometimes nearly obliterated by extension of dark gc; unf cinnamon-brown, basal markings as on ups; unh discal band and marginal area cinnamon-brown, *basal and pd spots white in transverse series*. ♀ similar.

Flight. May and August in two broods in southern range, a single brood in May/June in north.

Habitat. A lowland species, usually in woodland clearings, rarely to 4,000 ft. Larval food plants cowslips and primroses.

Distribution. Throughout C. Europe to 60°N, including England, S. Sweden and Baltic countries, but local. Spain, local, from Guadarrama northwards. Rare in Italy except on southern Alpine slopes. Absent from S. Spain, Ireland and Mediterranean islands excepting Sicily.

Variation. Northern races are small, ♂fw 13/14mm.; southern races often larger, especially in N. Italy with ♂fw 16/17mm., f. *praestans* Verity Pl. 14. In *second brood* often with extended dark markings f. *schwingenschussi* Rebel Pl. 21.

LYCAENIDAE
Leach 1815

The Blues, Coppers and Hairstreaks that comprise this very extensive family are small or very small butterflies, the males characteristically blue, coppery or brown, females normally less brilliant. Some 100 species occur in the region. Structural characters are remarkably uniform throughout the family. Specific identification may be difficult. The best characters are found on the undersides, especially of the hind-wings, in the precise arrangement of the small markings, spots and striae, which are usually identical in both sexes.

CIGARITIS ZOHRA   *Donzel's Silver-line*
Range. Restricted to N. Africa.   Map 231

C. zohra Donzel 1847 **TL:** Algeria   Pl. 52
Description. ♂ fw 12/13 mm., upf small black spot in cell, pd row irregular, spot in s 4 displaced distad; uph discoidal spot large; uns *gc of hw and costa of fw white*; unh with many brown silver-centred spots, the *crowded pd series sharply angled at v 4*, base sometimes entirely black. ♀ similar.
Flight. March/June depending upon locality and season.
Habitat. Mountains up to 5,500 ft., exact information not available. Larval food plant unknown.
Distribution. Morocco; Anosseur, Ifrane. Algeria; Sebdou, Saida, Kralfallh. Tunisia.
Variation. Ups markings variable; upf spots may be reduced to discoidal spot, costal and marginal spots; uns gc may be grey-brown, f. *jugurtha* Oberthur. Minor local variation is considerable.

Similar species. *C. allardi* p. 233, unh macular markings in straight rows. *C. siphax* below, unh spots smaller, gc usually darker, often reddish.

CIGARITIS SIPHAX   *Common Silver-line*
Range. Confined to Algeria and Tunisia.   Map 232

C. siphax Lucas 1847 **TL:** Algeria   Pl. 52
Description. ♂ fw 12/13 mm., ups marginal markings not well defined; upf pd spots irregular, spot in s 4 displaced distad; uns *gc of apex of fw and all hw some shade of brown*, often with reddish tint, with *obscure small round silver-centred spots* arranged as in *C. zohra*. ♀ similar.
Flight. March or later, sometimes in two broods April/May and September.
Habitat. Dry hillsides at moderate altitudes.
Distribution. Algeria; Bône, Aflou, Collo, Khenchela. Tunisia; Ain Draham. Not reported from Morocco.

Variation. On ups all markings are variable, esp. black marginal spots which are sometimes obsolete; uns gc of hw varies from brown to near purple.

Similar species. *C. zohra* p. 232.

CIGARITIS ALLARDI *Allard's Silver-line*
Range. Confined to N. Africa. Map 233

C. allardi Oberthur 1909 TL: Sebdou, Algeria Pl. 52
Description. ♂fw 12mm., upf black spots in oblique discoidal row with twin spots in s4, 5 isolated; submarginal spots large and regular on both wings; unh gc white, with large silver-centred *spots in straight basal, discal and pd rows.* ♀ similar.
Flight. May.
Habitat. No information; food plant unknown.
Distribution. Algeria; Sebdou, Masser Mines, Djebel Maktar at 5–6,000 ft., Abu Safra. Morocco.
Variation. In Morocco larger, more brightly coloured, ups black markings larger.

Similar species. *C. zohra* p. 232.

THECLA BETULAE *Brown Hairstreak*
Sw: Björksnabbvinge G: Nierenfleck or Birkenfalter Sp: Topacio
Range. C. and S. Europe and across Asia to Amurland and Korea.
Map 234

T. betulae Linnaeus 1758 TL: Sweden (Verity 1943) Pl. 50
Description. ♂fw 17/18mm., ups gc brown; upf with vertical mark at cell-end followed by orange patch, sometimes poorly developed; uph with small orange marks on margin at v1 and v2; uns orange-yellow, darkened towards outer margins; unf a narrow mark at cell-end, pd transverse line white; *unh with short discal and complete pd white transverse lines* with darker orange between, and narrow dark marginal line before white fringe. ♀ larger, upf with wide orange-red pd transverse band; uns gc more intense orange-red, markings more brilliant.
Flight. July/August.
Habitat. In light woodland at low to moderate altitudes. Larval food plants sloe, plum, birch, etc.
Distribution. C. and N. Europe to 62°N, including Ireland and England, from N. Spain and Pyrenees eastwards to Bulgaria. Italy, not south of Rome. Absent from S. Balkans, S. Italy, Mediterranean islands, Portugal and S. Spain.

QUERCUSIA QUERCUS *Purple Hairstreak*

Sw: Eksnabbvinge G: Eichenfalter Sp: Nazarena
Range. Europe and N. Africa and across Russia and Asia Minor to Armenia.   Map 235

Q. quercus quercus Linnaeus 1758 TL: England (Verity 1943) Pl. 50
Description. ♂fw 12/14mm., ups *both wings gleaming purple-blue* with black marginal borders; uns gc dove grey with white transverse pd line on each wing and obscure sub-marginal markings; unf yellow marks at anal angle in s1 and s2 (3), best marked in N. Europe; unh anal lobe and circle round black spot in s2 both yellow. ♀ gleaming royal blue in s1b and in cell; unh submarginal markings more distinct.
Flight. July/August.
Habitat. In woodlands from lowlands to 5,000 ft. Larval food plant oak, rarely ash.
Distribution. Throughout Europe to 60°N, including Britain, Mediterranean islands and Crete. Replaced in SW. by following subspecies.

Q. quercus iberica Staudinger 1901 TL: S. Spain and   Pl. 50
Morocco.
Description. Ups like *Q. q. quercus*; uns gc very pale-grey, markings reduced, often vestigial; unh black spot in s2 often absent.
Flight. June/July.
Habitat. Flies around ash and oak trees from 3–7,000 ft.
Distribution. Portugal. Spain, widely distributed in C. and S. districts. Morocco and Algeria, common.

LAEOSOPIS ROBORIS *Spanish Purple Hairstreak*

Sp: Moradilla del Fresno
Range. Restricted to Portugal, Spain and SE. France.   Map 236

L. roboris Esper 1793 TL: 'Frankfurt am Main' (error)   Pl. 50
Description. ♂fw 12/15mm., upf dark purple-blue with wide black marginal borders; uph black with basal purple patch, sometimes small; uns yellow-grey with yellow marginal borders and small black marginal dots between veins. ♀ larger, fw more rounded; upf a shining blue patch in s1b extending into cell; uph black; uns marginal markings better defined with broken silver antemarginal line on hw and black marginal spots capped with blue-white chevrons, sometimes partly developed also in ♂.
Flight. End May/June/early July.
Habitat. From sea-level to nearly 5,000 ft., on mountains, flying round ash trees, esp. small isolated trees. Larval food plant ash (*Fraxinus excelsior*).
Distribution. France, widely distributed in Provence, Cevennes and E. Pyrenees. Spain, esp. in N. and C. Spain, less common or absent near eastern seaboard and in SW, absent from Galicia. Portugal, not recorded from southern provinces.

NORDMANNIA ACACIAE *Sloe Hairstreak*

Sp: Sin Perfume
Range. From Spain across S. Europe and S. Russia to Asia Minor.

Map 237

N. acaciae Fabricius 1787 TL: S. Russia Pl. 50
Description. ♂fw 14/16mm., without sex-brand; hw tail on v2 often short; ups dark brown; upf unmarked; uns gc paler brown; unf white pd stripe often faintly marked and broken, darker shade at anal angle in s1b very common; unh white pd line better developed, *marginal lunules in s1a–s3 orange*, that in s2 with *black marginal spot*. ♀ similar, with *black anal tuft*.
Flight. June/July.
Habitat. Rough ground around sloe bushes, from sea-level to 5,000 ft. Larval food plant sloe (*Prunus spinosa*).
Distribution. S. Europe to 48°N, in S. Germany to 51°N, and eastwards to Balkans. France, north to Rennes, local, common in Jura. Switzerland, local in southern Cantons. S. Germany. Tirol. Italy, widely distributed through Apennines. Spain, local but not rare.

Similar species. *N. ilicis* below, larger, uns gc darker; unh submarginal lunules darker red, orange mark in s2 and black spot less prominent; ♀ without black anal tuft.

NORDMANNIA ILICIS *Ilex Hairstreak*

Sw: Järneksnabbvinge G: Steineichenfalter Sp: Querquera serrana
Range. Europe to S. Sweden, Asia Minor, Lebanon Map 238

N. ilicis Esper 1779 TL: Erlangen, Germany Pl. 50
Description. ♂fw 16/18mm., upf without sex-brand; ups dark brown; upf with or without orange discal mark; uns paler with slightly irregular series of white pd striae, best developed on hw; unh *marginal lunules red* usually *bordered with black internally and externally* and followed by white marginal line. ♀ often larger, markings brighter, upf with or without orange discal patch; unh red submarginal lunules generally larger.
Flight. June/July.
Habitat. On rough slopes among oaks of various species, from lowlands to 5,000 ft. Larval food plants oaks, usually on smaller bushy species.
Distribution. S. and C. Europe to about 58°N, including S. Sweden, widely distributed to Balkans and Greece, but more local and often scarce in its northern range. In Spain local in Cantabrian Mts., Cuenca, Teruel and Guadarrama. Absent from Britain, Corsica, Sardinia, Crete, S. Spain and Portugal.
Variation. On upf the orange discal patch is rare in ♂, inconstant in ♀ in northern and eastern ranges, becoming increasingly common in Pyrenees, and constant in Cantabrian Mts. and C. Spain in both sexes, f. *cerri* Huebner Pl. 50.

Similar species. *N. acaciae* p. 235, *N. esculi* below, unh series of 5 small discrete red submarginal spots, their black lunules very inconspicuous.

NORDMANNIA ESCULI   *False Ilex Hairstreak*
Sp: Querquera
Range. Restricted to SW. Europe and N. Africa.   Map 239

N. esculi esculi Huebner 1804   TL: Portugal   p. 273
Description. ♂fw 15/17mm., resembles *N. ilicis*; upf without sex-brand; unh with *small, discrete bright red submarginal spots* in s1b–s5, only faintly edged black, white marginal line faint beyond v2. ♀ similar, often larger, ups sometimes with indistinct orange pd flush.
Flight. June/July.
Habitat. Lowlands to 4,000 ft. on rough ground flying over small sloe bushes. Larval food plant uncertain, perhaps *Prunus*.
Distribution. Spain and Portugal, except Galicia and northern coastal districts. France, E. Pyrenees and Provence including Alpes Maritimes. Occurs in Balearic islands.
Variation. In southern localities ♀ upf often with slight orange flush accompanied by traces of orange submarginal spots on uph.

N. esculi mauretanica Staudinger 1892   TL: Morocco   p. 273
Description. Ups like *N. e. esculi* but uns paler grey-brown, markings absent on fw and nearly so on hw. In some localities there is extensive development of orange ups flush even in ♂.
Flight. May/June.
Habitat. On flowery slopes at 5–6,000 ft., often common.
Distribution. In Middle Atlas in Morocco, Algeria and Tunisia.
Similar species. *N. ilicis* p. 235.

STRYMONIDIA SPINI   *Blue-spot Hairstreak*
G: Schlehenfalter   Sp: Mancha azul
Range. S. and C. Europe to Asia Minor, Lebanon, Iraq and Iran.
                                                                      Map 240

S. spini Schiffermueller 1775   TL: Vienna   Pl. 50
Description. ♂fw 14/16mm., ups dark brown; upf sometimes with slight orange discal flush, small oval sex-brand at cell-end; uph orange marginal spots on anal lobe and often in s2; uns paler with white pd stripe firmly marked across both wings; *unh conspicuous blue mark at anal angle*, anal lobe black, two or three orange marginal lunules. ♀ usually larger with markings better defined.
Flight. June/July.
Habitat. Rough places among bushes of *Rhamnus, Prunus*, etc., from lowlands to 6,000 ft., frequent in hilly country. Larval food plant sloe *Rhamnus* and perhaps other shrubby bushes.

Distribution. S. and C. Europe to 58°N, absent from NW., rare in N. Germany, Czechoslovakia and Poland. Italy, north of Naples. Absent from Sicily, Corsica, Sardinia, Elba and Crete.

Variation. In Pyrenees, Spain and Portugal females often have an orange suffusion on disc of fw which may spread widely over both wings, ♀-f. *vandalusica* Lederer Pl. 50, common in S. Spain, rarely well developed in N. and E. Europe.

STRYMONIDIA W-ALBUM *White-letter Hairstreak*

F: Le W-Blanc   Sw: Almsnabbvinge   G: Ulmenzipfelfalter
Sp: W-blanca
Range. C. Europe to Japan.   Map 241

S. w-album Knoch 1782 TL: Leipzig   Pl. 50
Description. ♂fw 15/16mm., upf with small sex-brand above cell-end; gc dark brown, sometimes with small orange mark on anal lobe of hw; uns brown, with firm white pd line across both wings, on hw directed to v2 with final zig-zag forming *characteristic letter* '*W*', a double line across s1a, four or five orange marginal lunules and a fine white marginal line. ♀ slightly larger, ups paler brown.
Flight. July, at low to moderate altitudes.
Habitat. Near woodlands or isolated trees, visits flowers of bramble, etc. Larval food plants lime, elm and other trees, commonly wych elm in S. England.
Distribution. C. Europe to 60°N, including S. England and Scandinavia. Absent from E. Pyrenees, Spain, Portugal and Mediterranean islands except Sicily.

Similar species. *S. pruni* below.

STRYMONIDIA PRUNI *Black Hairstreak*

Sw: Plommonsnabbvinge   G: Pflaumenfalter   Sp: Endrinera
Range. W. Europe through Siberia to Amurland and Korea.   Map 242

S. pruni Linnaeus 1758 TL: Germany (Verity 1943)   Pl. 50
Description. ♂fw 15/16mm., small sex-brand above cell-end; ups black; uph orange submarginal lunules in s1b–s4; uns gc golden-brown with transverse stripe of black-bordered white striae across both wings; *unh bright orange submarginal band edged internally with conspicuous black spots*, largest at anal angle and often continued on fw. into s1b and s2 ♀ similar, larger, upf often with slight orange discal suffusion.
Flight. End June/July or earlier.
Habitat. Flies near hedges and thickets of blackthorn at low altitudes. Larval food plants *Prunus*, esp. *Prunus spinosa*, plum and rarely other trees.
Distribution. C. Europe to about 58°N, widespread but local. England,

only in Midlands. N. Spain. France, from Basses Pyrénées northwards. Zealand and S. Sweden. Italy, only in Po delta. More common in E. Europe in Poland, Rumania and Balkans to Bulgaria, S. Finland, in suitable localities. Absent from Portugal, peninsular Italy, Greece and Mediterranean islands.

Similar species. *S. w-album* p. 237, uph without orange marks at anal angle; unh orange submarginal band bordered internally by black lunules which never extend to fw.

CALLOPHRYS RUBI   *Green Hairstreak*

Sw: Björnbärssnabbvinge   G: Brombeerzipfelfalter   Sp: Cejialba
Range. From W. Europe and N. Africa across Russia and Asia Minor to Siberia and Amurland.   Map 243

C. rubi Linnaeus 1758   TL: Sweden (Verity 1943)   Pl. 50
Description. ♂fw 13/15mm., ups brown to dull grey; uph fringes often slightly undulant and sometimes chequered dark at veins; uns green; unh pd row of small white spots, often incomplete; *frons green*; *eyes narrowly bordered white*. ♀ similar, ups sometimes paler brown.
Flight. March or later usually in a single brood; a partial second brood has been reported from N. Africa.
Habitat. Rough ground among gorse, heather, broom, etc., from sea-level to 7,000 ft. Larval food plants gorse, broom, ling, *Vaccinium*, etc.
Distribution. Common and widely distributed throughout Europe and N. Africa, including the Mediterranean islands; probably absent from Orkney and Shetland Isles and Crete.
Variation. Ups generally darker in N., often more ruddy in S. esp. in N. Africa, f. *fervida* Staudinger.
Similar species. *C. avis* below.

CALLOPHRYS AVIS   *Chapman's Green Hairstreak*

Sp: Cejirrubia
Range. Restricted to SW. Europe and N. Africa.   Map 244

C. avis Chapman 1909   TL: S. France and Morocco   Pl. 50
Description. ♂fw 16mm., resembles *C. rubi*; ups brighter reddish-brown; *frons and eye borders foxy-red*; uns white pd line broken only at veins, best marked near costa of hw, often vestigial on fw. ♀ similar.
Flight. April/May, in a single brood.
Habitat. Lowlands, but up to 5,000 ft. in N. Africa, flying in bushy places or near isolated strawberry trees. Larval food plant *Arbutus unedo* (Arbusier).
Distribution. France, only E. Pyrenees, Var, Alpes Maritimes. Spain

Portugal. Morocco; Tangier. Algeria; Khenchela, Zehroun, Algiers. Tunisia; Ain Draham.

Similar species. *C. rubi* p. 238, eyes edged white and scales on front of head green.

TOMARES BALLUS   *Provence Hairstreak*

Sp: Cardenillo

Range. From Spain and Morocco to Tripolitania, Cyrenaica and Egypt.
Map 245

T. ballus   Fabricius 1787   TL: Spain   Pl. 52
Description. ♂fw 14/15mm., apex pointed; ups dark grey with traces of orange submarginal spots on uph in s1b, 2; unf discal area orange-red with black discal and pd spots; *unh green* with grey marginal border. ♀ upf discal area and uph wide marginal band orange-red.
Flight. January/April in a single brood.
Habitat. On rough stony ground at low or moderate levels. Larval food plants possibly *Lotus hispidus*, perhaps other low plants.
Distribution. S. France in Var, Bouches du Rhône, Maritime Alps, E. Pyrenees. Spain, local but widely distributed. Portugal, in mountainous central areas. N. Africa, on coastal plain and foothills of Atlas Mts. in Morocco, Algeria and Tunisia.
Similar species. *T. mauretanicus* below, unh brown or grey.

TOMARES MAURETANICUS   *Moroccan Hairstreak*

Range. Restricted to N. Africa.   Map 246

T. mauretanicus   Lucas 1849   TL: Algeria   Pl. 52
Description. ♂fw 14/15mm., resembles *T. ballus*; ups smokey-brown, unmarked; unf smokey-grey, usually with orange patch below cell and black discal and pd spots in series; *unh gc grey to brown*, marked with series of darker spots, often indistinct. ♀upf orange with brown marginal borders; uns resembles ♂, variable.
Flight. January/March.
Habitat. At low altitudes on coastal plain. Larval food plants *Heydisarum pallidum* and *Hippocrepis multisiliquosa*.
Distribution. Morocco, Algeria, Tunisia.
Similar species. *T. ballus* above.

LYCAENA HELLE   *Violet Copper*

Sw: Violett Guldvinge   G: Blauschillernder Feuerfalter
Range. C. and N. Europe across Russia and Siberia to Amurland.
Map 247

PLATE 41

2a

2b

1a

1b

1c

1d

2c

3b

6a

3a

5a

6b

4

5b

7

PLATE 42

1. Erebia alberganus   *Almond-eyed Ringlet*   **174**

    1a. *E. a. tyrsus* ♂. Lanceolate orange postdiscal spots large on both surfaces, white pupilled ocelli small. ♀ similar, uns suffused yellow.

    1b. *E. a. alberganus* ♂. Ups orange postdiscal oval spots smaller, less bright, uns markings much smaller but ocelli retain white pupils.

    1c. *E. a. phorcys* ♂. Large, like *E. a. tyrsus* but unh postdiscal spots pale yellow, and ocelli lightly tinged orange.

    1d. *E. a. alberganus* f. *caradjae* ♂. Small, fulvous markings inconspicuous, lanceolate on unf only.

2. Erebia ottomana   *Ottoman Brassy Ringlet*   **185**

    2a. *E. o. bureschi* ♂. Large, unh silvery postdiscal band enclosing 3 round black ocellar spots.

    2b. *E. o. balcanica* ♀. Ups postdiscal markings orange-yellow, brown ground-colour paler; unh pale yellow-grey, markings obscure.

    2c. *E. o. tardenota* ♂. Smaller, unh dove-grey banded with brown.

3. Erebia cassioides   *Common Brassy Ringlet*   **183**

    3a. *E. cassioides* ♂. Fw pointed; upf fulvous band short, twin apical ocelli prominent; uph postdiscal ocelli present.

    3b. *E. cassioides* ♀. Ups paler; ocelli well developed on both wings; unh yellowish-grey marbled brown. **See also Pl. 44.**

4. Erebia nivalis   *de Lesse's Brassy Ringlet*   **185**
E. nivalis ♂. Fw not pointed; upf fulvous band extends into cell; unh bright blue-grey marbled darker grey.

5. Erebia tyndarus   *Swiss Brassy Ringlet*   **183**

    5a. *E. tyndarus* ♀. Fw short, not pointed; upf ocelli very small; uph lacks ocelli.

    5b. *E. tyndarus* ♂. Like ♀ but brighter; upf ocelli small; uph lacks ocelli.

6. Erebia hispania   *Spanish Brassy Ringlet*   **184**

    6a. *E. h. hispania* ♂. Large; upf postdiscal band orange with large twin ocelli. ♀ unh yellowish, darker markings better defined.

    6b. *E. h. rondoui* ♂. Like *E. h. hispania* but smaller; upf orange postdiscal band wider; uns grey, usually with darker postdiscal line. ♀ ups more brightly marked; unh dark postdiscal line prominent.

7. Erebia calcaria   *Lorkovic's Brassy Ringlet*   **185**
E. calcaria ♂. Fw short; upf very dark, ocelli small; unh grey with dark postdiscal line and small dark submarginal marking.

L. helle   Schiffermueller 1775   TL: Vienna   Pls. 4, 51
   syn: *amphidamas* Esper 1780.

Description. ♂fw 12/14mm., upf orange gc almost wholly obscured by *strong violet gloss*, three discal and all pd spots black; uph dark grey with orange submarginal lunules bordered by small black spots, all suffused violet; unf orange-yellow with markings as ups and complete submarginal series; unh gc yellow-grey with small dark spots at base and on disc, complete pd series and prominent orange submarginal band enclosed by proximal and distal black spots, the former bordered internally by white lunules. ♀fw less pointed, markings better defined, without violet suffusion ups.

Flight. End May/October, in one or two broods according to locality.

Habitat. Damp meadows and marshy places from lowlands to 5,000 ft. Larval food plants knot grass (*Polygonum*).

Distribution. C. and N. Europe, local in widely scattered colonies. France, in Doubs, Jura, E. Pyrenees, Mont Dore. Belgium; Ardennes. Switzerland, in NE. on marshes of Jura, Urschweiz, Oberland, etc. Germany, mostly on the peat-mosses of Bavaria, becoming scarce, absent in north-west Poland. Baltic countries. Czechoslovakia. Fennoscandia, widely distributed to North Cape in a single annual brood; absent from S. Sweden.

LYCAENA PHLAEAS   *Small Copper*

F: Le Bronzé   Sw: Liten Guldvinge   G: Feuerfalter   Sp: Manto bicolor
Range. Europe and N. Africa through temperate Asia to Japan. Abyssinia. Eastern States of N. America.   Map 248

L. phlaeas phlaeas   Linnaeus 1761   TL: Westermannia, Sweden   Pl. 51
Description. ♂fw 12/15mm., ups gleaming reddish-gold with small black spots in cell, the irregular pd series and marginal border black; hw with triangular anal lobe and often a short projection at v2; uph dark grey with red submarginal band from anal lobe to s5, bordered by small black spots on margin; unf gc orange, black markings as on upf, each spot bordered yellow, marginal border grey-brown; *unh grey-brown with small scattered dark spots and inconspicuous red submarginal lunules.* ♀ similar, often larger, fw less pointed.

Flight. February/March and later in two or more broods.

Habitat. Flowery banks from sea level to 6,000 ft. Larval food plants dock and sorrel, also knot grass (*Polygonum*).

Distribution. Europe and N. Africa including Mediterranean and Atlantic islands.

Variation. In hot localities specimens of second and later broods are more or less heavily suffused dark grey on ups, and anal tails of hw are longer, f. *elea* Fabricius, a seasonal form. Small blue spots may occur on uph, f. *caeruleopunctata* Rühl. Rare specimens occur in which ups gc is white or pale golden or the pattern of ups black spots is abnormal.

L. phlaeas polaris Courvoisier 1911 TL: Norwegian Lapland   Pl. 51
Description. Resembles *L. p. phlaeas* on ups; differs in the pale grey gc of unh with dark spots prominent, esp. the irregular pd series; f. *caeruleopunctata* not uncommon.
Flight and **Habitat.** End June/July, in a single brood.
Distribution. Arctic Europe, Bodö, Saltdalen, Abisko, Porsanger, etc.

LYCAENA DISPAR *Large Copper*
G: Grosser Feuerfalter Sw: Stor Guldvinge
Range. Western Europe, formerly including England (TL of *L. dispar* Haworth 1803), across Russia to Amurland.   Map 249

L. dispar batava Oberthur 1920 TL: Friesland   Pl. 51
Description. ♂fw 18/20mm., ups burnished red-gold with narrow black discoidal bar and black marginal borders; unf orange with nearly evenly aligned row of pd spots and small black marginal marks before the grey marginal border; *unh gc pale blue-grey*, with wide red submarginal band extending from anal angle to v6 and pale ringed black spots in usual pattern. ♀ larger, upf red, not burnished, with discal series, but *without submarginal series* of black spots, black marginal borders wide; uph black with wide orange submarginal band; uns as in male.
Flight. June/July, in a single brood.
Habitat. Marshes and fens. Larval food plants docks, esp. *Rumex hydrolapathum* and *R. aquaticus.*
Distribution. Friesland in N. Holland, confined to a few localities. A small colony of this subspecies is maintained at Woodwalton Fen, Huntingdonshire, England. *L. dispar dispar* formerly occurred in England in fens of Huntingdonshire and Cambridgeshire, but has been extinct since 1848.

L. dispar rutila Werneberg 1864 TL: Env. Berlin   Pl. 51
Description. ♂fw 17/18mm., *first brood* smaller than *L. d. batava* in both sexes; unh grey gc slightly yellowish, orange submarginal band paler, narrower and not reaching v6. *Second brood* specimens often small, ♂fw 16/17mm., and ♀ with smaller black markings; unh orange submarginal band narrow and pale.
Flight. May/June and August/September in most lowland localities, a single brood in some northern localities and at higher altitudes.
Habitat. Formerly generally distributed in rough country with damp places and wet ditches, becoming increasingly rare throughout Europe. Larval food plants docks (as for *L. d. batava*).
Distribution. France, very local in Aube, Haute Marne, Alsace, Nièvre and Côte d'Or, Gironde, etc. Germany, widely distributed near Berlin and northwards to Baltic coast. Czechoslovakia. Hungary. Rumania. Balkans, esp. on lowlands near the R. Save and in Bulgaria. Italy, still found in marshy places in N. Italy; formerly occurred near Rome.

Similar species. *H. virgaureae* below, unh with white discal spots or band.

HEODES VIRGAUREAE *Scarce Copper*

F: Argus Satiné Sw: Vitfläckig Guldvinge G: Dukatenfalter
Sp: Manto de Oro
Range. From Europe and Asia Minor through C. Asia to Mongolia.
Map 250

H. virgaureae virgaureae Linnaeus 1758 TL: Sweden
(Verity 1943) Pl. 51
Description. ♂fw 16/17mm., ups gleaming red-gold, unspotted; upf black marginal border widest near apex; uph narrow black marginal border fusing with black spots between veins; unf black spots in usual pattern and marginal border grey; unh yellow-grey with small black spots, *pd spots bordered distally white*, submarginal band ill defined, orange. ♀ups with rather large black spots in usual pattern; uph black spots conspicuous only in pd area; uns resembles ♂.
Flight. July/August in a single brood.
Habitat. Flowery meadows from lowlands to 5,000 ft., attracted to flowers of golden rod. Larval food plants docks (*Rumex*).
Distribution. Common locally in C. and N. Europe; also in Balkans, esp. in mountains. Absent from Britain and from Italy south of Abruzzi.
Variation. Generally smaller in N. Europe; at high latitudes in Lapland, f. *oranulus* Freyer, very small, ♂fw 11/13mm., ups yellow-gold; ♀uph suffused dark grey with orange submarginal band. In S. Europe larger, ♂fw 17/19mm.

H. virgaureae montanus Meyer-Dür 1851 TL: Rhône Glacier, Pl. 52
Switzerland.
Description. ♂fw 15/16mm., small, black marginal borders wider; ups sometimes with small black discoidal spot. ♀ups heavily suffused grey, with usual golden colour sometimes obliterated.
Flight. July/August.
Habitat. Mountains, at high altitudes of 6,000 ft. or more, flying on flowery slopes.
Distribution. On the higher groups of the southern Alps from the Dauphiné to Gross Glockner, esp. in Oetztal Alps and Ortler group.

H. virgaureae miegii Vogel 1857 TL: Guadarrama, C. Spain Pl. 51
Description. ♂fw 17/18mm., large, upf black marginal border wide, black discoidal spot present and also with three or four small black pd spots in s4, 5, 6; uph black marginal spots larger, small pd spots occasionally present. ♀ups gc clear orange-yellow with minimal dark suffusion and prominent black markings.
Flight and Habitat as for *H. v. virgaureae*.

Distribution. C. Spain, La Granja, etc., and northwards to southern slopes of Cantabrian Mts., when it merges with *H.v. virgaureae*.
Similar species. *H. ottomanus* below, *T. thetis* p. 248, *L. dispar* p. 243.

HEODES OTTOMANUS *Grecian Copper*
Range. Southern Balkans, Greece and Asia Minor.   Map 251

H. ottomanus Lefèbvre 1830 TL: Greece   Pl. 51
Description. ♂fw 14/15mm., hw with marginal tooth (♂) or tail (♀) at v2; ups gleaming red-gold like *H. virgaureae*; upf black marginal border widest at apex, small black spots at cell-end and in s4–6; uph black marginal border fused with round black marginal spots between veins near anal angle; uns resembles *L. phlaeas*, gc yellow-grey; *unh broad red submarginal lunules* present in s1a–s5, *no white pd spots*. ♀ups resembles *H. virgaureae*; uns as in ♂.
Flight. March/April and end June/July in two broods.
Habitat. Rough places and flowery meadows at low to moderate levels. Larval food plants not known.
Distribution. Southern Balkans, including Montenegro, Albania and SE. Yugoslavia. In Greece esp. on Mt. Parnassus and south of the Gulf of Corinth.
Variation. Hw tails at v2 said to be more pronounced in *second brood*, in which also unh appears to be more yellow than grey.
Similar species. *H. virgaureae* p. 244, slightly larger and easily recognised by white pd spots on unh.

HEODES TITYRUS *Sooty Copper*
Sw: Dansk Guldvinge G: Bienenfalter Sp: Manto oscuro
Range. From W. Europe through Russia and Transcaucasus to Altai Mts.   Map 252

H. tityrus tityrus Poda 1761 TL: Graz, S. Austria   Pl. 52
  syn: *dorilis* Hufnagel 1766; *circe* Schiffermueller 1775 (invalid homonym)
Description. ♂fw 14/16mm., hw with marked anal lobe; *ups dark grey-brown*, fringes white; upf obscurely marked with darker spots in usual pattern; uph orange lunules in s1b–s3 or 4 vestigial; unf with black spots as above and traces of orange in submarginal area; unh yellow-grey with irregular small black spots, orange submarginal band more definite. ♀upf gc orange with usual pattern of black spots; uph dark brown, orange submarginal band conspicuous and enclosing round black spots *that barely touch margins*; uns resembles ♂ but more brightly marked.
Flight. April/May and August/September in two broods, a partial third brood has been reported from S. Europe.
Habitat. In flowery meadows, usually in lowlands but sometimes to 5,000 ft. in S. Europe. Larval food plant dock (*Rumex*).

Distribution. C. and S. Europe to about 54°N. Spain, local in Cantabrian Mts. and Catalonia, e.g., Montseny. Absent from Fennoscandia, Britain, Mediterranean islands except Sicily, and S. Spain.

H. tityrus bleusei Oberthur 1896   TL: Escorial and Madrid, Spain.
Description. ♂ups with orange gc as in ♀ and rather large black markings. In second (summer) brood with well-developed tails on hw.
Flight. April and July.
Habitat. Flowery meadows and banks at low altitudes.
Distribution. Known only from C. Spain, uncommon.

H. tityrus subalpinus Speyer 1851   TL: Innsbruck, N. Tirol   Pl. 52
Description. Ups dark grey, unmarked except for a darker cell-bar, fringes brilliant white; uns gc pale, rather yellowish-grey with markings as in *H. t. tityrus* but small; ♀ similar but fw more rounded. Forms intermediate between *H.t. tityrus* and *H.t. subalpinus*, with traces of ups markings esp. common in ♀, are not rare. Most colonies can be referred without difficulty to one or the other.
Flight. End June/July in a single brood.
Habitat. Mountain meadows at 4–7,000 ft. occasionally at lower levels.
Distribution. Alps, from Basses Alpes to Hohe Tauern.

Similar species. *T. thersamon* ♀ p. 247, uph marginal black spots fuse with marginal line.

HEODES ALCIPHRON   *Purple-shot Copper*

G: Violetter Feuerfalter   Sp: Manto de Purporo
Range. From W. Europe across Asia Minor to Iran.   Map 253

C. alciphron alciphron Rottemburg 1775   TL: Berlin   Pl. 52
Description. ♂fw 16/18 mm., ups gleaming reddish-orange heavily suffused violet, but in most specimens gc is clear near costa of hw; upf dark spots in usual pattern, pd row irregular, not always well defined, sometimes absent; uph dark cell-bar and pd spots sometimes vestigial; uns pattern of dark spots more complete on both wings; unh gc pale grey with orange submarginal band. ♀fw broad, less pointed; ups dark brown with *irregular pd row of darker spots*; uph with orange submarginal lunules in s1b–s6; uns markings as in male, but unf gc orange.
Flight. June/July in a single brood.
Habitat. Flowery banks and meadows, lowlands to 3,000 ft. Larval food plants dock (*Rumex*).
Distribution. France in Alsace and Jura. Germany, northwards to Baltic coast but absent in NW.   Czechoslovakia, Altvater Mt., Brno, etc., and eastwards to Hungary, Rumania and Balkans to Greece. Absent from Britain and Fennoscandia.

H. alciphron melibaeus Staudinger 1879 TL: Greece
Description. ♂fw 17/18mm., like *H. a alciphron* but ups violet suffusion reduced, with pale golden gc slightly veiled by grey suffusion, most marked on fw; usual black markings often scanty or vestigial; uns gc pale grey. ♀ larger, ups brown with usual markings; uph orange submarginal band conspicuous; sometimes traces of orange on upf disc.
Flight and Habitat. As for *H. a. alciphron*, common in mountains up to 5,000 ft.
Distribution. Rumania and Balkans to Greece; the dominant form in the Near East.

H. alciphron gordius Sulzer 1776 TL: Graubünden, Pl. 52
Switzerland
Description. Resembles *H. a. alciphron*; ♂ups violet suffusion reduced, black spots large and well defined; uns colour tones brighter. ♀ups gc orange-yellow, fuscous suffusion slight or absent.
Flight. June/August.
Habitat. Mountains of S. Europe, flying at 4–6,000 ft.
Distribution. The common form in S. Europe. France, in C and S. districts, and on all mountains from Alpes Maritimes to Dolomites. Spain, Portugal, Italy, including peninsular Italy. Absent from Balkans and Mediterranean islands except Sicily.

H. alciphron heracleanus Blachier 1913 TL: High Atlas, Morocco Pl. 52
Description. ♂fw 18/19mm., ups pale orange-yellow without violet suffusion. ♀ larger with fw to 21 mm, yellow to orange, black markings large and prominent.
Flight. June.
Habitat. High alpine meadows at 8–9,000 ft.
Distribution. Known only from the High Atlas (Toubkal massif).

Similar species. *P. hippothoe eurydame* (♀ only) p. 249, fw black pd spots in nearly evenly curved row.

THERSAMONIA THERSAMON *Lesser Fiery Copper*
Range. From Italy and E. Europe across W. Asia to Iraq and Iran.

Map 254

T. thersamon Esper 1784 TL: Sarepta, S. Russia Pl. 51
Description. ♂fw 14/16mm., ups gc rather pale gleaming gold with narrow black marginal borders; upf unmarked; uph discal area slightly dusky, sometimes faintly flushed violet, golden submarginal band enclosing black marginal spots which fuse with black border; unf with spots in usual pattern; unh grey with broken orange submarginal band and small dark spots. ♀ups with usual pattern of black spots complete on both wings; uph often darker, with bright orange submarginal band; uns like ♂.

Flight. April/May and July/August in two broods.
Habitat. Waste places among grass and flowers, lowlands to 4,000 ft.
Larval food plants dock and broom (*Rumex, Sarothamnus*).
Distribution. E. Europe, widely distributed but local in Austria, Czecho-
slovakia, Hungary, Rumania and Balkans including Greece and Turkey.
Italy; Liguria, Emilia, Lombardy and various localities in the Abruzzi.
Reports from NE. Italy need confirmation.
Variation. Specimens of *second brood* usually have a short tail on hw at
v2, f. *omphale* Klug.

Similar species. *T. phoebus* below. *H. tityrus* ♀ p. 245.

THERSAMONIA PHOEBUS   *Moroccan Copper*
Range. Confined to High Atlas in W. Morocco.   Map 255

T. phoebus Blachier 1908   TL: High Atlas, Morocco   Pl. 51
Description. ♂fw 14mm., ups gc golden; upf with narrow black marginal
border and small black spots in usual pattern; uph pd and submarginal
spots close together, followed by orange submarginal band and black
marginal spots, wing-margin slightly wavy near pointed anal lobe; unf
black spots larger, pale-ringed; unh gc pale yellow-grey with prominent
orange sub-marginal band. ♀ups gc paler, black spots larger; uph slightly
suffused fuscous; uns as in ♂.
Flight. May or later with prolonged emergence.
Habitat. Lowlands to 5,000 ft. Larval food plants docks (*Rumex*).
Distribution. W. Morocco, Asni, Marrakesh, etc.

Similar species. *T. thersamon* p. 247, slightly larger, upf ♂ without black
spots; ♀unh markings more bold; does not occur in Africa.

THERSAMONIA THETIS   *Fiery Copper*
Range. From Greece through W. Asia to Iraq and Iran.   Map 256

T. thetis   Klug 1834   TL: Syria   Pl. 51
Description. ♂fw 15/16mm., ups fiery red-gold; upf marginal spots touch-
ing narrow black apically expanded border; uph black marginal border
narrow with black antemarginal spots between each vein; unf gc pale
yellow-grey with black spots in usual pattern; unh pale grey, faintly
spotted, with faintly yellow submarginal band. ♀ups with usual markings
of black spots; uns as male. In both sexes a filamentous tail may be present
at v2 of hw, probably only in second brood, f. *caudata* Staudinger.
Flight. July.
Habitat. Flies at 5,000 ft. or more in mountains, attracted by thyme. Larval
food plant not known.
Distribution. In Europe only in Greece, Mt. Veluchi, Kaljaccuda, etc.,
perhaps also in SE. Yugoslavia (Skopje).

Similar species. *H. virgaureae* p. 244, unh with white discal spots.

PALAEOCHRYSOPHANUS HIPPOTHOE *Purple-edged Copper*
Sw: Violettkantad Guldvinge G: Kleiner Ampferfeuerfalter
Sp: Manto de Cobre
Range. W. Europe and through Russia and Siberia to the Amur.
Map 257

P. hippothoe hippothoe Linnaeus 1761 TL: Sweden (Lowland) Pl. 51
Description. ♂fw 16/17mm., ups rather *dark red-gold with black marginal borders*; upf shot purple along costa and with black discoidal stria; uph very dark and shot purple below cell, traces of orange at anal angle; uns gc grey or yellow-grey with usual markings of small black spots. ♀upf gc paler, less burnished, often suffused dark fuscous, with small black pd spots in nearly even curve; uph black with orange submarginal band enclosing black spots, f. *caeruleopunctata* Rühl, common.
Flight. June/July in a single brood.
Habitat. Damp meadows and bogs from lowlands to 5,000 ft. Larval food plants docks and snakeweed (*Polygonum bistorta*).
Distribution. C. and N. Europe, esp. in mountains, to 66°N. Spain; Cantabrian Mts., Riaño, Sierra Mancilla (Burgos), Sierra Moncayo, very local. N. Italy in Po Valley. Absent from C. and S. Spain, NW. France, S. Alps and peninsular Italy.

P. hippothoe stiberi Gerhard 1853 TL: Lapland Pl. 51
Description. Resembles *P. h. hippothoe*; ♂ups gc more golden (paler); unf gc orange-yellow with smaller black spots. ♀upf orange-yellow without usual black suffusion, black spots small; uph orange submarginal band more distinct from anal angle to s5.
Flight. July.
Habitat. Coastal districts and mountain valleys.
Distribution. Fennoscandia, in northern districts, from Dovrefjeld to North Cape and N. Finland.

P. hippothoe eurydame Hoffmannsegg 1806 TL: Mountains Pl. 51
near Geneva.
  syn: *eurybia* Ochsenheimer 1808
Description. ♂fw 16/17mm., ups differs from *P. h. hippothoe* in brighter orange-golden gc, black wing-borders narrower and without purple reflections, upf discoidal spot vestigial or absent. ♀ups generally completely dusky, orange markings vestigial if present.
Flight. July/August.
Habitat. Alpine meadows from 5,000 ft. upwards.
Distribution. Maritime Alps to Oetztal and high Dolomites. Italy, local on higher Apennines southwards to Caserta. Replaced by *P.h. hippothoe*

north of Rhône Valley, in Pyrenees and in eastern Alps of Austria. Distinction between *P.h. hippothoe* and *P.h. eurydame* is generally well defined but intermediate forms may occur where they meet.

P. hippothoe leonhardi Fruhstorfer 1917 TL: Rilo Mts.,   Pl. 51
Bulgaria.
   syn: *candens* auct.
Description. ♂fw 17/19 mm., large, otherwise indistinguishable from *P. h. hippothoe* by external characters but genitalia differ; ups purple reflections usually well marked; upf black discoidal spot present; uph dark area includes s 3. ♀ resembles *P.h. hippothoe* ♀, unh fawn-grey, markings inconspicuous.
Flight. End June/July in a single brood.
Habitat. Mountain meadows at 3–5,000 ft. Larval food plants docks.
Distribution . Replaces *P.h. hippothoe* in Balkan countries from Albania and SE. Yugoslavia and Greece to Croatia. A form of *P. hippothoe*, possibly *P. h. leonhardi*, has been taken in Rumania.

Similar species. *Heodes alciphron* p. 246 (♀ only); upf pd row of black spots less regular; unh grey, markings prominent.

LAMPIDES BOETICUS   *Long-tailed Blue*
Sp: Canela Estriada
Range. Nearly world-wide in warm countries.   Map 258

L. boeticus Linnaeus 1767 TL: Algeria   Pl. 53
Description. ♂fw 15/18 mm., fw apex pointed; hw tailed at v2; ups violet-blue with hairy appearance due to numerous androconia, dark marginal border narrow; uph violet-blue; uns gc fawn-grey with transverse white and dark grey stripes; *unh with wide white pd stripe* and small black and peacock-green marginal ocelli in s 1c and s 2. ♀ups brown, basal and discal areas violet-blue; uns resembles ♂.
Flight. Throughout summer months in succession of broods according to locality.
Habitat. Flowery banks and rough places from lowlands to 6,000 ft. or more. Larval food plants Leguminosae, esp. *Colutea*, living in seed-pods.
Distribution. Strongly migratory, resident in S. Europe and N. Africa, ranging N. in late summer to reach France, Belgium, Switzerland, Germany and occasionally England.

Similar species. *S. pirithous* below.

SYNTARUCUS PIRITHOUS   *Lang's Short-tailed Blue*
Sp: Gris Estriada
Range. N. Africa and S. Europe to Egypt, Lebanon and Asia Minor.
    Map 259

S. pirithous Linnaeus 1767 **TL**: Algeria Pl. 53
  syn: *telicanus* Lang 1789
Description. ♂fw 12/13 mm., ups blue with narrow dark marginal borders; ups without dark discoidal spot; uph obscure dark marginal spots in s1b, 2; *uns* both wings with light brown *complicated slightly variable pattern of pale transverse stripes*; unh with conspicuous green ocelli with black centres and ringed orange in s1b, 2. ♀ups grey-brown; upf with blue flush over middle third, and dark discal and pd spots; uph a faint blue basal flush and a dark round marginal spot in s2; uns as ♂.
Flight. March and throughout summer.
Habitat. Flowery banks and waste ground, usually at low altitudes. Larval food plants small Leguminosae, broom, etc.
Distribution. S. Europe, esp. coastal regions, including all the larger Mediterranean islands and extending northwards to southern Alpine slopes. Morocco. Algeria. Tunisia.
Similar species. *L. boeticus* p. 250, unh with conspicuous white pd band.

CYCLYRIUS WEBBIANUS *Canary Blue*
Range. Confined to Canary Islands. No map

C. webbianus Brullé 1839 **TL**: Canary Islands Pl. 52
Description. ♂fw 14/15 mm., ups deep violet-blue with rather wide black borders; unf gc light orange-brown with slightly darker spots and white subapical mark; unh grey-brown with obscure white discal markings and brilliant white pd band. ♀ups golden-brown with darker marginal borders and discoidal spot, wing-bases flushed blue; uns as in ♂.
Flight. March and later throughout the summer.
Habitat. Open ground from sea-level to 10,000 ft. on Tenerife. Larval food plant not known.
Distribution. Canary Islands, on Tenerife, Gran Canary, La Palma and Gomera.

TARUCUS THEOPHRASTUS *Common Tiger Blue*
Sp: Laberinto
Range. S. Spain and throughout Africa, Asia Minor, Iraq, Arabia and east to India. Map 260

T. theophrastus Fabricius 1793 **TL**: Morocco Pl. 53
Description. ♂fw 10/11 mm., ups blue with fine black marginal lines; upf a dark oblong discoidal spot; uph a small black marginal mark in s2, often also another at anal angle; *uns pd line macular on both wings.* ♀ups brown; upf obscure dark discal markings show through from uns, white pd spot in 4, often another in s5; uph discal spots very obscure, usually with line of grey or white spots in s2–4, dark marginal ocelli often conspicuous, wing-bases slightly flushed blue.

Flight. April/May and later in several broods.
Habitat. Flies around thorn bushes in very hot localities at low altitudes. Larval food plant *Zizyphus vulgaris*, a spiny shrub common in SE. Europe.
Distribution. S. Spain; Cadiz, Jaen, Almeria, Murcia. Morocco, Algeria, Tunisia, usually in lowlands near coast.

Similar species. *T. balkanicus* below, ♂ups with distinct dark discal markings; ♀ups without white pd spots on fw or hw. *T. rosaceus* below, uns dark pd marks fused into narrow continuous line on both wings.

TARUCUS ROSACEUS *Mediterranean Tiger Blue*

Range. Algeria, Tunisia and desert oases of N. Africa and Arabia, widely distributed in W. Asia to Iraq and Iran. Map 261

T. rosaceus Austaut 1885 TL: Alexandria, Egypt   Pl. 13
syn: *mediterraneae* B-Baker 1917
Description. ♂fw 9/11 mm., ups resembles *T. theophrastus* but with faint pinkish tint; upf dark discoidal mark more linear and less conspicuous; unf black pd marks usually fused into *slightly irregular continuous line from* v1–7, slightly broken at crossing of v6; unh pd marks fused into continuous dark line from inner margin to v8. ♀ups resembles *T. theophrastus*; upf blue basal suffusion more extensive with clear white pd marks in s3, 4, 5 and smaller marks behind a row of three dark pd spots; uph white lunules capping black marginal spots much better defined; uns resembles ♂.
Flight. Probably flies throughout summer in Algeria and Tunisia.
Habitat. Lowlands, probably to foothills, but food plant does not extend far into mountains. Larval food plant *Zizyphus spina-christi* (Iraq).
Distribution. Tunisia and Algeria (Biskra).
Similar species. *T. theophrastus* p. 251; *T. balkanicus* below, upf dark discal markings present.

TARUCUS BALKANICUS *Little Tiger Blue*

Range. Coastal regions of N. Africa, Balkans and Asia Minor to Lebanon and Iran. Map 262

T. balkanicus Freyer 1845 TL: 'Turkey' (probably Balkans)   Pl. 53
Description. ♂fw 9/11 mm., ups gc lilac-blue; *upf with obvious dark discoidal and pd spots*, and dark marginal borders; uph small discoidal stria usually distinct, marginal border dark, often with obscure darker submarginal spots; unh black spots of pd band joined to form a continuous line. ♀ups dark brown, wing-bases flushed blue, discoidal and pd markings obscure on dark gc; upf without white pd spot in s4, 5; uph without white pd spots, marginal ocelli dark, rarely well-formed.
Flight. April/May and later, in two or three broods throughout summer

Habitat. Flies around bushes of Christ's Thorn in hot localities, at low altitudes in Balkans. Larval food plant *Paliurus spina-christi*.

Distribution. Balkans, widely distributed in hot districts in Dalmatia, Montenegro, Albania and Greece. Rumania, reported from Dobrugea. Algeria. Tunisia. Distribution not well known owing to confusion with *T. rosaceus* and *T. theophrastus*.

Similar species. *T. theophrastus* p. 251 and *T. rosaceus* p. 252.

AZANUS JESOUS *African Babul Blue*
Range. Widely distributed in Africa, Egypt, Syria, etc.   Map 263

A. jesous Guérin 1849 TL: Abyssinia   Pl. 52
Description. ♂fw 11/12mm., ups pale shining blue with rosy reflections and a narrow dark border to both wings; uph dark marginal spot in s2; uns gc pale brown with white transverse striae; unf short brown stripe below costa from base, and white transverse striae; unh short black basal bar and *conspicuous round black spots*, *i.e.* four sub-basal, one on costa at two-thirds, and six sub-marginally in s1c to s6, two ocelli with peacock-green pupils in s1c, 2. ♀ups light brown often with pale suffusion enclosing discoidal spot; uph marginal spots in s1c. 2, larger and darker; uns as in male.
Flight. April and throughout summer.
Habitat. Flies around mimosa bushes at low altitudes. Larval food plants *Acacia*, perhaps also lucerne.
Distribution. Morocco, in western areas.

ZIZEERIA KNYSNA *African Grass Blue*
Range. Africa, Tropical Asia and Australia; Canary Islands, S. Portugal and S. Spain.   Map 264

Z. knysna knysna Trimen 1862 TL: Cape Town and   Pl. 54
Plettenberg Bay
  syn: *lysimon* Huebner 1805 (invalid homonym)
Description. ♂fw 10/12mm., ups violet blue with *wide dark marginal borders*, otherwise unmarked; uns pale fawn with discal and marginal markings in slightly darker shade of fawn. ♀ups brown with restricted and variable patches of blue above inner margins of both wings; uns as in ♂.
Flight. In N. Africa, etc., in two broods, April/June and August, but variable with locality.
Habitat. Moist places beside streams, etc., at low altitudes. Larval food plants *Oxalis*, *Medicago*, etc.
Distribution. S. Portugal. Spain, local in provinces of Malaga, Granada, Cadiz, Seville. N. Africa; Morocco, Algeria, not recorded from Tunisia. Canary Islands.

Variation. Size of specimens varies slightly in most localities, constantly large in the Canary Islands.

Z. knysna karsandra Moore 1865 TL: NW. India
Description. Indistinguishable from *Z. k. knysna* except by a small character in the male genitalia.
Flight and Habitat as for *Z. k. knysna*.
Distribution. E. Algeria, Tunisia, Sicily and Crete; widely distributed through tropical Asia and most of Australia.
Note. *Z. knysna karsandra* is considered a distinct species by some authors.
Similar species. *C. lorquinii* p. 259.

EVERES ARGIADES   *Short-tailed Blue*

Sp: Naranjitas Rabicorta   Sw: Kortsvansad Blåvinge
Range. From Cantabrian Mts. and France across Europe and Asia to Japan; also from coast to coast in N. America (*E. a. comyntas* Godart).
Map 265

E. argiades Pallas 1771   **TL: Samara, S. Russia (April)**   Pl. 53
Description. ♂ fw 10/15 mm., *first brood* ups violet-blue with narrow black marginal borders; uph antemarginal spots sometimes present in s1b–4; uns gc pale grey; unf pd spots in regular series very slightly curved; *unh marginal spots in s1c, s2 both filled orange*. ♀ups black with blue basal suffusion and orange spot at anal angle of hw. *Second brood* (f. *tiresias* Rottemburg) larger, ♂ fw 12/15 mm., ups darker tone of blue; ♀ups little or no blue basal suffusion but often with orange anal lunules.
Flight. April and later in two or more broods.
Habitat. Flowery banks and meadows, often in damp places, from lowlands to 1,500 ft. Larval food plants small Leguminosae, esp. medick, trefoil, etc.
Distribution. From Cantabrian Mts. and Pyrenees to 52°N and eastwards through Europe, Sicily and Greece. Reports from Sardinia and Corsica need confirmation. Absent from C. and S. Spain and NW. Europe. Has been taken occasionally in Britain, Holland, N. Germany, Finland, etc., as a vagrant.

Similar species. *E. alcetas* p. 255, unh without orange anal lunules.

EVERES DECOLORATUS   *Eastern Short-tailed Blue*

Range. Restricted to SE. Europe.   Map 266

E. decoloratus Staudinger 1886   TL: Vienna, Hungary, Bulgaria Pl. 53
   syn: *sebrus* Huebner 1824 (rejected name)
Description. ♂ fw 12/13 mm., ups gc bright blue with black marginal borders about 1 mm. wide and extending along veins; *upf with black discoidal spot*; uns gc very pale grey with small white-ringed spots in the usual

pattern; unf spot in s2 of pd series displaced slightly basad; unh markings often vestigial, without orange anal lunules; hw tail at v2 very short. ♀ ups both wings black or dark grey, unmarked; uns as in ♂.
Flight. April/September, usually in two broods, but information imperfect.
Habitat. Flowery banks, usually in hilly country, lowlands to 3,000 ft. Larval food plant medick (*Medicago lupulina*).
Distribution. Local in Lower Austria, Rumania, Croatia and in Albania and Bulgaria, probably widely distributed within this area.
Variation. Fresh specimens are bright blue, but the blue scales wear off and worn specimens look rough and darker, with fuscous scales along veins more obvious.

Similar species. *E. alcetas* below, upf without discoidal spot and black marginal line very narrow, linear.

EVERES ALCETAS *Provençal Short-tailed Blue*
Sp: Rabicorta
Range. Spain and across S. Europe to Bulgaria; not recorded from Asia Minor.   Map 267

E. alcetas Hoffmannsegg 1804 **TL: Austria**   Pl. 53
   syn: *coritas* Ochsenheimer 1808
Description. ♂ fw 13/16mm., hw with short tail at v2; ups clear violet-blue, *black marginal lines exceedingly narrow*; *upf without discoidal spot*; uph an antemarginal black spot in s2; uns gc pearl-grey, spots small, often partly obsolete; unh small black marginal spot in s2 constant. ♀ups gc black, unmarked; uns resembles ♂.
Flight. April/September in two or three broods.
Habitat. Flowery banks, lowlands to 3,000 ft. or more. Larval food plants small Leguminosae esp. *Coronilla varia*.
Distribution. Local in C. Spain and S. France and in scattered colonies throughout southern Europe; northwards to Isère, Rhône valley and southern slopes of Alps; Corsica, across Balkans to Bulgaria.

Similar species. *E. argiades* p. 254; *E. decoloratus* p. 254; *C. argiolus* p. 259; *C. osiris* p. 258 uns without marginal markings.

CUPIDO MINIMUS *Little Blue*
Sw: Liten Blåvinge Sp: Deunde Oscuro G: Zwergbläuling
Range. From C. Spain and France through Europe and Asia to Amurland and Mongolia.   Map 268

C. minimus minimus Fuessly 1775 **TL: Switzerland**   Pl. 53
   syn: *alsus* Schiffermueller 1775
Description. ♂ fw 10/12mm., *ups dark brown with silver-blue scales*

PLATE 43

1. Erebia pronoe　*The Water Ringlet*　

　1a. *E. p. pronoe* ♂. Ups fulvous bands well developed; unh violet-grey with wide dark-brown discal band.

　1b. *E. p. pronoe* ♀. Smaller, ups paler; unh yellow-brown with pale grey postdiscal band.

　1c. *E. p. vergy* ♂. Ups fulvous markings vestigial; uns as in *E. p. pronoe.*

　1d. *E. p. vergy* ♀. Ups paler brown, ocelli and fulvous bands vestigial or absent; unh ground-colour yellowish-brown.

2. Erebia stirius　*The Styrian Ringlet*　

　2a. *E. s. stirius* ♂. Ups black, fulvous markings restricted, white ocellar pupils brilliant; unh smooth dark brown, postdiscal area slightly paler, ocelli small.

　2b. *E. s. stirius* ♀. Ups brightly marked; unh postdiscal area pale grey, ocelli prominent.

　2c. *E. s. morula* ♂. Small; ups fulvous postdiscal markings narrow, ocelli greatly reduced.

3. Erebia styx　*The Stygian Ringlet*　

　3a. *E. s. styx* ♂. Ups like *E. s. stirius*; ups fulvous markings slightly more extensive; unh dark brown marbled paler.

　3b. *E. s. styx* ♀. Ups paler, fringes slightly chequered; unh yellow-brown, with dark marbling, ocelli small or absent.

　3c. *E. s. trentae* ♂. Large; ups very dark, fulvous markings narrow; uph ocelli often prominent; unh postdiscal band marbled pale grey. For ♀ see Pl. 44.

1a

1b

1c

1d

2a

2b

3a

3b

3c

2c

PLATE 44

1. **Erebia manto**   *Manto Ringlet*   158
   E. m. manto ♀-form *bubastis*. Unh basal and postdiscal markings
   white on pale yellow-grey ground-colour. See also Pls. **28, 38, 39.**

2. **Erebia serotina**   *Descimon's Ringlet*   166
   E.serotina ♂. Upf fulvous-red postdiscal band narrow; apical ocelli
   very small, blind; unh postdiscal area paler.

3. **Erebia gorge**   *Silky Ringlet*   178
   3a. *E. g. erynis* ♂. Upf tawny bands wide, lacking ocelli; unh dark,
       postdiscal area paler. See also Pl. 37.
   3b. *E. g. ramondi* ♀. Uph submarginal ocelli prominent; brightly
       marked. For ♂ see Pl. **37.**

4. **Erebia medusa**   *The Woodland Ringlet*   171
   E. m. psodea ♀. Ups postdiscal bands yellow, wide, crossed by dark
   veins; uph with 5 or 6 ocelli. See also Pl. 40.

5. **Erebia styx**   *The Stygian Ringlet*   190
   E. s. trentae ♀. Ups ocelli large, prominent; unh pale grey, brightly
   marbled darker, discal band well defined. For ♂ see Pl. **43.**

6. **Erebia meolans**   *The Piedmont Ringlet*   198
   E. m. meolans ♀. Ups like ♂ (Pl. 39) but paler, more brightly
   marked; unh brown, postdiscal band pale grey.

7. **Erebia phegea**   *Dalmatian Ringlet*   201
   E. p. dalmata ♂. Upf twin ocelli large, oblique, smaller postdiscal
   ocelli present in all other spaces of both wings.

8. **Erebia cassioides**   *Common Brassy Ringlet*   183
   8a. *E. c.* f. *pseudomurina* ♂. Ups like *E. c. cassioides* (Pl. 42); unh
       grey, markings vestigial.
   8b. *E. c. arvernensis* ♀. Like *E. c. cassioides* (Pl. **42**), but larger;
       unh yellowish.

9. **Erebia pandrose**   *The Dewy Ringlet*   200
   E. pandrose ♀-form *roberti*. Unh discal band and marginal markings dark brown. See also Pl. 39.

10. **Erebia pharte**   *The Blind Ringlet*   166
    10a. *E. pharte eupompa* ♀. Ups medium brown, yellow markings
        conspicuous; uns flushed yellow. See also Pl. 38.
    10b. *E. pharte phartina* ♂. Small, markings very obscure on both
        surfaces. See also Pl. 38.

11. **Erebia aethiops**   *Scotch Argus*   168
    E. a. f. *caledonia* ♀. Small; unh brown, pale postdiscal band yellow-
    ish. See also Pl. 39.

scattered over both wings, often concentrated between veins of fw and over lower half of hw; uns pale grey, sometimes with slightly blue basal flush, with usual markings of small, white-ringed spots; unf pd series nearly straight, parallel with outer margin; unh pd series sinuous, spot in s6 usually displaced basad, a small marginal dot in s2. ♀ similar but blue scales absent on ups.

Flight. End April/September, a single brood appearing late at high altitudes, perhaps two broods in some lowland localities. In England usually a single brood in June.

Habitat. Grassy banks from sea-level to 8,000 ft. Larval food plants various small Leguminosae, feeding upon flowers and seeds.

Distribution. Widely distributed, often common, throughout Europe, esp. on calcareous soils, to 69°N, including Ireland. N. Spain to Cuenca. Absent from S. Spain, Portugal and Mediterranean islands except Sicily.

Variation. The blue scaling on ♂ups may be very extensive or almost, but never quite, absent. Large specimens with fw to 14 mm. occur at high altitudes among others of average size, f. *alsoides* Gerhard.

C. minimus trinacriae Verity 1919 TL: Palermo, Sicily
Description. ♂fw 8/9 mm., ups very dark (black) and without blue scales. ♀ similar.
Flight. April/May. A single brood only has been recorded.
Habitat. Mountainous country from 600–4,000 ft.
Distribution. Sicily in Madonie Mts., Mt. Salvatore (Petralia), Trapani, San Martino della Scala, etc.

Similar species. *Everes*, all species pp. 254–5, hw with short tail; *C. carswelli* p. 259, unh discal spots in s2–5 in a straight row, ups in ♂ with occasional purple-blue scales; *C. osiris* below; *C. lorquinii* p. 259.

CUPIDO OSIRIS   *Osiris Blue*

Sp: Deunde Mayor
Range. From Spain and Provence through S. Europe and Asia Minor to C. Asia.   Map 269

C. osiris Meigen 1829 TL: not known.   Pl. 53
  syn: *sebrus* auct.
Description. ♂fw 12/15 mm., *ups gc violet-blue*, unmarked, with *narrow black marginal lines*; uns light grey with markings as in *C. minimus*; unh often with slight blue basal flush. ♀ups dark brown sometimes with blue flush upf; uns as in ♂.
Flight. End May and later, in one or two broods.
Habitat. Flowery banks, usually in mountainous country, flying from 1,500–6,000 ft., rarely at lower altitudes. Larval food plants small Leguminosae, esp. *Onobrychis*, perhaps also *Lathyrus*.
Distribution. N. and C. Spain. France, in Var and N. to Isère, Savoie, also

Ardéche, Gard, Hérault and Bouches du Rhône. Switzerland, Valais and Jura. Italy, Piedmont and Apennines S. to Lazio. Hungary, Rumania and Balkans including Albania, Bulgaria and Greece. A local species and often overlooked.

Similar species. *C. minimus* p. 257, ♀ never with violet-blue flush upf; *C. semiargus* p. 290; *Everes* pp. 254-5 all species.

CUPIDO LORQUINII *Lorquin's Blue*

Sp: Deunde Azul
Range. Restricted to N. Africa, Spain and Portugal. Map 270

C. lorquinii Herrich-Schaeffer 1847 TL: not stated Pl. 53
Description. ♂ fw 11/14mm., *ups violet-blue* with *broad black marginal borders* extending basad along veins, otherwise unmarked; uns small white-ringed dark spots arranged as in *C. minimus*, series sometimes incomplete. ♀ ups dark grey, sometimes with a few blue scales.
Flight. May/June in a single brood.
Habitat. Flies over short grass at roadsides, etc., to 5,000 ft. Larval food plants not recorded.
Distribution. S. Spain, local near Malaga, Seville, Granada, etc. Portugal in Estremadura. Morocco. Algeria.

Similar species. *C. minimus* p. 257, gc not violet-blue; *Z. knysna* p. 253, ups marginal borders wider, uns gc fawn-brown with marginal markings present.

CUPIDO CARSWELLI *Carswell's Little Blue*

Range. Known only from Murcia. Map 271

C. carswelli Stempffer 1927 TL: Sierra de Espuña, Spain
Description. ♂ fw 11mm., resembles *C. minimus*; ups brown with *a few purple-blue scales near wing-bases*; unh pd spots in s2-5 in straight row. ♀ ups dark grey-brown.
Flight. May.
Habitat. Flies over short grass at 4,000 ft.
Distribution. Local in Sierra de Espuña, Murcia.

Similar species. *C. minimus* p. 257. Care should be taken to identify the blue basal scales on ups in *carswelli*, since the relative positions of spots on nh are slightly variable.

CELASTRINA ARGIOLUS *Holly Blue*

w: Tosteblåvinge G: Faulbaumfalter Sp: Najade
Range. From N. Africa throughout Europe to C. Asia and Japan; from coast to coast in N. America and southwards to New Mexico. Map 272

C. argiolus Linnaeus 1758 TL: England (Verity 1943) Pl. 52
Description. ♂ fw 13/17mm., *first brood* ups shining pale sky blue with fine

PLATE 45

1a 1b

1c 2a

3a 2b

3b 4c

4a 4b

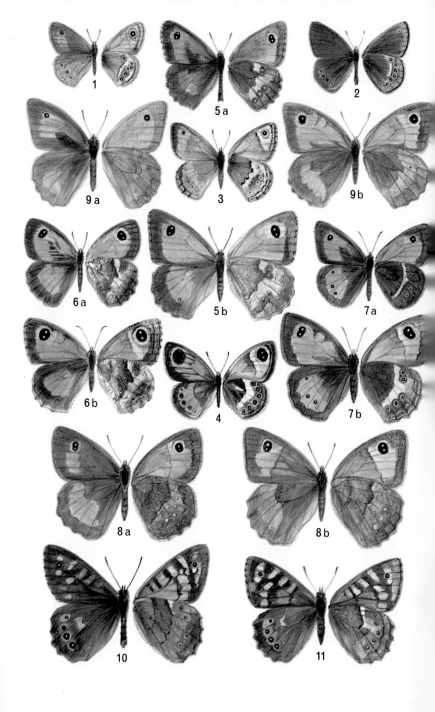

PLATE 46

1. **Coenonympha austauti** *Austaut's Algerian Heath* 218
   C. austauti ♂. Upf apical ocellus large; uph postdiscal pale stripe almost straight, 5 ocelli in curved series. ♀ similar.

2. **Coenonympha hero** *Scarce Heath* 222
   C. hero ♂. Ups dark grey-brown; unh submarginal ocelli tinged orange, preceded by white transverse band. ♀ similar.

3. **Coenonympha pamphilus** *Small Heath* 214
   C. p. thyrsis ♂. Ups like *C. pamphilus* (Pl. 48); uph minute postdiscal spots in spaces 2, 3, 4 not constant; unh pale buff with darker markings.

4. **Coenonympha vaucheri** *Vaucher's Heath* 218
   C. vaucheri ♂. Upf slightly dusky, apical ocellus blind, very large. ♀ lacks dusky ups suffusion; otherwise similar.

5. **Pyronia tithonus** *Gatekeeper* 210
   5a. *P. tithonus* ♂. Ups orange-brown; upf apical ocellus with twin white pupils, black sex-brand prominent; unh yellowish with postdiscal ocelli.
   5b. *P. tithonus* ♀. Larger; upf paler orange, lacking sex-brand; uns as in ♂.

6. **Pyronia cecilia** *Southern Gatekeeper* 210
   6a. *P. cecilia* ♂. Ups like *P. tithonus*; upf sex-brand conspicuous, divided by veins; unh brown, marbled pale grey, ocelli absent.
   6b. *P. cecilia* ♀. Larger; upf lacks sex-brand, otherwise as in ♂.

7. **Pyronia bathseba** *Spanish Gatekeeper* 211
   7a. *P. b. bathseba* ♂. Small; unh brown with prominent yellow discal stripe; ocelli obscure.
   7b. *P. b. pardilloi* ♀. Larger; unh yellow discal stripe wider, ocelli more prominent.

8. **Pyronia janiroides** *False Meadow Brown* 211
   8a. *P. janiroides* ♂. Upf orange postdiscal area narrow, limited by obscure dark sex-brand; unh brown, postdiscal ocelli very small, yellow.
   8b. *P. janiroides* ♀. Ups postdiscal areas broadly yellow; upf lacks dark sex-brand; uns as in ♂.

9. **Maniola nurag** *Sardinian Meadow Brown* 203
   9a. *M. nurag* ♂. Like *M. jurtina* (Pl. 45) but smaller; ups postdiscal fulvous areas extensive; upf dark sex-brand prominent.
   9b. *M. nurag* ♀. Like *M. jurtina* but smaller; ups fulvous areas extensive.

10. **Pararge xiphia** *Madeiran Speckled Wood* 227
    P. xiphia ♂. Fw pointed; ups orange markings small, subdued; unh discal band bounded by yellow mark on costa. ♀ similar.

11. **Pararge xiphioides** *Canary Speckled Wood* 22
    P. xiphioides ♂. Like *P. aegeria* (Pl. 49); unh basal area bounded by white costal mark. ♀ similar.

black marginal line slightly expanded at apex of fw; *uns white* with faintly blue shading at wing-bases, marked in the usual pattern with very small black spots often partly obsolete, *unf pd series displaced towards outer margin*, marginal markings obscure if present. ♀ups blue paler, upf dark marginal border includes apex and outer margin, base and discal areas broadly blue. In *second brood* ♀ups darker blue, upf dark border extensive, blue area reduced; uph costa usually dark.

Flight. April/May and July/August in two broods.

Habitat. Common in light woodland from lowlands to 5,000 ft. or more. Larval food plants various shrubs and trees esp. ivy, holly and buckthorn.

Distribution. Throughout the region except in N.W. Scandinavia.

Similar species. *E. alcetas* p. 255, distinguished by presence of short tail on hw at v2.

GLAUCOPSYCHE ALEXIS   *Green-underside Blue*

Sw: Klöverblåvinge Sp: Manchas verdes

Range. From W. Europe across Russia and C. Asia to Amurland.

Map 273

G. alexis alexis Poda 1761 **TL:** Graz, Austria   Pl. 53
  syn: *cyllarus* Rottemburg 1775

Description. ♂fw 13/18mm., ups blue, black marginal borders 1–2mm. wide; uns pale grey *without marginal markings*; unf black pd spots variable, usually prominent in a curved series, *large in s2*, diminishing in size to costa; unh basal area green, pd spots usually small, often obsolete. ♀ups brown with variable blue basal flush.

Flight. April/June in a single brood.

Habitat. Flowery banks near woodland among hills and mountains; lowlands to 4,000 ft. Larval food plants *Astragalus*, *Cytisus* and other small Leguminosae.

Distribution. Widely distributed in W. and N. Europe to 66°N but rare in north. Absent or occasional in N. Germany and Denmark, absent from Britain, S. Spain and Portugal.

G. alexis melanoposmater Verity 1928 **TL:** Aflou, Algeria

Description. ♂fw 13/15mm., ups black marginal borders narrow; unh green flush reduced or absent, black pd spots vestigial or absent. ♀ups basal areas of both wings generally blue.

Flight and Habitat. No information.

Distribution. Algeria. Not recorded from Morocco or Tunisia.

Similar species. *G. melanops* below.

GLAUCOPSYCHE MELANOPS   *Black-eyed Blue*

Sp: Escamas azules

Range. Confined to SW. Europe and N. Africa.   Map 274

G. melanops melanops Boisduval 1828 TL: Aix-en-Provence
Description. ♂fw 11/13mm., ups resembles *G. alexis*, sometimes paler blue; uns pale brown with *traces of marginal markings; unf black pd spots prominent*; unh narrowly dark grey at base, pd spots small but rarely absent. ♀ups grey-brown to black, usually with basal blue suffusions.
Flight. April/May in a single brood.
Habitat. Heaths and light woodland with broom and heather, rarely above 2,500 ft. Larval food plants *Dorycnium, Genista, Lotus*, in the flowers.
Distribution. SE. France in Ardêche, Var, Basses Alpes, Bouches-du-Rhône; E. Pyrenees, Hte Garonne; N. Italy, Liguria.

G. melanops algirica Heyne 1895 TL: Algeria Pl. 54
Description. ♂fw 14/16mm., larger, ups dark marginal borders wider; uns marginal markings better defined; unh with faintly marked grey sub-marginal lunules and antemarginal spots in each space. ♀ups blue basal suffusion generally reduced.
Flight. March/April/May.
Habitat. Among tall broom, to 3,000 ft. in Spain, to 6,500 ft. in N. Africa.
Distribution. C. and S. Spain, Morocco, Algeria, Tunisia. Transitional to *G. m. melanops* in Catalonia.

Similar species. *G. alexis* p. 262, ups very similar; uns gc pale grey and marginal markings absent, unh suffused green except in Algeria.

TURANANA PANAGAEA *Odd-spot Blue*
Range. Greece and Asia Minor (TL of *L. panagaea* Herrich-Schaeffer 1852) to Turkestan. Map 275

T. panagaea taygetica Rebel 1902 TL: Mt. Taygetos, Greece Pl. 52
Description. ♂fw 10/11mm., ups blue with black marginal borders about 2mm. wide and a small discoidal stria; uns gc light grey-brown; unf with large black pd spots, *spot in s3 esp. large and displaced distad*, a narrow black discoidal stria and marginal markings; unh with basal and pd black spots in series, large marginal spot in s2 and marginal markings. ♀ups brown.
Flight. May/June/July in a single brood.
Habitat. Hilly and mountainous districts at 3–7,000 ft. Larval food plant not known.
Distribution. Greece, on Mt. Chelmos and Taygetos Mts.

MACULINEA ALCON *Alcon Blue*
Sw: Alkonblåvinge Sp: Hormiguera
Range. From N. Spain and France across Europe to C. Asia. Map 276

M. alcon alcon Schiffermueller 1775 TL: Vienna Pl. 54
Description. ♂fw 17/19mm., ups pale rather dull blue with black marginal

borders 1–2 mm. wide, *otherwise unmarked*; uns gc light brown with darker light-ringed spots arranged in the usual pattern; *unh without blue or green basal dusting*. ♀ups heavily suffused grey-brown, sometimes flushed blue at wing-bases; upf an obscure discoidal spot and small pd spots often present.

Flight. July in a single brood.

Habitat. Damp meadows and marshy places, lowlands to 3,000 ft. Larval food plant *Gentiana pneumonanthe*, later in ants' nests.

Distribution. Widely distributed but very local in C. Europe. France, esp. in NE. Belgium. Switzerland. Most common in Germany, esp. on moorlands in Bavaria. S. Sweden. Denmark and east to Rumania and Balkans. N. Italy.

M. alcon rebeli Hirschke 1904   TL: Styrian Alps   Pl. 54

Description. ♂ups brighter blue, black marginal borders generally narrower and better defined, often slightly chequered; uns gc grey-brown, markings more distinct and usually with slight blue-green flush at base of hw. ♀ups basal areas blue, discoidal and black pd spots distinct.

Flight. End June/July.

Habitat. Meadows and grass slopes at 4–6,000 ft., sometimes at lower altitudes in France, often in dry localities. Larval food plants *Gentiana cruciata* and *G. germanica*.

Distribution. France, esp. Massif Central and SE. Alps; E. Pyrenees (Aulus). Denmark, very local. Switzerland and, chiefly as a mountain insect, through C. Europe, the Dolomites and Apennines. Spain, known from a few localities near Soria, Teruel and Santander.

Similar species. *M. arion*, uns grey rather than brown, ♂ nearly always with black discal spots upf; unh with wide basal blue-green flush and well-defined discal and marginal markings.

Note. Typical *M.a. alcon* and *M.a. rebeli* are so different that some authors have regarded them as distinct species, in spite of the fact that they are linked by intermediates.

MACULINEA ARION   *Large Blue*

Sw: Svartfläckig Blåvinge   G: Schwarzflecken Blauling
Sp: Hormiguera de lunares
Range. From W. Europe across Russia and Siberia to China.   Map 277

M. arion arion Linnaeus 1758   TL: Nuremberg, Germany   Pl. 54
(Fruhstorfer)

Description. ♂fw 16/20 mm., ups bright gleaming blue, fringes white, black marginal borders broad; *upf pd series of elongate black spots* variable but rarely absent; uph small black pd spots inconstant; *uns gc grey to grey-brown with usual markings, fringes chequered; unh blue-green* *basal suffusion usually extensive.* ♀ similar, ups black discal markings often larger.

Flight. June/July in a single brood.

Habitat. Rough grassy places with thyme from sea-level to 6,000 ft. Larval food plant thyme (*Thymus serpyllum*), later in ants' nests.

Distribution. Widely distributed in C. Europe to 62°N, including Pyrenees, Balkans and Greece. Very local in S. England; a mountain species in central Spain. Absent from Norway, S. Spain, Portugal and Mediterranean islands except Corsica.

M. arion obscura Christ 1878 TL: Zermatt and Liestal, Pl. 54
Switzerland

Description. Ups pd areas heavily suffused dark grey, markings sometimes nearly obliterated, blue shade present only at wing-bases.

Flight. July.

Habitat. Mountains from 4,000 ft. upwards.

Distribution. Predominant form in Alps of SE. France, Switzerland south of Rhône valley and Austria.

M. arion ligurica Wagner 1904 TL: Ligurian coastal region

Description. Often of large size, resembling *M. a. arion*; ups gc pale gleaming blue with black markings crisply defined; uph black marginal spots often present; uns gc pale grey, sometimes yellowish; unh blue-green basal flush reduced. ♀ups black markings generally large, sometimes confluent.

Flight. End June/July.

Habitat. Lowlands to moderate levels.

Distribution. Coastal regions of French and Italian Riviera from Nice to Genoa and inland to Modena and Florence; recorded also from Corsica.

Variation. Broadly speaking blue races occur at low or moderate altitudes, dark forms at higher levels in mountains, but this is not invariable. Variation in the extent of dark suffusion is clinal throughout the whole species, with the two major forms distributed in somewhat haphazard manner, more suggestive of ecological modifications than of geographical sub-species.

Similar species. *M. alcon* p. 263, *M. teleius* below.

MACULINEA TELEIUS *Scarce Large Blue*

Sp: Limbada

Range. From France through C. Europe and Asia to Japan. Map 278

M. teleius Bergstrasser 1779 TL: Hanau, W. Germany p. 54
syn: *euphemus* Huebner 1800

Description. ♂fw 16/18 mm., ups pale grey-blue, slightly paler in sub-marginal areas before the rather wide black marginal borders which extend basad along veins; upf black pd spots small, often reduced, sometimes absent; *uns gc pale brown*, usual markings rather faint except pd spots which are black and prominent; *unh without blue-green basal flush.* ♀ups, wide dusky suffusion along costa and outer margins; upf dark pd spots more constant; uns gc slightly darker shade of brown.

Flight. July.

Habitat. Marshy meadows and moorland from lowlands to 6,000 ft. Larval food plant *Sanguisorba officinalis*, later in ants' nests.

Distribution, Very local in C. Europe to 53°N (Berlin). France, chiefly in NE. Switzerland, not S. of Rhône valley. Italy, in southern foothills of Alps from Susa to Carniola. Absent from Rumania and Balkans.

Similar species. *M. arion* p. 264, ups blue gc brighter, with larger black markings, uns gc grey rather than brown, with extensive unh blue flush. *M. nausithous* below, uns cinnamon-brown, no marginal markings.

MACULINEA NAUSITHOUS   *Dusky Large Blue*

Range. From N. Spain and France across C. Europe in widely scattered colonies to the Urals and Caucasus.   Map 279

M. nausithous Bergstrasser 1779   TL: Hanau, W. Germany   Pl. 54
  syn: *arcas* Rottemburg 1775 (invalid homonym)

Description. ♂fw 17/18mm., ups resembles *M. teleius* but gc slightly darker tone of blue, black marginal borders 3mm. wide, pd spots often small, partly obscured; *uns cinnamon brown*, black pd spots in complete series but *no marginal markings.* ♀ups dark brown, unmarked, fringes brown; vestigial blue basal flush occasionally present.

Flight. July.

Habitat. Marshy lowlands, often beside lakes. Larval food plant *Sanguisorba officinalis*, later in ants' nests.

Distribution. Very local in C. Europe to 52°N. France, chiefly in NE near Dijon, Colmar, etc. N. Switzerland, Weesen, Berne, etc. Spain, an isolated colony near Soria. More widely distributed in Bavaria and C. Germany, Austria and Czechoslovakia. Absent from N. Germany, Denmark, Tirol and Balkans; occurrence in N. Italy needs confirmation.

Similar species. *M. teleius* p. 265.

IOLANA IOLAS   *Iolas Blue*

Sp: Espantalobos

Range. From N. Africa and C. Spain through S. Europe and Asia Minor to Iran.   Map 280

I. iolas Ochsenheimer 1816   TL: Hungary   Pl. 53

Description. ♂fw 18/21 mm., ups lustrous violet-blue with narrow black marginal borders, otherwise unmarked; uns pale grey; unf discoidal stria sent, also a series of black white-ringed *pd spots close to and parallel* *with outer margin*; unh with blue-grey basal flush and black basal and pd spots, marginal spots usually vestigial on both wings. ♀ups variable, usually blue with wide fuscous marginal borders often extending almost to base on both wings.

Flight. May/June usually in a single brood, a scanty late brood has been recorded in August/September.

Habitat. Rocky places and open woodland from lowlands to 6,000 ft. Larval food plant senna (*Colutea*).

Distribution. Spain, local in Sierra Nevada and Sierra Alta (Albarracin). France, Provence. Switzerland, only in Rhône valley. From Apennines and S. slopes of Alps to Hungary, Rumania, Balkans and Greece. Algeria. Not recorded from Morocco.

PHILOTES BATON *Baton Blue*

Sp: Falso Abencerragus

Range. From Spain across S. and C. Europe to Asia Minor, Iran, Afghanistan and Chitral. Map 281

P. baton baton Bergstrasser 1779 TL: Hanau, Germany Pl. 53

Description. ♂fw 10/12mm., *ups light powder blue*; upf narrow marginal borders and discoidal spot black; uph antemarginal spots black; uns gc light grey to grey-brown with prominent dark spots; *unh conspicuous orange submarginal lunules* in s1b–5 surmounted by small black lunules. ♀ups black with variable blue basal flush.

Flight. April/June and July/September in two broods at low levels, a single brood at high altitudes.

Habitat. Flowery banks among thyme, lowlands to 7,000 ft. Larval food plant thyme.

Distribution. Widely distributed in C. Europe to 48°N, southwards to Pyrenees, Cantabrian Mts. and Portugal. Widely distributed in Italy, including Sicily. Corsica and Sardinia.

Variation. There is little difference between first and second broods. In E. Pyrenees and NE. Spain unh orange submarginal lunules small or vestigial, transitional to following subspecies.

P. baton panoptes Huebner 1813 TL: Spain Pl. 53

Description. ♂fw 9/11mm., ups gc slightly deeper blue; uns gc grey-brown, dark discal spots clearly white-ringed and marginal markings narrow; unh *orange submarginal lunules vestigial or absent* submarginal and marginal dark lunules very close together. ♀ups dark brown with minimal blue basal flush.

Flight. April/May and July in two broods.

Habitat. Rough ground with thyme, 2,500–6,000 ft.

Distribution. Replaces *P. b. baton* in C. and S. Spain.

PLATE 47

1. **Coenonympha tullia** *The Large Heath* 212
   Upf without definite narrow dark border.
   1a. *C. t. rothliebii* ♂. Ups grey-brown, margins not dark; unh brightly marked, ocelli well developed in complete series.
   1b. *C. t. tiphon* ♂. Ups orange-brown; unh pale postdiscal band less prominent, ocelli smaller but series usually complete.
   1c. *C. t. demophile* ♂. Small; uns markings not well defined.
   1d. *C. t. scotica* ♂. Ups yellow-buff; uns pale postdiscal bands well developed, ocelli small or absent. ♀ similar.
   1e. *C. t. rhodopensis* f. *italica* ♂. Ups orange-buff unf postdiscal pale band absent (rarely vestigial); unh grey.
   1f. *C. t. rhodopensis* ♂. Like *C. t. italica*; unh often with postdiscal fulvous shade.

2. **Coenonympha glycerion** *Chestnut Heath* 221
   2a. ♂. Ups chestnut-brown; unh grey with small white postdiscal marks; ocelli small, sometimes vestigial.
   2b. ♀. Upf orange-buff; uph grey with yellow marginal line.

3. **Coenonympha leander** *Russian Heath* 221
   3a. *C. l. leander* ♂. Ups brown; upf base flushed buff; uph anal border buff; unf orange-buff, lacking grey marginal border.
   3b. *C. l. leander* ♀. Upf pale buff suffusion extensive; uph brown, buff anal border extending to space 4; uns as in ♂.

4. **Coenonympha iphioides** *Spanish Heath* 222
   4a. ♂. Uph orange marginal line vestigal; unf buff, with grey marginal border; unh grey, orange marginal line conspicuous.
   4b. ♀. Upf paler buff; uph orange marginal line complete; unh orange marginal line conspicuous.

5. **Coenonympha arcania** *Pearly Heath* 219
   5a. *C. a. arcania* ♂. Unh irregular white postdiscal band conspicuous; ocelli ringed yellow and black; ocellus in space 6 internal to band. ♀ similar.
   5b. *C. a. darwiniana* ♂. Unh ocellus in space 6 enclosed within more regular white postdiscal band; otherwise as in *C. a. arcania*.

6. **Coenonympha oedippus** *False Ringlet* 22.
   C. oedippus ♂. Ups dark brown; uns yellow-brown; unh ocellus in space 6 large, all ocelli ringed yellow. ♀ similar, ocelli larger.

7. **Coenonympha arcanioides** *Moroccan Pearly Heath* 22◦
   C. arcanioides ♂. Unh dark brown with narrow white stripe; ocelli obscure if present.

8. **Coenonympha gardetta** *Alpine Heath* 22
   8a. *C. g. macrophthalmica* ♂. Unh white submarginal band wide and regular, ocelli well developed and lacking rings.
   b. *C. g. gardetta* ♂. Unh grey, ocelli small or vestigial. ♀ similar.

1a   2c   2d

1b   2a   2b

3a   4   3b

5

6

7

8

PLATE 48

Similar species. *P. abencerragus* below, ♂ups darker (indigo) blue with wing-margins widely suffused dark fuscous, androconia scanty, about twice as long as wide (in *P. baton* abundant, small, rounded).

P. baton schiffermuelleri Hemming 1929   TL: Altenberg, Austria
syn: *P. b. vicrama* auct.
Description. Indistinguishable from *P. b. baton* by external characters, but ♂ genitalia differ.
Flight and **Habitat** as for *P.b. baton.*
Distribution. E. Europe to 62°N in Finland, C. Germany, Czechoslovakia; Alto Adige in Italy, Austria and eastwards to Balkans and Greece.
Similar species. *P. bavius* below, uph with orange submarginal lunules.

PHILOTES ABENCERRAGUS   *False Baton Blue*
Sp: Abencerraje
Range. From Spain and Morocco across N. Africa to Egypt and Jordan.
Map 282

P. abencerragus Pierret 1837   TL: Morocco   Pl. 53
Description. ♂fw 9/11 mm., resembles *P. baton panoptes*; fringes strongly chequered; ups gc *lustrous dark steel blue*, with dark marginal borders rather widely suffused; upf discoidal spot sometimes outlined white; uph costa broadly grey, antemarginal spots usually distinct; uns gc grey-brown, white-ringed dark spots strongly marked in regular series; unh submarginal and antemarginal markings close together, sometimes with traces of orange between. ♀ups dark grey with minimal blue basal dusting.
Flight. April/May, perhaps a second brood in summer (not recorded).
Habitat. Rough places among heather (*Erica arborea*), etc., 2,500–4,000 ft. in Spain, to 6,500 ft. in N. Africa. Larval food plants not recorded.
Distribution. Morocco, not rare in Middle and High Atlas. Algeria. Tunisia. Portugal, Alemtejo to Sierra de Estrela. S. Spain, widely distributed but very local from Aranjuez southwards.
Variation. In African specimens (High Atlas) uns gc slightly paler yellowish-grey than in Spanish specimens.
Similar species. *P. baton panoptes* p. 267.

PHILOTES BAVIUS   *Bavius Blue*
Range. Morocco and Algeria; Hungary, Greece, Asia Minor and S. Russia (*Lycaena bavius* Eversmann 1832 TL: S. Urals).   Map 283

P. bavius hungaricus Dioszegy 1913   TL: Hungary   Not figured
Description. ♂fw 12/15 mm., fringes white, chequered dark; ups gc violet-blue with broad diffuse fuscous marginal borders; *uph bright orange submarginal lunules in s1c, 2, 3* surrounding black antemarginal spots; uns markings jet-black and prominent; unh gc almost white with wide orange-

red submarginal band; androconia abundant. ♀ups suffused black, blue restricted to basal areas; uns as in ♂.
Flight. May, probably a second brood in July/August.
Habitat. Rough flowery places from lowlands to 3,000 ft. Larval food plant *Salvia argentea*.
Distribution. Hungary. Rumania, Cluj district (Transylvania). Greece, Mt. Chelmos.

P. bavius fatma Oberthur 1890 TL: Lambessa, Algeria Pl. 53
Description. Resembles *P. b. hungaricus*; ♂ups black marginal borders and antemarginal black dots better defined; uph series of orange submarginal lunules prominent and complete from s1b–7. ♀ups blue suffusion extensive.
Flight. April/May. A late brood has not been recorded.
Habitat. Woodland margins with *Salvia* at 5–6,000 ft.
Distribution. Algeria. Morocco, Middle Atlas, Anosseur, Ifrane, etc.
Similar species. *P. baton* p. 267.

SCOLITANTIDES ORION *Chequered Blue*
Sp: Banda Naranja   Sw: Fetörtsblåvinge
Range. From Spain and C. France across Europe and C. Asia to Japan.
Map 284

S. orion Pallas 1771 TL: Volga, Russia Pl. 53
Description. ♂fw 13/16mm., white fringes heavily chequered; *first brood* ups dark grey, markings variable, black discoidal spot and submarginal lunules rather brightly outlined in blue; upf with blue basal flush; *uns white with large jet black markings*; unh submarginal band bright orange, prominent. In *second brood* ♂ often larger but ups darker with obscure markings, blue restricted to basal flush on upf. ♀ ups usually black, with or without vestigial markings.
Flight. May/June and August in two broods in southern localities, a single brood in July in N. Europe.
Habitat. Rough places with low vegetation, lowlands to 3,000 ft. Larval food plant stonecrop (*Sedum telephium* and *S. album*).
Distribution. In two widely separated areas; (1) S. Europe to 50°N, from Spain, France, Switzerland and Sicily to Hungary, Rumania and Balkans with Greece. (2) Finland and S. Scandinavia. Apparently absent from peninsular Italy, Mediterranean islands and Portugal.
Variation. Scandinavian specimens are more brightly marked than those from S. Europe.

FREYERIA TROCHYLUS *Grass Jewel*
Range. SE. Europe and widely distributed in tropical and sub-tropical Asia and Africa.
Map 285

PLATE 49

1. Lasiommata maera   *Large Wall Brown*   228

  1a. *L. m. maera* ♂. Ups dull brown; upf with a single transverse cell-bar or none, sex-brand not prominent; uph lacks dark discal stripe.

  1b. *L. m. maera* ♀. Like ♂ but upf postdiscal fulvous markings well defined.

  1c. *L. m. adrasta* ♂. Larger; ups postdiscal areas bright fulvous; upf sex-brand prominent.

  1d. *L. m. adrasta* ♀. Upf broadly orange with light brown markings and prominent apical ocellus.

2. Lasiommata petropolitana   *Northern Wall Brown*   229

  2a. *L. petropolitana* ♂ ⎱ Like *L. m. maera*, but smaller and uph with
  2b. *L. petropolitana* ♀ ⎰ dark angled discal line, sometimes obscure.

3. Pararge aegeria   *Speckled Wood*   226

  3a. *P. a. aegeria* ♂. Ups bright orange-fulvous with dark brown markings.

  3b. *P. a. tircis* ♀. Ups like *P. a. aegeria* but ground-colour cream-white.

4. Lasiommata megera   *Wall Butterfly*   227

  4a. *L. m. megera* ♂. Ups bright fulvous; upf with two dark bars in cell; sex-brand prominent.

  4b. *L. m. megera* ♀. Like ♂ but upf lacks sex-brand and ground-colour slightly paler.

  4c. *L. m. paramegaera* ♂. Like *L. m. megera* but smaller; ups dark postdiscal striae vestigial or absent.

  4d. *L. m. paramegaera* ♀. Like ♂ but upf lacks dark sex-brand.

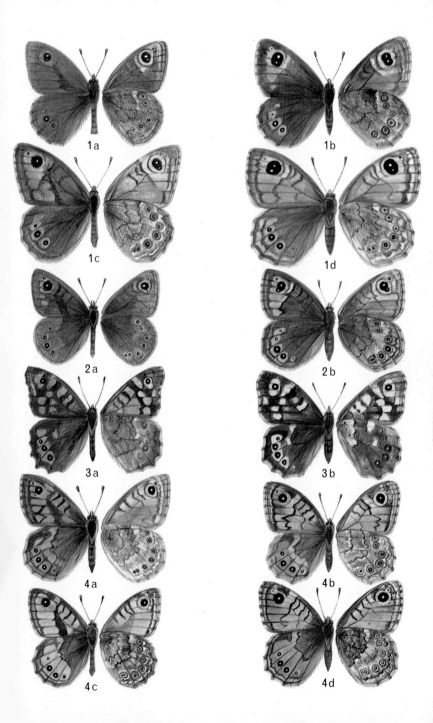

PLATE 50

1. Nordmannia ilicis   *Ilex Hairstreak*   235

    1a. *N. i. ilicis* ♂. Ups fw dark brown; unh red submarginal spots black-bordered internally and externally; no sex-brand.
    1b. *N. ilicis* f. *cerri* ♀. Upf postdiscal area orange.

2. Nordmannia esculi   *False Ilex Hairstreak*   236

    2a. *N. e. esculi* ♂. Unh red spots smaller, without black borders.
    2b. *N. e. mauretanica* ♀. Unh grey, markings vestigial.

3. Nordmannia acaciae   *Sloe Hairstreak*   235

    3a. *N. acaciae* ♂. Like *N. ilicis*; unh orange submarginal lunules enclosing black spots near anal angle; no sex-brand.
    3b. *N. acaciae* ♀. Apex of abdomen with black hair tuft.

4. Strymonidia spini   *Blue-spot Hairstreak*   236

    4a. ♂. Anal angle black with blue spot above. Sex-brand present.
    4b. *S. s.* ♀-f. *vandalusica*. Ups postdiscal areas broadly orange.

5. Strymonidia w-album   *White-letter Hairstreak*   237
    S. w-album ♂. Unh white postdiscal line forming W-mark in anal area. Sex-brand present. ♀ similar, often larger.

6. Strymonidia pruni   *Black Hairstreak*   237
    S. pruni ♀. Uph with orange submarginal lunules in spaces 1c-4; unh orange submarginal band bordered internally with black spots. ♂. smaller, upf without orange flush, sex-brand present.

7. Callophrys rubi   *Green Hairstreak*   238
    C. rubi ♂. Frons green, eyes bordered white.

8. Callophrys avis   *Chapman's Green Hairstreak*   238
    C. avis ♂. Like *C. rubi*; frons red, eyes bordered red.

9. Thecla betulae   *Brown Hairstreak*   233

    9a. ♀. Upf with postdiscal orange band.
    9b. ♂. Upf dark brown with or without vestigial orange mark.

10. Laeosopis roboris   *Spanish Purple Hairstreak*   234

    10a. *L. roboris* ♂. Upf base and disc blue.
    10b. *L. roboris* ♀. Like ♂ but upf blue at base only.

11. Quercusia quercus   *Purple Hairstreak*   234

    11a. *Q. q. quercus* ♂. Ups violet-blue with narrow black marginal borders; uns with postdiscal white lines, anal spots orange.
    11b. *Q. q. iberica* ♀. Ups blue restricted to fw in space 1b. and cell; uns markings vestigial.

F. trochylus Freyer 1844 TL: Turkey   Pl. 53
Description. ♂fw 8/9mm., ups gc brown; upf unmarked; uph 2–4 conspicuous orange lunules surmounting dark marginal spots near anal angle; uns pale grey-brown with usual markings; unh orange marginal band in s 1c–4 enclosing four round *black ocelli ringed in shining green*. Sexes similar.
Flight. March or later, perhaps with continuous emergence through summer.
Habitat. Barren stony ground from lowlands to moderate altitudes, flying near the ground, fond of settling on stones. Larval food plant heliotrope. Larva said to be attended by ants of the genus *Pheidole*.
Distribution. Greece (Peloponnesus), Crete and Turkey.

PLEBEJUS VOGELII *Vogel's Blue*
Range. Confined to Morocco.   Map 286

P. vogelii Oberthur 1920 TL: Taghzeft Pass, Middle Atlas   Pl. 55
Description. ♂fw 12/14mm., *ups pale grey-brown with chequered fringes*; upf black discoidal spot large, conspicuous orange submarginal line divided by veins into separate lunules, each enclosed internally and externally by black lunules, a fine white terminal line; uph similar, with very small discoidal stria; unf discoidal and pd spots very large; unh spots small, marginal borders not well defined. ♀ similar, ups often with small bluish-white marks internal to marginal borders.
Flight. August/September, a single brood only is recorded.
Habitat and Distribution. Only known from Morocco. It flies in the Middle Atlas near the Taghzeft Pass on rough stony ground at an altitude of 7,000 ft. Larval food plant not known.

PLEBEJUS MARTINI *Martin's Blue*
Range. Confined to Morocco and Algeria.   Map 287

P. martini martini Allard 1867 TL: Algeria   Pls. 4, 55
Description. ♂fw 14/15mm., ups resembles *P.p.sephirus*, lavender-blue with fine black marginal lines, otherwise unmarked; *uns gc pale grey-brown* with faint blue-grey basal shade; unf with usual markings, black pd spots prominent; unh markings smaller, *orange submarginal lunules very small*, inconspicuous. ♀ups dark brown with blue basal flush; uph with orange submarginal lunules in s1, 2, 3, 4 (5) and with black marginal spots in s 1–4; uns rather brown than grey with marginal markings better developed.
Flight. May, in a single brood.
Habitat. Rough places with heather, etc., at 5–7,000 ft. Larval food plant not recorded.
Distribution. Algeria, common in east, Lambessa, Batna, Khenchela. Morocco, in Middle and High Atlas and in El Rif, very local and rare.

Variation. Some Moroccan specimens have large pd spots on unf transitional to *P. m. allardi*.

P. martini allardi Oberthur TL: Oran, Algeria Pl. 4
Description. On ups resembles *P. m. martini* but uns black discoidal and postdiscal spots greatly enlarged. This was described as a distinct species, but probably correctly placed as a local form of *P. martini*.
Distribution. Only known from Algeria.

PLEBEJUS PYLAON *Zephyr Blue*

Sp: Niña de Astragalo
Range. From Spain eastwards with occasional scattered colonies through S. Europe including S. Russia (*Lycaena pylaon* Fischer 1832 TL: Sarepta); more widely distributed in W. Asia to Iran. Map 288

P. pylaon sephirus Frivaldsky 1835 TL: Slivno, Bulgaria Pl. 54
Description. ♂fw 14/17mm., ups clear violet-blue with *narrow black marginal lines*; *uph small black antemarginal spot constant in s*2, occasional in s1b, 3, 4; uns gc pale grey-brown; unh with prominent orange submarginal bands bordered proximally with black V-marks, black antemarginal spots *without silver scales*. ♀ups brown; uph two or more orange submarginal lunules each with black antemarginal spot; uns as in ♂.
Flight. End May/June according to altitude, in a single brood.
Habitat. Flowery banks from lowlands to 5,000 ft. Larval food plant vetch (*Astragalus*).
Distribution. Greece (Parnassus, Chelmos). Bulgaria (Sliven, Pirin Mts.). Albania. Hungary, in a restricted area in the foothills of the Siebenburgen, Cluj, Temisoara.

P. pylaon trappi Verity 1927 TL: Simplon Pl. 54
syn: *lycidas* Trapp 1863 (invalid homonym)
Description. ♂fw 14/17mm., ups gc darker blue with wider black margins; uph three or more black antemarginal spots; uns gc pale grey-brown with usual markings; *unh with well-marked white shade between pd spots and orange submarginal lunules*. ♀ resembles *P. p. sephirus*; ups often with slight blue basal suffusion; uph orange submarginal lunules often vestigial or absent.
Flight. End June/July in a single brood.
Habitat. Sheltered grassy places in mountains at 4–5,000 ft. Larval food plant vetch (*Astragalus excapus*).
Distribution. S. Switzerland esp. Simplon, Gemmi, Saastal, Zermatt, etc. Savoie Alps. Slightly smaller in Valnontey (Aosta).

P. pylaon hespericus Rambur 1839 TL: Sierra de Alfacar, Pl. 54
Andalusia
Description. ♂fw 14/15mm., resembles *P. p. sephirus*; *ups pale shining*

blue; uph with black antemarginal spots in s1–3; uns gc yellow-grey with markings as in *sephirus*. ♀ups paler brown, orange submarginal lunules on hw well marked.

Flight. May.

Habitat. Sheltered places in mountains at 3–4,000 ft. Larval food plant *Astragalus arragonensis*.

Distribution. Spain. Now extinct in Sierra de Alfacar. Teruel, very local at Albarracin, etc., also reported from Murcia. In Toledo, Aranjuez etc., slightly larger, ♂fw 16mm., ups blue not quite so pale, f. *galani* Agenjo.

Similar species. *L. idas* p. 277 and *P. argus* below are distinguished by peacock-blue scales in unh submarginal spots; *L. escheri* p. 297, ups blue less violet-tinted and unh white suffusion between pd spots and orange lunules reduced to white streak along v4; uph without black marginal spots. *K. eurypilus* p. 280.

PLEBEJUS ARGUS *Silver-studded Blue*

Sw: Allmän Blåvinge   G: Geiskleefalter   Sp: Niña hocecillas
Range. Throughout Europe and temperate Asia to Japan.   Map 289

P. argus argus Linnaeus 1758   TL: S. Sweden (Verity 1943)   Pl. 55
Description. ♂fw 12/15mm., resembles *L. idas* Linnaeus, *fore-tibia with strong spine*; *ups rather deep blue with black marginal borders about 1 mm. wide*; uph small black marginal spots between veins; uns gc variable, light grey to smoky grey with usual markings of black white-ringed spots and orange submarginal lunules; unh black antemarginal spots with green pupils ('silver-studded'). ♀ups brown with or without orange submarginal lunules and often with blue basal suffusion, fringes white at apex of fw; uns medium brown, white band between pd spots and submarginal markings prominent.

Flight. May or later with two broods in C. Europe, a single brood in N. Europe.

Habitat. Grassy banks and heaths from sea-level to moderate altitudes. Larval food plants Leguminosae, flowers of gorse, broom, bird's foot trefoil, ling, bog bilberry, etc.

Distribution. Europe to 68°N. Absent from Scotland, Ireland, Sicily, Sardinia, Elba.

Variation. Minor local variation is common. In C. Europe generally the ups black marginal borders often wider, ♀ rarely with blue basal flush, f. *aegon* Schiffermueller. In England variable, on southern heaths uns darker grey-brown and ♀ without blue ups flush.

P. argus aegidion   Meisner 1818   TL: Grimsel Pass, Switzerland
Description. ♂fw 12/13mm. ups resembles *P. a. argus* but black marginal

borders 3mm. wide; uns gc medium grey with usual markings. ♀ups brown, orange submarginal markings often obscure, rarely absent.
Flight. July/August in a single brood.
Habitat. Alpine meadows and grass slopes at 5,000 ft. and above.
Variation. Below 5,000 ft. in S. Alps distinctive characters often less marked, becoming transitional to *P.a. argus*.
Distribution. Generally distributed in higher Alps.

P. argus hypochionus Rambur 1858 TL: Andalucia   Pl. 55
Description. ♂fw 14/17mm., fw slightly pointed; ups marginal borders 1–2mm. wide but often less where antemarginal black spots are clearly defined; uns gc nearly white with markings conspicuous; unh white band between pd spots and submarginal lunules disappears in pale gc. ♀ups orange submarginal lunules generally large, esp. uph.
Flight. June/July in a single brood.
Habitat. Mountain slopes from 4,000 ft. upwards.
Distribution. C. and S. Spain, widely distributed.
Variation. In N. Spain, Cantabrian Mts., Sierra de la Demanda, etc., variable, in some colonies ups brilliant pale blue.

P. argus corsicus Bellier 1862 TL: Corsica   Pl. 55
Description. ♂fw 13/14mm., ups resembles *P. a. argus* in size and general appearance; uns gc grey-brown with pale markings appearing as white rings with centres scarcely darkened. ♀ups generally with blue basal suffusions; uns slightly darker brown, otherwise resembling ♂.
Flight, Habitat and Distribution. In Corsica and Sardinia, rather local in forest clearings, etc., flying in July.

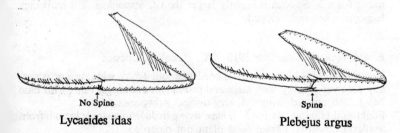

No Spine   Spine
Lycaeides idas   Plebejus argus

Similar species. *Lycaeides idas* below, *L. argyrognomon* p. 279; in these male foreleg is without tibial spine. *Plebejus pylaon* p. 275.

LYCAEIDES IDAS *Idas Blue*

Sw: Föränderlig Blåvinge Sp: Niña Esmaltada
Range. W. Europe including Fennoscandia to Altai Mts. Range somewhat uncertain owing to confusion with *L. argyrognomon*.   Map 290

L. idas idas Linnaeus 1761   TL: Sweden   Pls. 54, 55
Description. ♂fw 14/16mm., like *P. argus*, but fore tibia without spine; ups bright blue, both wings with *characteristic narrow black borders*; uns gc pale grey, often with yellowish tint, but variable, markings generally small and rather inconspicuous; unh black marginal spots with blue-green pupils. ♀ups brown with or without basal blue flush, orange sub-marginal lunules often prominent esp. on uph; uns gc pale brown with markings often larger, orange marginal bands brighter and more extensive.
Flight. June/July with a single brood in N. and C. Europe, usually two broods in S.
Habitat. Rough ground and mountain slopes from lowlands to 4,000 ft. Larval food plants various Leguminosae. The larvae are associated symbiotically with ants, e.g., *Lasius niger, Formica cinerea*, etc., and pupate within their nests where they also hibernate.
Distribution. From Spain to the North Cape and eastwards throughout Europe. Absent from Britain, Sardinia, Sicily and smaller Mediterranean islands.
Variation. *L. idas* is widely distributed in W. Europe and many local forms have been described and named. In general the variation shows a clinal series, with intergrading local forms and subspecies not well defined. Size is variable, at low altitudes often large, espcially in N. Italy, in the striking form *opulentus* Verity, ♂ fw 15/16mm; in the Pyrenees and Alps common but rather local at altitudes of 3-5,000 ft., of moderate size, male ups dark, borders narrow, ♀ often with blue basal flush, f. *alpinus* Berce Pl. 54 single-brooded; at high altitudes in the Alps smaller, ♂ fw 11/13mm, f. *haefelfingeri* Beuret Pl. 55. In arctic regions a similar small form occurs, f. *lapponicus* Gerhard Pls. 54, 55. The nominate subspecies *L. i. idas* Linnaeus from S. Sweden is slightly larger than f. *lapponicus*, uns markings larger and better developed.

L. idas bellieri   Oberthur 1910   TL: Bastelica, Corsica

Description. Ups black marginal borders about 1mm. wide; uns gc generally pale yellow-grey with large and prominent markings. ♀ups with blue basal flush on both wings. A very distinct subspecies.
Flight and Habitat. As for *L. i. idas*, flying in July in a single brood, from sea-level upwards. Larval food plant not recorded.
Distribution. Corsica, in mountains but more local than *P. argus corsicus*.

Similar species. *P. argus* p. 276, usually small and with wider black marginal borders, uns markings small and unf pd spot in s2 more displaced basad; ♂ *fore-tibia with terminal spine*; androconial scales more oval in *P. argus*; male genitalia distinctive. *L. argyrognomon* p. 279, large and colour brilliant; unh black chevrons before orange submarginal lunules nearly flat (larger and sagittate in *idas*).

LYCAEIDES ARGYROGNOMON   *Reverdin's Blue*

Sw: Kronärtblåvinge

Range. From France and Switzerland across C. Europe and S. Russia to Amurland and perhaps to Japan. **Map 291**

L. argyrognomon Bergstrasser 1779 **TL**: Hanau, Germany **Pl. 54**
syn: *ismenias* Meigen 1829 (invalid homonym); *aegus* Chapman 1917.
Description. Closely resembles *L. idas* but often larger; identification by external characters is difficult and often uncertain, but usually possible by noting the following distinctive features:
   (1) Ups gc in ♂ is very clear bright blue, esp. noticeable in fresh specimens.
   (2) Uns gc in ♂ is usually white, often with a bluish tint.
   (3) Unh the black V-marks proximal to orange submarginal lunules are gently curved (sagittate in *idas*). This is probably the most reliable specific character, present in both sexes, but not always well defined.
Flight. May/June and July/August, usually in two broods.
Habitat. Flowery banks, from lowlands to 3,500 ft. Larval food plant *Coronilla*.
Distribution. France, mostly in N. and E., Seine-et-Marne, Seine-et-Oise, Marne, Aisne, Hte Savoie, Isère esp. near Rhône valley. Norway, very local near Oslo; recorded also from S. Sweden. Switzerland in Jura and near Geneva. Italy, widely distributed but local. More common in Austria, Hungary, Rumania. Recorded from Greece (Mt. Olympus and Pindus Mts.). Absent from Denmark, Britain, NW. and SW. Europe and Mediterranean islands.
Similar species. *L. idas* p. 277; *P. argus* p. 276.

VACCINIINA OPTILETE   *Cranberry Blue*

Sw: Violett Blåvinge

Range. Central Alps and arctic Europe to Japan. **Map 292**

V. optilete Knoch 1781 **TL**: Braunschweig, Germany **Pl. 55**
Description. ♂ fw 13/15mm., *ups deep violet-blue* with narrow black marginal lines, otherwise unmarked; uns gc dull grey, usual markings regular, prominent and dark; *unh with blue-scaled red submarginal spot in s2* sometimes also in s1c and s3. ♀ups dark brown with some violet basal suffusion; uph a small orange submarginal spot sometimes present in s2; uns resembles ♂.
Flight. July in a single brood.
Habitat. Moorlands and mountain slopes with *Vaccinium* from lowlands to 7,000 ft. Larval food plant *Vaccinium oxycoccus* (cranberry), esp. the flowers, and other *Vaccinium* species.
Distribution. Fennoscandia and Baltic countries, generally common on *Vaccinium* slopes to North Cape; Denmark; C. Europe, local on peat

moorlands in Germany, Czechoslovakia and Rumania (Bukowina). Alps, present as a high alpine species from Savoie to Grossglockner. Balkans, only in Yugoslavia, Crni Vrh and Schar Planina. Absent from Vosges, Jura, Pyrenees, Apennines, and Julian Alps.

Variation. At high altitudes in Alps and in arctic regions often slightly smaller and with uns markings less prominent; ♀uph orange marginal spot in s2 absent.

KRETANIA EURYPILUS *Eastern Brown Argus*
Range. S. Greece and widely distributed in W. Asia.   Map 293

K. eurypilus Freyer 1852 TL: Amasia, Turkey   Pl. 13
Description. ♂fw 15/17mm., ups brown with white fringes; upf unmarked; uph usually with two or three marginal orange lunules capping black antemarginal spots in s1c, s2 and s3 but variable; uns gc pale fawn with usual markings; unf no spot in cell; unh *pd spots evenly curved in regular series* followed by white band before orange submarginal lunules; ♀ similar, ups orange submarginal lunules in s1c and s2 larger; uns more strongly marked.
Flight. July in a single brood.
Habitat. Rough stony ground flying at 5,500–6,000 ft. Larval food plant not known.
Distribution. Greece, a few specimens have been recorded from Mt. Chelmos in Peloponnesus.

Similar species. *A. agestis* p. 281, unh pd series of spots broken between s5–6, no white band before orange submarginal lunules. *P. pylaon* p. 275, unh antemarginal spots in s1c and s2 generally without blue-green scales.
Note. This species is included with some reserve. Few specimens have been taken in Greece, and resemblance in ♀ to *P. pylaon* is very close. It is not certain that identification has been confirmed yet by examination of the male genitalia.

KRETANIA PSYLORITA *Cretan Argus*
Range. Known only from Crete.   Map 294

K. psylorita Freyer 1845 TL: Mt. Ida, Crete   Pl. 56
Description. ♂fw 13mm., ups light brown; upf with or without small orange submarginal lunules; uph with small antemarginal spots surmounted by orange lunules but all markings very faint and small; uns gc very pale brown, unf no spot in cell; *unh pd series strongly curved but all markings very small, and faint*; silver scales sometimes present on the marginal dark spots. ♀ similar, ups and uns yellow submarginal lunules better developed.
Flight. June.
Habitat and Distribution. Known only from Crete, flying on Mt. Ida at 3–6,000 ft., low-flying and shy.

EUMEDONIA EUMEDON   *Geranium Argus*

Sw: Brun Blåvinge

Range. From Cantabrian Mts. and Pyrenees to North Cape and across Europe and Asia to the Pacific.   Map 295

E. eumedon Esper 1780   TL: Erlangen, W. Germany   Pl. 56
 syn: *chiron* Rottemburg 1775 (invalid homonym)

Description. ♂fw 14/16mm., ups dark brown, unmarked; uns grey to grey-brown with usual markings; unf no spot in cell, pd series in s1b-5 in straight row but often incomplete, marginal markings variable; unh with blue basal suffusion, *a short white streak along v5* from discoidal spot to pd spots, submarginal orange lunules often inconspicuous. ♀ larger, uph generally with traces of orange marginal lunules near anal angle; uns all markings well developed.

Flight. June/July in a single brood.

Habitat. Hilly or mountainous country, lowlands to 8,000 ft. Larval food plants *Geranium* esp. *G. pratense*.

Distribution. Spain, in Cantabrian Mts. France, Pyrenees, Massif Central, Jura; widely spread from Alps to N. Cape; peninsular Italy and Sicily; Balkans. Absent from Portugal, S. Spain, NW. Europe (including Denmark) and Mediterranean islands except Sicily.

Variation. In SE. Europe often large, uns gc brownish (yellow-brown) rather than grey, orange submarginal lunules and other markings all well developed. In arctic regions usually small, unh markings inconspicuous, f. *borealis* Wahlgren, similar in Alps at high altitudes. The unh white streak may be absent, f. *fylgia* Spångberg, usually found flying with typical specimens, rare in W. Europe but more common and sometimes confusing in Balkans.

ARICIA AGESTIS   *Brown Argus*

Sw: Rödflackig Blävinge   Sp: Morena Serrana

Range. N. Spain and eastwards across Europe to Iran, Siberia and Amurland.   Map 296

A. agestis agestis Schiffermueller 1775   TL: Vienna   Pl. 55
 syn. *astrarche* Bergsträsser 1779; *medon* Hufnagel 1776 (invalid homonym)

Description. ♂ fw 12/14 mm., *ups dark brown with orange marginal lunules usually in complete series*; upf discoidal spot dark; uns variable, often grey cr grey-brown, with black white-ringed discoidal and pd spots and series of bright orange-red submarginal spots; unf lacking basal spot; unh pd spot in s6 displaced basad, a white mark on v4. ♀ similar, fw less pointed, often slightly larger.

Flight. April or later, usually in 2 annual broods but often 3 broods in S. Europe.

Habitat. Heaths and open places from lowlands to 3,000 ft. Larval food-plants rock-rose and various Geraniaceae, e.g. Stork's Bill (*Erodium*).

Distribution. S. and C. Europe to about 56°N lat., including Britain and S. Scandinavia. Widely distributed esp. on calcareous soils. Absent from S. and C. Spain, Portugal, Balearic Islands and Ireland.

Variation. In S. Europe including Sardinia, Corsica, Elba, Greece and Malta ups orange marginal lunules often larger, f. *calida* Bellier.

Similar Species. *A. artaxerxes* and subpecies, usually at high altitudes in S. or C. Europe, ups number of orange marginal lunules reduced. There is no reliable constant distinctive character. ♀♀ of many Polyommatine species. *A. cramera*, distinctive character present in ♂ genitalia.

ARICIA ARTAXERXES   *Mountain Argus*

Range. From N. Spain, Sicily and the Balkans to Fennoscandia and eastwards to the Altai Mts. in several subspecies.   Map 297

A. artaxerxes artaxerxes Fabricius 1793 TL: Anglia (Scotland)   Pl. 55

Description. ♂ fw 11/12 mm., narrow, pointed; ups orange marginal lunules reduced in number, series incomplete, sometimes absent, *discoidal spot white*; uns gc grey, markings in usual pattern but all spots white, sometimes with vestigial black pupils, orange submarginal lunules in complete series on both wings. ♀ similar, ups orange submarginal lunules slightly larger.

Flight. Late June/July in a single brood.

Habitat. Sheltered moorland localities. Larval food plant Rock Rose.

Distribution. Scotland, in Fife, Forfar, etc. and in local colonies to Cromarty Firth and Sutherland; occasional in England in Durham and Lancashire.

Variation. In N. England small, ups orange lunules reduced but upf often without the white discoidal spot which may appear in about 10% of individuals, more commonly in ♀; uns spots usually with small black pupils, f. *salmacis* Stephens. Rare individuals with upf white discoidal spot have been reported from various localities in S. England and in S. Sweden, outside the range of this subspecies.

A. artaxerxes allous   Geyer 1837   TL: Alps of Provence   Pl. 55
    syn: *inhonora* Jachontov 1909

Description. Like *A. agestis*; ♂ fw 12/14 mm., ups dark brown; upf unmarked or with small orange submarginal lunules in incomplete series; uph orange marginal lunules commonly present in s1c, s2 and s3 but variable; fringes not chequered; uns pale grey-brown with markings as in *A. agestis*. ♀ similar, fw apex less pointed.

Flight. June/July/August in a single brood.

Habitat. A mountain butterfly in C. Europe flying at 4-7,000 ft.; at lower altitudes north of the Alps, a lowland species in the far north.

Distribution. Pyrenees and Alps of C. Europe extending northwards through Fennoscandia far into the Arctic and eastwards to Sicily and Greece. Absent from the Tatra and Carpathians.

Variation. Small and usually with greatly reduced or absent ups markings in the far north (*inhonora* Jachontov). Large races with ♂ fw 14/16 mm. occur in Denmark, S. Sweden, Poland, etc., flying at low altitudes, and there perhaps indistinguishable from *A. a. montensis* described below.

A. artaxerxes montensis Verity 1928 TL: Andalusia. Pl. 55
 syn: *montana* Heyne 1895 (invalid homonym). *nevadensis* Oberthur 1910 (invalid homonym).

Description. Like *A. a. allous* but larger, ♂ fw 14/16 mm., upf orange submarginal lunules reduced or absent; uph submarginal orange lunules usually present; unh pale yellow-grey, sometimes inclining to brown, pd spot in s6 often very slightly displaced basad. ♀ ups paler brown, large orange marginal lunules in complere series on both wings; uns gc inclined more to brown.

Flight. June/July in a single brood.

Habitat. A mountain butterfly in N. Africa and in S.W. Europe, flying on flowery slopes at 3-8,000 ft.

Distribution. Morocco, Algeria and Tunisia in Atlas Mts. Spain, widely distributed on mountains. France, in Pyrenees and Massif Central and thence to S.W. Alps. Less Common in Jura and Vosges. Yugoslavia and Greece.

Variation. In N. Spain, Pyrenees and S.W. Alps often smaller, when distinction from *A. a. allous* may be difficult or impossible.

A. a. montensis is considered specifically distinct by some authors.

ARICIA CRAMERA *Southern Brown Argus*

Sp: Morena
Range. Canary Islands and N. Africa, Spain and Portugal   Map 298

A. cramera Eschscholtz 1821 TL: Canary Islands   Pl. 55
 syn: *canariensis* Blachier 1889
Description. ♂fw 11/13mm., small, *ups dark brown with full series of bright*

orange marginal lunules; uns grey (*first brood*) or brown (*later broods*), unh pd series of spots usually distinctly broken by basal displacement of spot in s6. ♀ slightly larger, ups orange marginal spots larger and in complete series; uns with usual markings resembling ♂. Fringes chequered black and white in both sexes.

Flight. April and later in two or more broods.

Habitat. Rough ground and rocky slopes to 6,000 ft. Larval food plants not recorded.

Distribution. Canary Isles, on Tenerife, G. Canary, La Palma, Gomera. Morocco and Algeria, often common in Atlas Mts., not recorded from Tunisia. Spain, widely distributed northwards to R. Ebro (Soria and Saragossa). Portugal, Sierra de Estrela, Sierra de Gata.

Variation. The summer broods of *A. cramera* are recognisable at once by their small size and bright cinnamon-brown unh gc.

Similar species. *A. artaxerxes montensis* p. 283 usually larger, ups orange marginal lunules not well developed, reduced in number and sometimes absent; uns gc paler, grey or yellow-grey to café-au-lait. *A. agestis* esp. f. *calida* distinguishable by genitalia.

ARICIA MORRONENSIS   *Spanish Argus*

Sp: Morena Española
Range. Confined to Spain.   Map 299

A. morronensis Ribbe 1910   TL: Mt. Morron, Murcia   Pl. 55
  syn: *idas* Rambur 1840 (invalid homonym); *ramburi* Verity 1913

Description. ♂fw 13/15mm., *apex of fw not pointed*, outer margin convex, fringes lightly chequered; ups brown; upf dark discoidal spot sometimes ringed white; uph vestigial orange marginal lunules in s2, 3; uns pale coffee-brown with usual markings of small white-ringed dark spots; *unf pd spot in s6 displaced basad*; unh pd spot in s6 displaced basad; small inconspicuous orange-yellow submarginal lunules present on both wings. ♀ similar.

Flight. July/early August in a single brood.

Habitat. Rough stony slopes at 6,500 ft. in S. Spain, to 3-4,000 ft. farther north. Larval food plant not recorded.

Distribution. Spain, widely distributed but always extremely local in isolated colonies, Sierra Nevada, Sierra de Espuña, Sierra Priete, Casayo, Ordesa, etc.

Variation. Different colonies vary slightly in size, development of orange ups lunules, etc,; northern specimens are larger.

Similar species. *A. cramera* p. 283; *A. artaxerxes* p. 282, apex of fw more pointed, ups orange submarginal lunules more numerous; uns submarginal lunules orange-red.

ARICIA NICIAS   *Silvery Argus*

Sp: Borde Amplio   Sw: Donzels Blåvinge
Range. Pyrenees and SW. Alps, Finland and Russia.   Map 300

A. nicias Meigen 1830   TL: Rhetian Alps (Verity 1943)   Pl. 55
syn: *donzelii* Boisduval 1832

Description. ♂fw 11/12mm., *ups pale silvery blue* with wide fuscous marginal borders; upf discoidal spot very small, uph often absent; unh gc pale grey with usual markings small, sometimes incomplete or indistinct, marginal markings vestigial if present, pd spot in s6 slightly if at all displaced basad, a wedge-shaped white mark wide distally along v4. ♀ups brown with light brown fringes; uns resembles ♂. Androconia present on upf in ♂.
Flight. July in a single brood.
Habitat. Mountains at 3–5,000 ft. in S. Europe, a lowland species in north. Larval food plants *Geranium*, esp. *G. silvaticum* and *G. pratense*, meadow cranes-bill.
Distribution. E. Pyrenees and S. Alps of France, Switzerland and eastwards to Stilfserjoch and Franzenshohe. Also over a wide area in S. Finland and E. Sweden.
Variation. In N. distribution area ♂ups with narrower, better defined fuscous borders.
Similar species. *A. glandon* p. 286, larger, unh markings differ without a white streak along v4; *A. damon* p. 294, much larger, ups ♂ brilliant blue, unh gc brown with white streak along v4 extending to base.

ARICIA ANTEROS   *Blue Argus*

Range. Balkan Peninsula and eastwards to Iran.   Map 301

A. anteros Freyer 1839   TL: Constantinople   Pl. 55
Description. ♂fw 15/16mm., *ups gleaming pale blue* with black marginal borders about 2mm. wide; orange submarginal lunules generally prominent on both wings; *upf a small black discoidal spot*; uph small round antemarginal spots usually present; uns gc pale grey-brown with usual markings; unf no spot in cell; unh spot in s6 slightly displaced basad, with gap before spot in s5. ♀ups brown, orange submarginal spots usually present on hw, sometimes also on fw; upf discoidal spot black; uns gc brown or yellow-brown. Androconia present on upf in ♂.
Flight. June/early July in a single brood.
Habitat. Mountains, flying over rough flowery slopes, commonly at 3–5,000 ft., rarely at lower levels. Larval food plant not known.
Distribution. Bulgaria, in Rilo and Rhodope Mts. Albania. Yugoslavia, Velebit Mts., and through Croatia to Dobrugea but scarce and local in northern Balkans. Greece.
Similar species. *P. eros* p. 311 and *P. eroides* p. 310, on ups resemblance is

close but discoidal spots absent, unf with spot in cell; unh pd spots in regular series, no gap between spots in s 5 and s 6.

ALBULINA ORBITULUS   *Alpine Argus*
Sw: Fjällvickerblåvinge
Range. Alps and Norway to C. Asia.   Map 302

A. orbitulus de Prunner 1798   TL: Piedmont, N. Italy   Pl. 55
   syn: *pheretes* Huebner 1805
Description. ♂fw 12/14mm., ups gc shining sky-blue with black marginal lines, otherwise unmarked; uns gc grey; unf usual markings reduced and inconspicuous, sometimes absent, no spot in cell, discoidal and pd spots small, white-ringed, spot in s1b absent, *no marginal markings*; *unh spots white without black pupils*, large, pd series broken, spots in s4 and s5 displaced distad, pd spots often elongate oval, marginal markings vestigial. ♀ups brown often with slight blue basal suffusion; uns gc light brown with variable markings as in ♂.
Flight. July/August in a single brood.
Habitat. High alpine meadows from 5,500 ft. upwards. Larval food plants *Astragalus alpinus* and *A. frigidus*.
Distribution. Basses Alpes to Savoie and eastwards to Grossglockner, on nearly all high mountains. Norway in Jotunfjeld and Dovrefjeld flying at 3–4,000 ft. Sweden in Jämtland. Absent from Carpathians, Karawanken Mts. and Balkans.
Variation. Markings on uns are variable individually but racial variation is not marked.

AGRIADES GLANDON   *Glandon Blue*
Sp: Poco Brillo
Range. Sierra Nevada, Pyrenees, Alps and Balkans.   Map 303

A. glandon glandon de Prunner 1798   TL: W. Alps (Col du   Pl. 56
Glandon?)
   syn: *orbitulus* Esper 1800 (invalid homonym)
Description. ♂fw 13/15mm., ups shining pale greenish-blue with wide ill-defined *fuscous marginal borders* which often suffuse broadly across fw and less often across costal area of hw, discoidal spots small if present; uph sometimes with small brown antemarginal spots; unf gc pale grey-brown, cell-spot, discoidal and pd spots black, *marginal markings grey, obscure*; unh with large white discoidal spot, basal and pd spots usually well defined, except spots in s4, 5, often small and without black pupils, small yellow submarginal lunules rarely absent in s2 (3). ♀ often small, ups brown; uns resembles ♂ but gc darker and markings better defined.
Flight. July/August in a single brood.

Habitat. Mountains at 6–8,000 ft. flying over short grass slopes. Larval food plants *Androsace, Soldanella* (Primulaceae).
Distribution. Pyrenees and Basses Alpes through C. and S. Alps to Gross Glockner.
Variation. Size and extent of ups fuscous suffusion vary slightly, with darkest races at very high altitudes. In the Bavarian Alps, f. *alboocellatus* Osthelder, unh spots mostly without black pupils, perhaps better graded as a subspecies. In ♀ and more rarely in ♂upf discoidal and pd spots may be ringed white.

A. glandon dardanus Freyer 1844 TL: Turkey (Balkans?) Pl. 56
Description. ♂fw 11/12mm., ups grey-blue gc more extensive, fuscous marginal borders narrow; markings resemble those of *A. g. glandon* but unh pd spots in s4, 5 vestigial or absent.
Flight and Habitat as for *glandon.*
Distribution. Known only from Vran Planina and Cvrstniča in Hercegovina.

A. glandon zullichi Hemming 1933 TL: Sierra Nevada Pl. 56
syn: *nevadensis* Zullich 1928 (invalid homonym)
Description. ♂fw 12mm., resembles *A. g. glandon*; ups brown with restricted blue basal suffusion, discoidal spots present on both wings; uph submarginal lunules present but obscure in s1b–6; uns gc pale brown; unh pd spots in s6, 7 with brown pupils, remaining spots represented by elongate white chevrons just proximal to submarginal lunules.
Flight. July/August.
Habitat and Distribution. E. Sierra Nevada flying at 8,000 ft. Habitat appears to be very restricted.
Similar species. *A. pyrenaicus* p. 290, ♂ups pale silvery grey with narrow dark marginal borders; in both sexes unf submarginal spots black (grey in *glandon*). *A. aquilo* below, N. Scandinavia only; *A. nicias* p. 285.

AGRIADES AQUILO *Arctic Blue*
Sw: Högnordisk Blåvinge
Range. N. Scandinavia and probably also in arctic regions of Asia and Canada. Map 304

A. aquilo Boisduval 1832 TL: North Cape Pl. 56
Description. ♂fw 10/11 mm., *ups smooth shining pale grey* with slightly blue flush shading into narrow brown outer marginal borders, discoidal spots very small, marginal markings faint or absent; uns pale grey, markings as in *A. glandon*; unf submarginal spots dark and usually complete; unh markings white, rarely with vestigial black pupils, pd spots joined to submarginal lunules to form long white stripes. ♀ups brown with **pale sub-**

PLATE 51

1. **Heodes virgaureae** *Scarce Copper* See also Pl. 52   244
   - 1a. *H. v. miegii* ♂. Upf with discoidal and pd black spots.
   - 1b. *H. v. virgaureae* ♀. Ups black markings heavy and complete.
   - 1c. *H. v. virgaureae* ♂. Unh discal spots followed by white marks.

2. **Heodes ottomanus** *Grecian Copper*   245
   - ♂. Ups like *H. v. miegii* but unh lacks white postdiscal marks.

3. **Palaeochrysophanus hippothoe** *Purple-edged Copper*   249
   - 3a. *P. h. hippothoe* ♂. Uph flushed violet; upf with discoidal black spot.
   - 3b. *P. h. hippothoe* ♀. Upf black markings complete, pd spots in almost straight row (distinction from *Heodes alciphron*).
   - 3c. *P. h. eurydame* ♂. Ups red-gold; uph no violet; upf lacks discoidal black spot.
   - 3d. *P. h. eurydame* ♀. Ups markings lost in dark suffusion.
   - 3e. *P. h. leonhardi* ♂. Like *P. h. hippothoe* but larger.
   - 3f. *P. h. stiberi* ♀. Upf pale golden with small back markings.

4. **Lycaena phlaeas** *Small Copper*   242
   - 4a. *L. p. phlaeas* ♂. Upf gc gold; unh gc brown.
   - 4b. *L. p. polaris* ♂. Upf gc pale gold; unh gc pale grey.

5. **Lycaena helle** *Violet Copper*   239
   - ♂. Ups densely suffused violet. For ♀ see Pl. 4.

6. **Lycaena dispar** *Large Copper*   243
   - 6a. *L. d. rutila* ♂. Ups black bars at cell-ends; unh gc pale blue-grey.
   - 6b. *L. d. batava* ♀. Large; unh pale blue-grey; red margins much wider.

7. **Thersamonia thetis** *Fiery Copper*   248
   - ♂. Upf black marginal border expanded at apex; unh pale grey.

8. **Thersamonia thersamon** *Lesser Fiery Copper*   247
   - 8a. ♂. Uph dusky (variable) with red-gold marginal band.
   - 8b. ♀ Upf black markings complete; uph gc black.

9. **Thersamonia phoebus** *Moroccan Copper*   248
   - 9a. ♂. Small; ups gc pale golden; upf with small black spots.
   - 9b. ♀. Ups like ♂ but uph suffused grey.

PLATE 52

marginal markings and vestigial pd spots on fw in some specimens; uns resembles ♂
Flight. End June/July.
Habitat. Sheltered grassy places at low altitudes. Larval food plant *Astragalus alpinus*.
Distribution. Arctic Norway, local near coast from 66°N to North Cape, e.g., Tromsö, Saltdalen, Porsanger. N. Finland, Kilpisjärvi.
Similar species. *A. glandon* p. 286, larger; ups gc blue.
Note. *A. aquilo* is sometimes regarded as a subspecies of *A. glandon*.

AGRIADES PYRENAICUS *Gavarnie Blue*

Sp: Niña Gris
Range. Cantabrian Mts., C. Pyrenees; Balkans to Iran.   Map 305

A. pyrenaicus pyrenaicus Boisduval 1840   TL: Pyrenees   Pl. 56
Description. ♂fw 13/14mm., ups *pale silvery grey* with narrow black marginal lines; upf discoidal spot small, black and round; unf resembles *glandon* but pd spot in s6 displaced slightly basad, 3-5 *black submarginal lunules*; unh basal and pd spot in s7 white but often with black pupils, remaining discal and pd spots white without black pupils, outer margin white with small yellow lunule in s2. ♀ups brown, uph often with traces of submarginal pale lunules; uns as in ♂.
Flight. July.
Habitat. Flies over grass slopes at 6,000 ft. or more. Larval food plant *Androsace villosa*.
Distribution. Htes Pyrénées, Cauterets, Gavarnie, etc. Absent from Andorra and E. Pyrenees.

A. pyrenaicus asturiensis Oberthur 1910   TL: Picos de Europa   Pl. 56

Description. Ups gc slightly paler grey, black marginal lines preceded by obscure white marks between veins; uph usually with white submarginal lunules and small black antemarginal spots. ♀upf discoidal spot white-ringed, larger, and pale marginal marks small; uph submarginal lunules more prominent; uns resembles ♂.
Flight and **Habitat** as for *A. p. pyrenaicus*.
Distribution. Cantabrian Mts. on Picos de Europa, not recorded elsewhere.

Similar species. *A. glandon* p. 286.

CYANIRIS SEMIARGUS *Mazarine Blue*

Sw: Ängsblåvinge   Sp: Falsa Limbada
Range. Morocco and throughout temperate Europe and Asia to Mongolia.   Map 306

C. semiargus Rottemburg 1775 **TL:** Saxony, Germany Pl. 55
syn: *acis* Schiffermueller 1775

Description. ♂fw 14/17mm., ups dull violet-blue, ill-defined black marginal borders 1–2mm. wide, somewhat diffused basad along veins; uns gc pale grey-brown with blue basal flush; *unf* without spot in cell, discoidal stria and *pd spots present but marginal markings absent*; unh markings as on unf with additional basal spot in s7, traces of marginal markings near anal angle sometimes present. ♀ups brown, unmarked; uns gc brown, markings as in ♂.

Flight. End June/July/August in a single brood depending upon altitude.

Habitat. Flowery meadows and alpine slopes from sea-level to 6,000 ft.; will congregate in scores at wet places on paths. Larval food plants *Trifolium, Anthyllis, Melilotus, Armeria,* etc.; larva hibernates when small.

Distribution. Widely distributed and often common throughout W. Europe to 68°N, but local in mountains and often rare in Spain and Portugal. Morocco, very local in High Atlas and Middle Atlas, flying at 7–8,000 ft. Now extinct in Britain. Records from Corsica and Sardinia need confirmation.

Variation. Minimal. In Greece and Bulgaria occasionally with one or more obscure orange lunules at unh anal angle.

Similar species. *Cupido osiris* p. 258, ups gc similar but black marginal borders linear and well defined; uns gc pale grey (more brown in *semiargus*) with smaller markings; unf pd spots in nearly straight row. *C. helena* below.

CYANIRIS HELENA *Greek Mazarine Blue*
Range. Greece, Asia Minor, Lebanon and Iraq. Map 307

C. helena Staudinger 1862 **TL:** Mt. Taygetos, S. Greece Pl. 55
Description. ♂fw 13/14mm., resembles *C. semiargus*; ups violet-blue with narrow black marginal borders; *uph sometimes with traces of orange lunules near anal angle*; uns gc pale grey; unf a small discoidal stria, pd spots small, in nearly straight row close to indistinct submarginal and marginal markings; unh with blue basal suffusion, pd spots in very even curved series close to *orange submarginal lunules* at least *in s1c to s3*. ♀ups brown, sometimes with blue basal suffusion; upf with orange lunules in s1b to 3; uph with 3 to 5 orange marginal lunules in s1c to s4 or 5 often forming a band; uns as in ♂.

Flight. June/July, in a single brood.

Habitat. Mountains at 4–5,000 ft. Larval food plant not known.

Distribution. Greece, recorded from Mt. Chelmos, Zachlorou, Kalavryta, Taygetos Mts.

Similar species. *C. semiargus* above, unh without orange submarginal band.

Note. *C. helena* is a striking little butterfly often ranked as a subspecies of *C. semiargus*. It appears to be very local and uncommon.

PLATE 53

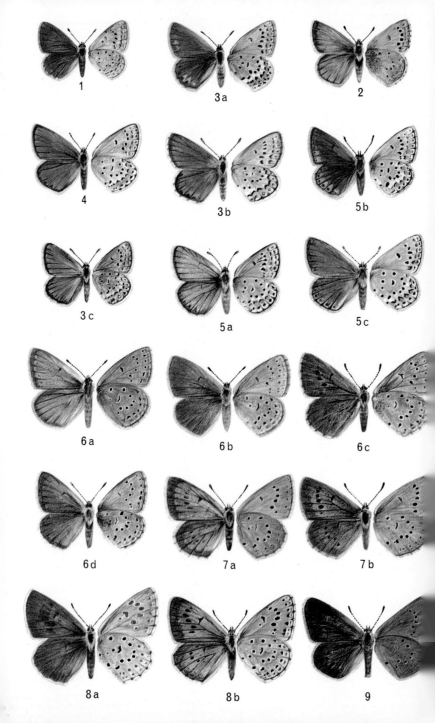

PLATE 54

1. **Zizeeria knysna**   *African Grass Blue*   253
   Z. knysna ♂. Ups violet blue, margins broadly brown; uns markings small; ♀ ups brown; uns as in ♂.

2. **Glaucopsyche melanops**   *Black-eyed Blue*   262
   G. m. algirica ♂. Ups blue; unf postdiscal spots large, submarginal markings present. ♀ ups brown, wing-bases suffused blue.

3. **Lycaeides idas**   *Idas Blue*   277
   3a. *L. i. f. alpinus* ♀. Ups brown, submarginal lunules yellow (variable); uns pale brown; unf lacks cell-spot; unh marginal spots near anal angle with blue-green scales.
   3b. *L. i. f. alpinus* ♂. Ups blue, black marginal line narrow; uns ground-colour pale grey, markings as in ♀.
   3c. *L. i. f. lapponicus* ♂. Small, like *L. i. alpinus*; uns ground-colour darker grey, markings small. ♀ ups brown, often with blue basal suffusions; uns as in ♂. See also Pl. 55.

4. **Lycaeides argyrognomon**   *Reverdin's Blue*   279
   L. argyrognomon ♂. Ups deep blue; unh ground-colour pale bluegrey; (male genitalia distinctive). ♀ brown, wing-bases usually blue.

5. **Plebejus pylaon**   *Zephyr Blue*   275
   5a. *P. p. hespericus* ♂. Ups pale gleaming blue; uns pale grey; unh spots at anal angle black, lacking green scales. ♀ ups brown; uns pale brown, otherwise as in ♂.
   5b. *P. p. sephirus* ♀. Like *L. idas* ♀; orange submarginal lunules well developed.
   5c. *P. p. trappi* ♂. Larger; ups deeper blue; uns as in *P. p. hespericus*; unf no cell-spots; unh pale postdiscal band usually prominent.

6. **Maculinea alcon**   *Alcon Blue*   263
   6a. *M, a. alcon* ♂. Ups pale blue; uns brown, lacking blue basal shade; unh no spot at base of space 1c.
   6b. *M. a. alcon* ♀. Ups brown, blue basal flush small if present.
   6c. *M. a. rebeli* ♀. Ups brown, wing-bases rather widely blue.
   6d. *M. a. rebeli* ♂. Like *M. a. alcon* but ups bright blue; uns ground-colour pale grey-brown, unh often with small blue basal flush.

7. **Maculinea teleius**   *Scarce Large Blue*   265
   7a. *M. teleius* ♂. Ups pale blue, brown borders wide, black postdiscal spots present; unh brown, no blue-green basal flush.
   7b. *M. teleius* ♀. Ups darker blue, postdiscal black spots larger.

8. **Maculinea arion**   *Large Blue*   264
   8a. *M. a. obscura* ♂. Ups heavily suffused grey-brown except over basal areas; unh with spot at base of space 1c.
   8b. *M. a. arion* ♂. Ups blue, no brown suffusion.

9. **Maculinea nausithous**   *Dusky Large Blue*   266
   M. nausithous ♂. Ups very dark, fringes brown; uns coffee-brown. ♀ ups brown, otherwise similar.

AGRODIAETUS DAMON   *Damon Blue*

Sp: Azul Cintada

Range. From Spain locally through S. and C. Europe, Russia and Armenia to Altai Mts.   Map 308

A. damon Schiffermueller 1775   TL: Vienna   Pl. 57

Description. ♂fw 15/17mm., ups gc pale shining blue with wide fuscous margins which extend basad along veins, no sex brand; unf gc yellow-grey with simple markings of discoidal stria and five or six pd spots all dark and white-ringed; *unh* slightly darker, more brown, with a *firm narrow pale stripe from base along* v4 nearly to margin, basal and pd markings small or vestigial. ♀ usually slightly smaller; ups gc brown, often with a few blue scales on thorax and at wing-bases; uns gc café-au-lait with markings as in ♂.

Flight. July/August in a single brood.

Habitat. Usually in mountains on calcareous soils, from valleys to 7,000 ft. Larval food plant sainfoin (*Onobrychis*).

Distribution. Widely distributed in Europe in scattered localised colonies. Spain, Cuenca. France, in C. Pyrenees, Lozère, Provence to Savoie, thence through C. Europe to 52°N in Bavaria. In Balkans recorded from Dalmatia, Bosnia and Macedonia. Rare in S. Italy; absent from S. Spain, Portugal and Mediterranean islands.

Variation. There is little evidence of local variation in W. Europe.

Similar species. *A. dolus* below; ups very pale blue or white with large brown androconial patch; unh white streak not prominent on pale gc; ♀uph veins darkened and obscure dark marginal spots present. *A. nicias* p. 285.

AGRODIAETUS DOLUS   *Furry Blue*

Sp: Velludita Fimbria Clara

Range. Confined to SW. Europe and Italy.   Map 309

A. dolus dolus Huebner 1823   TL: Maritime Alps   Pl. 57
(Verity 1943)

Description. ♂fw 17/19mm., *ups gc very pale blue* with fuscous marginal borders; base of fw with extensive *pale brown androconial* area which appears slightly rough; uph with fuscous marginal shades between veins; uns gc pale yellow-grey; unf pd spots conspicuous; unh standard markings often incomplete, the white streak along v4 sometimes indistinct. ♀ups brown, veins lined darker; uph with darker marginal spots between veins; uns gc darker brown than ♂; fringes pale.

Flight. Mid-July/August in a single brood.

Habitat. Hilly or mountainous districts from low levels to 6,000 ft. Larval food plant sainfoin and lucerne (*Onobrychis* and *Medicago sativa*).

Distribution. France, in Provence, very local in Var, Alpes Maritimes, Bouches du Rhône, etc.

A. dolus vittatus Oberthur 1892 TL: Lozère, France
Description. ♂fw 16/17mm., slightly smaller than *A. d. dolus*, ups gc pale grey with extensive fuscous suffusion along all veins, suffused blue at wing-bases only; uns gc pale grey-brown, deeper in tone on hw where white streak along v4 is clearly defined. ♀uns medium brown, considerably darker than in *A.d. dolus*.
Flight. Mid-July/August in a single brood.
Habitat. Rough ground at low levels.
Distribution. Lozère, Aveyron, Florac, Mende, Peyreleau, Balsièges, etc.

A. dolus virgilius Oberthur 1910 TL: Sulmona, Abruzzi   Pl. 57
Description. ♂fw 16/17mm., ups gc white, with narrow fuscous marginal lines somewhat shaded basad and along veins,extensive basal androconial area rough and brown, thorax and wing-bases blue; uph gc white with fuscous marginal line and variable fuscous marginal shading, veins lined dark esp. v6 and v7, dark antemarginal spots vestigial, base flushed blue; uns gc very pale cream, unh white streak along v4 rarely definite. ♀ resembles *A. d. dolus*, uns slightly darker brown; unh white streak usually absent.
Flight and **Habitat** as for *A.d. dolus*.
Distribution. Peninsular Italy, Bologna, Sulmona, l'Aquila, Sorrento, Roccaraso, Mt. Majella, Monti Sibillini, etc., with minor variation in different colonies.

Similar species. *A. damon* p. 294.

AGRODIAETUS AINSAE *Forster's Furry Blue*
Range. Restricted to northern Spain.   Map 310

A. ainsae Forster 1961 TL: Ainsa, N. Spain
Description. ♂fw 15/16mm., small, ups gc pale shining blue shading to white, indistinguishable from *A. dolus* except by small size.
Flight and **Habitat.** As for *A. dolus*.
Distribution. N. Spain, recorded from Ainsa, Jaca, Huesca, Burgos.
Note. *A. ainsae* is distinguished specifically from *A. dolus* by its lower chromosome number.

AGRODIAETUS ADMETUS *Anomalous Blue*
Range. E. Europe and Asia Minor.   Map 311

A. admetus Esper 1785 TL: Hungary   Pl. 57
Description. ♂fw 15/19mm., ups brown, unmarked, base and discal areas of fw covered by *patch of hairy androconial scales*; uns gc pale brown, sub-

marginal markings definite; unf without spot in cell, discoidal stria and pd
spots black, pale ringed, marginal spots paler brown, faint; unh usual
markings present, *sometimes with wedge-shaped white pd mark on v4.* ♀
often smaller, ups gc paler, smooth brown; uph generally with obscure
orange marginal lunules near anal angle; uns markings brighter and better
developed than in ♂, wedge-shaped white pd mark on v4 often present.
Flight. End June/July in a single brood.
Habitat. Hot rocky slopes, at low or moderate altitudes. Larval food plant
sainfoin (*Onobrychis*).
Distribution. Hungary. Czechoslovakia. Rumania, Dobrudscha. Bulgaria,
Karlovo. SE. Yugoslavia, Skopje. Greece, Parnassus, Taygetos Mts.
Usually very local in widely scattered colonies.
Similar species. *A. ripartii* below; *A. fabressei* below.

AGRODIAETUS FABRESSEI   *Oberthur's Anomalous Blue*
Range. Confined to central Spain.   Map 312

A. fabressei   Oberthur 1910   TL: Albarracin, C. Spain
Description. ♂ fw 17/18 mm., resembles *A. admetus* but differs in more
pointed fw; uns brown gc darker café-au-lait, discal markings bolder,
marginal markings fainter; outer margin of hw not evenly rounded but
with a slight bulge at v5, 6. ♀ smaller, unh often with short wedge-shaped
white mark on v4.
Flight. End June/August.
Habitat. Hot rocky mountain slopes at 3–4,000 ft. Larval food plant not
recorded.
Distribution. C. Spain in Province of Teruel, Albarracin, Noguera, etc.
Similar species. *A. admetus* p. 295, scarcely separable by external characters, distinguished by chromosome numbers.

AGRODIAETUS RIPARTII   *Ripart's Anomalous Blue*
Sp: Velludita Fimbria Oscura
Range. From Spain in widely separated colonies across S. Europe to Asia
Minor.   Map 313

A. ripartii   Freyer 1830   TL: Spain   Pl. 57
Description. ♂ fw 14/17 mm., resembles *A. admetus*; ups brown, unmarked;
upf basal areas covered by rough hairy patch of androconial scales; uns
pale yellow-grey with usual discal markings of white-ringed dark spots,
marginal markings vestigial or absent; unh with narrow pale stripe from
base of wing along v4. ♀ smaller, ups gc slightly paler; uph often with
orange lunules near anal area; uns darker grey-brown, markings bolder
esp. unf pd spots; unh white streak conspicuous, slightly expanded distally, marginal markings usually absent; fringes dark.
Flight. End July/August.

Habitat. Hot rocky slopes with rough vegetation, lowlands to 3,000 ft. or more, often flying with *A. admetus* in E. Europe. Larval food plant *Onobrychis* esp. *O. saxatilis*.

Distribution. Spain, Jaca. France, in Alpes Maritimes and Basses Alpes. Italy, only known near Oulz in N. Piedmont. Bulgaria, Sliven, Karlovo. SE. Yugoslavia, Prilep, Skopje. Albania. Greece. Absent from Hungary.

Similar species. *A. admetus* p. 295 and *A. fabressei* p. 296.

AGRODIAETUS COELESTINUS. See page 311.

PLEBICULA ESCHERI *Escher's Blue*

Range. S. Europe and Morocco. Map 314

P. escheri escheri Huebner 1823 TL: Var, S. France Pl. 57
(Verity 1943)
    syn: *agestor* Godart 1824

Description. ♂fw 17/19mm., *ups deep sky-blue*, fw costa and veins often paler, with fine black marginal lines; *hw fringe half chequered*, outer margin appears slightly wavy; uns gc grey with standard markings; unh with blue basal suffusion. ♀ups brown; series of *orange submarginal lunules generally complete and prominent*, sometimes missing on fw; uph marginal blue scaling rare; uns gc brown with bold markings as in ♂. Unf without cell-spot.
Flight. End June/July in a single brood.
Habitat. From lowlands to 6,000 ft., generally in mountainous districts. Larval food plants *Astragalus*.
Distribution. Spain and Portugal, generally distributed in mountainous districts. France, in C. and E. Pyrenees, Provence to Savoie and Hautes Alpes, Cantal, Lozère, Bouches du Rhône, Lot and Charente Inf. Switzerland, only in Rhône valley and Alps of Valais, Tessin and perhaps farther east. Italy, generally common in Alps of Piedmont and Ligurian Apennines and E. to Alto Adige (Bolzano, etc.).

P. escheri splendens Stefanelli 1904 TL: Florence
Description. ♂fw 15/17mm., ups gleaming pale sky blue; uns gc pale grey with small markings. ♀ups orange submarginal lunules well developed.
Flight. End June/early July.
Habitat. Rocky places with flowers at altitudes of 1,000 ft. or little more.
Distribution. Ligurian and Emilian Apennines, sometimes flying with more typical specimens, Florence, Genoa, Portofino, Arquarta Scrivia, Reggio, etc., in some colonies small, ♂fw 15/16mm., f. *altivolans* Verity Pl. 57.

P. escheri dalmatica Speyer 1882 TL: Dalmatia Pl. 13
    syn: *olympena* Verity 1936
Description. ♂fw 17/20mm., large, gc paler sky blue than in *P. e. escheri*,

black marginal border 1–2 mm. wide, not linear; uns gc paler, nearly white.
♀ resembles *P.e. splendens.*
Flight. June.
Habitat. Flies at moderate levels in hilly country.
Distribution. Dalmatia, Hercegovina, Blagai, Stolác. Greece, Mt. Olympus, Mt. Chelmos, Taygetos Mts.

Similar species. *L. bellargus* p. 309, fw fringes chequered, unf with spot in cell. *P. thersites* p. 302, smaller, ups gc violet-blue, unh pd spots smaller; ♀uph without full series of orange submarginal lunules. *Plebejus pylaon* p. 275.

PLEBICULA DORYLAS   *Turquoise Blue*
Sp: Niña Turquesa   Sw: Honungsklöverblåvinge
Range. From Spain through S. Europe to Asia Minor.   Map 315

P. dorylas Schiffermueller 1775   TL: Vienna   Pl. 56
   syn: *argester* Bergstrasser 1779; *hylas* Esper 1793 (invalid homonym)
Description. ♂fw 15/17 mm., ups *gleaming pale blue*, the narrow black marginal lines extending slightly basad along veins; uns gc pale olive-buff to grey with usual markings; unf no spot in cell, *margins broadly white, antemarginal markings vestigial*; unh markings small on slightly darker gc, a wedge-shaped white mark on v4. ♀ups brown, sometimes with blue basal suffusion, orange submarginal lunules usually present on hw, rare on fw; uns gc brown with markings as in ♂.
Flight. May/July and August/September in two broods at low levels, a single brood in July/August at high altitudes.
Habitat. Flowery slopes and meadows commonly at 3–5,000 ft. Larval food plants *Melilotus, Trifolium, Thymus, Anthyllis.*
Distribution. S. and C. Europe to Baltic. Very local in Spain, Cuenca, Burgos, etc.; more widely distributed from Pyrenees through Alps to Carpathians, Balkans and Greece; local in S. Sweden, Latvia and Lithuania. Reported from Sicily. Absent from NW. Europe, S. Italy and Mediterranean islands except perhaps Sicily.
Variation. There is slight individual variation in the shade of blue on ♂ups. Local variation is not well marked.

Similar species. In *P. thersites* p. 302, ♀uns marginal markings well developed. *P. golgus* below. *P. nivescens* p. 299.

PLEBICULA GOLGUS   *Nevada Blue*
Range. Confined to S. Spain.   Map 31●

P. golgus Huebner 1813   TL: S. Spain   Pl. 5●
Description. ♂fw 13/15 mm., resembles *P. dorylas* but smaller; fw ape● pointed, *ups gc deeper blue* with fine black marginal lines; uns gc yellow grey; unf white marginal band enclosing antemarginal small dark spots

unh yellow lunules vestigial, antemarginal spots small. ♀ups brown; uph
with or without small orange submarginal lunules; uns gc darker yellow-
grey with markings better developed, orange submarginal lunules present
on both wings.

Flight. July.

Habitat and **Distribution.** Known only from Sierra Nevada, flying at
altitudes of 7–8,000 ft.

Similar species. *P. dorylas* p. 298, ups gc pale blue; uns gc pale grey,
marginal markings vestigial in white marginal band.

PLEBICULA NIVESCENS *Mother-of-Pearl Blue*

Sp: Niña de Nacar

Range. Confined to Spain.   Map 317

P. nivescens Keferstein 1851 TL: Sierra de Alfacar   Pl. 56
Description. ♂fw 15/18mm., resembles *P. dorylas*; *ups pale shining silvery-
grey*; upf marginal border dark grey 1–2mm. wide; uph black marginal
lines preceded by dark grey antemarginal spots; uns gc very pale grey,
hw yellowish with markings as in *P. dorylas*, but submarginal markings
sometimes more distinct. ♀ups brown with broad orange-yellow lunules
generally well developed on both wings; uns as in ♂ but gc yellow-grey.
Flight. June/July in a single brood.
Habitat. In mountains at 3–6,000 ft. Larval food plants not recorded.
Distribution. Spain, local but widely distributed from Granada to Catalonia and Leon, extending to Pyrenees at Aulus. Absent from W. Spain.
Similar species. *P. dorylas* p. 298, ♂ups definitely blue; ♀ best identified by
association with ♂. *L. albicans* p. 307, unf with spot in cell in both sexes.

PLEBICULA ATLANTICA *Atlas Blue*

Range. Confined to Morocco.   Map 318

P. atlantica Elwes 1905 TL: High Atlas, Morocco   Pl. 56
Description. ♂fw 14/17mm., ups resembles *P. dorylas*, *ups very pale sky
blue*; upf black marginal border about 1mm. wide; uph antemarginal
black spots usually present; unf gc yellow-grey, pd spots very large, in
ight curve; unh markings quite small, sometimes incomplete. ♀ups gc
brown, slightly suffused orange, submarginal orange lunules very large and
coalesced to form continuous bands on both wings, small black antemarginal spots present on uph; uns as in ♂.
Flight. End May/June and August/September in two broods, *second brood*
specimens small, ♂fw 13/14mm.
Habitat. Stony slopes and dry scrub areas at 7–8,000 ft. Larval food plant
not known.
Distribution. Morocco, Middle Atlas on Taghzeft Pass, High Atlas on
Toubkal Massif.

PLATE 55

1. **Aricia agestis** *Brown Argus*   281
   1a. *A. agestis* ♂. Ups orange submarginal lunules well developed.

2. **Aricia artaxerxes** *Mountain Argus*   282
   1b. *A. a. artaxerxes* ♂. Ups lunules not well developed; discoidal
       spot white; uns spots mostly white.
   2a. *A. a. allous* ♂. No orange lunules.
   2b. *A. a. montensis* ♂. Larger; orange lunules on both wings.
   2c. *A. a. allous* f. *semimontensis* ♂. Orange lunules on hw only.

3. **Aricia cramera** *Southern Brown Argus*   283
   ♀. Ups orange submarginal lunules large, complete. ♂ lunules
   smaller.

4. **Aricia nicias** *Silvery Argus*   285
   ♂. Unh with white stripe on vein 4. ♀ ups brown.

5. **Aricia anteros** *Blue Argus*   285
   ♂. Ups gleaming pale blue, dark borders. ♀ ups brown.

6. **Aricia morronensis** *Spanish Argus*   284
   ♂. Unh postdiscal spot in space 6 displaced basad. ♀ similar.

7. **Cyaniris semiargus** *Mazarine Blue*   290
   ♂. Ups violet blue; uns no marginal markings. ♀ ups brown, un-
   marked.

8. **Cyaniris helena** *Greek Mazarine Blue*   291
   ♂. Unh with large pale orange anal lunules. ♀ ups brown.

9. **Albulina orbitulus** *Alpine Argus*   286
   ♂. Unh basal and postdiscal spots white. ♀ ups brown.

10. **Plebejus argus** *Silver-studded Blue*   276
    10a. *P. a. argus* ♂. Ups black borders 1-2 mm. wide.
    10b. *P. a. corsicus* ♀. Unf spots only slightly darker than ground-
         colour.
    10c. *P. a. hypochionus* ♂. Larger; borders 2-3 mm. wide; uns
         ground-colour white.

11. **Plebejus vogelii** *Vogel's Blue*   27
    ♂. Ups pale brown with orange submarginal bands; upf black dis-
    coidal spot large. ♀ similar.

12. **Plebejus martini** *Martin's Blue*   27
    ♂. Ups lavender blue; unf black postdiscal spots bold. For ♀ see
    Pl. 4.

13. **Vacciniina optilete** *Cranberry Blue*   27
    ♂. Ups deep violet blue; unh spot in s2 red. ♀ similar.

14. **Polyommatus icarus** *Common Blue*   31
    ♂. Ups sky blue with fine black marginal lines; unf black spot
    present in cell. For ♀ see Pl. 4.

15. **Lycaeides idas** *Idas Blue*   27
    15a. *L. i.* f. *haefelfingeri* ♂. Small, ups blue with narrow black mar-
         ginal lines. See Fig. on p. 277.
    15b. *L. i.* f. *lapponicus* ♀. Ups blue basal suffusions wide; uph mar-
         ginal spots capped orange. For ♂ see Pl. 54.

1a

4

2c

2a

3

1b

2b

5

6

7

8

9

10a

10b

10c

13

11

14

15a

12

15b

PLATE 56

1. **Agriades glandon**   *Glandon Blue*   286
    1a. *A. g. glandon* ♂. Ups greenish blue; unf submarginal markings
          vestigial; unh most ocelli with black pupils.
    1b. *A. g. glandon* ♀. Ups brown; unh markings brown, as in ♂.
    1c. *A. g.* f. *alboocellatus* ♂. Unh white markings mostly lack pupils.
    1d. *A. g. dardanus* ♂. Small, with fewer dark spots.
    1e. *A. g. zullichi* ♂. Small; unh white spots mostly lack pupils.

2. **Agriades aquilo**   *Arctic Blue*   287
    A. aquilo ♂. Ups pale grey-blue; unh white markings large.

3. **Agriades pyrenaicus**   *Gavarnie Blue*   290
    3a. *A. p. pyrenaicus* ♂. Unf submarginal black spots distinct.
    3b. *A. p. asturiensis* ♂. Unf black markings larger.
    3c. *A. p. asturiensis* ♀. Ups pale brown; markings grey.

4. **Eumedonia eumedon**   *Geranium Argus*   281
    4a. *E. e. eumedon* ♂. Unh white postdiscal stripe on vein 5.
    4b. *E. e. eumedon* f. *borealis* ♂. Unh, white stripe on vein 5 vestigial
          or absent.

5. **Kretania psylorita**   *Cretan Argus*   280
    K. psylorita ♂. Ups brown; uph marginal lunules pale yellow; uns
    markings very small.

6. **Plebicula dorylas**   *Turquoise Blue*   298
    P. dorylas ♂. Ups sky-blue; uns margins white.

7. **Plebicula atlantica**   *Atlas Blue*   299
    7a. *P. atlantica* ♂. Ups like *P. dorylas*, but paler blue; uns as in ♀.
    7b. *P. atlantica* ♀. Ups brown, orange lunules very large.

8. **Plebicula nivescens**   *Mother-of-Pearl Blue*   299
    P. nivescens ♂. Ups pale shining silver-grey; uns as in *P. dorylas*.

9. **Plebicula golgus**   *Nevada Blue*   298
    ♂. Small, ups deep sky blue; uns pale grey-brown.

10. **Plebicula thersites**   *Chapman's Blue*   302
    ♂. Like *Polyommatus icarus*; **(Pl. 55)** but ups more violet and unf
    without black cell-spot. ♀ like *P. icarus* **(Pl. 4)** but uns as in *thersites*
    ♂.

11. **Plebicula amanda**   *Amanda's Blue*   302
    11a. *P. a. amanda* ♂. Large; uns pale grey, markings small.
    11b. *P. a. amanda* ♀. Uph submarginal lunules incomplete.
    11c. *P. a. abdulaziz* ♀. Ups submarginal lunules complete.

12. **Polyommatus eroides**   *Balkans Blue*   310
    ♂. Ups shining sky-blue, dark borders 2 mm. wide; unf with black
    spot in cell. ♀ ups brown.

13. **Polyommatus eros**   *Eros Blue*   311
    ♂. Small; ups gleaming sky blue; borders 1 mm.; ♀ ups brown.

14. **Meleageria daphnis**   *Meleager's Blue*   303
    14a. ♂. Hw outer margins slightly scalloped.
    14b. *M. d. daphnis* ♀-f. *steeveni*. Ups brown with markings grey.
          See also Pl. 57.

Similar species. There is no similar species in Morocco.

PLEBICULA AMANDA   *Amanda's Blue*

Sp: Niña Estriada   Sw: Silverfärgad Blåvinge

Range. From N. Africa and Spain widely distributed in Europe and W. Asia to Iran.   Map 319

P. amanda amanda   Schneider 1792   TL: S. Sweden   Pl. 56
    syn: *icarius* Esper (after 1792)

Description. ♂fw 16/19mm., ups gc sky blue; *upf margin widely suffused with fuscous which extends basad along veins*; uph with dark marginal line extending basad along veins, sometimes with obscure antemarginal dark spots; uns gc pale dove grey with blue basal flush; unf usual markings rather small, no spot in cell and marginal markings obscure; unh pd markings rather small, generally with orange submarginal lunules in s1c, 2, 3 followed by small dark antemarginal spots from s1c–7. ♀ups medium brown, often with extensive blue basal suffusion; uph orange submarginal lunules with marginal black spots in s1c–3; uns gc darker grey-brown, otherwise as in ♂.

Flight. End June/July in a single brood.

Habitat. Flowery banks, etc., from lowlands to 5,000 ft. in southern Europe; associated with larval food plant, tufted vetch (*Vicia cracca*). Hibernates as small larva.

Distribution. Absent from NW. Europe, Venezia Giulia and Carniola: otherwise widely distributed but local to 65°N, especially in mountains.

Variation. Local variation is not marked. Females widely suffused with blue are common in Scandinavia, rare in the Alps and Pyrenees, f. *isias* Fruhstorfer.

P. amanda abdelaziz   Blachier 1905   TL: Atlas Mts., Morocco   Pl. 56

Description. ♂ups blue gc slightly paler with slightly silvery tone; uns markings small; unh orange lunules in anal area vestigial or absent. ♀ups brown with large orange-yellow marginal lunules on both wings and a slight general orange suffusion in some specimens.

Flight. June, in a single brood.

Habitat. Mountain meadows at 6–8,000 ft.

Distribution. Morocco, Middle and High Atlas. Algeria.

Similar species. The large size and slightly dusky gleaming pale blue ups and dove-grey lightly marked uns are unlike any other species.

PLEBICULA THERSITES   *Chapman's Blue*

Sp: Celda Limpia

Range. N. Africa and S. Europe to Lebanon, Asia Minor, Iran and Thian Shan.   Map 320

P. thersites Cantener 1834 TL: Vosges, etc., NE. France **Pl. 56**
Description. ♂fw 13/16mm., resembles *P. icarus* but *androconia numerous*, ups bright blue generally with slightly violet tint, fringes white, not chequered; uns gc light grey to brown; unf no spot in cell, otherwise with usual markings; orange submarginal lunules generally well developed on both wings; unh blue basal flush usually well marked in early specimens, often absent in late broods, usual markings complete with white mark on v4. ♀ups brown, sometimes with blue basal suffusion; uph orange submarginal lunules present, often absent upf; uns gc light brown with markings as in ♂, white streak along v4 often conspicuous.
Flight. May and later in two or more broods.
Habitat. Flowery meadows esp. fields of sainfoin (*Onobrychis*), larval food plant, from lowlands to 5,000 ft.
Distribution. N. Africa, in Middle Atlas and High Atlas, flying there at 5-6,000 ft. Europe, widely distributed but local to 50°N. Not recorded from Mediterranean islands (except Sicily) or from Algeria.
Variation. In some localities females often have a slight ups basal blue flush.

Similar species. *Polyommatus icarus* p. 310, wing-markings and colour are nearly identical but on unf *P. icarus* has a spot in the cell, sometimes very small. The male androconia on upf in *P. thersites* produce a slightly furry appearance which is not present in *P. icarus*. *P. escheri* p. 297. *P. dorylas* p. 298.

MELEAGERIA DAPHNIS *Meleager's Blue*

Sp: Azul Bipuntada G: Zahnflügel Bläuling
Range. From southern France across S. Europe to Lebanon, Syria and Iran. **Map 321**

M. daphnis Schiffermueller 1775 TL: Vienna **Pls. 56, 57**
syn: *meleager* Esper 1779
Description. ♂fw 18/19mm., *outer margin of hw slightly scalloped between v2 and v3*; ups light shining blue with narrow black marginal borders, otherwise unmarked; uns gc pale grey, hw slightly darker, usual markings present with basal and discal spots black, marginal markings grey; unf no spot in cell; unh without orange submarginal lunules. ♀hw more deeply scalloped; ups deeper blue with dark discoidal spot, costal and marginal borders dark; uph with antemarginal spots; uns gc light brown with markings as in ♂, a white wedge-shaped pd mark on v4.
Flight. June in a single brood.
Habitat. Warm flowery slopes from lowlands to 4,500 ft. Larval food plants species of *Orobus, Thymus, Astragalus*.
Distribution. France, in Cevennes, Provence and Dauphiné. Switzerland, esp. Rhône valley. Italy, widely distributed in mountainous areas of Piedmont, southern slopes of Alps, peninsular Italy and Sicily. In E. Europe

PLATE 57

1. **Plebicula escheri**   *Escher's Blue*   **See also Pl. 13.**   297

   1a. *P. e. escheri* ♂. Bright blue, black marginal line narrow; uns boldly marked; unf no cell-spot.
   1b. *P. e. escheri* ♀. Ups brown, orange marginal lunules prominent.
   1c. *P. e. splendens* f. *altivolans* ♂. Smaller, ups paler blue.

2. **Meleageria daphnis**   *Meleager's Blue*   303
   ♀. Ups blue; hw scalloped. For ♂ see **Pl. 56.**

3. **Lysandra bellargus**   *Adonis Blue*   309
   ♂. Bright blue, fringes chequered; unf black cell-spot present. ♀ ups brown; uns as in ♂ but ground-colour darker. (Rarely, as in figure, unf cell-spot minute or absent.)

4. **Lysandra punctifera**   *Spotted Adonis Blue*   309
   ♂. Like *L. bellargus*; ♂ uph marginal black spots prominent.

5. **Lysandra caelestissima**   *Azure Chalk-hill Blue*   308
   ♂. Like *L. bellargus* but ♂ ups paler sky-blue.

6. **Lysandra coridon**   *Chalk-hill Blue*   306

   6a. *L. c. coridon* ♂. Ups pale silvery-blue. ♀ brown.
   6b. *L. c. coridon* ♀-f. *syngrapha*. Ups blue, borders brown; uph often with orange spots.
   6c. *L. c. asturiensis* ♂. Ups brighter blue.

7. **Lysandra albicans**   *Spanish Chalk-hill Blue*   **See also Pl. 13.**   307
   L. a. albicans ♂. Large: ups grey-white with darker marginal markings uns markings small. ♀ brown.

8. **Lysandra hispana**   *Provence Chalk-hill Blue*   307

   8a. ♂. Like *L. coridon*; ups silvery-blue, sometimes slightly yellowish.
   8b. ♀. Like *L. coridon*; ups brown.

9. **Agrodiaetus damon**   *Damon Blue*   294
   ♂. Ups pale shining blue; unh with firm white stripe in space 4. ♀ brown, uns as in ♂.

10. **Agrodiaetus dolus**   *Furry Blue*   294

    10a. *A. d. virgilia* ♂. Ups grey-white; upf with wide discal brown suffusion. ♀ ups brown; markings as in ♂.
    10b. *A. d. dolus* ♂. Like *A. d. virgilia* but ups pale blue.

11. **Agrodiaetus admetus**   *Anomalous Blue*   29
    ♂. Uns with postdiscal and submarginal markings.

12. **Agrodiaetus ripartii**   *Ripart's Anomalous Blue*   29
    ♂. Unh with long pale stripe submarginal markings absent. ♀ similar but smaller.

PLATE 58

PYRGUS Upf postdiscal white spots in spaces 4 and 5 displaced outwards; costal fold present in ♂.

1. **Pyrgus malvae** *Grizzled Skipper*   312
   ♂. Uph postdiscal spots clearly defined. ♀ similar.

2. **Pyrgus alveus** *Large Grizzled Skipper*   313
   2a. *P. a. alveus* ♂. Uph postdiscal spots usually small or absent.
   2b. *P. a. centralhispaniae* ♂. Uph pale markings more extensive.
   2c. *P. a. numidus* ♂. Large; ups markings large and complete.
   2d. *P. a. alveus* ♀. Ups yellowish; upf white markings very small.
   2e. *P. a. scandinavicus* ♂. Unh discal band usually complete.
   2f. *P. a. alticolus* ♂. Very small; upf white markings minute.

3. **Pyrgus foulquieri** *Foulquier's Grizzled Skipper*   316
   ♂. Resembles *P. a. centralhispaniae*; uph pale markings large.

4. **Pyrgus armoricanus** *Oberthur's Grizzled Skipper*   315
   4a. *P. a. armoricanus* ♂. Small; uph pale discal mark often prominent.
   4b. *P. a. maroccanus* ♂. Larger; ups markings larger.

5. **Pyrgus onopordi** *Rosy Grizzled Skipper*   318
   ♂. Unh "signe de Blachier" in space 1c (See text).

6. **Pyrgus cirsii** *Cinquefoil Skipper*   317
   ♂. Upf white cell-spot rectangular. See fig., p. 318.

7. **Pyrgus carlinae** *Carline Skipper*   317
   7a. *P. c. carlinae* ♂. Unh ground-colour often reddish, prominent marginal pale mark in space 4/5. See fig., p. 318.
   7b. *P. c. carlinae* ♀. Ups yellowish, white markings small.

8. **Pyrgus serratulae** *Olive Skipper*   316
   8a. *P. serratulae* ♂. Unh gc olive- to grey-green.
   8b. *P. serratulae* f. *major* ♂. Larger; unh gc often dark.
   8c. *P. serratulae* ♀. Ups white markings small or obsolete.

9. **Pyrgus fritillarius** *Safflower Skipper*   322
   ♂. Uph white post-discal spots in regular series. ♀ similar.

10. **Pyrgus sidae** *Yellow-banded Skipper*   319
    10a. *P. s. sidae* ♂. Large, unh bands bright yellow.
    10b. *P .s. occiduus* ♂. Smaller, unh bands paler yellow.

11. **Pyrgus centaureae** *Northern Grizzled Skipper*   323
    ♂. Unh ground-colour dark, veins lined white.

12. **Pyrgus andromedae** *Alpine Grizzled Skipper*   322
    ♂. Unh with white streak and round spot in space 1c.

13. **Pyrgus cacaliae** *Dusky Grizzled Skipper*   323
    ♂. Upf white spots very small.

more widely distributed to 50°N or beyond. Absent from Spain, Pyrenees.
Portugal and Mediterranean islands except Sicily.
Variation. A ♀ form in which ups is dark grey with markings obscurely
outlined in blue-grey, f. *steeveni* Treitschke Pl. 56, is common in the western range.

LYSANDRA CORIDON   *Chalk-hill Blue*
G: Silbergrüner Bläuling   Sp: Niña coridon
Range. Apparently confined to Europe.   Map 322

L. coridon coridon   Poda 1761   TL: Graz, Austria   Pl. 57
Description. ♂fw 15/18mm., fringes strongly chequered; ups gc pale
silvery blue; upf with fuscous marginal borders 2–3mm. wide; uph black
marginal line narrow, antemarginal spots round; uns standard markings
all present; unf gc pale grey; unh gc tinted brown with slight blue-green
basal suffusion, markings less conspicuous than on fw, orange submarginal
lunules often small and pale, the wedge-shaped white mark along v4 extending to submarginal lunules. ♀ups brown, sometimes with blue suffusion; uns
brown, markings as in ♂.
Flight. July/August in a single brood.
Habitat. Grass banks from sea-level to 6,000 ft., restricted to chalk and
limestone country. Larval food plants various Leguminosae, e.g., vetches
and trefoils, esp. *Hippocrepis comosa*; larva hibernates when small.
Distribution. From Pyrenees northwards to Baltic coast in Germany thence
generally distributed in calcareous areas through S. and C. Europe from
S. England to Sorrento in peninsular Italy and Balkans (rare and local).
Greece, on Mt. Olympus, Mt. Taygetos, etc. Absent from Ireland, NW.
Germany, Denmark, Scandinavia, C. and S. Spain, Portugal and Mediterranean islands.
Variation. Slight local variation occurs in size, intensity of markings and in
shade of blue gc. In females ups blue suffusion is common and very extensive in some areas, f. *syngrapha* Keferstein, rare in the Alps.

L. coridon asturiensis   Sagarra 1922   TL: Pajares, Cantabrian   Pl. 57
Mts.
Description. ♂fw 15/17mm., ups bright pale blue without the greyish tone
usually present in *L. c. coridon*; markings as in *coridon*. ♀ usually brown,
but f. *syngrapha* occurs in some colonies and may preponderate.
Flight. July/August in a single brood.
Habitat. Rough flowery slopes at 2,500–4,000 ft.
Distribution. N. Spain, Picos de Europa, Santander, Burgos, Jaca, etc.

Similar species. *L. hispana* p. 307, double-brooded, may be confused with
L. coridon, but is greyer, even slightly yellowish. *L. caelestissima* p. 308
resembles *L.c. asturiensis*, but is slightly deeper violet-blue on ups. In

L. coridon and *L. hispana* certain identification may be impossible without accurate data as to time and place of occurrence. *L. albicans* below, ups pale grey. *L. bellargus* ♀ p. 309, ups usually with darker blue basal scales.

LYSANDRA HISPANA *Provence Chalk-hill Blue*
Range. Confined to SE. France, N. Italy and NE. Spain.   Map 323

L. hispana Herrich-Schaeffer 1852   TL: Spain   Pl. 57
  syn: *rezneciki* Bartel 1905
Description. ♂fw 16/18mm., very similar to *L. coridon*, not easily distinguishable without data; *ups pale blue-grey, slightly yellowish in oblique light*; upf discoidal stria minute if present, fuscous borders variable, sometimes wide with included vestigial pale submarginal lunules, often preceded by a paler area of gc; uns boldly marked esp. on hw. ♀ups brown, indistinguishable from *L. coridon* without accompanying ♂; *syngrapha*-like forms of the female have not been recorded.
Flight. April/May and September in two broods.
Habitat. Grassy banks and foothills at low levels, not above 3,000 ft. Larval food plants not recorded.
Distribution. France in E. Pyrenees, Aude, Hérault, Ardèche, Drôme, Basses Alpes, Var and Alpes Maritimes. Spain in Catalonia, esp. env. of Barcelona. Italy, in Liguria and Emilia to Florence and Siena.

Similar species. *L. coridon* p. 306, emerges in July/August, between broods of *L. hispana*; *L. albicans* below.

LYSANDRA ALBICANS *Spanish Chalk-hill Blue*
Range. Confined to Spain and N. Africa.   Map 324

L. albicans albicans Herrich-Schaeffer 1851   TL: Spain   Pls. 13, 57
Description. ♂fw 18/21 mm., ups *palest silky grey*, thorax and wing-bases faintly blue; upf fuscous *marginal border broad, often double* and enclosing marginal spots vaguely ringed with pale grey; uph fuscous marginal spots conspicuous; unf gc white with standard markings small; unh gc variable, brown, yellowish or white, markings often small and faint. ♀ups brown, often with small discoidal spots, orange submarginal lunules usually present before dark antemarginal spots on both wings and sometimes preceded by grey-white markings; uns brown, boldly marked in standard pattern.
Flight. July/August in a single brood.
Habitat. Rocky slopes and rough grass, etc., at 3–5,000 ft. Larval food plants not recorded.
Distribution. Spain, except W. Spain, local but not rare from Malaga, Granada, Bailen, Toledo, Albarracin, Burgos, to Jaca, etc. Absent from Portugal.
Variation. Ups gc varies considerably, very pale and nearly without blue

basal flush in S. Spain; farther N. and at higher altitudes more grey than white and uns darker, unh esp. pale brown, f. *arragonensis* Gerhard Pl. 13. These colour variants appear to form a clinal series.

L. albicans berber Le Cerf 1932 TL: Middle Atlas
Description. ♂fw 16/18mm., small and ups very pale, with well-marked dusky marginal borders; uns very pale. ♀ups brown, undistinguished.
Flight. August.
Habitat. Mountains at 5–9,000 ft.
Distribution. Morocco, recorded from Kasr-el-Kebir, Timesmout, Tameghilt, Moussah ou Salah, all in Middle Atlas; not recorded from High Atlas.

Similar species. *L. coridon* p. 306, ♂ups definitely blue; *L. hispana* p. 307, only in NE. Spain, generally smaller, ♂ ups grey gc slightly more suffused blue but distinction difficult without data, first brood over before *albicans* begins to fly; females of both species lack the small pale grey discal and marginal markings generally present in ♀ *albicans*. *P. nivescens* p. 299.

LYSANDRA CAELESTISSIMA *Azure Chalk-hill Blue*
Range. Confined to C. Spain in Provinces Cuenca and Teruel.   Map 325

L. caelestissima Verity 1921 TL: Albarracin, Tragacete   Pl. 57
Description. ♂fw 15/18mm., resembles *L. coridon; ups sky blue with slightly violet tint*, a deeper colour and without the silvery gleam of *L. c. asturiensis*; upf dark marginal border narrow, about 1mm. wide but slightly suffused and obscuring black antemarginal spots; uph marginal border linear, black antemarginal spots free; uns resembles *L. coridon*. ♀ups brown, rather small with fw 14/16mm.
Flight. July/August in a single brood.
Habitat. Flowery mountain slopes at 5,000 ft. or more. Larval food plant not recorded.
Distribution. C. Spain, on the Montes Universales in Cuenca and Teruel, e.g., Albarracin, Tragacete, Bronchales, Cuenca, Valdemoro.
Variation. In some localities a slightly larger and paler form occurs, f. *caerulescens* Tutt, described originally as a form of *L. albicans* but with gc decidedly blue. This form is uncommon, usually occurring singly and nearly always flying with *caelestissima*. Its exact taxonomic status is uncertain at present.

Similar species. *L. coridon* p. 306 and *L. albicans* p. 307, never develop the pure sky blue of *caelestissima*. *L. bellargus* p. 309, ♂ups vivid sky blue with black linear marginal borders. *L. albicans* p. 307, ♀ distinguishable on ups by small pale discoidal and marginal markings.

LYSANDRA BELLARGUS *Adonis Blue*

G: Himmelblauer Bläuling   Sp: Niña Celeste Rastrillo
Range. Europe including Russia to Iraq and Iran.   Map 326

L. bellargus Rottemburg 1775   TL: W. Germany   Pl. 57
   syn: *adonis* Schiffermueller 1775
Description. ♂fw 14/17mm., *ups shining vivid sky blue* with fine black marginal lines, fringes white, chequered black; uph with small black antemarginal spots; uns gc light-brown to grey-brown with standard markings complete; unh with blue-green basal flush; ♀ups brown, often with blue suffusion, rarely extensive; uph orange submarginal lunules often conspicuous, sometimes present also on fw; uns gc darker brown, markings as in ♂, but blue basal suffusion reduced or absent.
Flight. May/June and July/August in two broods in most localities.
Habitat. Meadows, etc., from lowlands to 6,000 ft., restricted to calcareous areas. Larval food plant horse-shoe vetch (*Hippocrepis*), and various other small Leguminosae.
Distribution. Widely distributed in S. and C. Europe to 55°N and to Latvia, local in S. England, rare in S. Spain. Absent from Ireland, Italy S. of Naples, Mediterranean islands, and Greece S. of the Gulf of Corinth.
Variation. Racial variation is not marked; minor individual variation with fusion or absence of uns spots is not very uncommon. In rare females blue ups suffusion may be complete except on marginal borders, f. *ceronus* Esper.

Similar species. *L. coridon* p. 306, in ♀ only; blue scales or suffusion on ups pale silvery. *P. escheri* p. 297, ♀.
Note. In some localities where *L. coridon* and *L. bellargus* occur on the same ground rare specimens have occurred in which the blue ups gc is paler, intermediate in shade between these species, f. *polonus* Zeller. Nine such specimens examined by de Lesse had variable chromosome numbers (52-70) with abnormal meiosis patterns, and there seems little doubt that some at least of these pale forms are hybrids between *L. coridon* and *L. bellargus*.

LYSANDRA PUNCTIFERA *Spotted Adonis Blue*

Range. Confined to Morocco and Algeria.   Map 327

L. punctifera Oberthur 1876   TL: Lambessa, Algeria   Pl. 57
   syn: *punctigera* Oberthur 1909
Description. ♂fw 15/18mm., ups bright gleaming sky blue, resembling *L. bellargus*; *uph antemarginal black spots free, conspicuous*; uns gc brown with small blue basal flush, standard markings conspicuous esp. on fw but orange submarginal lunules rather small. ♀ups gc brown, blue suffusion often present, sometimes extensive; uns as in ♂. Fringes white, strongly chequered black in both sexes.
Flight. May/June and September/October, second brood very small.

Habitat. Flowery banks at 5–6,000 ft. in Middle Atlas, to 7,500 ft. in High Atlas. Larval food plant not recorded.
Distribution. Morocco, Algeria.
Similar species. None in Africa.

POLYOMMATUS ICARUS   *Common Blue*

Sw: Puktörneblåvinge   G: Hauhechelbläuling   Sp: Dos Puntos
Range. From Canary Islands and temperate N. Africa throughout Europe and temperate Asia.   Map 328

P. icarus   Rottemburg 1775   **TL:** Saxony, Germany   Pls. 4, 55
Description. ♂fw 14/18mm., size variable; ups *androconia absent*, gc light violet-blue with fine black marginal lines; uns gc grey with blue-green basal flush, markings well developed; *unf with spot in cell and second basal spot below this in s*1b, pd spots in regular sinuous curve and orange submarginal lunules more or less developed; unh with all usual markings and white flash on v4 beyond pd spot. ♀ups brown, often flushed blue, orange submarginal lunules generally in complete series across both wings; uph with black antemarginal spots between veins; uns gc brown, all markings better developed.
Flight. April or later in two or three broods in S. Europe, a single brood in June/July in the far north.
Habitat. Meadows and open spaces, lowlands to 6,000 ft. or more. Larval food plants small Leguminosae, esp. trefoil, vetches and clovers.
Distribution. N. Africa, Canary Islands, all Europe to North Cape and all Mediterranean islands; one of the commonest and most ubiquitous butterflies, flying in the High Atlas to 8,000 ft.
Variation. Seasonal variation is sometimes well marked late broods being small and pale. Individual variation (aberrations) causing the loss or fusion of markings on uns are not uncommon.

Similar species. *Plebicula thersites* p. 302, markings on both surfaces are nearly identical but on unf there is no spot in cell and on upf androconia are abundant (absent in *icarus*). *P. icarus* does occur without a spot in cell on unf but rarely, f. *icarinus* Scriba. *P. eros* p. 311, ♂ups pale silvery blue; ♀ smaller, ups blue basal scaling, if present, paler.

POLYOMMATUS EROIDES   *False Eros Blue*
Range. Poland and Czechoslovakia to Balkans and Asia Minor.
                                                              Map 329

P. eroides   Frivaldsky 1835   **TL:** Balkans   Pl. 56
Description. ♂fw 15/18mm., ups gleaming sky blue with *black marginal borders about 2mm. wide;* uph with round antemarginal spots against dark border in s1c–s5; uns closely resembles *P. icarus.* ♀ups brown with slightly

grey tint, without blue suffusion, orange submarginal lunules variable; uns gc brown, markings as in ♂.

Flight. End June/July in a single brood.

Habitat. Mountainous country at 4–6,000 ft.

Distribution. E. Prussia and Czechoslovakia. Balkans, in Albania and Bulgaria (Kostenetz, Pirin Mts., etc.) and Greece.

Similar species. *P. eros* below.

POLYOMMATUS EROS   *Eros Blue*

Sp: Niño Amoroso

Range. Pyrenees, Alps and Apennines to C. Asia.   Map 330

P. eros   Ochsenheimer 1808   TL: Alps of Tirol etc.   Pl. 56

Description. ♂fw 13/14mm., ups pale shining blue with *black marginal borders wide*; uns resembles *P. icarus* closely, unh with blue basal suffusion darker. ♀ups medium brown, often with light-blue basal suffusion; submarginal orange lunules and antemarginal dark spots very variable, rarely well developed; uns gc grey-brown with markings as in ♂, blue basal suffusion reduced.

Flight. July/August in a single brood.

Habitat. Mountains, on grass slopes at 5–8,000 ft., usually at alpine levels in Pyrenees and Alps, but from 4,000 ft. in Apennines. Larval food plants Leguminosae including *Oxytropis* and *Astragalus*.

Distribution. See map 330.

Similar species. *P. eroides* p. 310; *P. icarus* p. 310.

PLEBICULA COELESTINA   *Pontic Blue*

Range. Greece and eastwards across N. Turkey and S. Russia to the Caucasus.   No Map

P. c. coelestina   Eversmann 1848   TL: Sarepta, S. Russia   No figure

Description. ♂ ups deep blue, marginal borders 2–3 mm. wide, black, otherwise unmarked, fringes white; uns pale grey-brown; unf discoidal and pd black white-ringed spots in complete series; unh gleaming blue-green, basal suffusion extending to end of cell, discoidal spot and pd spots wun mplete and regular series, as on fw, submarginal markings absent. pi,os brown, vestiges of yellow marginal lunules present at anal angle of h♀c otherwise unmarked; unh with yellow submarginal lunules in short series.

Flight. June, in Greece, on mountains at 4–5000 ft.

Distribution. In Europe known only from the Peloponnesus, Greece.

Similar species. *C. semiargus*, p. 290.

HESPERIIDAE
Latreille 1809

Skippers

These are small butterflies which differ widely from all others in the following characters. In the imago the head is wide, antennae widely separated, thorax robust. All wing-veins arise directly from the wing-base or from the discoidal cell, and all run without branching to the costa or outer margin. The antennal club often ends in a pointed tip—the apiculus. Larvae are cylindrical or fusiform, and the larval head appears large in relation to the slender neck and narrow first body segment. So far as known, all European species live in shelters made of grass or leaves, in which they pupate. The family is cosmopolitan. Males of the genera *Pyrgus*, *Muschampia* and *Carcharodus* have the costa of the forewing folded over enclosing androconia.

PYRGUS MALVAE   *Grizzled Skipper*

F: Le Tacheté   Sw: Kattostvisslare   G: Malven-Würfelfleckenfalter
Sp: Ajedrezada menor
Range. Widely distributed throughout Europe and eastwards to Mongolia
and Amurland.   Map 331

P. malvae malvae Linnaeus 1758   TL: Aland Is, Finland   Pl. 58
Description. ♂fw 11/13 mm.; ups white markings and spots sharply defined on both wings; *uph with clear-cut row of small white pd spots*; unh gc brown, often with green or yellowish tint, discal row of pale marks often broken in s2 and 3. ♀ usually slightly larger otherwise similar.
Flight. April/June and July/August in two broods in southern districts; in N. Europe and at high altitudes more often a single brood in May/June or later.
Habitat. Flowery banks, bogs and meadows from sea-level to 6,000 ft. Food plants *Potentilla*, *Fragaria*, *Malva*, *Agrimonia*, etc.
Distribution. Central, northern and eastern Europe to 65°N. Absent from N. Scotland and Ireland.

P. malvae malvoides Elwes and Edwards 1897   TL: Biarritz
Description. Indistinguishable from *P. m. malvae* on external characters, but genitalia distinct.
Flight. April/June and July/August in two broods at low altitudes, a single brood in June/July at high altitudes.
Habitat. As for *P. m, malvae*.
Distribution. Throughout Spain and Portugal. France only in S. and SE. Switzerland in southern Alps to about 47°N. Istria and throughout Italy

to Sicily. Absent from Corsica, Sardinia, Malta and Balearic Islands.

The next seven species form a difficult group. They are all closely related, lack well-marked specific characters, and show considerable local variation. It may be impossible to make a confident specific determination by external features, but most species are easily identified by the male genitalia.

The widely distributed and variable species *Pyrgus alveus* provides a convenient standard for comparison of specific characters with those of other species.

PYRGUS ALVEUS *Large Grizzled Skipper*

F: Le Plain-Chant Sw: Kattunvisslare G: Halbwurfelfalter
Sp: Ajedrezada serrana
Range. From N. Africa and Spain through most of Europe to Caucasus, Altai Mts. and Siberia. Map 332

P. alveus alveus Huebner 1803 TL: Germany (Verity 1940) Pl. 58
Description. ♂fw 14/16mm.; ups gc dark grey-brown (nearly black when fresh) often with yellowish flush; upf white spots of small to moderate size; uph rectangular discal mark in s4 and 5, *small pd spots usually very obscure*; unh gc *olive-brown* to greenish, pale discal band usually complete, but *spots in s2, 3 small*. ♀upf white spots smaller, gc sometimes with golden reflection when fresh.
Flight. End June to August in a single brood.
Habitat. Flowery meadows, most often in hilly districts or in mountains at 3–6,000 ft., rarely below 3,000 ft. Larval food plants *Potentilla, Helianthemum, Rubus*, etc.
Distribution. France in Central Massif, Pyrenees, Jura, Vosges, thence through Alps and Balkans to SE. Yugoslavia; northwards through Belgium, Germany and Poland to the Baltic countries but local and usually rare in its northern range. Absent from Britain and Mediterranean islands except Sicily. Records from Greece need confirmation.

P. alveus centralitaliae Verity 1920 TL: Sibillini Mts., C. Italy
Description. ♂fw 14/15mm., often smaller than *P. a. alveus*; ups gc distinctly yellowish with pale markings well developed and often extensive on uph. ♀ pale markings reduced; unh sometimes mottled darker.
Flight and Habitat as for *P.a. alveus*.
Distribution. Peninsular Italy, only on high mountains in Marche and Abruzzi, variable, subspecific characters not always well developed. Spain, on most mountains south of Pyrenees, with transitional forms on Cantabrian Mts., where extension of pale markings on uph is more constant, especially characteristic in Castile, Aragon and Andalusia, f. *centralhispaniae* Verity Pl. 58. Occasional specimens with extensive pale mark-

ings occur in S. France, esp. in Pyrenees, Cevennes and northwards to Dijon.

Similar species. *P. fritillarius* p. 322 is easily confused with *P.a. centralitaliae* but on upf has pale spot in cell oblique, inclined very close to pale discoidal mark; in *alveus* these two spots are well separated. *P. foulquieri picenus* p. 316, distinction very difficult, perhaps impossible without dissection.

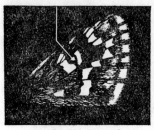

P. fritillarius upf   *P. alveus centralitaliae* upf

P. alveus alticolus   Rebel 1910   TL: High Alps (Stelvio)   Pl. 58
Description. ♂fw 12mm. or less; ups white spots reduced in number and size; unh markings small but complete. ♀ups basal hairs yellowish.
Flight. July/August in a single brood.
Habitat. Flies over short grass slopes at 6,000 ft. upwards.
Distribution. Pennine Alps, Grisons, Engadine, Brenner, Hohe Tauern, etc.
Variation. In its extreme development very small with fw 11mm. and ups markings minute f. *warrenensis* Verity. The taxonomic status of *alticolus* is uncertain.

P. alveus scandinavicus   Strand 1903   TL: Dovre, Norway   Pl. 58
    syn: *ballotae* Oberthur 1910

Description. ♂fw 11/12mm., small, upf markings well defined, usually also on hw; uns markings complete, often large, ♀ similar.
Flight. End June/July.
Habitat as for *P.a. alveus*.
Distribution. Fennoscandia, local but appears to be widely distributed to about 63°N.
Note. The small size and relatively large pale markings of *P.a. scandinavicus* are distinctive, recalling *P. armoricanus*. The genitalia characters are often unusual, but variable; possibly two species are present in Scandinavia. The taxonomic status of *scandinavicus* is uncertain; it is sometimes considered specifically distinct.

P. alveus numidus   Oberthur 1910   TL: Lambessa, Algeria   Pl. 58
Description. ♂fw 14/15mm.; slightly larger than *P. a. alveus*; ups white

markings well developed; uph discal and pd spots prominent; unh pale markings rather inconspicuous against pale yellowish gc. ♀ similar.
Flight. End May and August in two broods.
Habitat. Flowery slopes and meadows at 5–6,000 ft.
Distribution. Algeria (Lambessa). Morocco, Ifrane, Azrou, Anosseur, etc.; recorded from High Atlas.

Similar species. *P. armoricanus* below, smaller and broods emerge before and after *P. alveus*, flies commonly at lowland levels (*P. alveus* more in mountains); uph pale rectangular mark in s4 and 5 usually distinct; unh discal markings complete. *P. foulquieri* p. 316, compared with *P. alveus*, ups more hairy, pale spots and markings much better defined; distribution restricted. *P. serratulae* p. 316, smaller, unh smooth olive-brown, pale markings well defined.

PYRGUS ARMORICANUS *Oberthur's Grizzled Skipper*

Sp: Ajedrezaoa yunque   Sw: Fransk Blomvisslare
Range. From N. Africa and Europe to Iran.   Map 333

P. armoricanus armoricanus Oberthur 1910 TL: Rennes   Pl. 58
Description. ♂fw 12/14mm.; upf white markings complete; *uph pale markings usually present* and discal spot sometimes prominent; unh resembles *P. alveus* with pale discal band well defined esp. in s4, 5, 6 and with large round spot in s1c. ♀ similar or ups white spots may be reduced. Specimens of *second brood* are often small.
Flight. May/June and August/September in two broods in S. Europe, a single brood in June/July in parts of northern range.
Habitat. Flowery banks from lowlands to 4,000 ft. or more.
Distribution. Widely distributed across Europe to 60°N, rare and local in northern range. Spain and Portugal; Corsica, Sardinia and Sicily; Hungary, the Balkans and Greece. Recorded from Denmark in N. and S. Seeland and Bornholm.

Similar species. *P. alveus* p. 313.

P. armoricanus maroccanus Picard 1950 TL: Morocco   Pl. 58
Description. ♂fw 14mm., slightly larger than *P. a. armoricanus*; ups white markings more prominent; uph pale submarginal spots well defined. ♀ similar.
Flight. June; probably a second brood in late summer.
Habitat. Flowery banks and rough ground at 5–6,000 ft.
Distribution. Flies in Middle Atlas in Morocco and Algeria, not recorded from High Atlas.

Similar species. *P. onopordi* p. 318, easily separable by yellowish gc and distinctive unh marking in anal area. *P. alveus numidus* p. 314 is larger.

PYRGUS FOULQUIERI   *Foulquier's Grizzled Skipper*
Sp: Ajedrezada viril
Range. Confined to SW. Europe and Italy.   Map 334

P. foulquieri foulquieri   Oberthur 1910   TL: Larche, Basses Alpes   Pl. 58
syn: *bellieri* Oberthur 1910
Description. ♂fw 14/15mm., ups noticeably hairy at wing-bases; resembles
P. alveus centralitaliae, *uph pale markings complete* and only lightly suffused,
pd spots large, esp. in s2 and 3; unh gc yellow-brown, white markings
usually slightly more extensive than in *P. alveus.* ♀ups with marked yellow-
ish reflections and with smaller white markings.
Flight. Late July/August in a single brood.
Habitat. In mountains from valleys to 6,000 ft.
Distribution. France, widely distributed in south-east and in Central
Massif, Alpes Maritimes, Var, Bouches du Rhône, Isère and Hautes
Alpes, Lozère and Aveyron. Spain, Catalonia.

P. foulquieri picenus   Verity 1920   TL: Bolognola, C. Italy
Description. ♂fw 13/14mm., small, ups general colour tone paler yellowish,
ups pale markings complete; unh yellowish, usually slightly mottled
darker, white markings large and complete. ♀ similar.
Flight. July/August.
Habitat. Mountainous districts at 2–4,500 ft.
Distribution. Central Italy in Monti Sibillini, Abruzzi, Monte Aurunci,
etc., but very local.

Similar species. *P. alveus centralitaliae* Verity p. 313.

PYRGUS SERRATULAE   *Olive Skipper*
Sp: Ajedrezada verdosa   Sw: Ängskärevisslare
Range. From Spain across C. Europe to Transbaical.   Map 335

P. serratulae   Rambur 1839   TL: Spain   Pl. 58
Description. ♂fw 12/14mm., upf markings variable, white spots sometimes
very small; *uph pale markings generally obscure* or vestigial; *unh gc olive
to yellow-green without secondary mottling.* ♀ups white markings usually
very small, sometimes absent in s1b and s2 on upf, often with brassy
suffusion over the whole wing.
Flight. End June/August in a single brood, one of the first species to appear
in early summer.
Habitat. Usually in hilly or mountainous districts, from low levels (rare)
to 8,000 ft. in late summer. Larval food plants *Potentilla*, *Alchemilla*.
Distribution. S. and C. Europe to 52°N, occasional farther north, absent
from NW. France, Holland and NW. Germany; a mountain species in
peninsular Italy.
Variation. Size varies, large specimens, f. *major* Staudinger Pl. 85 with

fw 15/16mm. occur in lowlands in SW. France and elsewhere (Vendée, Gironde, Charente, etc.) and in Balkans (esp. Greece).

Similar species. Other small *Pyrgus* esp. *P. alveus*. The pattern of well-defined pale markings on a smooth olive-brown or yellowish unh gc is distinctive of *P. serratulae*. *P. fritillarius* p. 322, which often flies with *P. serratulae* in mid-June is larger and has well-defined small pale pd spots on uph.

PYRGUS CARLINAE *Carline Skipper*

Range. Confined to south-western Alps.   Map 336
P. carlinae Rambur 1839 TL: Dalecarlia (error)   Pl. 58
Description. ♂fw 13/14mm., *upf white cell mark narrow, divided, shaped like letter C* outwardly concave; uph pale markings obscure; *unh gc usually pale reddish-brown*, discal markings in s2 and s3 minute or absent, *white marginal mark on vein 5 prominent*. ♀ups usually with yellowish flush, white markings very small or partly obsolete.
Flight. July/August.
Habitat. Mountain pastures, often assembling in scores at damp places on paths, most common at 5–8,000 ft., occasional at lower altitudes. Larval food plant *Potentilla verna*.
Distribution. France, from Maritime Alps northwards to Savoie and on Italian slopes in Piedmont. Switzerland, on Alps of Valais and east to Ticino and Campiglio, northwards to Interlaken but uncommon north of Rhône valley.

Similar species. *P. serratulae* p. 316, which may fly at the same time and in the same localities; unh olive-grey without reddish tints and white marginal mark on vein 5 not especially prominent. *P. cirsii* below.

PYRGUS CIRSII *Cinquefoil Skipper*

Sp: Ajedrezada tórrida
Range. Confined to W. Europe.   Map 337

P. cirsii Rambur 1839 TL: Fontainebleau, France   Pl. 58
Description. ♂fw 13/14mm., upf all white markings prominent, *cell spot usually wide, rectangular*; *uph pale markings, esp. spot at base of s4 and 5*, and submarginal spots *distinct*, often yellowish; unh gc yellowish olive to reddish-brown, spots of discal band small, mark on margin on v5 brownish, inconspicuous; veins paler. ♀ similar.
Flight. Late July/August in a single brood.
Habitat. Flowery slopes, often at low altitudes, rarely above 4,500 ft. Larval food plant *Potentilla verna*, etc.
Distribution. Spain in Catalonia, Aragon, Andalusia, etc. France, E. Pyrenees, Central Massif and northwards to Paris, more common in SE., e.g., Var, Alpes Maritimes, Bouches du Rhône and northwards to Haute

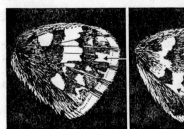  

P. carlinae unh   *P. onopordi* unh   *P. cirsii* upf

Savoie. Switzerland in Canton Vaud. Germany, Nurnberg (Pottenstein) and occasional in S. Bavaria. Not recorded with certainty from N. Italy.

Similar species. *P. carlinae* p. 317, ups white spots smaller, uph pale markings obscure, unh pale mark on margin on v5 prominent. *P. onopordi* below.

PYRGUS ONOPORDI   *Rosy Grizzled Skipper*

Sp: Ajedrezada Bigornia
Range. Confined to SW. Europe and N. Africa.   Map 338

P. onopordi Rambur 1839 TL: Granada, S. Spain   Pl. 58
Description. ♂fw 11/14mm., ups gc dark brown with slightly yellow tint; upf markings clearly defined; uph pale markings generally distinct, yellowish, esp. a pale mark near costa in s7; unh gc light yellow-brown, marbled darker, with yellow veins, a *prominent anvil-shaped discoidal spot in s4 and 5* and another large spot in 1c (signe de Blachier). ♀ usually slightly larger and ups darker, with fewer yellow scales.
Flight. April/June and July/September in two broods.
Habitat. Flowery meadows from lowlands to 4,500 ft. in Europe and to 5,500 ft. in N. Africa.
Distribution. SW. Europe to 46°N, including the Rhône valley and the southern slopes of the Alps, but commonest in Spain, Portugal, peninsular Italy and SE. France. N. Africa, widely distributed in Middle Atlas and High Atlas in Morocco and Algeria, up to 7,500 ft. Absent from Mediterranean islands.

Similar species. *P. cirsii* p. 317, which flies in late summer, ups darker, less yellow, upf white spots prominent, quadrate. *P. armoricanus* p. 315.

PYRGUS CINARAE   *Sandy Grizzled Skipper*
Range. C. Spain, S. Balkans and eastwards locally through S. Russia to Turkestan.   Map 339

P. cinarae cinarae Rambur 1839 **TL**: Sarepta Pl. 59
Description. ♂fw 15/16mm., ups gc very dark; *upf white spots large* esp. dumb-bell shaped spot near cell-end; uph two small basal spots, discal markings clear and well defined; unf white markings large; unh gc olive-brown, white spots conspicuous but not large. ♀ups *gc medium brown*; *ups pale markings less distinct and very small*; unh gc pale yellow-brown, white markings small, pearly, discrete.
Flight. End June.
Habitat. Dry stony slopes with scanty grass at 3,000 ft. Larval food plant not known.
Distribution. SE. Yugoslavia (Skopje). Albania. Bulgaria (Sliven).

P. cinarae clorinda Warren 1927 **TL**: Spain, Prov. Cuenca
Description. Differs from the eastern form in the slightly yellowish ups gc; unh gc definitely yellow. ♀ups with noticeable yellow flush.
Flight. July.
Habitat. In mountainous districts.
Distribution. C. Spain, local in Province Cuenca, e.g., Villacabras, Jardin Encatada, etc.

PYRGUS SIDAE *Yellow-banded Skipper*
Range. From Provence, C. Italy and Balkans to Asia Minor and Iran.
Map 340

P. sidae sidae Esper 1782 **TL**: Volga, S. Russia Pl. 58
Description. ♂fw 16/18mm., ups dark brown with greyish hair at wing-bases; upf cell-spot large, small submarginal spots usually all present; uph markings variable, pale spots sometimes prominent; *unh gc white, discal and pale pd bands bright yellow*; upf costal fold inconspicuous. ♀ similar, ups pale basal hair less conspicuous.
Flight. June/July in a single brood.
Habitat. Open places and flowery meadows, lowlands to 5,000 ft. Larval food plants Malvaceae, esp. *Abutilon avicennae.*
Distribution. Balkans; Bulgaria, Greece, Yugoslavia south of Mostar and Sarajevo. Rumania, Dobrogea, Banat.

P. sidae occiduus Verity 1925 **TL**: Tuscany Pl. 58
Description. ♂fw 13/16mm., ups spots smaller; unh discal and pd bands pale yellow.
Flight. June/early July in a single brood.
Habitat. Flowery banks and meadows, from lowlands to 4,500 ft.
Distribution. Italy, local in Apennines from Modena to Monte Aurunci; Florence; Liguria, Alassio, Genoa District, etc.; records from Alto Adige need confirmation. France, only in Provence, i.e., Alpes Maritimes, Var, Basses Alpes, Bouches du Rhône and Hérault.

PLATE 59

1a

1b

6

2a

2b

2c

2d

3

5

7a

7b

8

9

4

10a

10b

11

12

13

14a

14b

15

16

PLATE 60

1. **Heteropterus morpheus** *Large Chequered Skipper*   332
   ♂. Unh with large dark-circled white spots.

2. **Carterocephalus palaemon** *Chequered Skipper*   332
   ♂. Ups gc black with orange-yellow markings.

3. **Carterocephalus silvicolus** *Northern Chequered Skipper*   333

   3a. ♂. Upf yellow with dark markings.
   3b. ♀. Upf dark markings larger.

4. **Ochlodes venatus** *Large Skipper*   336

   4a. *O. v. faunus* ♂. Upf sex brand prominent; unh markings pale yellow, obscure.
   4b. *O. v. faunus* f. *alpinus* ♀. Ups gc darker.

5. **Hesperia comma** *Silver-spotted Skipper*   336

   5a. ♂. Unh gc greenish, marking silver-white; sex-brand large.
   5b. ♀. Slightly larger, lacks sex-brand.

6. **Thymelicus lineola** *Essex Skipper*   335

   6a. ♂. Sex-brand short; antennal tip black.
   6b. ♀. Resembles ♂ but lacking sex-brand.

7. **Thymelicus sylvestris** *Small Skipper*   335

   7a. *T. s. sylvestris* ♂. Sex-brand longer; antennal tip fulvous.
   7b. *T. s. syriacus* ♂. Large; ups bright fulvous-yellow.

8. **Thymelicus hamza** *Moroccan Small Skipper*   334

   8a. ♂. Sex-brand long; uph veins not lined black.
   8b. ♀ Upf shaded darker above inner margin.

9. **Thymelicus acteon** *Lulworth Skipper*   333

   9a. *T. a. acteon* ♂. Upf postdiscal spots faint; gc often clouded grey.
   9b. *T. a. acteon* ♀. Ups gc darker (variable).
   9c. *T. a. christi* ♂. Small; ups with bright, distinct markings.

10. **Gegenes pumilio** *Pigmy Skipper*   337

    10a. ♂. Small; ups very dark, unmarked.
    10b. ♀. Ups paler; upf with small discal spots.

11. **Gegenes nostrodamus** *Mediterranean Skipper*   337

    11a. ♂. Larger; ups brown, unmarked; unh greyish.
    11b. ♀. Often larger; upf with pale discal spots.

12. **Borbo borbonica** *Zeller's Skipper*   338
    B. b. zelleri ♂. Ups very dark; upf discal markings vitreous.

F.G.B.B.E.—X

PYRGUS FRITILLARIUS *Safflower Skipper*

G: Dunkelbrauner Dickkopffalter   Sp: Ajedrezada
Range. S. and C. Europe, S. Russia to C. Asia.   Map 341

P. fritillarius Poda 1761 TL: Graz, Austria   Pl. 58
    syn: *carthami* Huebner 1819
Description. ♂fw 15/17mm., ups gc dark charcoal-grey with pale hair at
wing-bases; upf usual white markings well developed; uph submarginal
pale spots generally well defined; unh gc yellow-grey, *white markings
narrowly bordered darker grey with distinctive mottled appearance.* ♀
similar, often larger, ups pale downy hair absent.
Flight. End June to early September in a single prolonged brood.
Habitat. Flowery banks and meadows from lowlands to 5,000 ft. or more.
Larval food plants mallow, *Potentilla*, *Althaea*, etc.
Distribution. Generally distributed and often abundant in S. and C. Europe
northwards to Baltic. Absent from Britain, Denmark, Holland, NW.
Germany, NW. France, and Mediterranean islands. Reported from Sicily.
Variation. In S. Spain ups often brightly marked with larger white spots,
f. *nevadensis* Oberthur.

Similar species. *P. alveus* p. 313.

PYRGUS ANDROMEDAE *Alpine Grizzled Skipper*

Sw: Blomvisslare   Sp: Ajedrezada admirada
Range. Confined to Europe.   Map 342

P. andromedae Wallengren 1853 TL: Dovre, Norway   Pl. 58
Description. ♂fw 13/15mm., ups resembles *P. alveus*; upf white spots well
defined in standard pattern, *small spot present at base of s*2 with twin
longitudinal spots just below in s1b;
uph pale markings generally heavily
obscured; unh gc olive-brown to yellowish, discoidal spot large and extended basad along median vein, gc
dark grey in s1a–1b with prominent
round white spot in s1c and a short
white streak above it (Text fig). ♀
generally similar.
Flight. June/July in a single brood.
Habitat. Rough hillsides, moorland,
etc., often near water; flies from

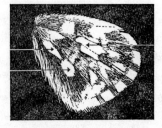

P. andromedae unh

5,000 ft. upwards in Pyrenees and Alps, at low altitudes in N. Norway
Larval food plants not known.
Distribution. Scandinavia, on main mountain system from Dovre to Nort
Cape, most common within the Arctic Circle. C. and S. Europe, occurs a
high levels on all principal mountain ranges from C. Pyrenees throug

Alps to Grossglockner and Julian Alps (Triglav) and northwards to
Bavaria; Bosnia and SE. Yugoslavia (Schar Planina), probably widely
distributed. Absent from Portugal, Spain, including Cantabrian Mts.,
E. Pyrenees (?), peninsular Italy and Greece, Tatra Mts. and Carpathians.

Similar species. *P. centaureae* below, upf lacks small white spot at base of
s2; unh dark grey, veins lined white. *P. cacaliae* below, ups white spots
generally very small; upf lacks white spot at base of s2 and twin white
marks below it; unh markings often rather indistinct.

PYRGUS CACALIAE   *Dusky Grizzled Skipper*

Sp: Ajedrezada oscura
Range. Confined to Europe.   Map 343

P. cacaliae Rambur 1839 TL: 'Alps'   Pl. 58
Description. ♂fw 13/15 mm., ups gc grey-brown; upf white spots often very
small, sometimes partly absent or minute, *no white spot at base of s2*; unh
gc grey to grey-brown, markings white, not sharply defined, inner margin
scarcely darker, a white spot in s1c and a short white streak above it. ♀
similar.
Flight. End June/July/August in a single brood, flight lasts about four
weeks.
Habitat. Only on high mountains at alpine levels from 6,000 ft. upwards.
Larval food plant *Tussilago farfara*.
Distribution. Alpes Maritimes and eastwards to Grosser Sau Alp and Gross
Glockner, northwards to Allgäuer Alps; recorded from Rilo Dagh in
Bulgaria and local in Rumania in S. Carpathians (Bucegi Mts.). Also re-
ported in Pyrenees.
Variation. Upf white spots larger in Carpathians.
Similar species. *P. andromedae* p. 322.

PYRGUS CENTAUREAE   *Northern Grizzled Skipper*

Sw: Klintvisslare
Range. N. Scandinavia and Arctic Russia, Altai Mts., Sajan Mts. N.
America widely distributed in arctic regions and extending to Appalach-
ians and through Rocky Mts. to S. Colorado (Pike's Peak).   Map 344

P. centaureae Rambur 1839 TL: Lapland   Pl. 58
Description. ♂fw 13/15 mm., ups dark grey, usually clouded with pale hair;
upf white spots well developed in usual pattern but *no spot at base of s2*;
uph white markings prominent, including pd spots, a conspicuous pale
mark in s7 near costa; unh gc rather dark grey, pale markings bold, *veins
lined white*, the large discal spot produced basad along median vein. ♀
similar.
Flight. June/July depending upon climate; flies in a single brood.

Habitat. Heathy bogs and tundra, from sea-level to 3,000 ft., in moun
tainous districts. Larval food plant *Rubus chamaemorus*.
Distribution. Fennoscandia, widely distributed except in cultivated souther
districts.

Similar species. *P. andromedae* p. 322.

SPIALIA SERTORIUS   *Red Underwing Skipper*
Sp: Sertorio
Range. N. Africa, S. Europe, W. Asia to Chitral, Altai Mts., Tibet an
Amur.   Map 34

S. sertorius sertorius Hoffmannsegg 1804 TL: Germany   Pl. 5
(Hemming 1936)
   syn: *sao* Huebner (invalid homonym); *hibiscae* Hemming 1936
Description. ♂fw 11/13mm., ups dark brown to black, white spots small
upf pd spots often absent in s4 or s5 or both, submarginal series generall
complete; uph discoidal spot small; unf dark grey; unh *brick red*, les
commonly yellowish, discal band of white spots sharply curved wit
large round spots on costa in s7, 8, *discoidal spot curved.* ♀ similar, usuall
larger.
Flight. April/May/June and July/August in two broods; in late broods ofte
very small.
Habitat. Rough ground and mountainsides from lowlands to 5,000 ft. i
its southern range. Larval food plants *Sanguisorba, Rubus, Potentilla.*
Distribution. Widely distributed from Spain and Portugal through S. an
C. Europe to 52°N, eastwards to Bavaria, Trieste, peninsular Italy. Re
ported from Czechoslovakia, N. Hungary and on two recent occasion
from Corsica. Absent from Britain, N. France, Belgium north o
Ardennes.

S. sertorius orbifer Huebner 1823 TL: not stated   Pl. 5
Description. ♂fw 11/14mm., ups white submarginal spots better defined
series often complete on fw; unf pale elongate mark at base of cell larger
unh pale olive-grey with large white markings, costal spot round, con
spicuous. ♀ similar, usually larger.
Flight and **Habitat** as for *S. s. sertorius.*
Distribution. E. Europe including much of Hungary (Buda), Rumania
Istria (Pola), Sicily and all Balkan countries. The distributional frontiers o
S.s. sertorius and *S.s. orbifer* are imperfectly known.

S. sertorius therapne Rambur 1832 TL: Corsica   Pl. 5
Description. ♂fw 9/10mm., the smallest European Skipper; ups dar
brown shaded yellow, pale markings all yellowish and rather large, esp
upf cell-spot which is more or less square; submarginal spots rarely present

uns red-brown with pale markings arranged as in *S. s. sertorius*. ♀ slightly larger.

Flight. April and September in two broods.

Habitat. Mountainous country to 5,000 ft. Larval food plant not known.

Distribution. Confined to Corsica and Sardinia. Typical *S.s. sertorius* has been reported from Corsica more than once, and specimens taken at Corte and Evisa have been described as being intermediate between it and *S.s. therapne*.

S. sertorius ali Oberthur 1881 TL: Morocco   Pl. 59

Description. ♂ fw 9/11 mm., ups markings slightly larger and faintly shaded yellow; *unh pale brown marbled with dark striae*, white markings sometimes nacreous, the discoidal spot prominent with pointed proximal and distal projections, veins conspicuously pale brown. ♀ similar.

Flight. April/June and September in two broods.

Habitat. Rough mountain sides and flowery slopes. Larval food plant not known.

Distribution. Morocco, in Middle Atlas, High Atlas and El Rif. Algeria. Tunisia. Widespread but rarely common.

Similar species. *S. phlomidis* below, larger, uph discoidal spot large and rectangular, unh large pale costal spot not round.

SPIALIA PHLOMIDIS *Persian Skipper*

Range. From S. Balkans through S. Russia and Asia Minor to Iran.

Map 346

S. phlomidis Herrich-Schaeffer 1845 TL: Sea of Marmora,   Pl. 59
Turkey

Description. ♂ fw 14/15 mm., ups gc black, markings as in *S. sertorius* but white spots larger, base of costa white, a white mark at base of s1b; uph discoidal spot large, rectangular, submarginal spot in s4 large; *unh gc pale olive-grey*, white markings well defined, *costal spot not round* but *linked to white discoidal spot*. ♀ similar.

Flight. June/early July. No record of a second brood.

Habitat. Flies at low or moderate altitudes in rough flowery places.

Distribution. Greece, SE. Yugoslavia and Albania. A very local species.

Similar species. *S. sertorius* p. 324. *S. doris* below, smaller, unh white mark in s7 well separated from large discoidal spot.

SPIALIA DORIS *Aden Skipper*

Range. High Atlas of Morocco, Egypt, Somaliland (Tajora, TL of *S. doris* Walker 1870) and Arabia to India.

Map 347

S. doris daphne Evans 1949 TL: High Atlas, Ziz Valley   Pl. 59

Description. ♂ fw 12 mm., very similar to *S. phlomidis* but smaller and fw more pointed; ups gc black, white markings large; upf white crescentic discoidal spot and subapical spots well marked, base of costa grey; uph discoidal spot large, square; uns gc dull greenish-grey, markings as on ups; unf costal area pale grey; *unh spot in s7 well separated from large white discoidal spot.* ♀ similar.

Flight. April/May and September.

Habitat. Dry valleys with sparse vegetation. Food plant in Egypt *Convolvulus lanatus.*

Distribution. Morocco, southern slopes of High Atlas, Ziz Valley at 3–4,000 ft., El Aioun du Drââ, 1,500 ft.

Similar species. *S. phlomidis* p. 325.

MUSCHAMPIA TESSELLUM *Tessellated Skipper*

Range. S. Balkans, S. Russia and eastwards to Iran and Amurland.

Map 348

M. tessellum Huebner 1803 TL: S. Russia Pl. 59

Description. ♂fw 16/18 mm., ups gc dark grey, *white markings large, fully developed on both wings*; upf a single pair of discal spots in s1b; uns gc pale olive-brown, darker at base of fw, white markings as above. ♀ similar.

Flight. End May/June in a single brood.

Habitat. Flowery meadows from lowlands to 3,000 ft. or more. Larval food plant not known.

Distribution. S. Balkans in Greece and SE. Yugoslavia.

Note. The form *nomas* Lederer, with uns of both wings nearly white and inconspicuous markings, has not yet been found in Europe although common in Asia Minor.

Similar species. *M. cribrellum* below, smaller, markings larger, upf normally with two pairs of discal spots in s1b.

MUSCHAMPIA CRIBRELLUM *Spinose Skipper*

Range. From Rumania across S. Russia to Altai Mts. and Amurland.

Map 349

M. cribrellum Eversmann 1841 TL: S. Russia Pl. 59

Description. ♂fw 13/16 mm., resembles *M. tessellum*, slightly smaller but markings larger, clear white and sharply defined; upf two pairs of discal spots in s1b; unh gc olive-yellow, *white markings large and tending to coalesce*, esp. those in submarginal area.

Flight. End May/June.

Habitat. No information.

Distribution. In Europe known only from W. Rumania on Pannonian plain at Cluj and Hunedoara.

Similar species. *M. tessellum* above.

MUSCHAMPIA PROTO   *Large Grizzled Skipper*

Sp: Polvillo dorado

Range. From N. Africa, Portugal and Spain through S. Europe to Asia
Minor.   Map 350

M. proto Ochsenheimer 1816   TL: Portugal   Pl. 59
Description. ♂fw 14/15mm.; ups gc dark grey, often somewhat obscured
by yellowish hair, discal spots white or yellowish, well developed, *submarginal markings lunular, indistinct*; unh gc variable, yellow-grey to
sandy-red, pale markings as above in white or sandy, often indistinct. ♀
similar, but ups without yellow hair.
Flight. April/May or later, in a single brood, but emergence sometimes
occurs at intervals throughout summer.
Habitat. Waste ground in lowlands or lower mountain slopes; to 5,500 ft.
in Morocco. Larval food plant *Phlomis*.
Distribution. Portugal. Spain (common). France, many localities in
Provence, esp. near coast, rare north of Hautes Alpes. Italy and Sicily.
Greece, on Mt. Taygetos, Mt. Parnassus, etc. Morocco. Algeria, Constantine, not rare.
Variation. In spring and early summer often large, with unh gc olive-grey;
in late summer often smaller with unh gc brown or red-brown. Large forms
with ♂fw 15/17mm., f. *fulvosatura* Verity Pl. 59, are common in Morocco.

Similar species. *M. mohammed* below, in N. Africa, ups markings more
yellow-brown; unh with some spaces filled dark brown, veins lined pale
brown. *M. leuzeae* p. 328.

MUSCHAMPIA MOHAMMED   *Barbary Skipper*

Range. Confined to Morocco and Algeria.   Map 351

M. mohammed Oberthur 1887   TL: Lambessa, Algeria   Pl. 59
Description. ♂fw 15/16mm., resembles *M. proto*; outer margin of hw
distinctly wavy; ups all markings better defined, yellowish; small sub-
marginal spots generally distinct; unh gc brown or red-brown, *veins paler*,
in pd area *some spaces filled dark brown* esp. s1c, 2, 3, white markings small,
sometimes partially ringed black, prominent pale discal spot usually
shining (nacreous).
Flight. March/June and August/September in two broods.
Habitat. Rough places and flowery banks at 5–6,000 ft. Food plant
Phlomis.
Distribution. Morocco, Azrou. Algeria, Aflou, Teniet-el-Haad, etc.
Variation. *First brood* small, ♂fw about 14mm., f. *caid* Le Cerf, unh gc
dark brown. The *second brood* described above is larger with unh red-
brown.

Similar species. *M. proto* above.

MUSCHAMPIA LEUZEAE   *Algerian Grizzled Skipper*
Range. Confined to Algeria.   Map 352

M. leuzeae Oberthur 1881   TL: Algeria   Pl. 59
Description. ♂fw 15mm., ups resembles *M. proto*; ups gc dark grey; upf
discal spot in cell very large; uph white markings reduced; uns both wings
suffused pale grey with rather obscure markings; *unh gc pale grey*, white
discal band narrow but regular and complete, submarginal pale spots
present, pattern faintly reticulate.
Flight. May and July.
Habitat. Flowery meadows.
Distribution. Algeria.

Similar species. *M. proto* p. 327, uph discal markings less complete; upf
discal cell-spot smaller; unh markings not reticulate.

CARCHARODUS ALCEAE   *Mallow Skipper*

Sp: Piquitos castana
Range. From N. Africa and Spain through S. and C. Europe to C. Asia.
                                                                    Map 353

C. alceae Esper 1780   TL: Germany   Pl. 59
Description. ♂fw 13/16mm., ups gc brown marbled darker brown and
grey; upf hyaline cell-spot very narrow, sometimes absent; *uph with vague
paler discal and pd markings*; uns gc paler brown; *unf without hair-tuft*;
unh a small white or yellow spot near base of cell, spots in s 1c, 2, 4, 5 and
7 forming a discal row, traces of submarginal series. ♀ often larger, otherwise similar.
Flight. April/May and later in two or three broods throughout summer.
Habitat. Flowery banks, etc., to 5,000 ft. usually in hilly country. Larval
food plants *Malva, Althaea, Hibiscus*, etc.
Distribution. N. Africa, widely distributed in Morocco, Algeria and Tunisia. S. and C. Europe to 52°N. Absent from Denmark, Fennoscandia,
Baltic countries, N. Germany and Britain.
Variation. Seasonal changes may be marked. Specimens of the *first brood*
are usually dark; in warm districts *second and third broods* are often
paler brown. In S. Italy, Sicily, etc., the last brood (September) is very
dark and small, ♂fw 13/14mm.

Similar species. *C. flocciferus* p. 330, hw markings better defined, esp. uph
discoidal spot; ♂ with hair pencil on unf from v1 near base.

CARCHARODUS LAVATHERAE   *Marbled Skipper*

G: Ziestfalter   Sp: Piquitos clara
Range. From N. Africa through S. Europe to Asia Minor.   Map 354

C. lavatherae Esper 1780 TL: S. France Pl. 59

Description. ♂fw 14/17mm., upf light olive-brown often suffused greenish and marbled darker, with white streaks at outer margin esp. in s4 and s5, vitreous spots prominent esp. cell-spot and spot in s2; uph darker with *conspicuous white discal spots*, pd spots sagittate, pointed basad; uns very pale greenish-white, slightly darker in discal areas, markings vestigial. ♂unf without hair-tuft. ♀ similar.

Flight. May/June or later, usually a single brood, but second broods have been reported.

Habitat. Dry flowery slopes esp. on calcareous soils, usually in hilly districts, from lowlands to 5,000 ft. or more. Larval food plant *Stachys*.

Distribution. S. and C. districts of Europe to 50°N, local and scarce N. of the Alps. Absent from Corsica, Sardinia, Sicily. N. Africa, widely distributed through the Middle Atlas in Morocco, Algeria and Tunisia.

Variation. In Spain and S. Balkans gc may be darker, more grey-brown.

CARCHARODUS BOETICUS *Southern Marbled Skipper*

Sp: Piquitos

Range. N. Africa, SW. Europe and C. Italy; Asia Minor to Iran.

Map 355

C. boeticus boeticus Rambur 1839 TL: Andalusia Pl. 59
   syn: *marrubii* Rambur 1840

Description. ♂fw 13/14mm., upf grey, slightly marbled darker grey-brown, a narrow pale grey discal band limiting a darker basal area, hyaline spots not large; uph darker brown, usually with small pale basal spot and discal and pd series of pale spots and lunules, the discoidal spot generally prominent; unf gc grey-brown with paler veins; unh pale yellow-grey, *veins, basal spots, discal spots and pd lunules* all almost white and *together producing a reticulate pattern*; fringes chequered. ♀ similar. ♂unf *with hair-tuft*.

Flight. May to September/October in two or three broods.

Habitat. Rough places and flowery slopes to 5,000 ft., usually in hot localities, most frequent among mountains. Larval food plants *Marrubium vulgare, Ballota foetida*, etc.

Distribution. Portugal. Spain, south of Pyrenees and Cantabrian Mts. France in E. Pyrenees and Provence. Switzerland in a single brood in Valais. N. Italy, Susa, and very local in Apennines and Sicily. Records from Yugoslavia and Greece need confirmation.

Variation. Colour varies through the seasons; in *first brood* (May) dark on ups; *second brood* (end June) paler grey-brown, often inclining to sandy; *late broods* (August/September) light sandy brown. The hair-tuft on unf also varies, being large and dark in early summer but pale sandy-brown and sometimes small in late broods.

C. boeticus stauderi Reverdin 1913 TL: El Kantara, Algeria   Pl. 5
Description. ♂fw 13/14mm., like *C. b. boeticus* in size and appearance; unl
pale veins and lattice pattern usually rather less well developed. The dis
tinctive character is a slight difference in the structure of the male geni
talia.
Flight and Habit as for *C. boeticus*.
Distribution. N. Africa, from Morocco to Cyrenaica, flying in the Middl
Atlas. Not known from Europe.

Similar species. *C. flocciferus* below and *C. orientalis* below, unh marking
are not reticulate.

CARCHARODUS FLOCCIFERUS *Tufted Skipper*
Sp: Piquitos serrana
Range. From Spain across S. Europe to Bulgaria.   Map. 35

C. flocciferus Zeller 1847 TL: Sicily   Pl. 5
  syn: *alchymillae* Hemming 1936; *altheae* Huebner 1803 (invali
homonym.)
Description. ♂fw 14/16mm.; ups gc dark grey-brown marbled with darke
striae which form a wide band across fw before the vitreous cell-spot
uph basal and discal spots pale, pd markings vague; unf grey-brown, paler
with white marginal striae and *prominent dark hair-tuft*; *unh grey-brown*
white markings better defined than on ups, including small submargina
spots. ♀ similar.
Flight. End May/June and end July/August in two broods.
Habitat. Flowery banks and rough ground esp. among mountains to
6,000 ft., less common at low levels. Larval food plants *Marrubium,
Stachys.*
Distribution. S. and C. Europe to 48°N, somewhat farther N. along Rhine
into Baden and eastwards to SE. Yugoslavia and Bulgaria. Reports from
Greece need confirmation. Absent or scarce in N. and W. France, S.
Spain, Portugal, Corsica and Sardinia.

Similar species. *C. alceae* p. 328; *C. boeticus* p. 329; *C. orientalis* below.

CARCHARODUS ORIENTALIS *Oriental Skipper*
Range. From Montenegro and Greece widely distributed in W. Asia to
Iran.   Map 357

C. orientalis Reverdin 1913 TL: S. Greece   Pl. 59
Description. ♂fw 14/15mm., ups gc variable, usually grey rather than
brown, often slightly yellowish; upf markings as in *C. flocciferus*; uph white
discal and submarginal markings well developed, often complete; unf gc
grey; *unh gc pale grey with obscure white markings.* ♀ similar. ♂unf dark
hair-tuft generally conspicuous.
Flight. April onwards, probably in two broods.

Habitat. Flowery meadows usually in mountainous country, to 4,000 ft. Larval food plant not recorded.

Distribution. Montenegro, Albania, Greece.

Note. Perhaps better regarded as a subspecies of *C. flocciferus*, but genitalia are distinct. Specimens intermediate between *C. flocciferus* and *C. orientalis* have been reported.

Similar species. *C. flocciferus* p. 330, unh gc dark grey-brown. *C. boeticus* p. 329.

ERYNNIS TAGES *Dingy Skipper*

F: La Grisette Sw: Skogssmygare G: Dunkler Dickkopffalter Sp: Cervantes

Range. Europe to 62°N, thence across Russia and Siberia to China.

Map 358

E. tages Linnaeus 1758 TL: Europe Pl. 59

Description. ♂fw 13/14mm., ups gc brown; upf three white dots on costa near apex, *complete series of white marginal dots*, oblique sub-basal and pd sinuous dark brown bands enclosing powdered pale grey area; uph white marginal dots as on fw and white or yellowish pd spots in some specimens; uns paler brown with white marginal dots on both wings, otherwise unmarked. ♀ similar. ♂ with costal fold.

Flight. May/June or later with a partial or complete second brood in some southern localities.

Habitat. Flowery banks to 6,000 ft., often associated with calcareous soils. Larval food plants *Lotus corniculatus*, *Eryngium*, *Coronilla*, etc.

Distribution. S. and C. Europe to Britain and S. Scandinavia, local in N. Germany and rare in Lithuania. Ireland, in limestone districts of Co. Clare, Galway and Co. Mayo, brightly variegated, ups dark brown and pale grey, f. *baynesi* Huggins Pl. 59.

Variation. Colour forms range from typical dark brown through medium brown, f. *brunnea* Tutt, to grey, f. *clarus* Caradja. Of these, f. *brunnea*, with vestigial ups markings, is very common in S. Europe.

Similar species. *E. marloyi* below (Greece only), upf dark transverse bands distinct, ♂ without costal fold.

ERYNNIS MARLOYI *Inky Skipper*

Range. S. Balkans through Asia Minor and Syria to Iran and Chitral.

Map 359

E. marloyi Boisduval 1834 TL: S. Greece Pl. 59

Description. ♂fw 14/15mm., ups dark brown, *marginal white dots inconspicuous or absent*; upf narrow black sub-basal and oblique pd transverse black bands mixed with grey, with two or three white dots before apex;

uph unmarked; unf white dots before apex as on ups. ♀ often larger, up
gc paler. ♂ without costal fold.

Flight. May/June, perhaps a second brood in some places.

Habitat. Mountainous districts to 6,000 ft. or more. Larval food plant no
recorded.

Distribution. In Europe only in Greece, Albania and SE. Yugoslavia.

Similar species. *E. tages* p. 331.

HETEROPTERUS MORPHEUS   *Large Chequered Skipper*

F: Le Miroir   G: Finsterling   Sp: Espejitos   Sw: Spegelsmygare
Range. From N. Spain through much of S. and C. Europe and C. Asia to
Amurland and Korea.   Map 36(

H. morpheus   Pallas 1771   TL: Samara, S. Russia   Pl. 6(
  syn: *steropes* Schiffermueller 1775

Description. ♂ fw 16/18 mm., ups dark brown; upf with three or four smal
yellow pre-apical spots near costa; uph unmarked; unf with yellow mark
ings at apex and along outer margin; unh gc yellow with twelve larg
whitish black-ringed spots, wide black band down inner margin an
black marginal line. ♀ upf yellow apical markings larger; fringes chequere
black and white; uns as in ♂.

Flight. End June/July in a single brood.

Habitat. Shady roads and woodland walks to 1,500 ft. Larval food plan
Brachypodium and other grasses, esp. *Molinia coerulea*.

Distribution. Local in widely dispersed colonies. Spain in coastal area nea
Santander. France, only N. and W. of Central Massif and S. to Basse
Pyrénées. Switzerland in warm valleys of Ticino. Italy, in Piedmont and E
to Alto Adige and Gorizia, also in Lazio, not rare in damp places. Mor
widely distributed in N. Germany and Lithuania. Bosnia, Serbia and
Rumania. Recorded also from Jersey, NW. Germany, Holland and
Denmark. Throughout its extensive range geographical variation is negli-
gible.

CARTEROCEPHALUS PALAEMON   *Chequered Skipper*

F: L'Echiquier   Sw: Gulfläckig Glanssmygare   G: Grosswegerichfalter
Range. From W. Europe across C. and N. Asia to Japan; N. America.

                                                                    Map 361

C. palaemon   Pallas 1771   TL: Russia   Pl. 6(
Description. ♂ fw 14 mm., *upf dark brown with large basal and pd dark yellow
spots*, small submarginal spots in series; uph one basal and two disca
spots all large and a row of small pd spots, all yellow; unh dark brownish
powdered yellow, yellow markings as on ups but paler on hw. ♀ ups g
more grey, markings in paler yellow.

Flight. June/July in a single brood.

Habitat. Usually in light woodland, to 5,000 ft. in S. Alps. Larval food plants grasses esp. *Bromus*.
Distribution. Widely distributed in NE. and C. Europe, extending across N. and C. France with colonies in Pyrenees, England and Scotland. A very local species absent from large areas including Denmark, peninsular Italy, SE. France and Spain. In Balkans recorded from Bosnia, Hercegovina and Bulgaria.
Similar species. *C. silvicolus* below, upf gc yellow with dark markings; uph with an additional yellow spot near costa.

CARTEROCEPHALUS SILVICOLUS
Northern Chequered Skipper

Sw: Svartfläckig Glanssmygare
Range. Fennoscandia and through Siberia to Amurland and Kamschatka.
Map 362

C. silvicolus   Meigen 1829   TL: Brunswick, Germany   Pl. 60
   syn: *sylvius* Knoch 1781   (invalid homonym)
Description. ♂fw 12/13mm., *upf gc light yellow with discal and very small submarginal spots* all black; uph gc black with yellow discal and submarginal spots arranged as in *C. palaemon* but with prominent *additional spot near costa*; uns markings as on ups. ♀upf dark markings greatly extended, basal area and outer margin dark.
Flight. End June/July in a single brood.
Habitat. Woodland and warm valleys with abundant vegetation at low altitudes. Food plants *Cynosurus* and other woodland grasses.
Distribution. Fennoscandia, not in mountainous districts, extending through Baltic countries including N. Poland, to Neubrandenburg and Holstein.
Similar species. *C. palaemon* p. 332.

THYMELICUS ACTEON   *Lulworth Skipper*

Sp: Dorada oscura
Range. From Canary Islands and N. Africa across S. and C. Europe to Cyprus, Lebanon and Asia Minor.   Map 363

T. acteon acteon   Rottemburg 1775   TL: Lansberg-an-der-   Pl. 60
Warthe, Germany
Description. ♂fw 11/13mm., ups gc dusky fulvous; upf a yellow streak in cell and a *bowed series of small yellow pd spots* in s3–9, often very obscure; uph unmarked; uns gc uniformly orange-yellow, except the black base of s1 on unf. ♀ similar. In both sexes palpi are white below with orange hair in front; hw with distinct anal lobe. ♂ with prominent sex-brand on upf from wing-base across v1 to v3.
Flight. May or later in a single brood.

Habitat. Grass banks and meadows to 5,000 ft., usually in damp places. Food plant Brome grass.
Distribution. Local in S. and C. Europe to 48°N; England only near coast in Dorset, Devon; rare or occasional in Alps of N. Italy; absent from Corsica and Sardinia.
Variation. In some districts gc is paler, more yellow, esp. in SW. Alps; gc much darker in NW. Spain and Portugal f. *virescens* Agenjo.

T. acteon oranus Evans 1949   TL: Algeria
Description. ♂fw 10/11mm., ups gc darker, slightly greenish with yellow marking distinct, esp. in ♀ in which a yellow discal band on upf is usual; uns both wings sometimes slightly shaded grey.
Flight. May or later in a single brood.
Habitat. Grassy banks, etc., in damp places in Atlas Mts. at 4–6,000 ft.
Distribution. Morocco. Algeria. Tunisia. Widely distributed.

T. acteon christi Rebel 1894   TL: Canary Islands   Pl. 60
Description. ♂fw 10/11mm., ups gc darker, all markings better defined in orange-yellow, including uph discal band; uns disc of fw orange with indistinct markings as on upf, dark grey in s1; unh s1b and s1c orange.
Flight. April and throughout summer.
Habitat. Grass banks, etc., to 6,000 ft. or more.
Distribution. Canary Islands, recorded from Tenerife, Gran Canary, La Palma, Gomera.

Similar species. *T. hamza* below, ♂ups gc brighter foxy-red; upf lacks pale pd spots; unh grey except fulvous inner marginal area.

THYMELICUS HAMZA   *Moroccan Small Skipper*
Range. N. Africa, Asia Minor, Cyprus and Turkestan.   Map 364

T. hamza Oberthur 1876   TL: Oran, Algeria   Pl. 60
Description. ♂fw 11/13mm., resembles *T. acteon*; ups bright fulvous; upf with slightly paler fulvous shade through cell and beyond, no trace of pd band; sex-brand continuous from v1–v3; uns bright fulvous; unh *greyish between v2 and v7*. ♀ similar, ups paler.
Flight. May/June in a single brood.
Habitat. Flowery places and rough slopes at 5–6,000 ft. Larval food plants not known.
Distribution. Local in Morocco, Algeria and Tunisia. Not reported from Europe.

Similar species. *T. acteon* p. 333.

THYMELICUS LINEOLA *Essex Skipper*
Am: European Skipper   Sw: Litten Tåtelsmygare
G: Schwarzkolbiger Dickkopffalter   Sp: Dorada linea corta
Range. From N. Africa across Europe and C. Asia to Amurland; also in
N. America, probably introduced.   Map 365

T. lineola lineola Ochsenheimer 1808   TL: Germany   Pl. 60
Description. ♂fw 12/14mm., ups gc fulvous; upf unmarked except for
narrow dark inconspicuous sex-brand, broken at v2, and not reaching v3;
unf fulvous, apex usually yellow-grey, a conspicuous black basal mark
below cell; unh pale yellow-grey with fulvous streak in s2. *Tip of antenna
black* beneath. ♀ similar.
Flight. End May to August in a single brood.
Habitat. Grassy banks and meadows to 6,000 ft. Larval food plants
various grasses.
Distribution. Widespread in S. and C. Europe to 62°N, including S.
England.

T. lineola semicolon Staudinger 1892   TL: Lambessa, Algeria
Description. ♂fw 13mm., ups resembles *T. l. lineola* but veins conspicuously
lined black beyond cell and dark marginal borders wider; upf sex-brand
larger; uns as in *T. l. lineola.* ♀ups gc paler with slight general fuscous
suffusion.
Flight and **Habitat** as for *T.l. lineola.*
Distribution. Widely distributed in Morocco and Algeria; not recorded
from Tunisia.
Variation. In some southern European localities extremely small with
♀fw 10mm. Large races, ♂fw 14mm., are common in E. Europe.
Similar species. *T. sylvestris* below, ups gc clear orange with little dark
suffusion along veins; in ♂upf black sex-brand conspicuous, slightly
curved; tip of antenna fulvous beneath.

THYMELICUS SYLVESTRIS *Small Skipper*
F: La Bande Noire   G: Ockergelber Braundickkopffalter
Sp: Dorada linea larga   Sw: Stor Tåtelsmygare
Range. From Morocco and Spain across Europe and Asia Minor to Iran.
                                                                    Map 366

T. sylvestris Poda 1761   TL: Graz, Austria   Pl. 60
    syn: *flava* Pontoppidan 1763; *thaumas* Hufnagel 1766
Description. ♂fw 13/15mm., ups clear fulvous yellow, outer margins and
veins lightly lined black; upf *conspicuous black sex-brand* below cell *from
v1 to v3*; uph costa dark grey, otherwise unmarked; uns fulvous, tip of fw
and most of hw greyish. *Tip of antenna fulvous* beneath. ♀ similar.
Flight. June or later in a single brood.

Habitat. Grass banks and meadows to 6,000 ft. or more. Larval food plants various grasses, *Aira, Piptatherum, Holcus,* etc.
Distribution. Generally common throughout Europe to 56°N. N. Africa, common in Atlas Mts. in Morocco and Algeria, not recorded from Tunisia. Absent from N. England.
Variation. Very large, brilliant races occur in S. Europe, ♂fw 15/16mm., f. *syriacus* Tutt Pl. 60.
Similar species. *T. lineola* p. 335.

HESPERIA COMMA *Silver-spotted Skipper*

F: le Comma Sw: Allmän Ängssmygare G: Kommafalter
Sp: Dorada manchas blancas
Range. From N. Africa and Spain through C. and N. Europe and temperate Asia to Western N. America. Map 367

H. comma comma Linnaeus 1758 TL: Sweden (Verity 1940) Pl. 60
Description. ♂fw 14/15mm., ups gc fulvous with wide dark brown borders on both wings; upf veins black, a conspicuous ridged black sex-brand, and small yellow sub-apical spots; hw anal lobe pronounced; uph discal area fulvous, with small paler pd spots; unf apex olive-green, pale spots as on ups; *unh olive-green with silvery discal spots.* ♀ups usually darker with markings more prominent; uns resembles ♂.
Flight. July/August in a single brood.
Habitat. Grass banks and meadows, on calcareous soils, from sea-level to 7,000 ft. or more. Larval food plants various grasses, esp. tussock grass.
Distribution. Widely distributed in suitable localities but local in Europe; rare in S. Spain; absent from S. Italy, Corsica, Sardinia, Ireland. In England, confined to chalk hills in S.

H. comma benuncas Oberthur 1912 TL: Algeria
Description. Unh white spots slightly larger and fused into an irregular pd band, veins often lined white. ♀ups fulvous markings sometimes extensive.
Flight. July.
Habitat. Mountainous districts of Morocco, Taohzeft Pass; Algeria, Djebel Aures, etc.
Similar species. *O. venatus* below, unh yellowish, pale markings indistinct.

OCHLODES VENATUS *Large Skipper*

F: le Sylvain Sw: Stor Ängssmygare
G: Rostfarbiger Dickkopffalter Sp: Dorada orla ancha
Range. From W. Europe through temperate Asia to China (TL of *Hesperia venata* Bremer and Grey 1857) and Japan. Map 368

O. venatus faunus Turati 1905 TL: Italy and S. France **Pl. 60**
  syn: *sylvanus* Esper 1779 (invalid homonym)

Description. ♂fw 14/17mm.; upf bright fulvous with wide dark outer margin, veins dark, a prominent black sex-brand without central ridge; uph fulvous with dark margins and a few faintly paler discal spots; unf paler fulvous with markings as on ups; *unh yellow*, variable discal spots faint, markings as on uph. ♀upf fulvous, base dusky and disc with series of dusky markings; uph dusky brown with series of paler discal spots; uns as in ♂.

Flight. June/July/August, in northern range a single brood, two or three broods reported from S. Italy.

Habitat. Grass banks and meadows to 6,000 ft. Larval food plants grasses, e.g., *Festuca, Poa, Triticum*, etc., also *Juncus*.

Distribution. Generally common throughout Europe to 64°N; records from Ireland need confirmation. Absent from all Mediterranean islands except Sicily.

Variation. In some northern localities and at high altitudes often smaller and ups gc darker, f. *alpinus* Hoffmann Pl. 60.

Similar species. *H. comma* p. 336.

GEGENES NOSTRODAMUS *Mediterranean Skipper*

Sp: Veloz de las Rieras
Range. From coastal districts of Mediterranean through Egypt and Asia Minor to Turkestan and India. Map 369

G. nostrodamus Fabricius 1793 TL: Morocco (Barbaria) **Pl. 60**
Description. ♂fw 15/16mm., ups *pale brown, unmarked*; unf paler with two or three indistinct pale discal spots; unh pale sandy-brown unmarked fading to white along inner margin. ♀upf with angled series of pale discal spots, very small on costa, larger in s1b, s2 and s3, repeated on uns; unh as in ♂, faint paler discal spots sometimes present.

Flight. May/October, most common in late summer.

Habitat. Hot dry paths and rocky gorges, usually at low altitudes, most often near sea. Larval food plant grasses.

Distribution. Recorded from many localities around Mediterranean coast including NE. coast of Morocco at Rabat, etc. Occurs in Spain N. to Saragossa.

Similar species. *G. pumilio* below, ups very dark brown. *B. borbonica* p. 338, ups very dark with vitreous spots.

GEGENES PUMILIO *Pigmy Skipper*

Range. From coastal districts of Mediterranean eastwards to Iran and Himalaya; also very generally throughout Africa. Map 370

G. pumilio Hoffmannsegg 1804   TL: Naples   Pl. 60
   syn: *pygmaeus* Cyrilli 1787 (invalid homonym); *aetna* Boisduval 1840;
   lefebvrei Rambur 1842
Description. ♂fw 14mm., outer margin of fw straight or slightly convex;
ups very dark brown, unmarked; uns pale grey-brown with indistinct pale pd
spots on both wings. ♀ups gc slightly paler with small indistinct pale pd
spots on fw; uns pale grey-brown, both wings with small pale pd spots.
Flight. April/October, flies throughout summer.
Habitat. At low altitudes, often resting on hot paths or rocks in full sun.
Larval food plant grasses.
Distribution. Recorded from many localities around the Mediterranean
coasts.

Similar species. *G. nostrodamus* p. 337; *B. borbonica* below.

BORBO BORBONICA   *Zeller's Skipper*
Sp: Veloz fenestrada
Range. Occasional along S. Mediterranean coast and widely distributed
in Egypt, Syria, Africa, Mauritius and Reunion (TL of *Hesperia borbonica*
Boisduval 1833).   Map 371

B. borbonica zelleri Lederer 1855   TL: Syria   Pl. 60
Description. ♂fw 14/15mm., palpi pale yellow-brown below; ups dark
brown; upf *with pd series of hyaline spots*, largest spot in s2, spot in s1b
yellow; uph unmarked; unf base and disc brown, apex and all hind-wing
rather bright yellow-brown, markings as on ups. ♀ generally larger and
similar, unh often with a few small pale spots.
Flight. September/October.
Habitat. At low altitudes near sea-coast.
Distribution. Algeria, Hussein Day. Morocco at Rabat. Gibraltar. There
are few Mediterranean records with satisfactory data.

Similar species. ♀*G. pumilio* p. 337, ♀*G. nostrodamus* p. 337, spots on fw
not hyaline.

Bibliography

Albania. REBEL, & ZERNY H. 1931. *Die Lepidopterenfauna Albaniens.* Denkschriften der mathem. naturw. Klasse *103*: 37-161 (Acad. d. Wissensch. in Wien).

Algeria. OBERTHUR, C. 1914. *Faune des Lépidoptères de la Barbarie.* Études de Lépidopterologie Comparée *10*: 1-459. Rennes.

Balkans. REBEL, H. 1903. *Studien über die Lepidopterenfauna der Balkanländer* 1. Bulgarien und Ostrumelien. Ann. naturh. Hofmuseum Wien *18*: 123-346.
2. Bosnien und Herzegovina. id. 1904. *19*: 97-377.
3. Montenegro. Albanien etc. id. 1913. *27*: 281-334.

Balearic Islands. REBEL, H. 1926. *Lepidopteren von den Balearen.* Iris. Dresden. *40*: 135-141; id. 1934. *48*: 122-126.

Belgium. HACKRAY, J. & SARLET, L. G. 1969 et seq. *Catalogue des Macrolépidoptères de Belgique.* Lambillionea, Suppl. to vol. *67* etc.

Corsica. LEESTMANS, R. 1965. *Étude biogéographique sur les Lépidoptères diurnes de la Corse.* Alexanor *4*: 17 et seq.

Crete. TRONIÇEK, E. 1949. *Contribution to the Knowledge of the Lepidopterological fauna of Crete.* Acta Ent. Mus. Nat. Prague *26* (358): pp. 15.

Czechoslovakia. HRUBY, K. 1964. *Prodromus Lepidopter Slovenska.* pp. 1-962. Bratislava.

Denmark. See under Finland.

Estonia. THOMSON, E. 1967. Die Grossschmetterlinge Estlands. Stollhamm.
VIIDALEPP, J. & MOLS, T. 1963. *Eesti Suurliblikate Määraja.* Eesti NSV Teaduste Akadeemia. Tartu.

Finland. NORDSTRÖM, F. 1955. *De Fennoskandiska Dagfjärilarnas Utbredning.* Acta Univ. Lund (2), *51.* Butterflies only, with excellent distribution maps.
LANGER, T. W. 1957. *Systematisk oversigt over de danske storsommerfugles* . . . Saertryk af Flora og Fauna 63:1-26. (English Summary).

France. LHOMME, L. 1923-1935. *Catalogue des Lépidoptères de France et de Belgique.* *1*: 1-114. Le Carriol. Lot. Out of date but still the standard work for the Lepidoptera of France.

Germany. FORSTER, W. & WOHLFAHRT, T. A. *Die Schmetterlinge Mitteleuropas.* *2*: 1-126. 1955. Tagfalter. Stuttgart.

Great Britain. HOWARTH, T. G. 1973. *South's British Butterflies.* pp. 1-320. London.

Greece. COUTSIS, J. G. 1969. *List of Grecian Butterflies.* Entomologist *102*: 264-268 id. 1972. Additional Records. Ent. Rec. 84: 145-151. A Collector's list with localities, etc.

Holland. LEMPKE, B. J. 1936, 1937. Tijdschr. Ent. *79*: 238-15, with supplements.

Italy. VERITY, R. 1940-1953. *Le Farfalle Diurne d'Italia.* 5 vol. Florence.

Morocco. OBERTHUR, C. 1922. *Les Lépidoptères du Maroc.* Études de Lépidopterologie Comparée *19*: 1-403. Rennes. Many coloured figures.

Hungary. GOZMANY, L. 1968. *Nappali Lepkek—Diurna.* Fauna Hungariae 91. pp. 1-204. Budapest.

Norway. See under Finland.

Poland. ROMANISZYN, J. 1929. *Fauna Motyli Polski* (Fauna Lepidopterorum Poloniae). pp. 1-555. Krakow.

Portugal. ZERKOWITZ, A. 1946. *The Lepidoptera of Portugal.* J. New York Ent. Soc. 54:51-87.

Pyrenees. RONDOU, P. 1932-1935. *Catalogue des Lépidoptères des Pyrénées.* Ann. Soc. Ent. Fr. *101*: 165-222. *105*: 253-255.
OBERTHUR, C. 1923. *Catalogue des Lépidoptères des Pyrénées-Orientales.* Études de Lépidopterologie Comparée 20: 1-54. Rennes.

Rumania. NICULESCU, E. 1961-1970. *Fauna Repub. Pop. Romine.* Lepidoptera 11: fasc. 5-7, 10. Bucharest (Rumanian Language).

Sardinia. HARTIG, F. & AMSEL, H. G. 1951. *Lepidoptera Sardinica.* Fragmenta Est *1*:1-152. Rome.

Scandinavia. See under Finland.

Sicily. MARIASI, M. 1939. *Fauna Lepidopterorum Siciliae.* Mem. Soc. ent. Ital *17*: 129-187.

Spain. MANLEY, W. B. L. & ALLCARD, H. G. 1970. *A Field Guide to the Butterflie. and Burnets of Spain.* Hampton, Middlesex.

Sweden. NORDSTRÖM, F. & WAHLGREN, E. 1935-1941. *Svenska Fjärilar.* pp. 1-353 Stockholm.

Switzerland. VORBRODT, K. & MÜLLER-RUTZ, J. 1911-1914 and later supplements *Die Schmetterlinge der Schweiz.* Bern.

Tunisia. CNEOUR, A. 1954. Macrolepidoptéres de Tunisie. 1-2: Bull. Soc. Sci. Nat Tunis. *7*: 207-239.

Yugoslavia. See under Balkans.

The following foreign editions of the present Field Guide have so far appeared. Thei translators have been at liberty to modify the text, and have in many cases introduce subspecies which we did not think necessary to include:

Denmark	*Europas dagsommerfugle*	Gads Forlag	Niels Peder Kristenser Svend Kaaber Niels L. Wolff
Holland	*Elseviers vlindergids*	Elsevier	B. J. Lempke, J. Huisenga
Germany	*Schmetterlinge Europas*	Paul Parey	Dr. Forster
France	*Guide des Papillons d'Europe*	Delachaux & Niestle	P. C. Rougeot
Norway	*En Felthandbok Sommerfugler*	Tiden Norsk Forlag	Magne Opheim
Spain	*Guia de Campo de las Mariposas de Espana y de Europa*	Omega	Olegario Escola
Sweden	*Europas fjärilar Dagfjärilar*	Almqvist & Wiksell	Per Douwes

Distribution Maps

Distribution maps are necessary in order to show accurately the ranges of the species without regard to national frontiers. On these maps the black areas show breeding ranges of each species so far as these are known. It has not been possible to make a distinction between resident breeding species and summer visitors, of which several occur regularly in central and northern Europe, i.e. immigrant species which arrive and breed every summer, but which are not able to survive through winter in northern regions. Many migrants disperse far beyond their breeding ranges and such additional areas of dispersal are shown by parallel black lines. In N. Africa, in Tripolitania, Cyrenaica and Fezzan, where some Palearctic butterflies are known to occur although actual distribution is not understood, the presence of such species is indicated by dots.

The maps are intended to show where each butterfly may be expected to occur in suitable habitats. They do not always show the extreme limits of occasional dispersal ("strays"), nor do they show areas of earlier occurrence in which today the species is extinct.

The Atlantic Islands are not included on the maps, but a butterfly's presence on any of them is indicated by initial letters as follows: **C**= Canary Islands; **M**=Madeira; **A**=Azores.

The preparation of distribution maps is extremely laborious, often difficult, and without doubt some maps now presented will be imperfect in details. Accurate corrections can be made only by entomologists with personal knowledge of the countries concerned and suggestions for improvements will be welcomed by Dr. L. G. Higgins, Focklesbrook Farm, Chobham, Woking, Surrey, England.

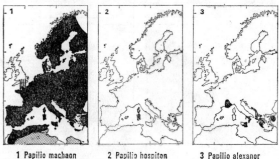

1 Papilio machaon   2 Papilio hospiton   3 Papilio alexanor

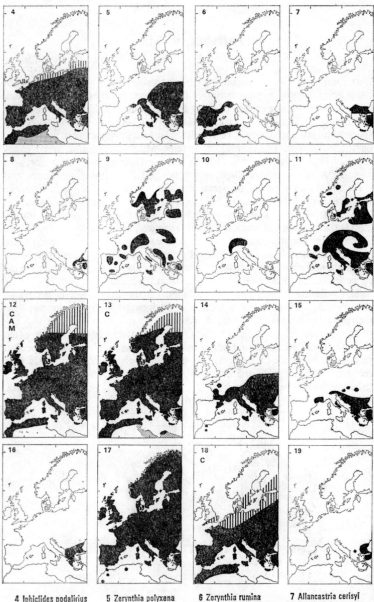

4 Iphiclides podalirius   5 Zerynthia polyxena   6 Zerynthia rumina   7 Allancastria cerisyi
8 Archon apollinus   9 Parnassius apollo   10 Parnassius phoebus   11 Parnassius mnemosyne
12 Pieris brassicae   13 Pieris rapae   14 Pieris mannii   15 Pieris ergane
16 Pieris krueperi   17 Pieris napi   18 Pontia daplidice   19 Pontia chloridice

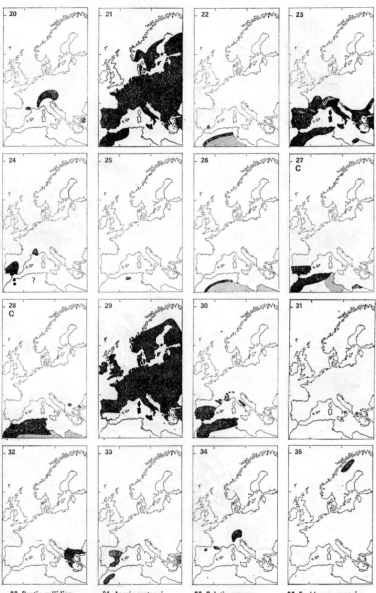

20 Pontia callidice
24 Euchloe tagis
28 Elphinstonia charlonia
32 Anthocharis gruneri

21 Aporia crataegi
25 Euchloe pechi
29 Anthocharis cardamines
33 Zegris eupheme

22 Colotis evagore
26 Euchloe falloui
30 Anthocharis belia
34 Colias phicomone

23 Euchloe a. ausonia (cross hatch); E.a. crameri (black)
27 Euchloe belemia
31 Anthocharis damone
35 Colias nastes

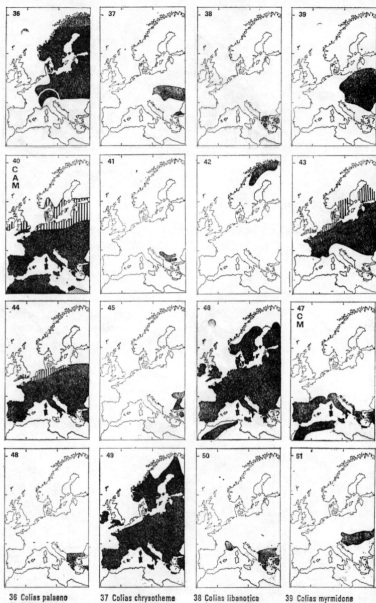

36 Colias palaeno
37 Colias chrysotheme
38 Colias libanotica
39 Colias myrmidone
40 Colias crocea
41 Colias balcanica
42 Colias hecla
43 Colias hyale
44 Colias australis
45 Colias erate
46 Gonepteryx rhamni
47 Gonepteryx cleopatra
48 Gonepteryx farinosa
49 Leptidea sinapis
50 Leptidea duponcheli
51 Leptidea morsei

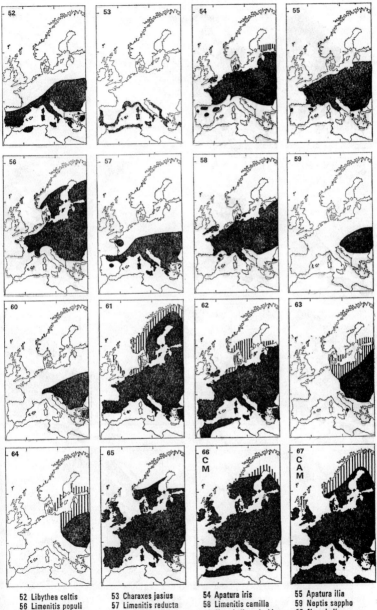

52 Libythea celtis
56 Limenitis populi
60 Neptis rivularis
64 Nymphalis vau-album

53 Charaxes jasius
57 Limenitis reducta
61 Nymphalis antiopa
65 Inachis io

54 Apatura iris
58 Limenitis camilla
62 Nymphalis polychloros
66 Vanessa atalanta

55 Apatura ilia
59 Neptis sappho
63 Nymphalis
   xanthomelas
67 Vanessa cardui

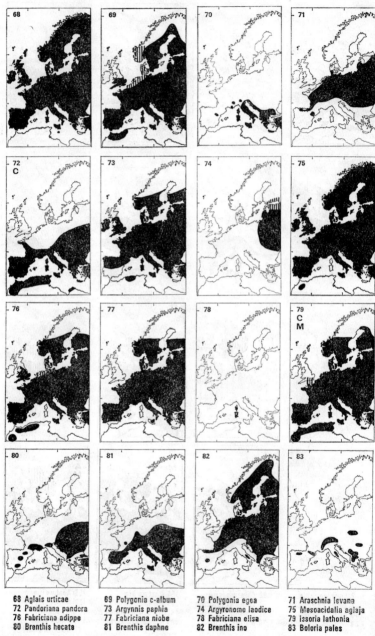

68 Aglais urticae
72 Pandoriana pandora
76 Fabriciana adippe
80 Brenthis hecate

69 Polygonia c-album
73 Argynnis paphia
77 Fabriciana niobe
81 Brenthis daphne

70 Polygonia egea
74 Argyronome laodice
78 Fabriciana elisa
82 Brenthis ino

71 Araschnia levana
75 Mesoacidalia aglaja
79 Issoria lathonia
83 Boloria pales

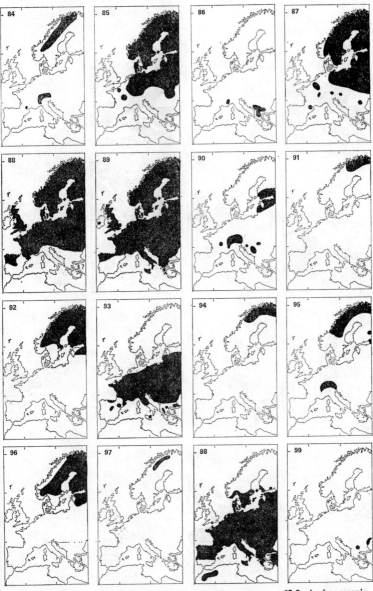

84 Boloria napaea
88 Clossiana selene
92 Clossiana freija
96 Clossiana frigga

85 Boloria aquilonaris
89 Clossiana euphrosyna
93 Clossiana dia
97 Clossiana improba

86 Boloria graeca
90 Clossiana titania
94 Clossiana polaris
98 Melitaea cinxia

87 Proclossiana eunomia
91 Clossiana chariclea
95 Clossiana thore
99 Melitaea arduinna

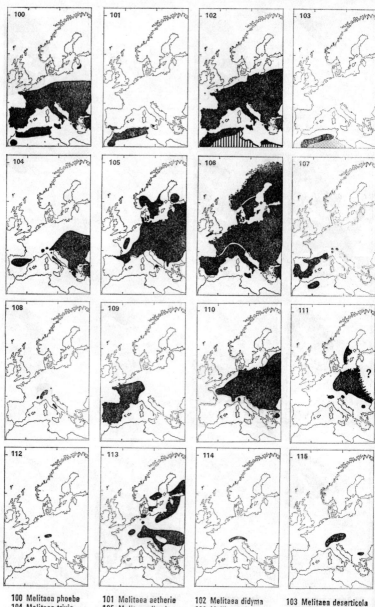

100 Melitaea phoebe
104 Melitaea trivia
108 Mellicta varia
112 Mellicta asteria

101 Melitaea aetherie
105 Melitaea diamina
109 Mellicta parthenoides
113 Euphydryas maturna

102 Melitaea didyma
106 Mellicta athalia
110 Mellicta aurelia
114 Euphydryas intermedia

103 Melitaea deserticola
107 Mellicta deione
111 Mellicta britomartis
115 Euphydryas cynthia

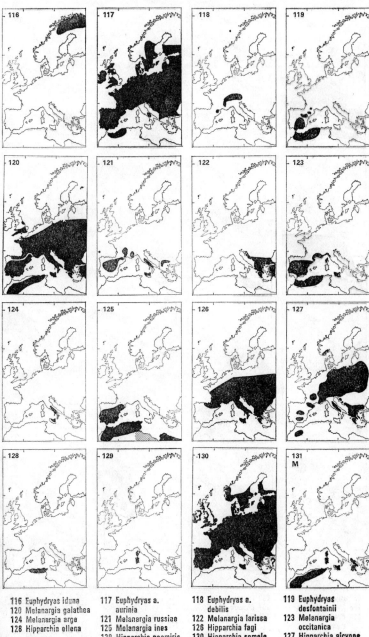

116 Euphydryas iduna
120 Melanargia galathea
124 Melanargia arge
128 Hipparchia ellena

117 Euphydryas a.
    aurinia
121 Melanargia russiae
125 Melanargia ines
129 Hipparchia neomiris

118 Euphydryas a.
    debilis
122 Melanargia larissa
126 Hipparchia fagi
130 Hipparchia semele

119 Euphydryas
    desfontainii
123 Melanargia
    occitanica
127 Hipparchia alcyone
131 Hipparchia aristaeus

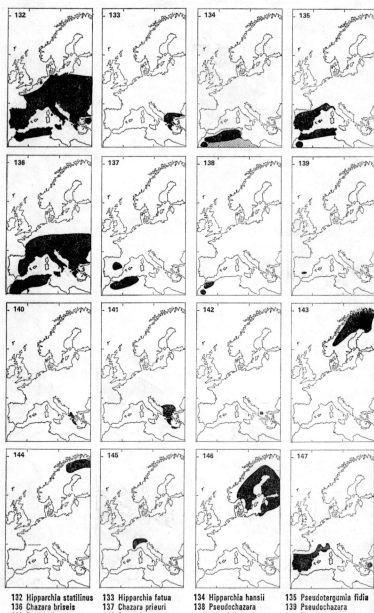

132 Hipparchia statilinus
136 Chazara briseis
140 Pseudochazara mamurra
144 Oeneis bore

133 Hipparchia fatua
137 Chazara prieuri
141 Pseudochazara anthelea
145 Oeneis glacialis

134 Hipparchia hansii
138 Pseudochazara atlantis
142 Pseudochazara geyeri
146 Oeneis jutta

135 Pseudotergumia fidia
139 Pseudochazara hippolyte
143 Oeneis norna
147 Satyrus actaea

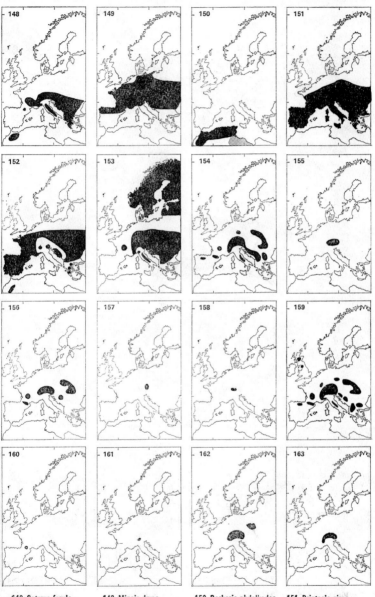

148 Satyrus ferula
149 Minois dryas
150 Berberia abdelkader
151 Brintesia circe
152 Arethusana arethusa
153 Erebia ligea
154 Erebia euryale
155 Erebia eriphyle
156 Erebia manto
157 Erebia claudina
158 Erebia flavofasciata
159 Erebia epiphron
160 Erebia serotina
161 Erebia christi
162 Erebia pharte
163 Erebia melampus

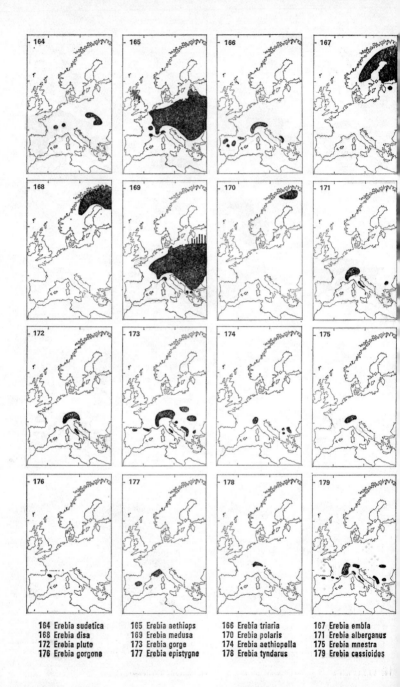

164 Erebia sudetica
168 Erebia disa
172 Erebia pluto
176 Erebia gorgone

165 Erebia aethiops
169 Erebia medusa
173 Erebia gorge
177 Erebia epistygne

166 Erebia triaria
170 Erebia polaris
174 Erebia aethiopella
178 Erebia tyndarus

167 Erebia embla
171 Erebia alberganus
175 Erebia mnestra
179 Erebia cassioides

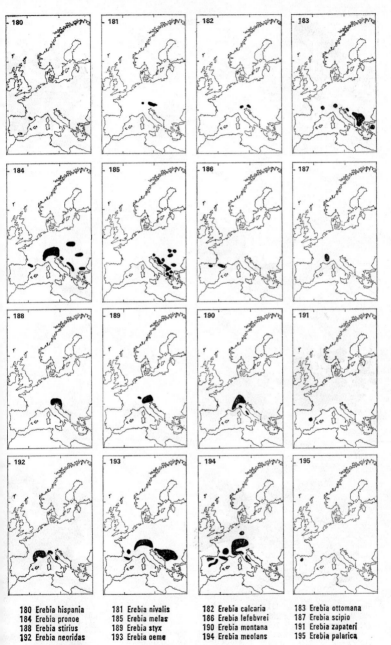

180 Erebia hispania
184 Erebia pronoe
188 Erebia stirius
192 Erebia neoridas

181 Erebia nivalis
185 Erebia melas
189 Erebia styx
193 Erebia oeme

182 Erebia calcaria
186 Erebia lefebvrei
190 Erebia montana
194 Erebia meolans

183 Erebia ottomana
187 Erebia scipio
191 Erebia zapateri
195 Erebia palarica

F.G.B.B.E.—Z

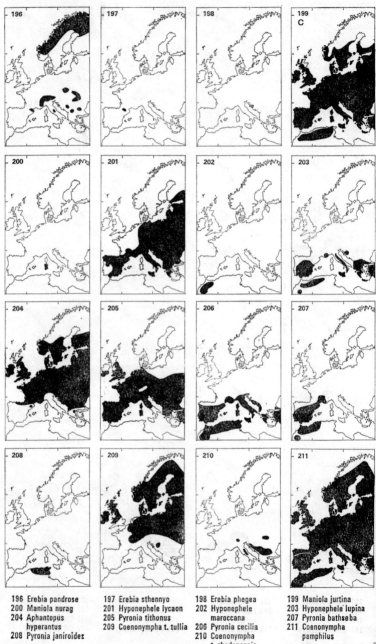

196 Erebia pandrose
200 Maniola nurag
204 Aphantopus
    hyperantus
208 Pyronia janiroïdes

197 Erebia sthennyo
201 Hyponephele lycaon
205 Pyronia tithonus
209 Coenonympha t. tullia

198 Erebia phegea
202 Hyponephele
    maroccana
206 Pyronia cecilia
210 Coenonympha
    t. rhodopensis

199 Maniola jurtina
203 Hyponephele lupina
207 Pyronia bathseba
211 Coenonympha
    pamphilus

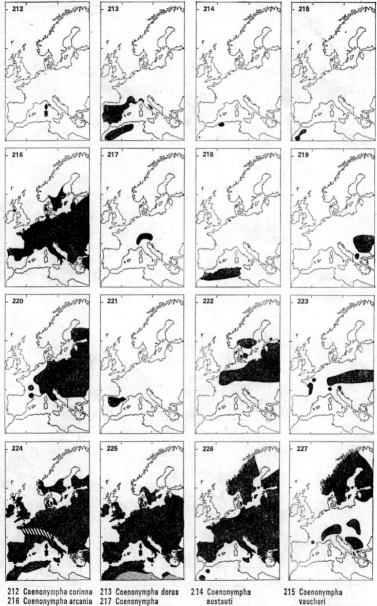

212 Coenonympha corinna
216 Coenonympha arcania
220 Coenonympha glycerion
224 Pararge aegeria

213 Coenonympha dorus
217 Coenonympha gardetta
221 Coenonympha iphioides
225 Lasiommata megera

214 Coenonympha austauti
218 Coenonympha arcanioides
222 Coenonympha hero
226 Lasiommata maera

215 Coenonympha vaucheri
219 Coenonympha leander
223 Coenonympha oedippus
227 Lasiommata petropolitana

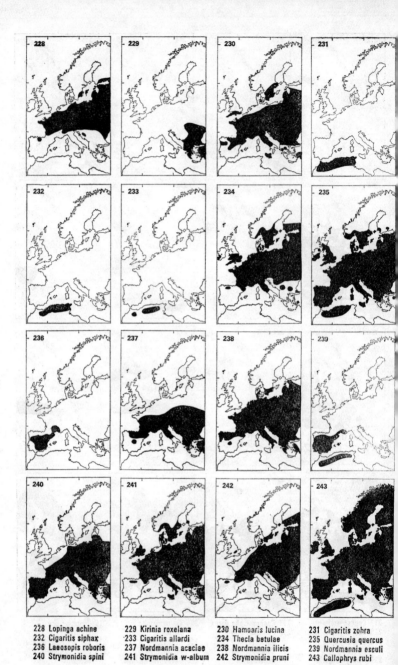

228 Lopinga achine
232 Cigaritis siphax
236 Laeosopis roboris
240 Strymonidia spini

229 Kirinia roxelana
233 Cigaritis allardi
237 Nordmannia acaciae
241 Strymonidia w-album

230 Hamoaris lucina
234 Thecla betulae
238 Nordmannia ilicis
242 Strymonidia pruni

231 Cigaritis zohra
235 Quercusia quercus
239 Nordmannia esculi
243 Callophrys rubi

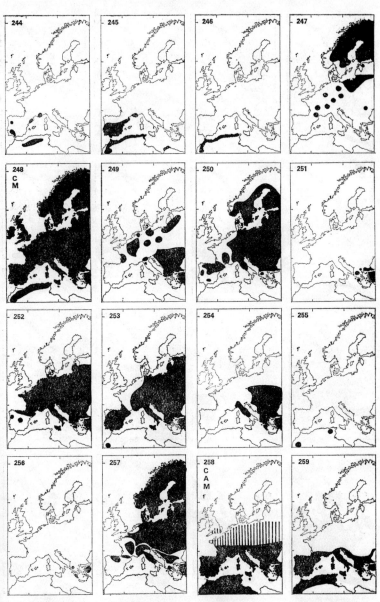

244 Callophrys avis
248 Lycaena phlaeas
252 Heodes tityrus
256 Thersamonia thetis

245 Tomares ballus
249 Lycaena dispar
253 Heodes alciphron
257 Palaeochrysophanus hippothoe

246 Tomares mauretanicus
250 Heodes virgaureae
254 Thersamonia thersamon
258 Lampides boeticus

247 Lycaena helle
251 Heodes ottomanus
255 Thersamonia phoebus
259 Syntarucus pirithous

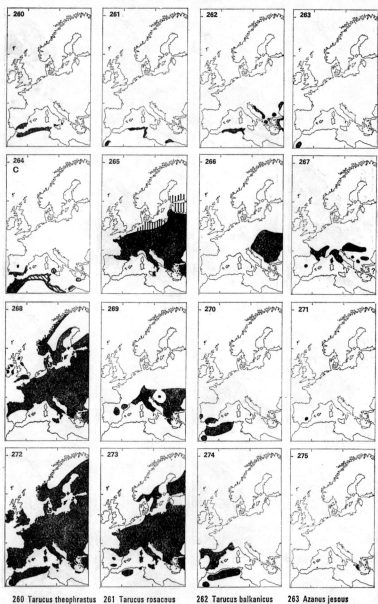

260 Tarucus theophrastus
264 Zizeeria k. knysna
(black)
Zizeeria k. karsandra
(cross hatch)
268 Cupido minimus
272 Celastrina argiolus

261 Tarucus rosaceus
265 Everes argiades
269 Cupido osiris
273 Glaucopsyche alexis

262 Tarucus balkanicus
266 Everes decoloratus
270 Cupido lorquinii
274 Glaucopsyche
melanops

263 Azanus jesous
267 Everes alcetas
271 Cupido carswell
275 Turanana panagea

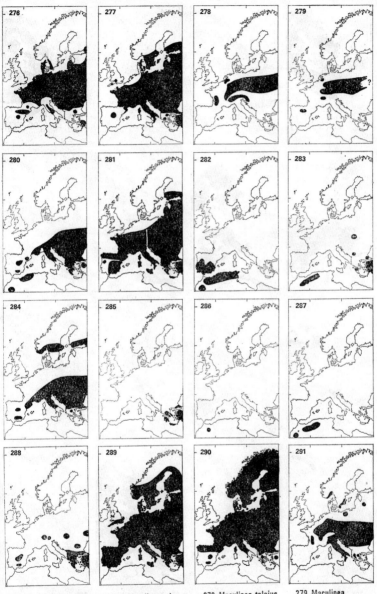

276 Maculinea alcon
280 Iolana iolas
284 Scolitantides orion
288 Plebejus pylaon

277 Maculinea arion
281 Philotes baton
285 Freyeria trochylus
289 Plebejus argus

278 Maculinea teleius
282 Philotes
abencerragus
286 Plebejus vogelii
290 Lycaeides idas

279 Maculinea
nausithous
283 Philotes bavius
287 Plebejus martini
291 Lycaeides
argyrognomon

292 Vacciniina optilete
296 Aricia agestis
300 Aricia nicias
304 Agriades aquilo

293 Kretania eurypilus
297 Aricia allous
301 Aricia anteros
305 Agriades pyrenaicus

294 Kretania psylorita
298 Aricia cramera
302 Albulina orbitulus
306 Cyaniris semiargus

295 Eumedonia eumedon
299 Aricia morronensis
303 Agriades glandon
307 Cyaniris helena

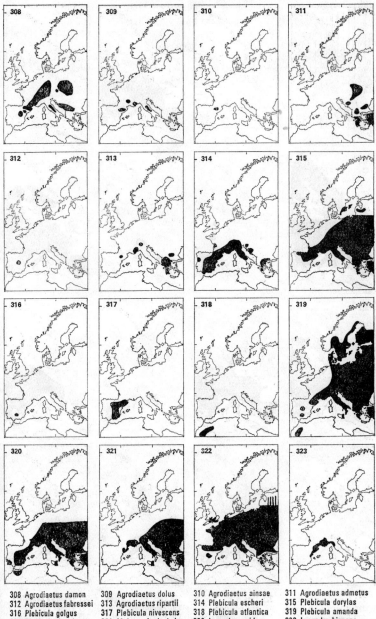

308 Agrodiaetus damon
312 Agrodiaetus fabressei
316 Plebicula golgus
320 Plebicula thersites
309 Agrodiaetus dolus
313 Agrodiaetus ripartii
317 Plebicula nivescens
321 Meleageria daphnis
310 Agrodiaetus ainsae
314 Plebicula escheri
318 Plebicula atlantica
322 Lysandra coridon
311 Agrodiaetus admetus
315 Plebicula dorylas
319 Plebicula amanda
323 Lysandra hispana

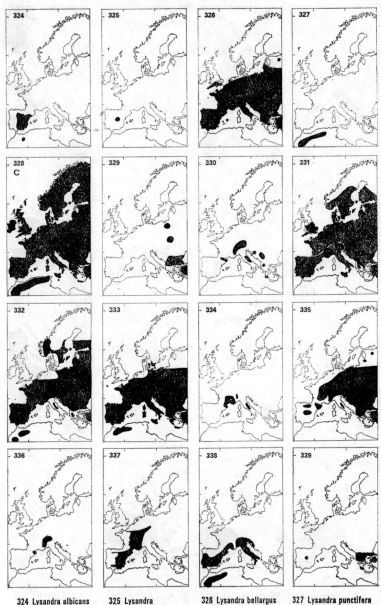

324 Lysandra albicans
328 Polyommatus icarus
332 Pyrgus alveus
336 Pyrgus carlinae

325 Lysandra
    caelestissima
329 Polyommatus eroides
333 Pyrgus armoricanus
337 Pyrgus cirsii

326 Lysandra bellargus
330 Polyommatus eros
334 Pyrgus foulquieri
338 Pyrgus onopordi

327 Lysandra punctifera
331 Pyrgus malvae
335 Pyrgus serratulae
339 Pyrgus cinarae

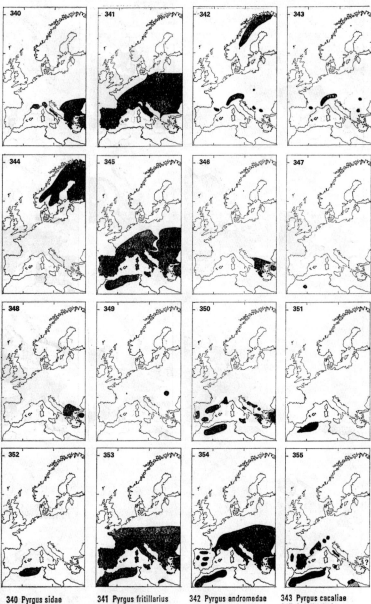

340 Pyrgus sidae
344 Pyrgus centaureae
348 Muschampia
    tessellum
352 Muschampia leuzeae

341 Pyrgus fritillarius
345 Spialia sertorius
349 Muschampia
    cribrellum
353 Carcharodus alceae

342 Pyrgus andromedae
346 Spialia phlomidis
350 Muschampia proto
354 Carcharodus
    lavatherae

343 Pyrgus cacaliae
347 Spialia doris
351 Muschampia
    mohammed
355 Carcharodus boeticus

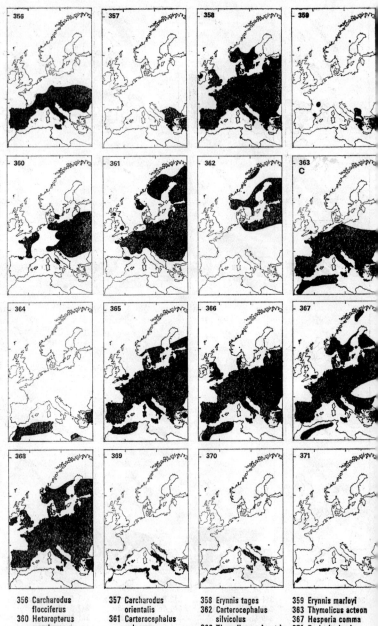

356 Carcharodus
    flocciferus
360 Heteropterus
    morpheus
364 Thymelicus hamza
368 Ochlodes venatus

357 Carcharodus
    orientalis
361 Carterocephalus
    palaemon
365 Thymelicus lineola
369 Gegenes nostrodamus

358 Erynnis tages
362 Carterocephalus
    silvicolus
366 Thymelicus sylvestris
370 Gegenes pumilio

359 Erynnis marloyi
363 Thymelicus acteon
367 Hesperia comma
371 Borbo borbonica

English Names Index

References in **bold** type are to plate numbers.

Index of Scientific Names

References in **bold** type are to plate numbers.
Names in *italics* are synonyms; *f.* = form.

INDEX

372